FIRST EDITION

SPOTLIGHT ON SOCIAL RESEARCH

ALEXANDER R. THOMAS

*State University of New York,
College at Oneonta*

POLLY J. SMITH

*University at Albany,
State University of New York*

Boston ■ New York ■ San Francisco
Mexico City ■ Montreal ■ Toronto ■ London ■ Madrid ■ Munich ■ Paris
Hong Kong ■ Singapore ■ Tokyo ■ Cape Town ■ Sydney

Editor in Chief: *Karen Hanson*
Series Editorial Assistant: *Andrea Christie*
Marketing Manager: *Judeth ball*
Production Editor: *Anna Socrates*
Editorial Production Service: *Matrix Productions Inc.*
Composition and Prepress Buyer: *Linda Cox*
Manufacturing Buyer: *JoAnne Sweeney*
Cover Administrator: *Kristina Mose-Libon*
Electronic Composition: *Modern Graphics*

Library of Congress Cataloging-in-Publication Data

Thomas, Alexander R., [date]
    Spotlight on social research / Alexander R. Thomas, Polly J. Smith.
       p. cm.
    Includes bibliographical references and index.
    ISBN 0-205-36806-9
    1. Social sciences—Research—Methodology. I. Smith, Polly J. II. Title.

H62.T444 2003
001.4′2—dc21

2002018537

Printed in the United States of America

10 9 8 7 6 5 4 3 2 1 08 07 06 04 03 02

For Jan DeAmicis,
mentor and inspiration to us both,
we hope you finally have the book
you were looking for

CONTENTS

PREFACE

Spotlight on Social Research is the result of a determined struggle to find an approach to teaching research methods that would result in basic research literacy. After using several traditional textbooks, we did not think the structure we had imposed was appropriate to a course where the stated goal is for each student to take away the necessary skills for reading, dissecting, and critiquing research. Many of the texts stressed the theoretical underpinnings of social research as nearly a third of their content, and this meant that a third of the course was also spent on theory. Like many other professors with whom we talked, we also looked at supplements to textbooks. They were very useful, but many were either focused on a particular topic or did not give much introduction to the methods themselves, again requiring the adoption of a textbook. We asked ourselves: What if a collection of readings could also feature short introductions to the research method?

Spotlight on Social Research is our attempt at such a book. It is first and foremost a collection of readings that illustrate the major research methods used in the social sciences. We have carefully picked each reading to provide a diverse selection of topics. The readings show the differing ways in which research design can vary even with the same basic research method. Not all experiments are the same, and these readings are meant to demonstrate this fact.

Spotlight on Social Research is also designed to be flexible. It can be used in conjunction with a standard textbook, or it can be used with other supplementary books, such as Gregg Lee Carter's *Doing Sociology with Student CHIP*, J. Mitchell Tewksbury's *Extreme Methods*, or Christine Hult's *Researching and Writing in the Social Sciences*. Or it may be used as a stand-alone text.

From the beginning we have considered this book an integral part of a course designed to help students learn research methods by doing research methods. Students can learn the principles of research by reading the short introductions presented here, reading and critiquing the research articles (all of which are from refereed academic journals), and possibly doing projects specifically designed by the instructor.

Jacqueline Groot got the ball rolling with Allyn & Bacon, and for that effort we are deeply appreciative. Jeff Lasser, also at Allyn & Bacon, has been very helpful to us novices at every step. Merrill Peterson at Matrix Productions has been indispensible in turning the manuscript into the book. Jan DeAmicis and John Johnsen at Utica College of Syracuse University and Jack Levin at Northeastern University have provided inspiration for this project. We need to thank all of them. And, of course, we need to thank the staff at the Milne Library at SUNY Oneonta for the invaluable assistance they have provided. Sue DeJoy, in the Department of Sociology at SUNY Oneonta, has been particularly helpful.

We would also like to thank Al and Barbara Thomas, Bob and Norma Smith, and Robert and Todd Mayton, whose patience and understanding were sorely needed and thankfully received.

Finally, we would like to thank the following reviewers for their helpful critiques: Keith F. Durkin, Ohio Northern University; Mark Edwards, Oregon State University; Patti A. Giuffre, Southwest Texas State University; and W. Lawrence Neuman, University of Wisconsin at Whitewhater.

CHAPTER 1

THE PURSUIT OF KNOWLEDGE

Consider, if you will, that cold you had last year. Runny nose, sore throat, scratchy eyes. That general feeling of "blah." And now think: What did you do to feel better? Whatever you did, it required knowledge of the common cold and how to address its symptoms. But where did that knowledge come from?

NONSCIENTIFIC APPROACHES TO KNOWLEDGE

Although science involves the search for knowledge, science is not the only approach to gaining knowledge. Other approaches include common sense, mysticism, and rationalism.

Common Sense

Common-sense knowledge is a reliance on what appears to be obvious. For instance, your cold last year did not just mail itself to you. Common sense dictates that you caught the cold from somebody else who had it, most likely someone with whom you spent time. As you recall your relations just prior to catching the cold, you remember that your father, roommate, and significant other's friend also had colds. Obviously, you caught the cold from one of them!

Common sense often leads people to the correct solution to a problem. Given these circumstances, you may well have caught the cold from your father, roommate, or significant other's friend. But common sense cannot tell you the specifics of how that happened. Science informs us that the common cold is caused by numerous viral infections and can be transmitted from one person to another by a variety of mechanisms, such as touch, sharing each other's glass, and the like. Such information, if known, is often included as part of common sense. Because of its reliance on the obvious, common sense does not readily help people understand the nonobvious. In actuality, you may have contacted that cold last year when the stranger standing next to you on the subway coughed.

Mysticism

"God bless you." This is the polite thing to say when someone sneezes, but why? As in many cultures, many Americans believed in the past (and some still do) that illness is the work of spirits or demons that have invaded the body. Because a sneeze is an early symptom of the onset of the common cold and many allergies, it was believed that an incantation to God to bless you could weaken the power of the spirit and help the patient remain healthy. Such sources of knowledge are related to *mysticism*.

Knowledge derived through mysticism relies on extraworldly sources for information. Often, mystical knowledge is believed to be transferred from extraworldly sources to an individual (or mystic) who has unique access to such knowledge. Mystical knowledge can be highly structured, as in the case of many religious traditions, or loosely structured, as is the case with psychics and spiritual mediums.

Rationalism

Knowledge can also be gained through rational means. *Rationalism* utilizes logic and complex systems of knowledge in order to understand aspects of the world. Perhaps the most famous example of rationalism is the following:

> All men are mortal.
> Socrates is a man.
> Therefore, Socrates is mortal.

In this example, it is proven that Socrates is a mortal by logically considering two statements that are true—that men are mortal and that Socrates is a man. If both statements are true, then it logically follows that Socrates is (or rather, was) a man. This conclusion is proven logically and without direct observation of Socrates.

Rationalism can be subject to errors in assumption. In other words, if a statement that is assumed to be true is in fact false, then any statements based on the assumption are possibly (but not necessarily) false as well. For instance, consider the following statement:

> *Events on Earth are influenced by the alignment of celestial bodies to one another.*

If the statement is true, then reading your daily horoscope might not be too bad an idea. If, however, the statement is false, then the entire logical system for gaining knowledge based on its truth (astrology) is possibly false. It is also possible that the logical system might not be false: It is possible that your horoscope rings true for another reason.

SCIENTIFIC KNOWLEDGE

Before discussing science, it is important to acknowledge that most people rely on a mixture of types of knowledge. Our common-sense knowledge that a cold can be passed from one person to the next also assumes that it is a virus that is being passed. Many psychics use astrology to help inform their decisions. Even many scientists are influenced by their religious views. That said, what is science?

Science is a way of gaining knowledge through systematic observation. This method contrasts to mysticism in that the knowledge is observable to anyone. Science is based on the idea that a particular phenomenon can be observed by anybody who repeats the conditions that brought it about. The practice of repeating a study to ensure that the phenomenon can be observed is called *replication*. Science is also systematic in that scientists consciously seek to observe a phenomenon. Scientific observations are specifically searched out in contrast to common-sense observations, which are often based on casual observation. Science also differs from rationalism in that it is based on observation. Although scientific theories are often rational, they need to be tested against observation to be considered accurate. In this sense, the mere deduction that Socrates is mortal is not entirely satisfactory; the theory needs to be tested. Luckily, there are some ethical constraints on science!

Scientific Method

Science relies upon the logic of the scientific method. The first aspect of the scientific method has already been discussed: that phenomenon need to be observable. This means that a study needs to be replicable: others can repeat the study and achieve the same results. Through an accumulation of such observable studies, certain properties of the phenomenon under study can be discerned. For instance, it has been repeatedly observed that water boils and evaporates, or turns from liquid to gas, at 100 degrees Celsius at sea level. The phenomenon is not only observable, but it can be repeated over and over again. In other words, the theory that water boils at 100 degrees Celsius is testable.

Not all scientific knowledge is so straightforward, however. Consider the theory that humans have evolved from an ancestor of both ourselves and the chimpanzee. In this case, the actual process of a human evolving from a common ancestor with chimpanzees has not been observed. So how do we know that this process has taken place? For starters, there has been direct observation of evolution through natural selection of microorganisms, so-called superbugs. Such bacteria have evolved in response to the introduction of antibiotics. As an antibiotic is introduced to a population of bacteria, it kills the organisms that are not resistant to the medication but spares those organisms that are drug resistant. In a classic example of natural selection, those left behind are free to reproduce and in time there is a population of drug-resistant bacteria. There is also a good, albeit incomplete, fossil record of species of protohumans dating back almost to the split with the ancestors of both humans and chimpanzees. In addition, there are numerous observable similarities between contemporary humans and chimpanzees. Our DNA is 99 percent similar, infants of both species look very similar and develop in similar ways, there are obvious physical similarities among adults of both species, and there are far more behavioral similarities than many people (and perhaps chimpanzees as well) would care to admit. From these numerous observations, it can be inferred that humans and chimpanzees share a common ancestor in our evolutionary past (Jones et al., 1992).

Consensus

The scientific method also depends on agreement or consensus among members of the scientific community about the properties of a particular phenomenon. Most scientists, for example, agree that the global climate has been getting warmer over the past century because of increased carbon dioxide emissions by humans. Consensus is not built easily, however, and it is not surprising that there are varying levels of agreement about particular phenomena throughout the sciences. It is difficult to imagine that a scientist living today would dispute that a molecule of water is composed of two atoms of hydrogen and one of oxygen. In contrast, a minority of scientists claim that global warming is not caused by increased carbon dioxide emissions by humans.

In some cases, there is simply not enough evidence for the formation of a consensus. For instance, there is little agreement on the ability of Neandertals, a species of humans that went extinct about twenty thousand years ago, to speak. Did they have language comparable to that of modern humans, did they use only gestures and vocalizations similar to those of other ape species (like chimpanzees), or were their language skills somewhere in between? Although most scientists would likely say somewhere in between, the exact placement of Neandertal language on the continuum between the two poles (no language vs. human language) remains uncertain (Maryanski & Turner, 1992).

The scientific community seeks agreement not only on factual information but on the definition of various phenomena. In fact, reaching a consensus about how a particular term should be defined or measured is often as contentious as the facts about a phenomenon. How should we define unemployment? Obviously, someone who wants a job and does not have one is unemployed. But what about someone who does not want a job? Or someone who wants to work full time but can only find part-time employment? Or someone who cannot find a job in her or his field and so takes a job in another field until one more desirable opens up? Different countries and social scientists measure unemployment differently because there is disagreement over how to define the concept of unemployment.

ASPECTS OF SCIENCE

With so much emphasis placed on the benefits of science and technology, many people have little knowledge of what constitutes science. There are many components of science, and the following are some of the most important.

Induction and Deduction

Science relies on the interplay of inductive reasoning (induction) and deductive reasoning (deduction). Inductive reasoning, which stresses observation and description, dates back to the Lyceum of the Greek philosopher Aristotle. This tradition is still found today in diverse scientific disciplines, from the descriptions of stars found in astronomy to the detailed observations of different cultures found in sociology and anthropology. The descriptions are often used as the foundation for general theories, and from them specific predictions are deduced and tested. Deductive reasoning, which stresses logic and mathematical representation, continues a tradition dating to Plato and his Academy in ancient Athens.

The seventeenth-century English philosopher Francis Bacon believed that a sufficiently large number of observations would yield theories to explain these observations. In this way, Bacon was suggesting that induction was the appropriate way to gain scientific knowledge. *Induction* works from specific observations about a phenomenon and theorizes general principles based on these observations. While observing that temperatures have been rising worldwide, one might theorize that global warming is caused by increased carbon dioxide emissions by humans. In social research, the practice of building theory based on observations is also called grounded theory.

In contrast, the French philosopher René Descartes argued about the same time that knowledge is best gained through deduction. *Deduction* begins with general statements about a phenomenon and makes specific predictions about it based on the general theory. Based on the general theory that global temperatures have been rising, one might predict that global temperatures were warmer during the 1990s than during the 1960s. This specific statement can then be tested for its accuracy.

In practice, science utilizes both approaches.

Quantitative versus Qualitative Data

Science utilizes observations, or data, in order to gain knowledge about phenomena. Data can be quantitative or qualitative.

Quantitative data are data that can be represented numerically. For instance, the median family income of a community is a number that represents the income gained by families in the 50th percentile—in other words, the exact middle—of all the incomes earned by all the families in a community in that year. If we know the median family income, we know that 50 percent made more and 50 percent made less. Using these figures in combination with other quantitative data, we can construct a good description of the community. But some things cannot be understood by looking at quantitative data alone.

Qualitative data are data that are represented by language, pictures, or other nonmathematical devices. The best representation of your hometown may not be a statistical profile but rather a picture of the Main Street or your own written description. These data cannot in their natural form be mathematically manipulated or represented in a table, but they can be useful in conveying knowledge.

Pure and Applied Research

Science also varies in terms of its purpose. Some scientific research is conducted for the sake or purpose of gaining knowledge. Such "knowledge for the sake of knowledge" is called *pure research*. For example, research conducted to understand the composition of a star has little practical value to everyday life on Earth. The purpose of conducting the research is to gain more knowledge—it may be tremendously useful information in the future, but it may not. The true utility of the knowledge is simply having it. In contrast, *applied research* is conducted with some practical purpose in mind. Determining whether or not a given land mass contains oil has a very practical application: extracting the oil. Often, pure research develops a body of knowledge that can then be used as the basis for applied research. Early work with electricity was often pure research, but the early theories were then used as the basis of applied research that revolutionized daily life.

Levels of Analysis

Science attempts to explain phenomena at various levels of observation. Macro-level observation examines large-scale phenomena, such as entire societies or cultures. Micro-level observation, in contrast, deals with small-scale phenomena, such as interactions between individuals. Some scientists also discuss a meso level of analysis—that is, a middle-range level of analysis between the micro and macro levels.

Units of Analysis

A *unit of analysis* is the unit that is actually being measured. It can be the individual, in which case the researcher measures the actions of individuals and tabulates the results. There are other units of analysis as well. Organizations, societies, and social institutions, among other things, can all be used as units of analysis, depending upon the research being conducted. Most surveys, for instance, ask individual people questions and tabulate the results. The individual is the unit of analysis. Other studies compare the poverty rates of different nations, and the nation is the unit of analysis.

Causation

Much research attempts to explain how a phenomenon operates, and this kind of explanation often relies on establishing causation. *Causation* is the concept that the action of a phenomenon affects the behavior of another. For causation to be established, three criteria need to be satisfied.

Relationship.   There needs to be a relationship between the action and reaction of the two phenomena. For instance, there is a proven relationship between the approach of a low pressure system in the atmosphere and the development of rain. This relationship is based on the fact that the low pressure system causes rain.

Relationships do not always exist because of causation, however. For instance, there is a relationship between the rate of ice cream consumption and the murder rate. This relationship does not exist because of causation, however, but rather because both phenomena are influenced by the weather. When a relationship between two phenomena exists because of a third variable that affects both, the relationship is said to be spurious.

Temporal Order.   In order to establish that one phenomenon causes another, the cause needs to occur before the effect. Obviously, the effect cannot take place before its cause.

Elimination of Alternatives.   In order to establish causation, possible alternative theories about the relationship need to be eliminated. As the fictional detective Sherlock Holmes noted, the remaining facts, no matter how seemingly implausible, must be correct.

Reliability and Validity

In order to measure phenomena, there needs to be an indicator or test of the phenomenon. Scientists need to measure the phenomena they study and are therefore concerned with the reliability and validity of the measurement.

Reliability refers to the consistency of the measurement. Measures need to be consistent over time. For instance, if an instrument to measure the blood alcohol content of an individual is reliable, it will read the same level of inebriation each time that individual has that blood alcohol content level. Measures also need to be representative; that is, they need to give the same results across different units of analysis. For instance, the blood alcohol content instrument needs to give consistent results for each individual who uses it.

Validity refers to the accuracy of the measure. An instrument used to measure blood alcohol content needs, in fact, to measure blood alcohol content. Not only does a measure need to be valid on the face of things, it also needs to measure the entire nature of the phenomenon. For instance, if a researcher defines a happy family as one in which family members are satisfied with other family members as a whole, the measure of happiness needs to include everyone. A measure concerned only with the relationship between the spouses would not be valid.

SOCIAL SCIENCE RESEARCH METHODS

Social science research utilizes a variety of methods, some of which are used in other sciences and some of which are not. Although each major method is discussed individually, many social scientists practice triangulation: the utilization of three or more distinct methods to research a phenomenon. The advantage of triangulation is that it benefits from the unique properties of each method, and thus a more full and accurate picture of the phenomenon emerges.

As stated earlier, scientific research utilizes both quantitative and qualitative data. Quantitative research methods result primarily in quantitative data, and qualitative research methods result primarily in qualitative data.

There are four major types of quantitative methods. The first, *experimentation*, or *experiments*, studies phenomena under tightly controlled settings. Survey methods gather an array of data from a wide variety of respondents. *Content analysis* studies themes found in the artifacts of a society, such as newspapers, cinema, and music. *Secondary data analysis* uses data collected for a purpose other than the study being conducted in order to understand phenomena.

There are two broad areas of qualitative research. *Historical comparative research* examines historical processes over time and/or compares different populations to one another. In *fieldwork*, the researcher collects data by coming into direct contact with the people being studied. Data are collected by conducting interviews, observing social life, and participating in group activities.

CONCLUSION

As you will see, each social science research method is unique. Each contains an entire body of knowledge focused on making research as precise as possible. And it seems likely that as time moves on, social research will become even more accurate.

CHAPTER 2

ELEMENTS OF RESEARCH

Science ultimately creates theories to explain various phenomena. A *theory* is a set of abstractions that organizes knowledge. That said, there are varying levels of abstraction, and theories are often related to one another through these abstractions.

THEORY

Paradigms

Paradigms, also called theoretical frameworks, are the most complex and encompassing of theories. A *paradigm* is a general framework for understanding a large array of phenomena. There are numerous paradigms in the social sciences, but the main three are functionalism, conflict theory, and interactionism.

Functionalism.   *Functionalism* assumes that a social organization operates according to the same basic principals as an organism. Just as an organism requires a mechanism for making decisions, so does a social organism (politics). Just as a person needs a way to distribute oxygen and nutrients throughout the body, a society needs a way to distribute food and shelter to its members (economics). Based on this assumption, functionalists tend to concern themselves with institutions. Institutions are components of a society that exist to perform some function that needs to be done. Functionalists are concerned with the equilibrium between various institutions in a society and the evolution of societies from "simple" to "complex."

Conflict Theory.   *Conflict theory* maintains that society is composed of groups that have opposing interests. Some groups hold power over others, and thus are capable of exploiting and controlling others. Members of groups that are not in power often struggle to gain power or at the very least act in a way that opposes the current order.

Those in power, conflict theorists say, attempt to hold onto their power through coercion or by convincing others of their superiority.

Interactionism.   *Interactionism* assumes that people collectively create their sense of reality through social interaction. People communicate with the aid of symbols, and those symbols guide others through their social world. As they interact, they perceive the world from their own unique vantage point and act on those perceptions. The way people think about themselves and the world around them is therefore heavily influenced by the interactions they have experienced.

Middle-Range Theories

Middle-range theories had their greatest spokesman in functionalist sociologist Robert King Merton (1968). Merton considered middle-range theory to be a link between the macro and micro level of observation. Merton's strain theory, for instance, attempted to explain how disequilibrium at the macro level (the society) causes conformity or deviance at the micro level (the individual). Merton proposed that a culture prescribes a set of goals (cultural goals) that individuals in the society share. He also proposed that each culture prescribes a set of acceptable means (institutional means) for achieving those goals. When a person accepts the cultural goals and the institutional means to achieving those goals as valid, the person will conform. If, in contrast, a person accepts the goals as valid but rejects the means of achieving the goals, he or she will use illegitimate means to achieve the goals, such as stealing or selling drugs. The person is said to be using the adaptation mode of innovation. Merton theorized four adaptation modes that lead to deviant behavior when a person does not accept both the goals and the legitimate means of achieving them.

Hypotheses

A *hypothesis* is a simple relationship between aspects of a phenomenon. Hypotheses are not abstract but rather specific statements about a phenomenon. The hypothesis is what is tested in a study.

Hypotheses are often derived from middle-range theories. For instance, based on the example of Robert Merton's strain theory just mentioned, it can be hypothesized that a person will be more likely to commit a crime if she or he perceives that the institutional means for achieving the cultural goals (e.g., success) are not available. The hypothesis can be expressed as follows:

> Individuals who believe that they do not have opportunities to succeed will be more likely to commit crime than those who perceive that they do have opportunities to succeed.

Notice that the hypothesis, because of its simplicity, can be tested.

RESEARCH DESIGN

In order to learn more about a phenomenon, scientists conduct research studies. Studies come in a variety of forms: quantitative and qualitative, inductive and deductive, present-day and historical. These studies have several components in common.

Variables

A *variable* is a concept that has two or more values. Gender is a variable because it has two values: male and female. Age is also a variable, although there are many values (1 year old, 2 years old, 3 years old, etc.). The specific values or categories of a variable are known as the *attributes* of that variable. Although variables are found in both quantitative and qualitative research, they are most often discussed in regard to quantitative methods. This is because variables, through their various values, are measurable.

A hypothesis discusses the relationships among variables, and as such different types of variables play a role in a hypothesis. Some variables act independently of other variables; the variable is not influenced by the other variables in a relationship but does exert influence on them. This variable is called the *independent variable:* a variable that influences other variables in a relationship but is independent of their influence. For example, it has been demonstrated that violent crime rates rise during the warm summer months (Cohn, 1990). This is because people are more likely to go out in public on warm days than when it is cold. In this case, the weather has an influence on crime, but crime does not influence the weather. The weather is an independent variable.

A *dependent variable* is a variable that is acted upon by the independent variable. The dependent variable is often the variable that the researcher is trying to explain. For instance, in the preceding example the dependent variable is crime—we are trying to explain fluctuations in the crime rate. The dependent variable is dependent upon the action of the independent variable; that is, the crime rate is dependent upon the weather.

A third type of variable, an *intervening variable,* acts as a causal link between the independent and dependent variables. In other words, the independent variable acts upon the intervening variable, which in turn acts on the dependent variable. In the example, note that the weather does not really directly cause violent crime. The weather actually influences the number of people in public, which influences the crime rate. In this case, the number of people in public is the intervening variable.

Levels of Measurement

Remember that variables can be measured, and that is why they are so central in research, especially quantitative research. It is important to note that variables are measured in different ways. The different ways in which variables are measured are called the levels of measurement.

Nominal Variables. *Nominal variables* act as labels for concepts. Consider gender: there are males and there are females. The two terms—*male* and *female*—are really just labels to discuss a series of traits attributable to being male or female. One need not use the words as labels; gender can be coded numerically as well. *Female* can be coded as 0, *male* as 1, or vice versa. Because the attribute is a label for something else, there is no mathematical relationship between the numbers. For instance, hair color may be coded as blonde, brunette, and redhead, or 1, 2, and 3, or 105, 204, and 328.

Ordinal Variables. *Ordinal variables* are similar to nominal variables in being essentially labels for a concept, but they introduce a ranking or ordering to the variable. Consider class level: freshman, sophomore, junior, or senior. The attributes in this variable are labels for a particular concept, but there is also a ranking. A sophomore has more college credits than a freshman but fewer than a junior. But also notice that it cannot be determined how many more or fewer credits the sophomore may have! One sophomore may have 32 credits—only three more than a freshman. Another sophomore may have 59 credits—only one fewer than a junior. Beyond the ranking there is little mathematical relationship between the attributes of ordinal variables.

Interval Variables. *Interval variables* are variables between which there is a set mathematical distance. The Fahrenheit scale, for instance, measures temperature in degrees. Each degree corresponds precisely to the same increase or decrease in temperature. Therefore, 50 degrees is 10 degrees warmer than 40 degrees, which is 10 degrees warmer than 30 degrees. In each case, 10 degrees represents the same difference in temperature—the interval is exactly the same between the degrees. Interval variables have a precise mathematical relationship between attributes and thus are useful for a variety of statistical techniques that are of no help with nominal and ordinal variables. One limitation of interval variables, however, is that there is no starting point or zero. Zero degrees Fahrenheit has no more or less meaning than 10 degrees Fahrenheit—it is just another number on the scale. Even 0 degrees Fahrenheit, which is the freezing point of water at sea level, is meaningful only as a label. It is still possible for the temperature to be colder than 0 degrees Celsius or 0 degrees Fahrenheit, and thus there is no true starting point for the scale.

Ratio Variables. *Ratio variables* are interval variables that do have a starting point or zero. The presence of a zero enables the variable to reflect a precise ratio between two attributes. Age is a ratio variable. For instance, 40 years old is twice as old as 20 years old.

SAMPLING

Population

A *population* consists of all the cases (people, organizations, etc.) that the researcher may wish to study. For instance, a researcher may wish to study life in Oneonta, New York. The unit of analysis in this case is the individual who lives in Oneonta, and the population is all the cases who satisfy the criteria of being an individual who lives in Oneonta. Of course, conducting interviews with each of the thousands of residents who live in the city, for example, would be costly and time consuming. In order to conduct research about populations in a more cost- and time-efficient manner, social scientists use sampling. The researcher is concerned with generalizability: the ability of the results of the study to be applied to the general population being studied.

A *sample* is a portion of a population that is chosen to represent the population as a whole. A sample has several advantages. Sampling saves the researcher time. If one were to interview all 14,000 residents of Oneonta, New York, the process would likely take years. If a sample of 500 residents were selected instead, the process would take less time. Sampling also saves money. Interviewing 500 Oneonta residents would take fewer interviewers, audio tape, paper for questionnaires, gas for getting to the interview, and so on than interviewing every single resident. In addition to saving the researcher both time and money, a well-designed and executed sample is often highly accurate.

The type of sampling used is dependent upon the type of research conducted. Qualitative researchers tend to use nonprobability sampling. *Nonprobability sampling* is the selection of cases for their potential of illuminating or complementing specific social processes. Max Weber, for instance, studied the economies of India, China, and Europe to understand the role of ideology in economic life, not because he randomly selected the three economic systems from a list of all societies. Quantitative researchers use probability sampling, or *random sampling*, because they are interested in drawing a sample that will be representative of the entire population.

Nonprobability Sampling

Qualitative researchers are often looking for samples on the basis of their relevance to the study of a particular topic. In many cases, this limiting of the topic requires that the sample not be random. For instance, if one wants to study how experienced drug users smoke marijuana, it is best to study experienced drug users. There are three major types of nonprobability sampling.

Purposive Sampling.   In purposive sampling, the researcher selects all cases that fit the criteria of the study. If the researcher wants to study drug dealers, it is not realistic to think that one can randomly sample from a list of prison inmates. This method would exclude dealers who have not been caught, for instance, or those who received sentences of probation. Instead, the sample should be selected by finding dealers in locales where they associate or with the aid of the police. Given that the sample is not random, the results of the study will not be generalizable to the population at large. However, purposive sampling is useful for gaining insights that can later be formalized and tested using other means. In other words, it is particularly appropriate for inductive research.

Snowball Sampling.   Like purposive sampling, snowball sampling is also useful for inductive research. Snowball sampling builds a sample by identifying individuals for the sample and then asking them for additional people for the sample. The additional people are in turn asked to add more cases to the sample. Snowball samples help researchers understand the relationships among members of a social network because the relationships can be plotted in a network sociogram.

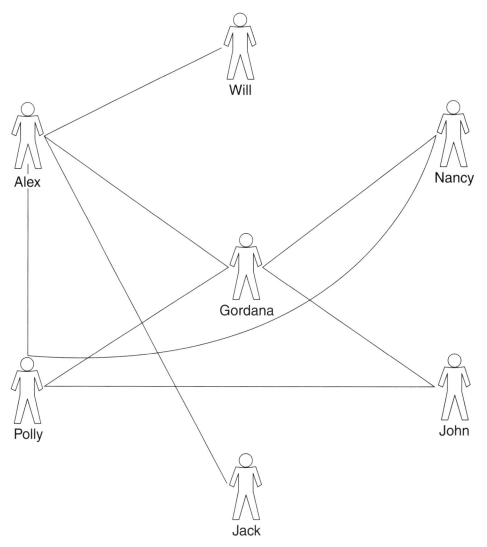

FIGURE 2.1 Network Sociogram. Network sociograms are useful for analyzing the relationships among people. From this sociogram, we can see that Alex knows Polly, Will, Gordana, and Jack but not Nancy or John. We can also see that Polly knows Alex, John, Gordana, and Nancy but not Will or Jack.

Theoretical Sampling. In theoretical sampling, the cases of a sample are chosen while the grounded theory of the study is developed. New cases are selected on the basis that they can illuminate or expand the theory.

Probability Sampling

Probability sampling is used most often in quantitative research. Whereas nonprobability samples are attempting to illuminate a particular aspect of social life, the goal of probability samples is generalizability.

The population, or universe, is the pool of cases the researcher wishes to study. It is an abstract concept because the population is never truly established, except in very small populations (e.g., a classroom). The population of Albany, New York, at 1:00 p.m. on April 1, 2000, is subject to debate. Who counts? Do those in the city for work, but who did not reside there, count? How about those who were born or died at that time? Or a resident who was in Boston at that time of day? Because of the abstract nature of population, researchers need to approximate the population. This is done using a sampling frame, a list that approximates the population. Sampling frames do not necessarily include everybody in a population, and they often contain cases that are no longer a part of the population, but an up-to-date sampling frame does approximate the population reasonably well. For instance, a list of telephone customers in Albany contains the names of people who have moved or died but does not contain the names of new residents. Nevertheless, this list approximates the population even though it is not an exact representation. Needless to say, the more up-to-date the sampling frame, the more accurate it will be.

In probability sampling, the researcher attempts to minimize sampling error. *Sampling error* is the difference between the population and the sample. For example, if a population is 51 percent female and 49 percent male, but the sample drawn contains a 50/50 ratio, the difference between the population and the sample is the sampling error.

The processes of choosing the sample from the sampling frame are numerous, although there are three that are most common: simple random, systematic, and stratified.

Simple Random. In simple random sampling, the cases to be included in the sample are picked randomly. Traditionally, this process was performed by assigning a number to every individual case in the sampling frame. The researcher would then choose numbers from a random number table—a table containing numbers picked in a mathematically random way so that the placement of each number in the table has the same probability of inclusion as the other numbers. The cases corresponding to the selected numbers were included in the sample. In recent years, however, this task of randomly selecting cases from a sampling frame has been given over to computers. Many telephone surveys, for instance, utilize computer software that automatically dials a randomly selected telephone number from the sampling frame.

Systematic.   Systematic sampling is similar to simple random sampling, but the selection of cases is somewhat different. As with simple random sampling, each case in the sampling frame is assigned a number. Unlike simple random, the selection is based on a sampling interval. The sampling interval (SI) is the number that is equal to the number of cases in the sampling frame (SF) divided by the number of cases to be included in the sample (S), as shown in Figure 2.2a. For instance, if a study requires a sample of 25 percent of a sampling frame of 1000 cases, the sample size should include 250 cases.

In this example the sampling interval is 4. The researcher randomly selects a starting point in the sampling frame and then selects every fourth case until the sample is complete. Systematic sampling works reasonably well for most research but is problematic when the data are cyclical. Cyclical data are data in which one or more properties of the case repeat in a pattern. If the data are cyclical, a systematic sample could bias the sample, as shown in Figure 2.2b.

Stratified.   The third major type of sampling is stratified sampling. In stratified sampling, the researcher uses existing data to determine the proportion of different sub-

2.2a. Systematic sampling starts by determining the sampling interval (SI):

$$SI = \frac{SF}{S}$$

So if the sampling frame (SF) is 1000 and the desired sample size (S) is 250,

$$SI = \frac{1000}{250}$$

the sampling interval is 4.

2.2b. But beware of cyclical data:

1	Male	
2	Female	Random Start Point = 3
3*	Male	SI = 4
4	Female	
5	Male	
6	Female	
7*	Male	
8	Female	
9	Male	
10	Female	
11*	Male	
12	Female	

FIGURE 2.2   Systematic Sampling
*Indicates cases to be included in sample.

populations within the overall population. For instance, a small city might contain a population that is 60 percent white, 20 percent black, 10 percent Hispanic-American, 5 percent Asian-American, and 5 percent belonging to other racial or ethnic backgrounds. In this case, simple random and systematic sampling may introduce sampling error, but a stratified sample would allow the researcher to ensure that the sample is representative of the population—that is, that it includes appropriate proportions of each of these groups. The researcher divides the sampling frame into strata and samples the sampling frame randomly, using either simple random or systematic sampling methods. By doing so, the researcher ensures that the overall sample is proportionate.

At times a researcher may find it necessary to oversample. Oversampling involves the purposeful selection of more cases of a particular subpopulation. For instance, in the previous example of a small city the Asian-American subpopulation is only 5 percent of the total population. If the sampling frame is 10,000, the total number of cases of Asian Americans in the sampling frame is only 500. If the researcher only samples 5 percent of the sampling frame, then only 25 Asian Americans will be included in the study. If this were to occur, each of the 25 cases would represent 4 percent of the Asian-American subpopulation. The researcher can increase the validity of the study by choosing 100 Asian Americans. The proportion of each stratum within the sample as a whole can be adjusted mathematically so that each subpopulation represents the proper proportion of the total population.

THE RESEARCH REPORT

The results of a research project need to be reported upon its completion. This is done through a variety of mechanisms. Research presentations are made at scientific conferences, and there are three major types of presentation. Poster sessions are displays of research made graphically, traditionally with posters but more recently with video and computer technology as well. Paper sessions are presentations in which a research paper is read to attendees. While paper sessions often feature visual aids, such as slides or posters, they are more focused on the oral presentation of the research than are poster sessions. Roundtable discussions are similar to paper sessions in that they involve oral presentation of a research paper, but the papers are often in an earlier stage of development. Roundtables allow researchers to discuss research projects in a relatively informal setting, enabling them to share concerns and their combined knowledge of the topic.

In addition to presentations, researchers can publish their work. Research reports are reports published by a company or research center that has generated the research. Journal articles, in contrast, are published in scholarly research journals that are (normally) independent of the institution and researchers conducting the research. Unlike most research reports, journal articles are refereed. The journal editor sends submitted articles to independent judges, who give an opinion about whether the article should be published, revised by the author and resubmitted for consideration, or simply not be published by that particular journal. The identity of the author is withheld from the referees in order to ensure a reasonably unbiased decision. Journal articles vary in length from about 5 to 35 pages. In contrast, monographs are books written about a specific research question. Most often, monographs attempt to summarize and expand on a body of research or present the results of a large-scale project that cannot be summarized within the constraints of a journal article. Many book publishers also referee monographs, but some do not.

In each of these types of research report, the format tends to vary according to the amount of time or space given to report the research, the type of research methods utilized, and the purpose of the research. Most reports, however, are based on a generic format that most scholars follow.

The first component of a research report is appropriately called an introduction. The introduction discusses the topic of the study and its significance to the wider scholarly community. The significance of the study includes any new advance to knowledge, implications for scientific theory, or ramifications for social policy, In short, the introduction is where the researcher explains why she or he conducted the study.

The literature review is the second component of a research report; it is a summary of past research and theories about the research topic. It is used to summarize the knowledge about a particular topic to date and often includes the specifics about how the current study fits into or advances the existing body of knowledge. Literature reviews are not mere summaries of past work, but rather essays that systematically analyze the relationships of past work to the present work. They are written in a thematic fashion. Each major orientation or trend in past research is analyzed as its own topic. For instance, a literature review will likely compare past research in light of differing theoretical traditions, methodological approaches, contrasting findings, and any other apparent themes in the literature to that point.

The literature review is followed by the methods section. The methods section outlines the steps taken to complete the study, such as the overall design of the study (e.g., whether it is a survey, experiment, etc.), a description of the population under study, and the sampling technique and the sampling frame utilized. Any special circumstances or considerations relevant to the research methods are also discussed in this section.

The goal of a research study is its findings, and they are reported in the section after the methods section. In quantitative research, the findings are often presented as statistical tables and analyzed. In qualitative research, the findings section often analyzes part of a narrative or is organized by themes supported with quotes from interviews.

The discussion section summarizes the significance of the findings. It is here that the relevance of the study within the context of the research discussed in the literature review is analyzed. The discussion section also proposes new avenues for further research. Policy recommendations, if relevant, are also made in the discussion section.

The final component of a research report is the conclusion. The conclusion acts as a summary of the significance of the entire study. In many studies, it is included as part of the discussion section. The conclusion should restate the important findings and their relevance to the field at large and should emphasize that the previous sections of the report did in fact examine all issues introduced in the introduction.

CONCLUSION

Each research method utilizes these components in slightly different ways. Surveys and experiments tend to be very explicit about the study aims and hypotheses. In contrast, fieldwork is often vague about explicit hypotheses. The reports for each type of research also vary. In general, quantitative research tends to adhere closely to the structure presented here, whereas qualitative research is often more loosely structured. Even within a research method, different studies will look very different in print. This variation in style will become more apparent as you continue reading this book.

CHAPTER 3

ETHICS

Consider the following research design:

> The purpose of the research is to ascertain the role of socialization in the development of personality. Volunteers will be cloned into one of three groups, two experimental and one control. The control group clones will be placed in family units; clones assigned to experimental group 1 will be placed in controlled environments that stress violence and depression; and experimental group 2 clones will be placed in controlled environments that provide for all conceivable needs and stress love and respect for others. Personality inventories will be administered to the clones in each group every year to determine the overall personality characteristics of each individual clone.

Sound unreasonable? In the early twenty-first century, cloning technology is developing at a rapid pace. Although it is likely that most scientists would consider each new clone as a new and unique individual who just happens to be genetically identical to another, that does not mean that every scientist would perceive clones in this way. And let's face it—cloning does present a unique opportunity to further study the role of genetics and socialization in the formation of personality. But wouldn't scientists realize the immorality of such an experimental design? Let's answer this question later.

CODE OF ETHICS

Scientists must adhere to professional codes of ethics. *Codes of ethics* are adopted by professional associations of each scientific discipline, including the American Sociological Association. Although each profession has its own code of ethics, there is considerable agreement on the main points of scientific ethics. The major consideration in all professions is to combat a sense of arrogance that has the potential to inform scientific research. It is thus not surprising that examples of violations of research ethics have often inspired the adoption of the official codes of ethics. But how do we know to adopt a rule against a certain act if no one has ever tried it before?

Voluntary Participation

Research subjects in a study need to be voluntary particpants. In other words, the people under study have a right to know that they are part of a scientific study. Throughout several decades of the twentieth century, African-American men who had tested positive for syphilis were allowed to go through life untreated. The effects of the disease on white men were known to researchers; the experiment investigated whether the effects were the same on black men. Modern medicine, of course, correctly predicted the effects to be the same. In order to prevent the research subjects from seeking treatment for the deadly disease, it is probable that they were not fully informed about the dangers of their conditions. The result of the Tuskegee syphilis experiment was that these men were allowed to suffer the effects of the disease in the name of science despite the fact that they could have been successfully treated (Jones, 1993).

The question of voluntary participation is contentious in certain types of fieldwork. As you will see in Chapter 9, fieldwork researchers must be concerned with the issue of disclosure: the notification of subjects that the researcher is involved in data collection for a scientific study. The issue often revolves around the effect the disclosure may have on those being studied. For instance, it may be argued that a researcher studying a street gang may put herself or himself at risk by disclosing the project or that disclosure may make subjects less willing to discuss certain elements of life that may be important to the study. In practice, however, gang researchers have successfully disclosed their research to gang members without adversely affecting their project (Padilla, 1992; Donaldson, 1993). Indeed, disclosure allows the researcher to ask questions that might otherwise seem strange.

There have been moments in history when subjects of other researchers were not voluntary participants. German physicians performed a range of unethical experiments on nonwilling Jewish subjects during World War II, for example.

Avoidance of Harm

Although it seems obvious, we must state plainly. Researchers cannot harm the subject of their research. Harm can take different forms. Physical harm involves harm directed at an individual's body. Emotional harm is directed at an individual's mental or emotional well-being. Financial harm is harm that reduces or inhibits one's financial well-being. Moral harm is harm that damages one's reputation and self-image. In addition to the researcher's producing such harm directly, it is also considered unethical for a researcher to create conditions under which harm can be caused to others.

Stanley Milgram (1974) was horrified by the willingness of ordinary German citizens to participate in the Holocaust during World War II. One refrain was heard from the perpetrators: Each claimed to be "just following orders." Milgram chose to study this obedience to authority by setting up an experiment during which subjects were asked to administer electric shocks ranging to 450 volts—deadly to humans. The supposed victim of the therapy was a confederate who was not actually being shocked, but the research subjects, most of whom were willing to administer a deadly shock to the stranger in the booth in front of them, were not aware of this. Subjects were faced with the ugly truth that they would kill a person merely because an authority figure asked them to do so—an uncomfortable truth that most people are never forced to confront. Because of the potential psychological damage of this revelation, there was considerable controversy over the ethics of the methods for years after the experiment.

The avoidance of harm also requires that researchers not deceive or mislead subjects. This is not always possible. Numerous experiments in social psychology, for instance, have relied upon concealing the true nature of the study or purposefully misleading the subject. In such cases, subjects need to be *debriefed*, or told the complete purpose of the study at the conclusion of the study.

Anonymity

Research subjects have a right to anonymity. Anonymity is associated with three distinct concepts: anonymity, confidentiality, and privacy. Anonymity refers to the right of an individual to not have his or her identity shared with others. The choice to become part of an experiment ultimately resides with the subject, and so does the decision to share this choice with others. Therefore, the fact that a person has chosen to be a subject in a research project does not in itself allow the researcher to disclose the subject's identity.

When Vidich and Bensman (1968) published their study of a small upstate New York town, they concealed the names of the people in the town and even the town itself. Using pseudonyms for people and places, they wrote in extreme detail about relationships between residents, the political structure of the town, and other such information. The problem was that the detail was perhaps too good. For instance, any reader with a protractor and knowledge of New York state geography could identify the town by reading the opening chapter of the book. Similarly, although most readers did not know the town judge, for instance, a town resident could figure out the identity of the individual being discussed.

Confidentiality is an outgrowth of the right to anonymity. A subject has the right to expect that any information disclosed to the researcher will not be revealed to others. This also means that research findings cannot be reported in a way that makes subjects' statements or secrets apparent to others.

Privacy refers to the right of subjects to choose their own level of disclosure. Agreeing to be a part of an interview, for instance, does not require subjects to discuss topics they do not wish to discuss. A subject may feel quite comfortable discussing finances and morality but not sex.

Reporting Findings

Scientists have an obligation to report the findings of their research. It may seem that the researcher would automatically want to report the findings, but this is not always the case.

At times, the findings of a study may suggest that a theory is wrong or suggest a course of action that some may find objectionable. Numerous studies have supported the theory that humans evolved from an ancestor of both ourselves and modern chimpanzees, but some find the notion of evolution through natural selection to be a challenge to their religious beliefs. Similarly, a study of youth crime may show juvenile crime to be declining, but this finding may undermine the platform of a candidate for elected office. In both cases, the researcher may find political pressure to alter or suppress findings. However, most professional codes of ethics require researchers to work independently of such considerations and release their findings despite the inconvenience to one or another party.

THE INTERNAL REVIEW BOARD

Ethical violations are not all the same. The Tuskegee syphilis experiment, for instance, is a shocking violation of professional ethics for two reasons (Jones, 1993). First, the harm caused by withholding treatment for these patients was a death sentence—no greater harm than that. Second, the research was unnecessary. The effects of syphilis were already known, and any difference between the progression of disease among blacks and whites could have been determined with a nonlethal disease, such as the common cold. The fact that the subjects were not told the full extent of the illness they were suffering calls into question whether they gave informed consent to participate. Without being fully informed about the disease, they could not make an informed decision. Therefore, it cannot be said that these subjects participated voluntarily.

Stanley Milgram's (1974) obedience study, however, did seek to investigate a valid research question. Historical (and not so historical) evidence shows that ordinary people are capable of atrocities, and Milgram sought to understand the psychological foundations of this behavior. He found that 65 percent were willing to administer a deadly shock without the urging of a mob, threat of force, or hatred. Milgram himself was shocked by the results, and it is difficult to argue that they are not significant. But that is not the question. The real question is: Was the advance of knowledge worth the price of the psychological damage experienced by some, if not all, of the subjects? Many argued that it was not, but Milgram was certainly not alone in his contention that the methods he used were not unethical.

In their study of a small town, Vidich and Bensman (1968) took steps to guarantee the anonymity of their subjects. In a sense, they failed to do so because they reported too much. This case does provide a warning to future researchers to pay more attention to issues regarding anonymity.

Often external review of the research design can help mitigate any potentially negative effects. In addition, past ethics violations have brought attention to the need for mechanisms to supervise researchers. Most institutions out of which research is conducted, such as colleges and universities, have adopted ethics codes of their own. In order to ensure that researchers follow ethics codes and the law, *internal review boards* were established to review research proposals before the beginning of a study involving human and other living subjects.

THE ANSWER

Our original question was: Wouldn't scientists realize the immorality of the experimental design utilizing clones? The answer: We don't know.

THE READINGS

Although these readings in ethics are quite different from each other, both address issues related to the nature of scientific research and scientists. Horace Miner's famous 1956 essay, "Body Ritual among the Nacirema," describes an unusual native society located in the Western hemisphere. In "Reporting Unethical Research Behavior," Neil Wenger and associates (1999) wanted to know whether scientists would consider particular types of research unethical and what they would do about it.

■ ■ ■ ■ ■ ▬▬▬▬▬▬▬▬▬▬▬▬▬▬▬▬▬▬▬▬▬▬▬▬

BODY RITUAL AMONG THE NACIREMA
Horace Miner
University of Michigan

In a landmass between the Atlantic and Pacific Oceans lives a curious people with an interesting set of rituals. In describing their rituals and the shrines found in their homes, some interesting questions arise about the ability of scientists to properly interpret the data on other cultures without tainting their analysis with their own culturally based biases. [ED.]

The anthropologist has become so familiar with the diversity of ways in which different peoples behave in similar situations that he is not apt to be surprised by even the most exotic customs. In fact, if all of the logically possible combinations of behavior have not been found somewhere in the world, he is apt to suspect that they must be present in some yet undescribed tribe. This point has, in fact, been expressed with respect to clan organization by Murdock (1949:71). In this light, the magical beliefs and practices of the Nacirema present such unusual aspects that it seems desirable to describe them as an example of the extremes to which human behavior can go.

Professor Linton first brought the ritual of the Nacirema to the attention of anthropologists twenty years ago (1936:326), but the culture of this people is still very poorly understood. They are a North American group living in the territory between the Canadian Cree, the Yaqui and Tarahumare of Mexico, and the Carib and Arawak of the Antilles. Little is known of their origin, although tradition states that they came from the east. According to Nacirema mythology, their nation was originated by a culture hero, Notgnihsaw, who is otherwise known for two great feats of strength—the throwing of a piece of wampum across the river Pa-To-Mac and the chopping down of a cherry tree in which the Spirit of Truth resided.

Nacirema culture is characterized by a highly developed market economy which has evolved in a rich natural habitat. While much of the people's time is devoted to economic pursuits, a large part of the fruits of these labors and a considerable portion of the day are spent in ritual activity. The focus of this activity is the human body, the appearance and health of which loom as a dominant concern in the ethos of the people. While such a concern is certainly not

From *American Anthropologist* v58, 503–507, June 1956.

unusual, its ceremonial aspects and associated philosophy are unique.

The fundamental belief underlying the whole system appears to be that the human body is ugly and that its natural tendency is to debility and disease. Incarcerated in such a body, man's only hope is to avert these characteristics through the use of the powerful influences of ritual and ceremony. Every household has one or more shrines devoted to this purpose. The more powerful individuals in the society have several shrines in their houses and, in fact, the opulence of a house is often referred to in terms of the number of such ritual centers it possesses. Most houses are of wattle and daub construction, but the shrine rooms of the more wealthy are walled with stone. Poorer families imitate the rich by applying pottery plaques to their shrine walls.

While each family has at least one such shrine, the rituals associated with it are not family ceremonies but are private and secret. The rites are normally only discussed with children, and then only during the period when they are being initiated into these mysteries. I was able, however, to establish sufficient rapport with the natives to examine these shrines and to have the rituals described to me.

The focal point of the shrine is a box or chest which is built into the wall. In this chest are kept the many charms and magical potions without which no native believes he could live. These preparations are secured from a variety of specialized practitioners. The most powerful of these are the medicine men, whose assistance must be rewarded with substantial gifts. However, the medicine men do not provide the curative potions for their clients, but decide what the ingredients should be and then write them down in an ancient and secret language. This writing is understood only by the medicine men and by the herbalists who, for another gift, provide the required charm.

The charm is not disposed of after it has served its purpose, but is placed in the charm-box of the household shrine. As these magical materials are specific for certain ills, and the real or imagined maladies of the people are many, the charm-box is usually full to overflowing. The magical packets are so numerous that people forget what their purposes were and fear to use

them again. While the natives are very vague on this point, we can only assume that the idea in retaining all the old magical materials is that their presence in the charm-box, before which the body rituals are conducted, will in some way protect the worshipper.

Beneath the charm-box is a small font. Each day every member of the family, in succession, enters the shrine room, bows his head before the charm-box, mingles different sorts of holy water in the font, and proceeds with a brief rite of ablution. The holy waters are secured from the Water Temple of the community, where the priests conduct elaborate ceremonies to make the liquid ritually pure.

In the hierarchy of magical practitioners, and below the medicine men in prestige, are specialists whose designation is best translated "holy-mouth-men." The Nacirema have an almost pathological horror of and fascination with the mouth, the condition of which is believed to have a supernatural influence on all social relationships. Were it not for the rituals of the mouth, they believe that their teeth would fall out, their gums bleed, their jaws shrink, their friends desert them, and their lovers reject them. They also believe that a strong relationship exists between oral and moral characteristics. For example, there is a ritual ablution of the mouth for children which is supposed to improve their moral fiber.

The daily body ritual performed by everyone includes a mouth-rite. Despite the fact that these people are so punctilious about care of the mouth, this rite involves a practice which strikes the uninitiated stranger as revolting. It was reported to me that the ritual consists of inserting a small bundle of hog hairs into the mouth, along with certain magical powders, and then moving the bundle in a highly formalized series of gestures.

In addition to the private mouth-rite, the people seek out a holy-mouth-man once or twice a year. These practitioners have an impressive set of paraphernalia, consisting of a variety of augers, awls, probes, and prods. The use of these objects in the exorcism of the evils of the mouth involve almost unbelievable ritual torture of the client. The holy-mouth-man opens the client's mouth and, using the above mentioned tools, enlarges any holes which decay may have created in the teeth. Magical materials are put into these holes. If there are no naturally occurring holes in the teeth, large sections of one or more teeth are gouged out so that the supernatural substance can be applied. In the client's view, the purpose of these ministrations is to arrest decay and to draw friends. The extremely sacred and traditional character of the rite is evident in the fact that the natives return to the holy-mouth-men year after year, despite the fact that their teeth continue to decay.

It is to be hoped that, when a thorough study of the Nacirema is made, there will be careful inquiry into the personality structure of these people. One has but to watch the gleam in the eye of a holy-mouth-man, as he jabs an awl into an exposed nerve, to suspect that a certain amount of sadism is involved. If this can be established, a very interesting pattern emerges, for most of the population shows definite masochistic tendencies. It was to these that Professor Linton referred in discussing a distinctive part of the daily body ritual which is performed only by men. This part of the rite involves scraping and lacerating the surface of the face with a sharp instrument. Special women's rites are performed only four times during each lunar month, but what they lack in frequency is made up in barbarity. As part of this ceremony, women bake their heads in small ovens for about an hour. The theoretically interesting point is that what seems to be a preponderantly masochistic people have developed sadistic specialists.

The medicine men have an imposing temple, or *latipso*, in every community of any size. The more elaborate ceremonies required to treat very sick patients can only be performed at this temple. These ceremonies involve not only the thaumaturge but a permanent group of vestal maidens who move sedately about the temple chambers in distinctive costume and headdress.

The *latipso* ceremonies are so harsh that it is phenomenal that a fair proportion of the really sick natives who enter the temple ever recover. Small children whose indoctrination is still incomplete have been known to resist attempts to take them to the temple because "that is where you go to die." Despite this fact, sick adults are not only willing but eager to undergo the protracted ritual purification, if they can afford to do so. No matter how ill the supplicant or how grave the emergency, the guardians of many temples will not admit a client if he cannot give a rich gift to the custodian. Even after one has gained admission and survived the ceremonies, the guardians will not permit the neophyte to leave until he makes still another gift.

The supplicant entering the temple is first stripped of all his or her clothes. In every-day life the Nacirema avoids exposure of his body and its natural functions. Bathing and excretory acts are performed only in the secrecy of the household shrine, where they are ritualized as part of the body-rites. Psychological shock results from the fact that body secrecy is suddenly lost upon entry into the *latipso*. A man, whose own wife has never seen him in an excretory act, suddenly finds himself naked and assisted by a vestal maiden while he performs his natural functions into a sacred vessel. This sort of ceremonial treatment is necessitated by the fact that the excreta are used by a diviner to ascertain the course and nature of the client's sickness. Female clients, on the other hand, find their naked bodies are subjected to the scrutiny, manipulation and prodding of the medicine men.

Few supplicants in the temple are well enough to do anything but lie on their hard beds. The daily ceremonies, like the rites of the holy-mouth-men, involve discomfort and torture. With ritual precision, the vestals awaken their miserable charges each dawn and roll them about on their beds of pain while performing ablutions, in the formal movements of which the maidens are highly trained. At other times they insert magic wands in the supplicant's mouth or force him to eat substances which are supposed to be healing. From time to time the medicine men come to their clients and jab magically treated needles into their flesh. The fact that these temple ceremonies may not cure, and may even kill the neophyte, in no way decreases the people's faith in the medicine men.

There remains one other kind of practitioner, known as a "listener." This witch-doctor has the power to exorcise the devils that lodge in the heads of people who have been bewitched.

The Nacirema believe that parents bewitch their own children. Mothers are particularly suspected of putting a curse on children while teaching them the secret body rituals. The counter-magic of the witch-doctor is unusual in its lack of ritual. The patient simply tells the "listener" all his troubles and fears, beginning with the earliest difficulties he can remember. The memory displayed by the Nacirema in these exorcism sessions is truly remarkable. It is not uncommon for the patient to bemoan the rejection he felt upon being weaned as a babe, and a few individuals even see their troubles going back to the traumatic effects of their own birth.

In conclusion, mention must be made of certain practices which have their base in native esthetics but which depend upon the pervasive aversion to the natural body and its functions. There are ritual fasts to make fat people thin and ceremonial feasts to make thin people fat. Still other rites are used to make women's breasts larger if they are small, and smaller if they are large. General dissatisfaction with breast shape is symbolized in the fact that the ideal form is virtually outside the range of human variation. A few women afflicted with almost inhuman hypermammary development are so idolized that they make a handsome living by simply going from village to village and permitting the natives to stare at them for a fee.

Reference has already been made to the fact that excretory functions are ritualized, routinized, and relegated to secrecy. Natural reproductive functions are similarly distorted.

Intercourse is taboo as a topic and scheduled as an act. Efforts are made to avoid pregnancy by the use of magical materials or by limiting intercourse to certain phases of the moon. Conception is actually very infrequent. When pregnant, women dress so as to hide their condition. Parturition takes place in secret, without friends or relatives to assist, and the majority of women do not nurse their infants.

Our review of the ritual life of the Nacirema has certainly shown them to be a magic-ridden people. It is hard to understand how they have managed to exist so long under the burdens which they have imposed upon themselves. But even such exotic customs as these take on real meaning when they are viewed with the insight provided by Malinowski when he wrote (1948:70):

> Looking from far and above, from our high places of safety in the developed civilization, it is easy to see all the crudity and irrelevance of magic. But without its power and guidance early man could not have mastered his practical difficulties as he has done, nor could man have advanced to the higher stages of civilization.

REFERENCES CITED

Linton, Ralph. 1936. *The Study of Man*. New York: D. Appleton-Century Co.
Malinowski, Bronislaw. 1948. *Magic, Science, and Religion*. Glencoe: The Free Press.
Murdock, George P. 1949. *Social Structure*. New York: The Macmillan Co.

■ ■ ■ ■ ■

REPORTING UNETHICAL RESEARCH BEHAVIOR

Neil S. Wenger, Stanley G. Korenman, Richard Berk, and Honghu Liu
University of California, Los Angeles

Scientists, as professionals, have a responsibility to self-regulate. However, whistleblowing is rare. We investigated scientists' infrequent disclosure of unethical behavior by studying their responses to scenarios describing unethical research acts and compared their responses to those of research administrators. A cross-sectional survey was administered to National Science Foundation–funded principal investigators and their institutions' repre-

From *Evaluation Review*, 23, 5 (October 1999): 553–70. Copyright © Sage Publications, Inc.

sentatives (IRs) to the Office of Research Integrity. Both scientists and IRs proposed to respond to nearly all research behaviors that they rated as unethical. Scientists more often proposed responses limited to the research team (58% vs. 25% of cases, p < .001) whereas IRs more often proposed to inform an administrator or dean, journal editor, funding agency, professional society, or reporter. The prior behavior and academic rank of the scenario protagonist were associated with responses, but consequences of the unethical behavior were not. Scientists appear to perceive that they uphold their responsibility to respond to unethical behavior by disclosures within the research team, whereas administrators propose to report to externally accountable individuals, raising the question of whether scientists' behavior constitutes professional self-regulation or cover up.

Scientists, as professionals, are supposed to report unethical research behavior (National Academy of Sciences Committee on the Conduct of Science 1995). They have the responsibility to self-regulate and to police the actions of fellow professionals (Sigma Xi 1991 and Flores 1988). Self-regulation sustains academic freedom and limits the influence of religion, politics, and other forces on scientific research (Ben-David 1991). However, *whistle-blowing*, informing about unethical scientific conduct, occurs infrequently. Publicized misconduct cases often reveal missed reporting opportunities.

Why whistle-blowing is uncommon is poorly understood. It might be due to a scientist's perception of collegiality (Swazey and Scher 1981) or related to the serious repercussions that may befall the informant (Lennane 1993). Alternatively, scientists may not accept the responsibility to police the actions of peers. To investigate scientists' self-regulation and whistle-blowing behaviors, we compared how scientists said they would respond to unethical research behavior and the responses of administrators responsible for the conduct of research.

METHODS
This study analyzes data derived from a project aimed at understanding the norms of scientists (Korenman et al. 1998). A computer-generated survey instrument was developed to elicit responses concerning a respondent's perception of whether specific research behaviors were ethical and, if not, whether and how the subject would respond to knowledge of the behavior. The survey was mailed to all 924 National Science Foundation principal investigators receiving grants from the Division of Molecular and Cellular Biology during 1993 or 1994 and to the 140 administrators responsible for the conduct of research (institutions' representatives, IRs) from the scientists' institutions. We evaluated whether respondents indicated that they would respond to the behavior and the response they proposed. Respondent and scenario-based factors associated with responses to unethical behavior were evaluated, and the responses of scientists and IRs were compared.

INSTRUMENT AND SURVEY TECHNIQUE
Each survey instrument contained 12 scenarios randomly selected from 8,364 possible scenarios. Following a fractional factorial design, scenarios were constructed with series of sentences derived from randomly assigned phrases, each consisting of one level from a dimension (Rossi and Nock 1982). The dimensions were the factors theoretically related to a respondent's reaction to research conduct in four domains: (a) performance and reporting of research, (b) appropriation of the ideas of others, (c) conflicts of interest/commitment, and (d) collegiality/sharing. The other dimensions contained in each scenario were the following: gender and status of the scientist, the harm and larger consequences resulting from the act, and whether this was a first-time offense. A full description of each of the dimensions and the levels within the dimensions is contained in the appendix.

For each scenario, respondents were asked whether the act was unethical and, if so, the degree to which it was unethical on a scale of 1 to 10 (the unethical score). Respondents rating an act as unethical were asked, If you knew about behavior like this, would you

- keep it to yourself?
- speak directly to the researcher about your concerns?

- indicate your misgiving about the behavior to your scientific colleagues?
- inform the editor of relevant journals?
- inform the researcher's immediate supervisor?
- inform the administrator or dean in the researcher's institution?
- inform the researcher's professional society?
- inform the researcher's funding agencies?
- contact a reporter for science, nature, or another professional journal?
- contact the lay media?
- other?

Respondents were instructed to choose as many responses as applicable. Then, they were asked whether punishment was appropriate for this behavior.

The survey, described in detail elsewhere (Korenman et al. 1998), included items asking respondents about demographic characteristics, academic position, and research experience. The survey was approved by the Institutional Review Board for administration without written informed consent.

ANALYSIS

The scenario was the unit of analysis. Only scenarios containing unethical behavior (that is, a behavior rated as unethical by the respondent) were evaluated in this study. The relationship of the response to the behavior and scenario dimensions was evaluated using simple means and proportions, yielding unbiased estimates due to the fractional factorial design (Hox, Kreft, and Hermkens 1991). To understand the response to a particular case of unethical behavior, we aggregated all the responses suggested for each case and categorized the patterns of response. The 21 most common response patterns account for 74% of all scenario cases. The mean unethical score and the proportion of respondents suggesting punishment was computed for each response pattern. The percentage of unethical cases attributable to each pattern was compared between scientists and IRs using chi-square tests. The relationship of each response to the protagonist's characteristics was evaluated for all domains combined using chi-square

tests. The relationship of each response to the specific unethical research behaviors was evaluated.

To understand the differences between scientists and IR proposed reporting, we performed logistic regression including as independent variables respondent academic rank, age and gender, scenario unethical score, the respondent's sample (scientist versus IR), and the interaction of sample and unethical score. The dependent variable was whether the respondent offered a response that included informing an administrator or individual external to researcher's group (a dean, a journal editor, a funding agency, a professional society, or a reporter) versus limiting information within researchers (informing no one or only the researcher and/or colleagues and/or a supervisor). In this analysis, intrarespondent correlation was accounted for using a modified maximum likelihood estimate (Huber 1967) that accumulates scenario information within respondent to increase the standard errors of the parameter estimates reflecting redundancy in correlated observations.

RESULTS

Sixty-nine percent (606) of scientists and 69% (91) of IRs returned completed surveys. Compared to nonresponders, survey responders were younger ($p < .001$), but there was no difference by gender or academic rank. Overall, 97% of respondents held a Ph.D. degree, their median age was 50 years, and 73% were male. Scientists were younger than IRs ($p = .001$), but there was no gender difference. Fifty-one percent of IRs were either the president, vice-president, or provost of their institution.

Respondents offered a response for 95% of behaviors that they rated unethical. They responded more often to research behavior they judged to be more unethical: 71% of acts rated 1 (on the 1 to 10 scale of unethical behavior), 88% of the acts rated 2, 92% of the acts rated 3, 95% to 96% of the acts rated 4 to 6, and 97% to 100% of the acts rated 7 to 10.

For 12% of cases, respondents indicated that their only action would be to speak with the researcher committing the act. For an additional 10%, respondents would speak only with the perpetrator and colleagues; and for 7%, respondents proposed to speak with colleagues only. Respondents felt that punishment was appropriate for 53%, 63%, and 61% of these cases, respectively. Punishment was suggested for nearly all protagonists in cases for which respondents proposed to inform an administrator and/or external party (e.g., journal editor or funder). Overall, respondents said they would inform a journal editor, funding agency, or professional society for 19%, 16%, and 4% of cases, respectively. Contacting the lay media was chosen for 0.5% of cases.

COMPARING RESPONSES TO UNETHICAL BEHAVIOR PROPOSED BY SCIENTISTS AND IRs

Institutional representatives proposed a response to 99% of the behaviors that they classified as unethical, and scientists proposed a response to 94% of unethical acts. IRs proposed different responses than scientists. Seventy-four percent of scientists proposed to speak to the researcher who committed the offense, compared to 67% of IRs (p = .001), and scientists proposed to discuss such issues with colleagues far more often than did IRs (58% versus 24%, p = .001).

The findings indicate that scientists more often proposed actions that were limited to the researcher and colleagues, whereas IRs proposed to involve administrators, deans, and others more often in revelations of the unethical behavior. For example, scientists would speak with only the researcher and colleagues in 12% of cases and only colleagues in 9% of cases; IRs proposed these actions in only 2% and 0.4% of cases, respectively. IRs proposed to discuss cases with the researcher, supervisor, and an administrator in 18% of cases, whereas scientists suggested this plan in only 3% of cases. Overall, scientists would limit reporting to researchers (researcher and/or colleagues and/or supervisor) or not report for 58% of cases, compared to only 25% for IRs (p < .001).

We developed a model of whether respondents said they would report the behavior outside of the group of researchers (inform an administrator or dean, a journal editor, a funding agency, a professional society, or a reporter) versus limiting reporting to the researchers (the researcher and/or colleagues and/or the supervisor). The logistic regression (Somers's D = 0.53), adjusting for respondent academic rank, age and gender, scenario unethical score, and the interaction between sample and unethical score revealed that IRs were significantly more likely to inform an administrator or external individual. Figure 2 displays the predicted percentage of cases that scientists and IRs would report to an administrator or external individual by the unethical level of the case. At every unethical level, IRs would report behavior outside the research group more often than would scientists.

RELATIONSHIP OF THE RESPONSE TO THE UNETHICAL ACT

Respondents matched responses with unethical acts. Responses including informing an administrator, dean, or journal editor were prescribed for cases with higher mean unethical score ratings. Informing an administrator or dean was proposed for 23% of the scenarios in which the protagonist made "an honest but serious mistake in reporting research results," whereas such a response was planned for 67% of scenarios in which "fabrication of data" occurred. Respondents proposed to inform the funding agency for 40% of scenarios depicting data fabrication but only 9% of scenarios in which the scientist picked "the best results to report, honestly believing them to be the correct ones." For each response (row) except "keeping it to yourself," the percentage of proposed responses across acts (columns) was significantly different by the chi-square test ($p \leq$ .001). Differences in how subjects said they would respond across the range of acts also was found for the other three behavior domains.

Although there was a direct relationship between response and the nature of the unethical act, the response was unrelated to the harm resulting from the unethical act. The exception to this was when a specific reporting act would serve to rectify the effect of the behavior. For example, respondents would report an unethical appropriation of ideas that resulted in a publication in a prestigious journal to a journal editor more often than if the act resulted in a grant or meeting presentation (27% versus 14% versus 13%, p = .001).

RELATIONSHIP OF RESPONSE TO THE PROTAGONIST'S CHARACTERISTICS

The type of response to unethical research behavior was not related to the gender of the protagonist. However, there was a relationship between the response and the academic status of the protagonist and whether this was repeated behavior. Compared to senior researchers, junior scientists were more likely to be spoken to directly. The unethical behavior of a tenured, prestigious head of a laboratory was more likely to be discussed with colleagues, a funding agency, and the scientific press. Scientists who committed prior offenses were more likely to be reported to colleagues, supervisors, administrators, editors, and funders, although they were less likely to be directly confronted.

DISCUSSION

This investigation into scientists' proposed responses to unethical research behavior reveals that scientists said they would act in response to 94% of research behaviors that they considered to be unethical. This finding is consistent with the scientists' professional responsibility to self-regulate and to ensure the validity of science—the so-called organized skepticism of Merton (1973). However, the findings appear to conflict with the perception that scientists do not reveal many of the unethical behaviors they discover or suspect (Engler et al. 1987).

These data shed light on the apparent discrepancy between scientists' actual and proposed actions. Although scientists nearly universally propose to report unethical behavior, in fully one third of the cases, the reporting was confined to the researcher, to colleagues, or to a combination of the two. If we add situations in which scientist respondents would report the behavior to the researcher's supervisor, 50% of cases would not be reported by scientist whistle-blowers beyond the researcher's immediate superior or colleagues. Reporting would be "constructive"—educational or a warning—and unlikely to generate a disciplinary response. This mode of response would not be viewed by external observers as an accountable reporting of the unethical behavior. These findings elucidate the paradox of scientists' purported willingness to respond to the unethical behavior but the rarity of observable whistle-blowing. This leads to the question, Is the proposed behavior self-regulation or cover-up?

Scientists felt that 69% of the cases in which they would report unethical behavior to some combination of the researcher, supervisor, and colleagues merited punishment. Because reporting the behavior to this internal group is unlikely to result in any administrative action or sanction, these findings suggest that scientist respondents perceived that their actions alone would confer punishment upon the perpetrator of the unethical act (Friedson 1970). Being mistrusted by one's colleagues or profession would be a devastating blow to scientists for whom trust and integrity are the foundation of transaction and communication (Fuchs and Westervelt 1996). Scientists may perceive that they are responding appropriately to unethical acts by informing perpetrators and colleagues. This theory is bolstered by the fact that acts in the minimally to moderately unethical range (mean scores of 4 to 6.5 on the 10-point scale) were handled in this fashion. Responses to behaviors rated as more unethical included scientists' notification of administrators and parties external to the research group.

An alternative explanation of these findings might be the cognitive dissonance between the commitment that scientists feel to the self-policing role as a professional and loyalty to colleagues and the profession. A scientist has an obligation of loyalty to fellow scientists (Swazey and Scher 1981). In addition, there is the potential that exposing research fraud could potentially harm science to a greater degree than the fraud itself (Wenger et al. 1997). The social pressures against external reporting of unethical behavior (Swazey and Scher 1981; Fuchs and Westervelt 1996), uncertainty about whether behaviors are unethical, and the harms that befall whistle-blowers may contribute to scientists' ambivalence.

Compared to scientists, IRs were significantly more likely to report unethical acts to administrators or other individuals who would act on the information, even after accounting for the unethical rating of the act. Not only did IRs propose to notify administrators and outside parties more often, but they proposed to do so for less unethical behaviors than did scientists. This calls into question precisely what is required of a profession to police itself and whether scientists are able to accomplish this.

There are no explicit rules for what behaviors need to be recognized and addressed for a profession to police itself. This is in part integral to the profession's members being the repository of the specialized knowledge, enabling the detection of unethical behavior. However, the very divergent perspectives on the appropriate response to unethical behavior of scientists and those charged with addressing research behavior at their institutions challenge scientists to justify their self-regulation behaviors. Some have suggested that professions alone are unable to self-regulate (Bayles 1981). Proposals to improve regulation include incorporation of lay individuals in the process of deciding on sanctions and creation of more explicit guidelines for reporting and punishment (Bayles 1981; Fox and Braxton 1994; Association of American Medical Colleges 1997). However, these data demonstrate that 50% of unethical behaviors would probably never come to the attention of review panels. These findings call on scientists and regulators to develop a common understanding of the reporting requirements for unethical behavior. Until that is possible, the usual conduct of the scientist will lead to the continued perception that reporting is incomplete.

This study is limited in several ways. The data were derived from a small homogeneous group of scientists; it has been shown that there is variation among the experiences of researchers in different disciplines (Swazey, Anderson, and Lewis 1993) and the findings may not be generalizable to other scientist groups. In addition, the findings are based on responses to scenarios rather than actual behavior. Scenario responses are not always consistent with actual behavior, although responses tend to reflect the direction and relative magnitude of a behavior (Jones, Gerrity, and Eary 1990). In addition, the findings appear to be consistent with the observed behavior of scientists (Hamilton 1992); social

desirability bias would lead to underestimation of the degree to which scientists would handle unethical behavior internally. The expected relationships found between the response to unethical behavior and unethical level of the act, protagonist academic position, and prior behavior, but not with protagonist gender and resultant harms, supports the validity of the survey data. Furthermore, IRs and scientists may perceive different duties to report research. Although IRs, as representatives to the Office of Research Integrity, have a duty to report scientific misconduct once an investigation has been initiated, their initial ethical responsibilities when discovering unethical behavior mirrors that of the scientist. Finally, this is an exploratory study. Further work should elucidate the differences between scientists and IRs found here and should evaluate the purpose and meaning underlying scientists' proposed responses to unethical behavior.

REFERENCES

ASSOCIATION OF AMERICAN MEDICAL COLLEGES. 1997. *Developing a code of ethics in research: A guide for scientific societies.* Washington, DC: Author.

BAYLES, M. D. 1981. Ensuring compliance. In *Professional ethics*. Belmont, CA: Wadsworth.

BEN-DAVID, J. 1991. The profession of science and its powers. In *Scientific growth: Essays on the social organization and ethos of science*, edited by G. Freudenthal. Berkeley: University of California Press.

ENGLER, R. L., J. W. COVELL, P. J. FRIEDMAN, P. S. KITCHER, and R. M. PETERS. 1987. Misrepresentation and responsibility in medical research. *New England Journal of Medicine* 317:1383-9.

FLORES, A. 1988. Introduction: What kind of person should a professional be? In *Professional ideals*, edited by A. Flores. Belmont, CA: Wadsworth.

FOX, M. F., and J. M. BRAXTON. 1994. Misconduct and social control in science. *Journal of Higher Education* 65:373-83.

FRIEDSON, E. 1970. *Profession of medicine: A study of the sociology of applied knowledge.* New York: Dodd, Mead.

FUCHS, S., and S. D. WESTERVELT. 1996. Fraud and trust in science. *Perspective in Biology and Medicine* 39:248-69.

HAMILTON, D. P. 1992. In the trenches, doubts about scientific integrity. *Science* 255:1636.

HOX, J. J., I. G. G. KREFT, P. L. J. HERMKENS. 1991. The analysis of factorial surveys. *Sociological Methods and Research* 4:493-510.

HUNDER, P. J. 1967. *The behavior of maximum likelihood estimates under nonstandard conditions*. Berkeley: University of California Press.

JONES, T. V., M. S. GERRITY, and J. EARY. 1990. Written case simulations: Do they predict physicians' behavior? *Journal of Clinical Epidemiology* 43:805-15.

KORENMAN, S. G., R. BERK, N. S. WENGER, and V. LEW. 1998. Evaluation of the research norms of scientists and administrators responsible for academic research integrity. *JAMA* 279:41-7.

LENNANE, K. J. 1993. "Whistleblowing": A health issue. *BMJ* 307:667-70.

MERTON, R. K. 1973. The normative structure of science. In *The Sociology of Science*, edited by N. W. Storer. Chicago: University of Chicago Press.

NATIONAL ACADEMY OF SCIENCES COMMITTEE ON THE CONDUCT OF SCIENCE. 1995. *On being a scientist: Responsible conduct in research*. Washington, DC: National Academy Press.

ROSSI, P. H., and S. L. NOCK 1982. *Measuring social judgments: The factorial survey approach*. Newbury Park, CA: Sage.

SIGMA XI, The Scientific Research Society. 1991. *Honor in science*, 2d ed. Research Triangle Park.

SWAZEY, J. P., M. S. ANDERSON, and K. S. LEWIS. 1993. Ethical problems in academic research. *American Scientist* 81:542-53.

SWAZEY, J. P., and S. R. SCHER, eds. 1981. The whistleblower as a deviant professional: Professional norms and responses to fraud in clinical research. In *Whistleblowing in biomedical research*. Washington, DC: President's Com- mission for the Study of Ethical Problems in Medicine and Biomedical and Behavioral Research.

WENGER, N. S., S. G. KORENMAN, R. BERK, and S. BERRY. 1997. The ethics of scientific research: An analysis of focus groups of scientists and institutional representatives. *Journal of Invest Medicine* 45:371-80.

COMMENTARY ON THE READINGS

Spell *Nacirema* backwards, and you have *American*. The essay begins much like any normal article based on anthropological fieldwork. But the rituals start to sound strangely familiar, even though the interpretation is all wrong. Bathrooms are not shrines, but an observer from another culture might well perceive them that way. Miner is trying to make an important point: Despite the skill, dedication, and best intentions of social scientists, interpretive mistakes are bound to happen. As social scientists have been raised and continue to live in their own cultures, it is all too easy to interpret the artifacts and practices of members of other cultures—and those of our own—through the lens of our cultural biases about "natives." Social scientists have an ethical obligation to remember that we are not perfect, that mistakes can be made, and often those mistakes in interpretation or judgment can have negative consequences.

Neil Wenger and associates have written a fine essay that not only illuminates the role of the scientific community in reporting unethical behavior, but provides an excellent example of a survey as well. The scientific community is organized to seek out and expand knowledge, and one aspect of this function is to police one another to ensure that research behavior is ethical. The good news in their study is that many scientists recognized the behaviors about which they were asked as unethical. But some might find their findings disturbing:

> Fifty percent of cases would not be reported by scientist whistle-blowers beyond the researcher's immediate superior or colleagues. . . . This mode of response would not be viewed by external observers as an accountable reporting of unethical behavior (562).

The results seem to indicate that the mere act of embarrassing the researcher in front of his or her peers is enough to halt the behavior and deter future behavior.

It is possible that most scientists would discuss the unethical behavior with the scientist first and then take more severe action if they were not satisfied with the researcher's response to their criticism. The authors also suggest that personal loyalty might interfere with the ethical obligations to report unethical behavior. Scientists are often friends with one another, and reporting unethical practices might be construed as a betrayal by some. In other cases, a scientist might be concerned that the disclosure of unethical research could have a more negative effect on science than the unethical behavior itself.

In sum, Wenger and associates demonstrate that the reporting of unethical research behavior is more complicated than one would necessarily suppose. There is some comfort to be taken in the finding that many of the situations they discussed were perceived as unethical. This perception of right and wrong most likely guides most scientists to conduct ethical research. And it's a good thing.

CONCLUSION

Ethics are not merely a matter of common sense. Ethical lapses can come about because a researcher deliberately acts unethically, but they can also occur because the researcher does not fully think through a study or acts with a sense of arrogance. This means that researchers need to constantly think about ethics in designing and carrying out research projects.

CHAPTER 4

EXPERIMENTS

Perhaps the image that first comes to mind when one thinks of a scientist is that of a laboratory and a white-coated individual holding a clipboard. Experiments are a key tool for all of the sciences, and the social sciences are no exception. The basic design of the experiment has also served as the inspiration for other research methods. It is thus a logical place to begin our investigation into research methods.

CONTROL

The key to understanding experimental methods is control. In an experiment, the researcher attempts to control all extraneous variables so that only the effects of the relevant variables are important. The experimenter tries to understand the effect that a given stimulus has on a particular phenomenon, and in order to do this all other variables that might have an effect on the phenomenon must be accounted for so that only the stimulus remains as the likely culprit. For example, if one wants to understand the effect of football on an individual's propensity to commit a violent act, a simple experiment could be arranged where subjects are exposed to a video of a football game and their level of interest in violence is measured afterwards. Such a design, however, would fail to control for a series of possible variables. The individual's background could be a significant variable, and so sampling would need to ensure a random selection of subjects. Also, the level of violence on the video would need to remain constant across all subjects so that the results would reflect the effects of the same game. Similarly, the environment in which the game is watched would need to be controlled—some people may become more excitable in the presence of others, regardless of what is on television. In other words, every variable that *might* influence an individual's propensity toward violence must be controlled so that the researcher can be certain that it is the effect of football itself that is being measured.

THE PLAYERS

Experiments have a number of personnel components. The experimenter, obviously, is the researcher. The people on whom the experiment is run are referred to as *subjects*. Subjects are generally sampled from an appropriate population, such as college students or the local community. While the experiment is taking place, the experimenter at times finds it necessary to have coconspirators who are not identified as working with the experimenter but rather in some other capacity. These coconspirators are called *confederates*. For instance, Solomon Asch (1958) conducted experiments in which a subject was placed at a table with a number of confederates posing as fellow subjects. The subject and confederates were shown a series of lines, one shorter than the rest, and asked if the lines were the same length. Each confederate answered "yes"—an obvious error—until the subject was finally asked for her or his opinion. The experiment tested the subjects' willingness to conform to social pressure, and the confederates were part of the experimental stimulus (see later).

In this experiment, Solomon Asch felt it necessary to conceal the true nature of the experiment. If the subjects had known what was being studied, this surely would have biased the results. Many experiments rely on such concealment of their true purposes, but subjects must be informed about the true nature of study at the earliest possible moment. Therefore, many experiments include a *debriefing* immediately after the experiment so that subjects may be informed about the purpose of the study.

CLASSICAL EXPERIMENTAL DESIGN

As discussed in Chapter 1, most research methods incorporate an independent and a dependent variable. In the classical experiment, the researcher attempts to isolate these two variables so that it can be said, "This experiment shows a relationship between watching football and violence," or "This experiment shows no relationship between watching football and violence." In the previous example, "viewing football" is the independent variable because we are interested in studying its influence on one's propensity to commit violence (the dependent variable).

The effect of the independent variable can be ascertained by measuring the dependent variable of each subject before and after the exposure to the independent variable. The measurement of the dependent variable before exposure to the independent variable is called a *pretest*, whereas the measurement that is done afterward is called the *posttest*. In our current example, one may choose to measure one's violence propensity with a questionnaire, physiological tests, or preferably some combination of both. The tests may show the following hypothetical results:

PRETEST	POSTTEST
85	85

This experiment shows no difference between the pretest and the posttest, and we may conclude that the independent variable had no effect on the dependent variable.

In other words, we measured no significant effect on violence propensity by viewing football. However, our experiment may also yield the following results:

PRETEST   **POSTTEST**
85   100

Here there is a significant difference between the pretest and the posttest. If a higher score indicates a higher propensity to violence, we may conclude that viewing football increases one's propensity to violence. Similarly, if we had a lower posttest score on the same scale, it would indicate a lower propensity to violence as a result of watching football.

In order to have a valid experiment, the subjects are divided into two groups: the control group and the experimental group. A *control group* is a group of subjects who are not exposed to the independent variable, or stimulus, whereas the *experimental group* is exposed to the stimulus. The initial sample obtained for conducting the experiment is divided, at random, between the two groups so that they are similar to each other in every way except for exposure to the stimulus. In the current example, we would want to ensure that, for instance, all football fans are not assigned to the control group and that the experimental group has no football fans. By assigning subjects randomly to the control and experimental groups, we minimize the possibility that the two groups are biased in any particular direction and thus have a more valid study. We then carry out the experiment.

Experimental group: Pretest → Exposure to stimulus → posttest
Control group: Pretest → No exposure to stimulus → posttest

In some cases, especially in medical research, a placebo may be used to simulate exposure to a stimulus but it does not contain the experimental stimulus. For instance, an experiment testing the effects of aspirin on a headache may administer a sugar pill to the control group while the experimental group receives aspirin. In pharmaceutical research, it has been found that some subjects will show a change from pretest to posttest even when given a placebo, the change being attributable to the power of one's mind when subjects *think* they are being given a substance that will work even when there is no chemical reason for it to do so. Although placebos are relatively rare in social research, the placebo effect must still be accounted for in experiments. Similarly, in social research one must be wary of the Hawthorne effect, wherein subjects will show a response simply because of the attention being given by the experimenter.

INTERPRETATION AND ANALYSIS

Experiments are interpreted by examining the results of the pretest and posttest. In a classical experiment, the result may be quite clear:

	PRETEST	POSTTEST
Experimental group	85	100
Control group	85	85

In this example, there is a very clear change in the experimental group but no change in the control group. In our football experiment, we can surmise that watching football has an effect on violence, for the control group (which did not watch football) showed no change in its posttest score. It is possible to use a placebo in this case, such as exposing the control group to a documentary about house cats, in which case the results may look more like this:

	PRETEST	POSTTEST
Experimental group	85	100
Control group	85	80

The control group does show some change as a result of watching a video, but the stimulus is different and so are the results. The changes may be the result of watching a video, any video, or they could be the result of watching a film about cats, but they are not the results of watching football as in the experimental group. Similarly, even with the absence of a placebo, there may still be some change in the posttest caused by the boredom of not watching a video.

VARIATIONS ON EXPERIMENTAL DESIGN

There are many variations on the classical experimental design, too numerous to discuss fully here. One way in which experiments may vary is based on blindness. In a single blind experiment, the researcher knows which individuals are assigned to the experimental and control groups, but the subjects do not. Subjects are rarely, if ever, told to which group they are assigned because this knowledge can bias the results. However, researchers are people too, and the knowledge of who is in what group can also bias the researcher's perception of effects. To guard against this effect, some experiments are double blind: Neither the researchers nor the subjects know to which group a subject is assigned.

Experiments could also vary by including more than one experimental group so that the effect of intervening variables can be tested. In some cases, more than one control group may be used, one with a placebo and one without. In still other cases, certain components of the classical experiment may be excluded. Classical experiments are often best conducted in a laboratory of some kind, but such an environment itself can bias the results for social scientists. To avoid this effect, quasi-experiments can be conducted that, while not controlling for extraneous variables, more precisely mimic real world scenarios. A quasi-experiment may, for instance, include only an experimental group (a one-group experiment) or not include a pretest (a static group experiment). In both cases, some level of validity is sacrificed for the relative ease of finding subjects or more accurately mimicking the real world.

THE READINGS

The following experiments are both variations on classical design but must necessarily work within the limits imposed by their subject matter. The first reading, "Placing Alcohol Warnings before, during, and after TV Beer Ads: Effects on Knowledge and Responses to the Ads and Warnings," by Michael Slater and colleagues (1994), tests a series of independent variables. The second reading, "Experimentally Manipulating Race: Perceptions of Police Brutality in an Arrest," by Jack Levin and Alex Thomas (1997), is an example of an "after-only" design that, because of the nature of the stimulus videotape, cannot include a pretest of the subjects.

■ ■ ■ ■ ■

PLACING ALCOHOL WARNINGS BEFORE, DURING, AND AFTER TV BEER ADS: EFFECTS ON KNOWLEDGE AND RESPONSES TO THE ADS AND THE WARNINGS

Michael D. Slater, Donna Rouner, David Karan, Kevin Murphy, and Frederick Beauvais
Colorado State University

This experiment compared the effects of warnings placed before, during, or after television beer advertisements. Warnings before or after the ads led to higher knowledge scores and fewer negative comments about the warning presentation than did warnings scrolled during the ads; warnings after and during but not before the ads significantly decreased positive comments about the ads. Earlier findings regarding effects of warning topic and quantitative information in the warnings were replicated.

INTRODUCTION

During the past decade, warnings have been mandated on alcohol container labels, and several U.S. senators have proposed legislation to require warnings on alcohol advertising similar to those required on cigarette advertising. However, beer—unlike cigarettes—is heavily advertised on television. If warnings are to be required with televised alcohol advertisements, several practical issues must be confronted, and the resulting policy decisions should be informed by empirical research. One such issue is how warnings are placed with respect to the television advertisement.

A warning in a print advertisement can be boxed and separated from the rest of the ad, and research suggests it can be overlooked in a visual scan of the page.[1] A warning accompanying a television advertisement may be harder to ignore. Presentation of information is typically sequential and controlled by the videotape editor, not by the eye movements of the viewer over a printed graphic image. Given the sequential nature of videotape, one important issue in designing warnings for ads is their sequencing relative to the ad. This study examines the effects of placing an alcohol warning before, during, or after a beer ad; on responses to the warning and responses to the ad; as well as on other outcomes such as recall and knowledge. In addition, this study serves to replicate ealier research which found distinctive interactions between alcohol warning topics and the presence or absence of quantitative information in the warnings.[2]

From *Journalism & Mass Communication Quarterly,* 76, 3 (Autumn 1999): 468–84. Copyright
© 1999 AEJMC.

Implications of the Sequential Placement of a Warning on Responses to and Recall of the Warning. There has been some research on the location of warnings within print cigarette ads.[3] We have located no parallel studies comparing the effects of placing warnings before or after a televised ad. Nonetheless, if warnings are paired with televised ads, there are two plausible placement strategies. For example, when advertisers include a responsible drinking slogan, it normally comes at the end of the ad. On the other hand, a Seagram's ad introduced in 1997 included a six-second warning regarding underage drinking at the beginning of the ad. There are important questions regarding placement of warnings before or after the ad. First, there are questions about how viewers respond to, and recall, the warnings themselves. Second, there are questions about effects of the warnings on responses to the advertisements, and on knowledge and attitudes relative to alcohol use. The second set of questions, unlike the first, can best be gauged in comparison to an advertisement-only, no-warning control condition. The two sets of questions, then, will be addressed separately below.

An alternative to placing the warning before or after an ad is including it during the advertisement. Obviously, many constraints operate on such a placement strategy. Warning text cannot occupy the screen to the exclusion of the ad, nor can a voice read the warning without interfering with the ad soundtrack. However, the use of scrolled text under television programming is now familiar to most viewers, most often in the form of weather advisories.[4] Such scrolled warnings were also used during the Persian Gulf war to indicate newscasts that were subject to Iraqi censorship. Research on the censorship disclaimers indicated that the scrolled messages reduced thought elaboration about the disclaimer, presumably by increasing cognitive load on the viewers.[5] It is likely that the same phenomenon would be found for scrolled warnings. Therefore,

> H1: Warnings scrolled under a televised beer ad will result in less thought elaboration about the warnings compared to warnings placed before or after the ad.

The ad and the warning, when presented sequentially rather than simultaneously, can be considered a paired set of stimuli. Therefore, the placement of the warning may also influence processing set, or the tendency to process social information either to remember it or to glean social impressions from it.[6] Because warnings are largely informational, people should process them as such and tend to remember their contents, whereas ads tend to be processed as social information, leading people to form impressions rather than remember details.[7] If the ad is processed with an impression set, then the presence of scrolled warnings would interfere with the viewer's processing goals,[8] which should prove frustrating or annoying to the viewer. Therefore,

> H2: Viewers will respond more negatively regarding the presentation of warnings scrolled under a televised beer ad than to the presentation of warnings before or after the ad.

Existing research does not provide clear guidance regarding implications of placement for recall of warning content. However, some inferences can be made. If scrolling a warning under an advertisement splits the viewer's attention and increases cognitive load, then recall of warnings should be less than when the warning is shown before or after the ad—assuming, of course, that recall of warnings is sensitive to such differences in cognitive effort. Also when an ad follows a warning, the ad might establish an impression set that interferes with the ability to remember the content of the warning seen just earlier. Therefore,

> H3: Recall for warning content will be lowest when the warning is scrolled under a televised beer advertisement, highest when the warning follows the ad, and be intermediate when the warning precedes the ad.

Treatment/Control Comparisons of Warning Effects. One of the most intriguing aspects of warnings is their possible impact on viewer responses to the televised beer advertisements. Treatment/control comparisons make it possible to assess the impact of warnings on responses to advertisements. For example, in the Newhagen studies discussed above, scrolled disclaimers tended to reduce memory for the televised story.[9] Therefore, we might expect reduced thought elaboration concerning the ads in the warning conditions, as compared to the control condition. In addition, scrolled disclaimers at the beginning of the news story tended to increase thought elaboration about the news story relative to disclaimers at the end of the story. Assuming that placement of warnings before or after the ad will have similar effects to placing a disclaimer at the beginning or end of a news story leads us to expect a similar pattern with respect to warnings. Finally, we might also expect that warnings scrolled during the ad will be directly competitive for cognitive resources with the ad, leading to the greatest reduction in thought elaboration concerning the ad. Therefore:

> H4: In the warning conditions, viewers will show the least thought elaboration about televised beer advertisements when the warning is scrolled during the ad, and will show the most thought elaboration when the warning is shown before the advertisement, with warnings after the ad showing intermediate values; the greatest elaboration will be found in the no-warning control condition.

The amount of thought elaboration does not speak to a more important question from the applied perspective: the effect of the warnings on the valence of responses to the ad. As mentioned earlier, warnings and ads can be thought of as paired stimuli. Therefore, the first stimulus processed may serve to prime attitudes that will be activated when the succeeding message is processed.[10] Previous research has found that alcohol warnings presented after the ad result in relatively less positive net responses to beer ads than when no warnings are present,[11] an effect that increased with repeated exposures to the warnings and ads. It would therefore seem plausible to expect that such an effect would be even more pronounced when the warning appeared before the ad, priming negative attitudes regarding alcohol use. Similarly, warnings scrolled dur-

ing the ad should result in relatively negative overall responses to the ad even more than for the before condition, as the negative attitudes are being primed simultaneously with the processing of the ad. Therefore,

> H5: Viewers will show (a) the fewest positive and most negative responses to the televised beer advertisements when the warning is scrolled during the ad, followed by when the warning precedes the ad and then by the condition in which warnings are after the ads, with the control condition showing the most positive and fewest negative responses to the ads; (b) this effect will increase with repetition of the ads and warnings.

Most research on alcohol warnings has focused on recall of the container warning label.[12] The one positive effect of alcohol warning exposure typically found is greater knowledge concerning alcohol risks, especially when the information in the warnings has novel elements.[13] Assuming that there is some novel information in the warnings, one should expect some knowledge effect due to warning exposure. However, this may vary by placement condition. As argued above, warnings shown simultaneously with the ads should result in greater difficulty processing the information in the warnings and the ads. Similarly, the ads will interfere least with learning information in warnings shown after the ads. Therefore,

> H6: Viewers will score highest in knowledge of information contained in the warnings when the warning is after the beer advertisement, followed by when the warning precedes the ad, and then by the condition in which warnings are scrolled during the ad, with the control condition showing the least knowledge about alcohol risks addressed in the warnings.

Evidence for some attitudinal effects of short-term warning exposure has also been found. Two studies of college students indicated that the container warning, when appended to print advertisements, actually served to increase perceived product benefits and/or reduce perceived risks.[14] Another study of college students, using televised advertisements and more specific, stronger warnings, found no such boomerang effect. The latter study also found evidence that the warnings decreased confidence in beliefs about the riskiness of alcohol among those students who tended to believe alcohol was relatively risk-free.[15] Given the use of warnings that are stronger and more specific than the container warning, we might expect:

> H7: Viewers in the warning conditions who believe beer to be relatively risk-free will show reduced confidence in their risk beliefs relative to controls.

Replication of Findings regarding Warning Topic and Quantitative Information. An earlier study showed that the effects of including quantitative information in warnings was contingent on the topic of the warning.[16] In particular, more positive responses were found to the quantitative versions of an alcohol and cancer warning than the non-quantitative version, with the opposite pattern for warnings about drinking and driving and alcohol/drug interactions. Topic effects were also found for negative responses to the warnings and for perceived risk of alcohol, in which drinking and driving warnings were best received, followed by alcohol/drug and alcohol/cancer warnings in that order.

The present study utilized these same warnings and many of the same dependent measures, permitting replication insofar as the topic and quantitative information variables do not interact with our present treatment conditions (that is, warning placement). Therefore:

> H8: Interactions between alcohol warning topic and the presence or absence of quantitative information in the warnings will be found concerning positive responses to the warnings; and topic effects will be found for (a) negative responses to the warnings, and (b) perceived product risks.

METHODS

This experiment used a 4 (warnings before, warnings during, warnings after, and no warn-

ings) × 3 (drunk-driving, alcohol and cancer, and alcohol/drug interactions warning topics) × 2 (warnings with and without quantitative information) factorial design. The warning placement factor was between subjects. The warning topic and quantitative information factors were within-subjects factors.

Stimuli Production and Presentation. For the before-ad and after-ad warning conditions, the warnings were presented in white reversed out of black background, with a professional announcer reading the warning text. For the during-ad warning, white text scrolled across the bottom of the screen beginning a few seconds after the beginning of the ad and concluding before the ad ended. Details on warning content and the warning development process are provided elsewhere.[17] Seven warnings were produced of each type, six representing the crossed topic by quantitative information factors and the seventh the container warning. Seven television beer ads were selected to accompany the warnings, selected from a random sampling of beer ads. The selection incorporated the restriction that no more than one ad be included from any one advertising campaign. The warnings and ads were counterbalanced using a 7 × 7 Greco-Latin template, which assured that stimulus order and sequence would be counterbalanced. To increase the realism of the viewing experience, the ads and warnings were presented in three "pods" of four ads, with a beer ad at the beginning and end of the pod and two randomly selected non-beer ads serving as filler; a seventh ad-warning pair concluded the presentation. The pods were presented during randomly selected sports programs, as nearly all beer advertisements are shown during sports programming.[18]

Procedure. Alcohol use information (see below) was collected on the telephone during the screener prior to agreement to participate in the on-site data collection session. Participants met in groups of three to seven in which they saw the stimulus tapes and provided open- and closed-end responses (see below) when the tape was stopped after each ad-warning pair. Posttest and demographic data were collected at the end of the videotape presentation.

Participants and Recruiting Procedures. A commercial market research company under the supervision of the investigators recruited participants in the experiment using a random telephone sample for a Western county that closely approximates national averages for many demographic variables. The reason for this procedure was that the policy implications of a study on warnings required the most representative participants that we could reasonably obtain, rather than the convenience samples typical of most experimental research. We offered a $35 incentive for participation in the experiment. We found that 57% of those persons who completed the screener and qualified for participation would in fact come to the university campus to participate in the research, and that 44.3% of the persons contacted would complete the screener. These response rates are quite high for recruitment to central location research, and, combined with the random digit dial recruitment strategy, suggest that the participants were in fact unusually representative by the standards of controlled experimental research.

Qualifying participants were required to be 21 to 65 years old and use alcohol a minimum of once a month. The sample was stratified to ensure equal gender representation. Heavier drinkers (14+ drinks per week) were quota-sampled to be proportionate to the national norm of 9%, based on the quantity/frequency measurement method.[19] Our sample reached within 1% of the quota without oversampling, which increased our confidence in the sample's representativeness. Participants included 181 males and 179 females. Nearly half—46.7%—of participants were between 21 and 34 years old, with the remainder falling between 35–65 years. Participants were 85% Euro-American, 4.2% Native American, 3.9% Latino, 5.3% other, with the remainder being African- or Asian-American. Lighter drinkers were about a quarter of the study population, with 26.7% of participants reporting having fewer than 1 drink per week, 54.2% consuming 1–7 drinks per week, and 19.1% consuming more than 7 drinks per week.

Measured Variables. Cognitive responses are the thoughts that arise in the recipient of a persuasive message in response to that message.

Research indicates that such responses mediate the persuasive impact of messages in general,[20] the impact of alcohol education messages on alcohol-related attitudes,[21] and the impact of alcohol warnings on associated attitudes.[22] Warning coding categories included the following: issue- or content-related comments, style- or presentation-related comments, nonspecific emotional reactions, and non-sequiturs. Responses in each category were also coded as being either positive (consistent with the alcohol warning message), neutral, or negative. The Cohen's kappa for intercoder reliability (using two coders with 10% of the sample) was .83 for polarity and .58 for category. Kappa is a conservative statistic, and kappas greater than .5 are considered adequate for analysis.[23] Responses to the advertisement were coded, for the purposes of this study, simply in terms of polarity, with a kappa of .97. Consistent with our earlier research, polarity was not collapsed into net scores. We have found in the context of warnings that analyzing positive and negative responses to warnings and advertisements independently is more productive than using a computed net polarity score.[24]

Two semantic-differential type items, using a 9-point response scale, were used after each message exposure to measure the perceived hazard and safety of the product (beer) advertised.[25] The risk items were combined into an index (Cronbach's alphas ranged from .63 to .74 across the 7 repetitions of these items in the repeated measures design). Confidence in these ratings was also assessed after each risk item, yielding alphas ranging from .84 to .92.[26]

Recall was measured via an open-ended item: "If you can recall even a part of any of the warnings you have just seen, please write down those warnings or phrases from those warnings." Correctly recalled phrases were summed to create an addictive scale of recall across all warnings. Two coders separately created counts on 10% of the sample, and achieved a Pearson's correlation of .84 on the recall count.

Knowledge of alcohol risks discussed in the warnings was assessed by summing correct responses to 7 true/false items that reflected the content of the alcohol warnings shown. Alcohol use was computed by combining a quantity of drinks per occasion measure and a frequency of

drinking measure into a standard quantity/fre-
quency measure indicating average number of
drinks per week.[27]

RESULTS

The first three hypotheses concerned effects of
warning placement on responses and recall of
warnings, in which the control condition was ir-
relevant. These hypotheses were tested using repeated measures analyses of variance, with
placement included as a between-subjects factor.[28] H1 proposed that there would be less
thought elaboration in response to warnings
scrolled during a beer advertisement relative to
warnings shown before or after the ad. Warning
placement did not in fact significantly affect the
number of thoughts about the warnings. H2 predicted that viewers would respond more negatively to the presentation style of warnings
scrolled under ads than to warnings before or
after the ads. This hypothesis was supported.
Planned contrasts using the scrolled condition as
the reference category indicated differences between the scrolled condition and both the before
and after conditions were statistically significant.
No interactions between warning placement and
the warning content variables (i.e., topic and
quantitative information) were found. It should
be noted, however, that the number of negative
comments about warning presentation were
highly skewed. While analyses of variance in
general are robust against violations of normal-
ity due to skewness and skedasticity, highly
skewed data can render probability estimates less
precise.[29] Therefore, as a check we also tested
the presence or absence of negative presentation
comments by condition using the chi-square statistic. Over half the viewers of the scrolled warnings made at least one negative comment about
presentation, compared to slightly more than a
third of those who saw warnings before the ads
and under a third of those who saw the warnings
after the ad. Such a test is particularly defensible
given the lack of effect of other treatment or design factors on this dependent variable. We also
examined other data, skewed to a lesser extent,
using square root transformations (e.g., H5
analyses). Since these analyses proved essentially
the same as the untransformed analyses, we report the untransformed versions here.

H3 predicted that recall for warning content would be lowest for the scrolled warning
and highest when the warning follows the ad.
There was no support for this hypothesis: recall
means were virtually the same for the three
treatment conditions.

H4 and H5 concerned the effects of warning placement on responses to the beer advertisements.[30] H4 predicted that viewers would
show the least thought elaboration about the ads
when warnings were scrolled under the ads, and
the most elaboration (except for the control condition) when warnings were shown before the
ads. the prediction was partially supported. A
planned polynomial contrast for the predicted
linear trend was significant. As predicted,
thought elaboration about the ads was highest in
the control condition and was highest among the
treatment conditions when the warning was
shown before the ad. However, thought elaboration about the ads tended to be slightly lower
when the warning followed the ad than when
warnings were scrolled.

H5 predicted that viewers would respond
most positively to the beer advertisements in the
control condition, followed by the warning after,
warning before, and the warning during conditions, in that order. H5 also predicted that the
effect would increase with repetition. H5 was
partially supported. The treatment main effects
were significant, as was the planned polynomial
contrast for the predicted linear trend, but the
rankings for warnings before and warnings after
were reversed. As treatment/control differences
were of particular interest here, we also ran contrasts with the control condition for each treatment condition. Positive responses to the ads
were significantly lower when warnings were
shown during and after the ad, but not when
warnings were shown before the ad. Warning effects on the number of negative responses to the
ad were not significant, nor was the treatment by
time interaction for either positive or negative
responses.

The next two hypotheses concerned treatment versus control effects on two cognitive/atti-
tudinal outcomes: knowledge and confidence in
beliefs about the riskiness of beer. H6 proposed
that viewers would show the greatest posttest
knowledge when the warning appeared after the

beer advertisement, followed by the condition in which the warning precedes the ad, then by the scrolled condition, and finally by the control condition. This hypothesis was supported. Planned polynomial contrasts indicated that the linear trend was much as predicted. However, there was very little difference between knowledge posttest scores and warnings being shown before or after the ad, with the warning before condition being marginally higher.

Given these knowledge effects, the absence of recall differences between the during and the other warning conditions was surprising. Therefore, we ran a correlation between the recall and knowledge measures to estimate the relationship between these two outcomes. The correlation between the two was statistically significant but small.

H7 predicted that viewers exposed to warnings who believe beer to be relatively risk-free would show reduced confidence relative to comparable viewers in the control condition. This hypothesis was not supported.[31]

Finally, H8 predicted that the interactions between warning topic and the presence or absence of quantitative information found in previous research on positive responses to the warnings[32] would be replicated here. The hypothesis was supported and the predicted interaction was found. The pattern of means suggested that quantitative warnings were preferred for the alcohol and cancer warnings, and that the reverse was true for the other topics—the same pattern found previously. Topic main effects paralleled the earlier study, with drinking and driving warnings receiving the most positive and least negative responses, with the opposite true of alcohol and cancer. As in the earlier study, there was no statistically significant interaction between quantitative information and topic on negative responses. However, there was such an interaction for perceived risk of alcohol, that suggested slightly higher perceived risks for the quantitative versus the non-quantitative version of the drinking and driving warning, and the opposite pattern for the drinking/drug interaction warning.

DISCUSSION
Comparisons of the warning treatment to the no-warning control support existing literature which suggests that alcohol warnings, especially those that contain new information, can be expected to increase knowledge.[33] In addition, previous research found that alcohol warnings paired with ads result in less positive responses to those ads.[34] Similar results were found in the present study.

More important, this study provides new insights into the effects of various alternative ways to place warnings on television ads. For example, warnings before and after the ad generated relatively few negative comments and resulted in relatively higher post-test knowledge scores compared to the scrolled warnings. However, warnings placed before the ads did not significantly reduce positive responses to the ads relative to no-warning controls. In contrast, warnings during and after the ad did reduce positive responses to the ads. Therefore, warnings before ads may prove an acceptable compromise option from both the public health and industry vantage points should warnings eventually be mandated. Warnings scrolled during the ads were the least effective warning variant in terms of knowledge levels at post-test and generated the most negative comments about warning presentation, as well as evidently interfering with the processing of the ads. As a result, scrolled warnings are the most problematic of the three options. However, it should be noted that these scrolled warnings did show a statistically significant difference from controls in post-test knowledge levels. The scrolled warnings, then, appear to be less effective but not ineffective as an informational tool.

It should also be noted that warnings after the ads reduced total thought elaboration about the ads even more than did warnings during the ad. This finding further underscores the relative undesirability of warnings after ads compared to warnings before the ads from the advertiser's perspective. One explanation for this result is that the warnings were more available in memory than the ads when warnings were shown last. The relative availability of the warnings in memory would tend to reduce the thoughts generated about the ads. If this interpretation is correct, it would suggest, per the theoretical issues discussed earlier, that recency and availability effects are more influential than response set influences in the context of ads and warnings. After all, warnings before the ads, which should have been more influential on ad responses from the response set perspective, had less impact on responses to the ad than did warnings shown during and after the ad. It may be that viewers are accustomed to having very different messages juxtaposed within the same pod of commercial messages, and are able to process the ad without prior warning messages greatly influencing their responses via response set or other priming mechanisms. Or, more simply, a six-second warning may not be enough to prime a response set.

As described above, there were differences in knowledge as a function of placement: warnings scrolled during the ads were associated with less knowledge. There were no such differences for the recall measure. These results suggest an interesting difference between recall and knowledge in the context of this study—a difference further attested by the weak correlation between the two measures. The gist of the warnings were relatively familiar. Therefore, it is possible that any warning exposure simply made whatever people already knew more salient in memory. As priming existing knowledge is not processing-intensive, warning placement might make little difference. As a result, no differences in recall would be apparent: the participant could typically reel off several already familiar points made in the warnings because they had been brought back to mind. On the other hand, the knowledge items required successfully having processed specific, and in some cases, new information. Acquisition of new information, assimilating it into existing knowledge structures or schemata, is cognitively demanding. Therefore, knowledge impacts would be less in the scrolled condition, in which cognitive capacity is challenged by having to process the ad and the warning simultaneously. Such knowledge gain apparently was not reflected in open-ended recall: it is easier to correctly recognize complex information based on a brief exposure than to repeat it without cuing in an open-ended response.

This study also largely confirmed earlier findings[35] that responses to quantitative information in warnings were contingent on the warning topic. In addition, the lack of topic or quantitative vs. non-quantitative content interactions with warning placement indicated that these effects were consistent across all those conditions.

Any controlled, laboratory study suffers from limitations to generalizability. This study is not exempted from that caveat, as participants self-selected in terms of willingness to participate. However, the use of random digit dial recruiting and incentives adequate to encourage participation does mean that this study population is far more diverse and less subject to systematic biases than the typical convenience sample used in experimental research. Certainly the close match between our recruited population and the expected percentage of heavy drinkers from national survey norms is encouraging in this respect.

In summary, these results are consistent with other studies of warnings in underscoring the importance of knowledge as an outcome. If knowledge gain is a principal benefit of warning exposure, then use of varied warnings providing various relevant facts may be preferred to single or generic warnings, and should be recommended to policymakers.[36] These results suggest, too, that measuring recall alone is insufficient to assess knowledge gain in an experimental context.

Most relevant to the intent of this study, these results provide guidance for policymakers regarding placement of warnings with respect to televised alcohol ads. Warnings scrolled during the ad result in lower post-test knowledge levels compared to other warning placements, and generate more negative responses to the warnings as well as fewer positive responses to the ads. As a result, they appear to be the least attractive of the three placement alternatives from either the industry or the public health perspective (unless the public health priority is to undermine the ad, rather than educate the audience). Warnings placed after the ads appear to be effective from the public health standpoint, in terms of minimizing negative comments about warnings and reducing positive responses to beer ads while producing good post-test knowledge levels. Warnings placed before the ads, however, also performed comparably well in terms of audience response and post-test knowledge scores, but did not reduce positive responses to the ads relative to controls at a statistically significant level. Therefore, warnings placed before televised ads may prove a viable compromise strategy should legislators or regulators again pursue inclusion of warnings with alcohol advertising.

NOTES

1. Gaurav Bhalla and John L. Lastovicka, "The Impact of Changing Cigarette Warning Message Content and Format," in *Advances in Consumer Research*, ed. Thomas C. Kinnear (Provo, UT: Association for Consumer Research, 1984), 305–310; Eddie M. Clark and Timothy C. Brock, "Warning Label Location, Advertising, and Cognitive Responding," in *Attention, Attitude, and Affect in Response to Advertising*, ed. Eddie M. Clark, Timothy C. Brock, and David W. Stewart (Hillsdale, NJ: Erlbaum, 1994), 287–99.

2. Michael D. Slater, David Karan, Donna Rouner, Frederick Beauvais, and Kevin Murphy, "Developing and Assessing Alcohol Warning Content: Responses to Quantitative Information and Behavioral Recommendations in Warnings with TV Ads," *Public Policy and Marketing* 17 (spring 1998): 48-60.

3. Clark and Brock, "Warning Label Location, Advertising, and Cognitive Responding."

4. One study did attempt to compare placement of alcohol warnings during versus after the advertisement; see Todd Barlow and Michael S. Wogalter, "Alcoholic Beverage Warnings in Magazine and Television Advertisements," *Journal of Consumer Research* 20 (June 1993): 147–56. In that study, the "during" condition was a warning superimposed on the last frame of the ad, which provided a still backdrop. This, of course, is little different from the after condition as compared to the scrolling approach. Barlow and Wogalter found no difference between their conditions and suggested that the during condition might better have been executed during the sound and motion of the advertisement.

5. John E. Newhagen, "Effects of Televised Government Censorship Disclaimers on Memory and Thought Elaboration During the Gulf War," *Journal of Broadcasting & Electronic Media* 38 (summer 1994): 339–51.

6. Robert S. Wyer and Thomas K. Srull, "Human Cognition in its Social Context," *Psychological Review* 93 (July 1986): 322–59.

7. Marion Friestad and Esther Thorson, "Remembering Ads: the Effects of Encoding Strategies, Retrieval Cues, and Emotional Response," *Journal of Consumer Psychology* 2 (1993): 1–23.

8. See, for a more complete discussion, Michael D. Slater, "Persuasion Processes Across Receiver Goals and Message Genres," *Communication Theory* 7 (1997): 125–48.

9. John E. Newhagen, "Effects of Censorship Disclaimers in Persian Gulf War Television News on Negative Thought Elaboration," *Communication Research* 21 (April 1994): 232–48; Newhagen, "Effects of Televised Government Censorship Disclaimers."

10. R. H. Fazio, D. M. Sanbonmatsu, M. C. Powell, and F. R. Kardes, "On the Automatic Activation of Attitudes," *Journal of Personality and Social Psychology* 50 (February 1986): 505–514.

11. Michael D. Slater and Melanie M. Domenech, "Alcohol Warnings in TV Beer Advertisements," *Journal of Studies on Alcohol* 156 (May 1995): 361–67.

12. Janet R. Hankin, Ira J. Firestone, James J. Sloan, Joel W. Ager, Allen C. Goodman, Robert J. Sokol, and Susan S. Martier, "The Impact of the Alcohol Warning Label on Drinking During Pregnancy," *Public Policy and Marketing* 12 (1993): 10–18; Michael E. Hilton, "An Overview of Recent Findings on Alcohol Beverage Labels," *Public Policy and Marketing* 12 (1993): 1–9; Robert N. Mayer, Ken R. Smith, and Debra L. Scammon, "Evaluating the Impact of Alcohol Warning Labels," *Advances in Consumer Research* 18 (1991) 706–714.

13. Andrea M. Fenaughty and David P. MacKinnon, "Immediate Effects of the Arizona

Alcohol Warning Poster," *Journal of Public Policy and Marketing* 12 (spring 1993): 69–77; Michael J. Kalsher, Steven W. Clarke, and Michael S. Wogalter, "Communication of Alcohol Facts and Hazards by a Warning Poster," *Journal of Public Policy and Marketing* 12 (spring 1993): 78–90; David P. MacKinnon, Mary Ann Pentz, and Alan W. Stacy, "The Alcohol Warning Label and Adolescents: The First Year," *American Journal of Public Health* 83 (April 1993): 585–87; Slater et al., "Developing and Assessing Alcohol Warning Content: Responses to Quantitative Information and Behavioral Recommendations in Warnings with TV Ads."

14. Deborah Blood and Leslie B. Snyder, "Why Warnings Boomerang: the Failure of the Surgeon General's Alcohol Warning to Affect Young Adults" (paper presented at the annual meeting of the International Communication Association, Health Communication Division, Washington, D.C., May 1993); Leslie B. Snyder and Deborah J. Blood, "Caution: Alcohol Advertising and the Surgeon General's Warnings May Have Adverse Effects on Young Adults," *Applied Communication Research* 20 (February 1992): 37–53.

15. Slater and Domenech, "Alcohol Warnings in TV Beer Advertisements."

16. Slater et al., "Developing and Assessing Alcohol Warning Content: Responses to Quantitative Information and Behavioral Recommendations in Warnings with TV Ads."

17. Slater et al., "Developing and Assessing Alcohol Warning Content: Responses to Quantitative Information and Behavioral Recommendations in Warnings with TV Ads."

18. Patricia A. Madden and Joel W. Grube, "The Frequency and Nature of Alcohol and Tobacco Advertising in Televised Sports, 1990–1992," *American Journal of Public Health* 84 (February 1994): 297–99.

19. Lorraine T. Midanik, "Comparing Usual Quantity/Frequency and Graduated Frequency Scales to Assess Yearly Alcohol Consumption: Results from the 1990 U.S.

National Alcohol Survey," *Addiction* 89 (April 1994): 407–412.

20. Richard E. Petty and John T. Cacioppo, *Communication and Persuasion: Central and Peripheral Routes to Attitude Change* (New York: Springer-Verlag, 1986).

21. Michael D. Slater and Donna Rouner, "Value Affirmative and Value Protective Processing of Alcohol Education Messages that Include Statistics or Anecdotes," *Communication Research* 23 (April 1996): 210–35.

22. J. Craig Andrews, Richard G. Netemeyer, and Srinivas Durvasala, "The Role of Cognitive Responses as Mediators of Alcohol Warning Label Effects," *Journal of Public Policy and Marketing* 12 (spring 1993): 57–68.

23. J. Richard Landis and Gary G. Koch, "The Measurement of Observer Agreement for Categorical Data," *Biometrics* 33 (March 1977): 159–74.

24. Slater et al., "Developing and Assessing Alcohol Warning Content: Responses to Quantitative Information and Behavioral Recommendations in Warnings with TV Ads."

25. Slater and Domenech, "Alcohol Warnings in TV Beer Advertisements"; Snyder and Blood, "Caution: Alcohol Advertising and the Surgeon General's Warnings May Have Adverse Effects on Young Adults."

26. Slater and Domenech, "Alcohol Warnings in TV Beer Advertisements."

27. Midanik, "Comparing Usual Quantity/Frequency and Graduated Frequency Scales to Assess Yearly Alcohol Consumption: Results from the 1990 U.S. National Alcohol Survey."

28. Multivariate analyses of variance were conducted prior to running the individual analyses of variance reported here; relevant effects were significant in the omnibus models. Total alcohol consumption was used as a covariate in all the analyses of variance reported.

29. Gene V. Glass, P. D. Peckham, and J. R. Sanders, "Consequences of Failure to Meet Assumptions Underlying the Fixed Effects Analysis of Variance and Covariance," *Review of Educational Research* 42 (summer

1972): 237–88.

30. These analyses of variance incorporated the control condition (as the control condition measured responses to advertisements but not of course responses to warnings) and used serial position as the repeated measures factor.

31. It should be noted that the adult population in this study rated beer consumption, on average, as much riskier than did the college students in the Slater and Domenech study; the lack of impact on confidence in risk estimates found here may be due to the adults' relatively more realistic risk assessments.

32. Slater et al., "Developing and Assessing Alcohol Warning Content: Responses to Quantitative Information and Behavioral Recommendations in Warnings with TV Ads."

33. Fenaughty and MacKinnon, "Immediate Effects of the Arizona Alcohol Warning Poster"; Kalsher, Clarke, and Wogalter, "Communication of Alcohol Facts and Hazards by a Warning Poster"; MacKinnon, Pentz, and Stacy, "The Alcohol Warning Label and Adolescents: The First Year"; Slater et al., "Developing and Assessing Alcohol Warning Content: Responses to Quantitative Information and Behavioral Recommendations in Warnings with TV Ads."

34. Slater and Domenech, "Alcohol Warnings in TV Beer Advertisements."

35. Slater et al., "Developing and Assessing Alcohol Warning Content: Responses to Quantitative Information and Behavioral Recommendations in Warnings with TV Ads."

36. Richard F. Beltramini, "Perceived Believability of Warning Label Information Presented in Cigarette Advertising," *Journal of Advertising* 17 (1988): 26–32; Barbara Loken and Beth Howard-Pitney, "Effectiveness of Cigarette Advertisements on Women: An Experimental Study," *Journal of Applied Psychology* 73 (August 1988): 378–82.

EXPERIMENTALLY MANIPULATING RACE: PERCEPTIONS OF POLICE BRUTALITY IN AN ARREST*

Jack Levin and Alexander R. Thomas
Northeastern University

This study was designed to test, in a controlled setting, the effects of racial identity of the police on perceptions of police brutality. We produced three videotapes, each showing a black male suspect being arrested by two police officers whose racial identity was varied. One version of the tape then was viewed by each randomly assigned subject, 28 white and 33 black college students. Subjects' perceptions of violence and illegality were influenced by the officers' racial identity: Both black and white subjects were significantly more likely to see violence and illegality when both arresting officers were white. Implications for social policy and future research were discussed.

Research on civil disturbances suggests that confrontations between white police and local resi-

From *Justice Quarterly, 14*, 3 (September 1997): 573–85. Copyright © 1997 Academy of Criminal Justice Sciences.

*We are grateful to Lt. Zoel A. Roy, Lt. Mark J. Porter, and Det. James V. Casinelli of the Division of Public Safety at Northeastern University for their participation in the experimental treatments; to Keith Motley and Jen Klein of Northeastern University for their valuable assistance; to Michael Markowitz at Widener University for his comments and suggestions; to Leonard Caplan for his technical skills in colorizing the videotapes; and to James A. Fox and Jack McDevitt of Northeastern University and to anonymous reviewers for their suggestions on improving the manuscript. Direct correspondence to the authors at the Department of Sociology & Anthropology, 500 Holmes Hall, Northeastern University, Boston, MA 02115.

dents often serve as a precipitating episode for riots in inner-city neighborhoods (Carter 1986, 1990; Schneider 1992; Smelser 1962; Weller 1985). In an early study, Knopf (1975) identified "police brutality" as a dominant content theme in the rumors circulated among blacks before and during a riot.

According to the report of the National Advisory Commission on Civil Disorders (1968), many of the riots of the 1960s in Harlem, Watts, Detroit, and other major cities were ignited by routine arrests of black citizens by white police officers. Civil disturbances occurring since 1980 have similarly involved charges of police brutality and racism during the arrest of minority residents (Jackson 1989). The most famous recent case was the videotaped beating of black motorist Rodney King on March 3, 1991, by white members of the Los Angeles Police Department. Many black Americans were convinced that the excessive violence and illegal procedures involved in King's arrest resulted specifically from racism—white police beating a black victim because of his race (Murty, Roebuck, and Armstrong 1994).

Perceptions of discrimination by the police and the criminal justice system against black Americans have been documented clearly (Allport 1979; Arnold 1971; Bullock 1961; Foley 1982; Malpass 1974; Miller, Rossi, and Simpson 1986; Nagel & Weitzman 1972; Thornberry 1973). In some cases, these perceptions are held so widely by black Americans that they have assumed the status of urban legends regarding conspiracy by police institutions (Turner 1993).

As in the Rodney King incident, the actual severity of police brutality often plays a role in molding public sentiment and galvanizing collective behavior. Even in the most benign circumstances, however, many black residents still may believe that the police use a double standard of justice when dealing with urban residents: one for blacks and another for whites. Research in social psychology has provided compelling evidence that individuals often "selectively perceive" a social situation to make it consistent with their stereotyped preconceptions (Bardach and Park 1996). In any particular encounter, even the most contradictory evidence may be ig-

nored or interpreted so as to support a sterotyped image of out-group behavior. In addition, simply knowing an individual's group identity (e.g., his or her race, ethnicity, or gender) may be enough to evoke a generalized belief about the group, which then leads the evaluator to regard that individual as guilty or criminal behavior (Bodenhausen 1987). Therefore, given the history of friction between the police and the minority community, the very presence of white arresting officers in a black neighborhood may be enough to generate a charge of police brutality (Hagen & Albonetti 1982).

The purpose of the present study was to examine, in a controlled setting, the effect of police officers' racial identity on perceptions of brutality when a black suspect is under arrest. According to previous research, brutal police behavior during an arrest is measured by the degree of force or violence as well as the illegality of a police response—in particular, by the use of "unnecessary," "excessive," and therefore "unlawful" force in subduing a suspect (Bouza 1990). As a result, we hypothesized that respondents who viewed the arrest of a black suspect would perceive significantly more police violence and illegality (i.e., brutality) when both arresting officers were white than when they were both black or when they were a black-and-white team.

METHOD

In attempting to manipulate police officers' racial identity during an arrest, we initially considered adopting a tactic widely employed in social psychology, namely varying the race of a paper-and-pencil stimulus target (in this case, the police officer) by informing the respondents that he is either black or white. This approach, however, not only is unnecessarily artificial but also lacks the visibility that is critical in assessing police brutality. As in Pearce's (1979) study of racial discrimination by real estate agents, we also considered filming different actors in the roles of black or white officers. Unfortunately this approach fails to control for variation in individual characteristics other than race (such as size, physical stature, personal grooming, and even gestures and expressions) that might account for differing perceptions of brutality.

Therefore, to simulate a realistic arrest, we finally decided to produce three videotaped arrest scenes in which the same actor played the role of a black suspect being arrested by two armed police officers. The police were actually members of a university campus security force who were instructed, for the purpose of staging the scene, to use standard operating procedures in making the "arrest." The "suspect" resisted slightly; thus the officers were obliged to use a moderate amount of force, but always "by the book."

We made the video recording using a household VHS camcorder with the same video quality as the equipment employed to videotape the Rodney King episode. The three arrest scenes were taped during a single evening on the floor of a large lecture hall. The camera was kept at a distance of 25-30 feet so that the actors' "skin color" could be discerned but not their physical features or age.

The three arrest situations were as close to identical as possible, with one exception. We varied the racial identity of the two arresting officers—two whites, one black and one white, or two blacks—by giving each one a full face mask to wear, consisting of either light- or dark-colored panty hose. The officers' other features were covered with police caps, uniforms, and gloves. Therefore respondents could use only the officers' facial features to determine racial identity. In all three conditions, the "black suspect" wore a dark mask. Thus respondents could not compare the artificial masks worn by police with the genuine facial characteristics of a black individual playing the role.

To eliminate any other differences between taped arrests, we removed the audio portion from all showings. In addition, as an indication that the level of violence was consistent across the arrest incidents, versions of all three tapes were colored red, which completely obscured the racial characteristics of the two officers and the suspect. A panel of 12 students, viewing the colorized videotapes in a pretest, detected no significant differences between the three scenes with respect to the degree of violence employed by the police officers (chi-square = .54, df = 2, p > .05).

In another pretest, we measured the realism of the taped arrest scenes by asking a panel of 13 judges (all graduate students) to view one of the three tapes and then to state whether it had been simulated. Only six of the 13 judges believed that the scene they observed had been artificially constructed; the other seven believed they might have viewed an actual arrest.

Sixty-one undergraduate students at Northeastern University—33 blacks and 28 whites, all between ages 18 and 23—volunteered to participate in the study. Each respondent was paid five dollars to view one of the three videotaped arrest scenes, randomly assigned, and then to answer a few qeustions about what they had seen.

The experiment was a 3×2 factorial design employing three levels of racial identity of police (two white vs. one white and one black vs. two black) and two levels of respondent's race (black vs. white). Thus all possible combinations of racial identities for both police and respondents were represented. Approximately one-third of all black respondents viewed each of the three racially varied videotapes; about one-third of all white respondents viewed each of these tapes.

The experiment was conducted in a meeting room at the university and was designed to simulate the "Rodney King effect," whereby witnesses viewed an arrest as recorded on videotape. Respondents were told only that they would view an arrest scene and then would be asked to answer a few questions about what they had observed. None were informed beforehand that the arrest was simulated for research. A tape was shown to one respondent at a time; roughly equal numbers of blacks and whites viewed each arrest scene. Then all respondents gave their answers to an "after only" measure of the dependent variables.

We measured both dependent variables by asking respondents to estimate the degree of violence and illegality (i.e., brutality) employed by police in the arrest they had viewed. All respondents answered on five-point, bipolar scales ranging from "violent" to "nonviolent" and from "illegal" to "legal." As a check on the effectiveness of the manipulation, respondents also were asked to indicate the racial identity—black or white—of the two police officers they had seen in the tape. All respondents included in the analysis identified the officers' race correctly. Immediately after their participation, respondents were debriefed individually. None realized the true intent of the study. Most expressed complete surprise when we informed them that the arresting officers' racial identity had been simulated with masks.

FINDINGS

A 3×2 analysis of variance for violence uncovered significant main effects for respondent's race and racial identity of the police.

A 3×2 analysis of variance for illegality yielded a main effect at a borderline level of significance for respondent's race and a significant main effect for racial identity of the police.

In both analyses, the interaction between racial identity of police and respondent's race was nonsignificant, an indication that the results obtained in main effect B applied to both black and white respondents.[1]

Tukey's multiple comparison of main-effect means revealed a consistent pattern of results for both dependent variable measures. As hypothesized, respondents perceived significantly greater violence and illegality when both police officers were white (violence: $\overline{X}$ = 3.32, n = 22; illegality: $\overline{X}$ = 3.36, n = 22) than when both were black (violence: $\overline{X}$ = 2.50, n = 14; illegality: $\overline{X}$ = 2.14, n = 14) or when one was black and the other white (violence: $\overline{X}$ = 2.72, n = 25; illegality: $\overline{X}$ = 2.32, n = 25). The difference between black/black and white/black officers was nonsignificant.

DISCUSSION

Because many black Americans tend to view the police as a tool of repression, it is not surprising that black respondents in our study were more likely than their white counterparts to perceive violence and illegality on the part of arresting officers. This finding is consistent with national survey evidence suggesting that black Americans are more likely than whites to believe that "police overreaction to crime" is a serious threat to Americans' rights and freedoms (U.S. Department of Justice 1995). National surveys also report that black Americans are much more likely than whites to express little or no confidence in the police and less likely to imagine any situation in which they would approve of a police officer "striking an adult male citizen" (U.S. Department of Justice 1995).

Results obtained in the present study strongly suggest in addition that perceptions of police violence and illegality during the arrest of black suspects are influenced by the racial identity of police on the scene. We found that respondents tended to perceive more brutality when both arresting officers were white than when at least one of the officers was black.

Witnesses may regard exclusively white police as "representatives of the white power structure" who illegitimately harass and batter black residents. If they do so, then the act of police brutality may be regarded as a race-specific crime, stereotypically committed by white rather than black police officers.[2] Our findings showed that the presence of a black officer along with a white partner tends to mitigate the negative perception of racial bias.

Our results applied not only to black but also to white respondents. Thus whites who witness the arrest of a black suspect are influenced in their perception of brutality, like their black counterparts, by the racial identity of the police. As a result, when the arresting officers are white, white residents may be as likely as those in the black community to perceive brutality based on racial bias. This finding may have practical implications for gaining the support of white Americans—those who serve on juries, vote, or hold powerful public offices—for policies and programs to change the role of the police in black communities. Many whites are likely to agree, for example, that a change in the complexion of a local police force might reduce the potential for racial conflict.

In the present study, the suspect's racial identity was held constant: In all three versions of the arrest, he was black. Therefore we can only speculate about the results we might have obtained for a white suspect under the same experimental conditions. Because black Americans are culturally stereotyped as violent, one might argue that the results obtained here would not apply to the case of police arresting a white suspect (Levin & McDevitt 1993). In the present study, however, white respondents associated police brutality with white, but not black, officers. Therefore the presence of a black officer at the scene of an arrest might well reduce the perception of brutality toward any suspect, regardless of race.

Experimental research is uniquely able to rule out spuriousness in establishing a causal relationship between two or more variables. An experimental approach gives investigators the advantage of manipulating an independent variable (in this case, racial identity of police) in order to observe its effects (in this case, on perceptions of brutality), carefully controlling for the impact of other possible variables. For example, there is reason to believe that perceptions of police brutality also may be influenced by factors such as previous experiences with the police and socioeconomic status. Because all respondents were assigned randomly to treatment groups, however, it is safe to assume that these other variables were not responsible for the results we obtained here.

At the same time, findings obtained through experimental research are often flawed by their lack of external validity. In the present study we constructed an artificial arrest situation to which only 61 respondents were exposed. Moreover, in the absence of random sampling, it becomes extremely problematic to generalize beyond the narrow confines of the experiment itself, regardless of how realistic it might have been. We simply do not know, for example, the relative effect of arrest interactions in relation to other potential causal factors such as political climate, perceptions of police conduct, and police professionalism. Future researchers might seek to broaden the external validity of this study by testing its applicability in a survey format under a variety of conditions and in the presence of a number of important variables.

Insofar as they are generalizable, however, our present findings may have important implications for effectively assigning police officers to inner-city neighborhoods, in which tensions run high and civil disturbances are likely to occur. Though only a few officers account for a large proportion of complaints of excessive force, a much larger number of officers are likely to be regarded as perpetrators of acts of brutality. Many complaints of excessive force ultimately are determined by police review to be "not sustained." Granted, some of these unverified complaints may reflect an "us versus them" attitude on the part of police, which supports a code of silence and even lying to protect fellow officers (NAACP and Criminal Justice Institute 1995). Yet on the basis of results obtained in the present study, one might hypothesize that at least some of the invalid complaints about police brutality reflect a stereotyped view of white police officers, who may be operating "by the book" but are not viewed in the black community as doing so.

Thus it might be expected that police-community relations will be strained severely whenever exclusively white police are stationed in such communities. On the other hand, the assignment of officers according to race (e.g., black police to black neighborhoods and white police to white neighborhoods) would create, among other things, a racially segregated police force. Therefore, we tentatively offer a modest proposal. Our results suggest that police-community tensions in black neighborhoods might be reduced without the need for segregated police forces by assigning teams of white and black officers. Fortunately, as a result of affirmative action guidelines, a growing number of agencies across the country have increased their hiring of black officers (Armstrong & Wood 1991). Future research may give such departments an additional incentive to continue their minority recruitment.

NOTES

1. Although not reported here, gender differences were found to be nonsigificant for the interaction effect (violence: $F = .84$, df = $2/49$, $p > .05$; illegality: $F = .04$, df = $2/49$, $p > .05$).

2. For a discussion of race-stereotypic crime, see Gordon (1990, 1993); Gordon et al. (1988); Sunnafrank and Fontes (1983).

REFERENCES

ALLPORT, G. W. 1979. *The Nature of Prejudice*. New York: Addison-Wesley.

Armstrong, S. & D. B. Wood. 1991. "Curbing Brutality Starts at the Top." *Christian Science Monitor*, March 25, p. 1.

Arnold, W. R. 1971. "Race and Ethnicity Relative to Other Factors in Juvenile Court Dispositions." *American Journal of Sociology* 77:211–27.

Bardach, L. & B. Park. 1996. "The Effect of In-Group/Out-Group Status on Memory for Consistent and Inconsistent Behavior of an Individual." *Personality and Social Psychology Bulletin* 22:169–78.

Bodenhausen, G. V. 1987. "Stereotypic Biases in Social Decision Making and Memory: Testing Process Models of Stereotype Use." *Journal of Personality and Social Psychology* 55:726–37.

Bouza, A. 1990. *The Police Mystique*. New York: Plenum.

Bullock, R. 1961. "Significance of the Racial Factor in the Length of Prison Sentences." *Journal of Criminal Law, Criminology, and Police Science* 52:411–15.

Carter, G. L. 1986. "In the Narrows of the 1960s U.S. Black Rioting." *Journal of Conflict Resolution* 30:115–27.

———. 1990. "Black Attitudes and the 1960s Black Riots: An Aggregate-Level Analysis of the Kerner Comission's '15 Cities' Data." *Sociological Quarterly* 31:269–86.

Foley, R. 1982. "The Effect of Race and Personality on Mock Jurors' Decisions." *Journal of Psychology* 112:47–53.

Gordon, R. A. 1990. "Attributions for Blue-Collar and White-Collar Crime: The Effects of Subject and Defendant Race on Simulated Juror Decisions." *Journal of Applied Social Psychology* 20:971–83.

———. 1993. "The Effect of Strong versus Weak Evidence on the Assessment of Race Stereotypic and Race Non-Stereotypic Crimes." *Journal of Applied Social Psychology* 23:734–49.

Gordon, R. A., T. A. Bindrim, M. L. McNicholas, T. L. Walden. 1988. "Perceptions of Blue-Collar and White-Collar Crime: The Effect of Defendant Race on Simulated Juror Decisions." *Journal of Social Psychology* 28:191–97.

Hagan, J. & C. Albonetti. 1982. "Race, Class, and the Perception of Criminal Injustice in America." *American Journal of Sociology* 88:329–55.

Jackson, P. I. 1989. *Minority Group Threat, Crime, and Policing*. New York: Praeger.

Knopf, T. A. 1975. *Rumors, Race, and Riots*. New Brunswick, NJ: Transaction Books.

Levin, J. & J. McDevitt. 1993. *Hate Crimes: The Rising Tide of Bigotry and Bloodshed*. New York: Plenum.

Malpass, R. S. 1974. "Racial Bias in Eyewitness Identification." *Personality and Social Psychology Bulletin* 1:42–44.

Miller, J. L., P. H. Rossi, & J. E. Simpson. 1986. "Perceptions of Justice: Race and Gender Differences in Judgments of Appropriate Prison Sentences." *Law and Society Review* 20:313–34.

Murty, K. S., J. B. Roebuck, and G. R. Armstrong. 1994. "The Black Community's Reaction to the 1992 Los Angeles Riot." *Deviant Behavior* 15:85–104.

Nagel, S. & L. J. Weitzman. 1972. "Double Standard of American Justice." *Society* 9:18–25.

National Advisory Commission on Civil Disorders. 1968. *Report on the National Advisory Commission on Civil Disorders*. Washington, DC: U.S. Government Printing Office.

National Association for the Advancement of Colored People and the Criminal Justice Institute. 1995. *Beyond the Rodney King Study: An Investigation of Police Misconduct in Minority Communities*. Boston: Northeastern University Press.

Pearce, D. M. 1969. "Gatekeepers and Homeseekers: Institutional Patterns in Racial Steering." *Social Problems* 26:325–42.

Schneider, H. J. 1992. "Criminology of Riots." *International Journal of Offender Therapy and Comparative Criminology* 36:173–86.

Smelser, N. 1962. *Theory of Collective Behavior*. New York: Free Press.

Sunnafrank, M. & N. E. Fontes. 1983. "General Crime Related Racial Stereotypes and Influence on Juridicial Decisions." *Cornell Journal of Social Relations* 17:1–15.

Thornberry, T. P. 1973. "Race, Socioeconomic Status, and Sentencing in the Juvenile Court System." *Journal of Criminal Law and Criminology* 64:90–98.

Turner, P. A. 1993. *I Heard It through the Grapevine*. Berkeley: U. of California Press.

U.S. Department of Justice. 1995. *Sourcebook of Criminal Justice Statistics—1994*. Washington, DC: Bureau of Justice Statistics.

COMMENTARY ON THE READINGS

In the first reading, Michael Slater and colleagues were testing the effectiveness of alcohol warnings during advertisements on television. To do this, they employed a design utilizing several variations, or factors, within the experiment. They were interested in the placement of the warning within the advertisement, and this included four factors: the warning before the main body of the advertisement, the warning appearing after the main body of the advertisement, the warning being scrolled along the bottom of the screen during the advertisement, and no warning at all. They were also interested in the effectiveness of different warning topics, and this category yielded three factors: warnings about drunk driving, about cancer, and about possible drug interactions. They also tested the effectiveness of advertisements with statistics, a category that included two factors: warnings with or without statistics.

The authors were very concerned with making their experiment more "lifelike." Experiments are good at isolating variables, but that efficiency can also make the experience seem less real for the experimental subject. Thus, much effort has been expended to make the experiment seem more real in order to have a valid experiment. This quest for realism in the laboratory is also found in the article by Jack Levin and Alex Thomas investigating the perceptions of police brutality. The experiment was conducted shortly after a 1991 incident in which members of the Los Angeles police department were videotaped using excessive violence against a black man, Rodney King, during an arrest situation. The incident eventually led to a series of riots in Los Angeles and elsewhere. The authors decided to mimic the effect of watching a videotaped arrest.

Because the experiment relied on using a videotaped scene, a pretest of the subjects could have biased the results by giving clues on what the videotape would be about and what was being tested. Therefore, they relied on an "after-only" design that tested their perceptions to the stimulus itself.

There are two dependent variables: the subject's perception of violence and the subject's perception of illegality on the arresting officers. These are being measured in regard to two independent variables: the racial identity of the arresting officers and the racial identity of the subjects themselves. The stimulus in this case was not the independent variable per se, but a videotape produced to mimic the tape shown in connection with the Rodney King case. To ensure that subjects were responding to the racial identity of the police, each actor played the same role in each production and the racial identity was altered with light or dark colored panty hose. To ensure that the three productions had the same level of violence and illegality, all were colorized and tested on subjects. Similarly, the videotape was also tested for realism before conducting the experiment with subjects.

After the data were collected, researchers in both experiments conducted a series of statistical tests to see if the results were significant. Slater and colleagues found that from the perspective of the alcohol industry it is more desirable to run the warning prior to the commercial than during or after. They learned this by testing the eight hypotheses they introduced during the literature review. Levin and Thomas found that the racial identity of the police officers was significant; that is, both white and black suspects were more likely to perceive violence and illegality when both arresting officers were white than when they were both black or in a black/white team.

CONCLUSION

It is common usage to refer to any piece of scientific research as an experiment. Of course, experiments do include a range of variation. However, experiments are something very specific; they are designed to isolate their variables and test the relationships among them. Although some other methods try to mimic the control found in experiments, these research methods do not emphasize control to the same degree that experiments do.

CHAPTER 5

SURVEYS

SURVEY RESEARCH METHODS

A *survey* is a research technique that utilizes a questionnaire to collect data on a sizable number of subjects. Surveys allow researchers to explore research questions that have not been addressed in the past using original data collected specifically to address their interests. Determining an appropriate sample population to be surveyed and developing a survey tool are two of the first steps a researcher must consider when using a survey method. In addition to an appropriate sample and an adequate tool, the actual method of survey administration must be determined and then carried out. Finally the data collected will be organized and analyzed according to the researchers' agenda. Each of these steps—survey sample, research tool, administration, and analysis—must be outlined in advance, considering the pros and cons of each available option.

The data collected from surveys are compiled based on the answers that people provide to questions. Questions may be asked in a person-to-person interview, in a telephone interview, or in a self-administered setting—such as a survey distributed by mail. In choosing one of these options, the researcher must consider costs and response rates as well as the reliability and validity of the responses obtained by each method of administration. Some commonly used surveys include those that are designed to measure public opinion, political inclination, and consumer preferences. The results of these surveys are published by newspapers and magazines and are used by politicians and marketers to guide their actions according to constituent or consumer preferences.

THE SAMPLE

One of the many choices a researcher must make in choosing a survey research method is the type of sampling to be used. Most researchers would agree that the best type of sample is a probability sample, but in many cases this kind of sample is impossible to obtain. The hardest part of drawing a probability sample is to ensure that all members of the population to be studied are known and that each member has an equal chance of being selected. If significant portions of the population are not included, the data collected will be neither reliable nor valid. It is important to identify the smaller subgroups of the population from which the sample will be drawn and make sure that the number included from each of these groups is large enough to maintain the reliability of the estimate.

QUESTIONNAIRE DEVELOPMENT

Developing the questionnaire to be used in a survey is crucial to the success of a survey. A survey is based on administering a questionnaire to a selected group of respondents. Guidelines for developing survey questions (Payne, 1951) and scaling techniques for questionnaires (Likert, 1932) that measure social phenomena were developed early in the use of surveys as measurement tools. The questionnaire consists of questions that have been developed with the consideration of the sample, research interests, and survey format in mind. The answers to the questions on a survey are generally used as measures or social indicators. Often, answers are coded and used to support or negate theoretical positions regarding the behavior, attitudes, emotions, perceptions, and opinions held by a given population. If survey data are to be reliable and valid, it is important that each person answering the questions posed is actually answering the same question. The choice of words and wording in general should communicate one and only one idea to the person answering the question. Wording that is not clear and words with duplicate meanings should be avoided. In the case of personal or telephone interviews, it is essential that each interviewer use the same words and wording in each interview. If a prompt to help the respondent understand the question is necessary, it needs to be consistent so that all respondents will receive the same prompt.

Standardized questions have become the norm in most surveys. Writing clear, concise questions that will generate usable responses is one of the most difficult parts of developing a research tool. Questions should be precise and ask about only one issue; asking about more than one issue per question may confuse the respondent and result in answers that are not appropriate. For example, a researcher who is interested in exploring the drug and alcohol use of college students during spring break must be sure that the questions regarding alcohol use are separate from those regarding drug use.

Respondents should be qualified and willing to answer the questions posed, and the questions should be relevant to respondents. In the study of the drug and alcohol use of college students during spring break, the researcher must be sure that the sample includes only college students and that those who did not participate in spring break are able to indicate this fact early in the questionnaire.

The use of negative terms should be avoided, and question wording should avoid influencing the respondent's selection. For instance, when inquiring about the use of marijuana, one would not ask, "Have you ever used the dangerous drug marijuana?" This wording may bias the respondent's answer because few people want to admit to using a dangerous substance; by referring to it as such the researcher places the drug in a negative context. In addition, by revealing her or his own bias that the drug is dangerous, the researcher risks losing credibility in some subjects' eyes—especially those who feel that marijuana is not dangerous.

The questions on a survey questionnaire may be open ended or closed ended. Open-ended questions allow the respondent to answer as he or she sees fit, while close-ended questions require the respondent to choose from answers provided by the researcher. In the spring break survey, the researcher may choose to allow the respondent to list all of the types of alcohol or drugs he or she consumed while on spring break, may choose to provide a list from which the respondent can select the drugs used, or may focus the study on only one or two specific drugs based on previous knowledge about those substances most likely to be used by college students. The questions on a survey may ask the respondent to agree or disagree with a series of statements or give their opinion about a given issue or statement. In an effort to determine how college students perceive their own condition or that of others while drinking, the researcher may ask the respondent how many drinks he or she would have consumed before being considered "buzzed," "drunk," or "gone." In this case, the word selected would depend on the researcher's perception of the terms the college students would use to refer to themselves or others.

In addition to question wording and relevance to the respondent, the ordering of questions and the format of the questionnaire may also influence the quality of the data collected. It is best to place easier and less intrusive questions at the beginning of the survey. For instance, the researcher would not want to begin the questionnaire on drug and alcohol use by asking the respondent how many days during spring break he/she had more than 10 drinks, but would begin by asking if the respondent attended spring break and where, or what his or her current college rank is. Surveys also require a disclosure statement that gives information about the purpose of the study, the researcher's qualifications, and the level of anonymity promised to the respondent. Such information gives respondents confidence that their responses will be useful and that their information will be kept confidential. The disclosure statement should be completed prior to the distribution of the questionnaire. In addition, the questionnaire should not include the respondent's name, social security number, or other identification so that specific responses cannot be traced to specific individuals.

SURVEY ADMINISTRATION

Surveys may be administered using a variety of methods, including personal interviews, telephone interviews, and self-administered questionnaires. Each of these methods has distinct advantages as well as disadvantages that have the ability to bias the data collected. The method of administration is just as important as drawing the sample and developing the survey tool in terms of its ability to influence the reliability and validity of the study overall.

The personal interview is a commonly used method of administering a survey. This method offers some considerable advantages. Personal interviews are often the best way to obtain the cooperation of respondents; people are often more willing to speak to a person standing in front of them than they are to respond to a piece of what they may consider junk mail. An interview format is also more effective than self-administration because an interviewer can work to assure that all questions are understood and answered appropriately. Interviewers also allow for the collection of multiple types of data—general and visual observations, self-administered sections, and question-and-answer segments. Finally personal interviews are generally longer than written questionnaires and allow the interviewer to develop a personal rapport with the respondent, making it easier to obtain answers to questions that have the potential to be viewed as sensitive. Personal interviews have disadvantages as well. In a large project, numerous interviewers are dispersed throughout the area of research, making it difficult to monitor their activities and get together for a meeting. Personal interviews are also very time consuming and, because of the number of interviewers, tend to be very expensive.

Telephone interviews are often the method of administration selected when personal interviews are viewed as too costly or time consuming. Random-digit dialing allows for random sampling of general populations. In addition, some populations are more easily accessed using telephone interviews than personal interviews, such as those who have inflexible schedules or are frequently on call at work. Managing and monitoring interview staff and the administration of the questionnaire are also more easily done with telephone interviews than with personal interviews. Finally, telephone interviews maintain many of the advantages of personal interviews while decreasing costs and time of data collection and avoiding the pitfalls of self-administration. Despite their numerous advantages, telephone interviews also have several limitations. The most obvious limitation is that not all potential respondents in a sample may have a telephone; this method excludes all members of a given population without a telephone. The amount of nonresponse is higher in telephone interviews than it is in personal interviews; it is easier to hang up on someone who wants to ask questions than it is to turn away an individual with whom one is standing face to face. In addition, the survey tool must be limited to asking questions—the use of visual aids and the general observations of the interviewer cannot be included—and the number of prompts and alternative questions is limited.

Surveys that are self-administered have several potential advantages over those completed in either of the interview formats reviewed here. If a survey is completed by the respondent, complex response categories and visual aides are easily designed into the survey tool and similar questions may be scattered throughout the questionnaire. In addition, the respondent is not faced with sharing his/her responses with another individual. However, these advantages come with several potential disadvantages. Open-ended questions are not particularly useful in a self-administered questionnaire, forcing the questions to be closed ended. This requires that the researcher be aware of all possible responses so that the respondent will not become discouraged and view the questionnaire as a waste of time. Self-administered questionnaires also carry the assumption that respondents have the literacy skills required to complete the questionnaire. Finally, there is no interviewer present to be sure that the respondent understands the questions or to make sure that all questions are completed with appropriate answers.

Surveys that are self-administered by mail have several advantages over the methods just discussed. Mailed surveys are relatively inexpensive and require fewer staff than either personal or telephone interviews. They make a diverse range of populations within reach and are able to reach those who, for whatever reason, may be inaccessible in person or by telephone. Mailed surveys also give respondents time to think about their answers, look up information they may not immediately know, consult others if they are unclear or do not understand (although this aspect may also be viewed as a disadvantage in some instances). Mailed surveys in particular suffer from the disadvantages related to the absence of an interviewer. They lack the ability to convince a respondent to cooperate and complete the questionnaire. They must also rely on the accuracy of mailing addresses. More recently, surveys have been administered online, with varying results. Online surveys are cheaper than mail surveys but are also less representative of the general population.

NONRESPONSE

One of the more trying aspects of the survey method is the constant dilemma of how to address *nonresponse*, or the failure to collect data from a subject. There are several situations in which nonresponse can occur. The first is when an individual selected to be in the sample refuses to participate. A college student may refuse to participate in the spring break survey, for instance. The second is when a respondent agrees to participate but fails to answer all of the questions on the survey. The third is when a respondent is not able to answer the questions posed because of a limitation—language barrier, illness, illiteracy, and so on. The final nonresponse situation is if the method of data collection—interview, mail, telephone—does not reach the selected respondent and thus he or she is not given the opportunity to respond to the questions on the survey. In administering a survey by mail, the researcher should plan on at least one follow-up mailing. Sending follow-up questionnaires is often necessary and may encourage respondents to complete the questionnaire, especially if a sense of urgency and importance is included.

Despite the method of data collection selected, nonresponse remains a critical issue to researchers, and major efforts are made to limit the extent of nonresponses encountered in the data collection process. The method of administration selected can have a great impact on the response rate of a survey—the percentage of the sample who complete the survey. Personal interviews typically have the best response rates, followed by telephone interviews. Mailed self-administered surveys typically have much lower response rates, even after a second mailing. However, a self-administered survey with a captive audience, such as a college class, has quite a good response rate. Nonresponse is a problem for researchers because the result can be a biased sample, and thus the reliability of the estimates drawn from the data collected will be decreased.

THE READINGS

The following two articles serve as examples of how the survey method can be applied by researchers. The first, "Neighborhood Associations: Their Issues, Their Allies, and Their Opponents," by John Logan and Gordana Rabrenovic (1990), seeks to examine neighborhood associations in an urban area as political actors. The second, "Inshopping by Residents of Small Communities," by James Pinkerton and colleagues (1995), explores consumer behavior in two rural communities.

▪ ▪ ▪ ▪ ▪ ▬▬▬▬▬▬▬▬▬▬▬▬▬▬▬▬▬▬▬▬▬▬▬▬▬▬▬▬▬▬▬▬▬▬▬▬▬▬▬

NEIGHBORHOOD ASSOCIATIONS: THEIR ISSUES, THEIR ALLIES, AND THEIR OPPONENTS

John R. Logan and Gordana Rabrenovic
State University of New York at Albany

We study neighborhood associations as local political actors. In our sample, most were formed around a single neighborhood issue, typically involving land-development projects. Their most common opponents include local government and business and real estate developers. The well-known growth-machine model is challenged in two ways. First, although growth issues are prominent in the establishment of neighborhood associations, in many cases they are joined or replaced by other kinds of issues (such as public services or safety). Second, local government is perceived as a political ally as often as it is seen as an opponent, and sometimes it is seen as both on the same issue.

More than 30 years ago, counter to then-current fashion, two social scientists, Form (1954) and Long (1958), argued that urban researchers should focus more directly on the various actors whose intentions, strategies, and interactions affect community development. As urban theory has veered away from the economic determinism and "invisible hand" metaphors of human ecology, consensus has grown among researchers regarding the need to understand land developers and realtors, financial institutions, associations of homeowners and tenant unions, and other po-

litical players. Although new theories are being based upon assumptions about the interests and activities of such players, great gaps exist in the research base.

In our study we examine one type of actor, the neighborhood association. For our purposes, a *neighborhood association* is defined as a civic organization oriented toward maintaining or improving the quality of life in a geographically delimited residential area. We are interested in the neighborhood association, not simply as a form of local voluntary organization, but more precisely as a distinctive form in which the common interests of residents of a bounded community area are expressed in American cities. The neighborhood association is not the only possible form; political party organizations, churches, union locals, ethnic clubs, and chapters of environmental groups can, and sometimes do, play this role. Nevertheless, in this country, the neighborhood association is commonly the vehicle through which neighbors learn about problems, formulate opinions, and seek to intervene in the political process to protect their local interests. Further, although at one time these organizations may have had largely social functions, the current tendency seems to be that instrumental political activities

From *Urban Affairs Quarterly*, 26, 1 (September 1990): 68–94. Copyright © 1990 Sage Publications, Inc.

predominate (Guest 1985; Crenson 1983; Goering 1979). In this study, then, we examine how and why these associations come into being, what issues become the focus of their attention, and how they understand the political context in which they act.

UP AGAINST THE GROWTH MACHINE

The most vivid account of the politics of urbanization is Molotch's (1976) model of the city as a growth machine (see also Logan and Molotch 1987). In this model, the central issue in local politics, the issue that captures the essense of locality, is the pursuit of ever more intensive growth. Political control is attributed to a coalition of progrowth entrepreneurs (aiming for profit from rent intensification), against whom the interests of city residents (desiring price stability and security of their daily activities in the neighborhood) seldom prevail.

Mollenkopf (1983) portrayed growth politics in similar fashion, although in his view, neighborhood mobilization has stalled the growth machine in a number of major cities. The neighborhood association is often the vehicle for such mobilization. Elkin (1985) and Fainstein and Fainstein (1983) also have emphasized the centrality of progrowth coalitions in urban politics. In their accounts, however, the greater oppositional role is played by lower-income and minority residents, and middle-class residents are viewed as important constituents whose interests often are protected by local regimes.

A parallel view of neighborhood associations has emerged from the geographic literature on locational conflicts (see especially, Cox 1981). Janelle (1977) emphasized transportation, high-density residential development, and commercial expansion as specific issues about which business and residents may have opposing views. Boyte (1980) stressed urban renewal and highway programs as the bases for urban confrontations in the 1960s.

Types of Issues

These researchers gave prominent attention to land-development questions. Others have given equal weight to issues of public service delivery—schools, crime prevention, traffic and parking regulation, and garbage collection (Davidson 1979; Thomas 1986; Burnett 1983; Lowe 1977). In one of the best empirical studies to date, Guest and Oropesa (1984) found that Seattle residents were most concerned with services and facilities (mentioned by 29.7% of respondents) and physical characteristics of the community environment, including streets and sewers (27.7%). Land-use change and zoning were mentioned by only 18.2%, which is a substantial percentage but is lower than might be expected based on the growth-politics literature. We must note, however, that these data refer to the concerns of individual residents, not the activities of neighborhood associations.

Thus one question that we must address is the relative importance of land-development issues and other sorts of issues for neighborhood associations. We will take two approaches. One is to explore the conditions in which associations were formed: when, in what political context, and on what issue or issues? But, as Arnold (1979, 15) pointed out, many associations are founded to address a single issue, but their concerns are broadened as they become permanent organizations. Therefore, we will also examine the current issues addressed by neighborhood associations.

The Balance of Power

A second question is how neighborhood associations fit into the local balance of forces. In the growth-machine model, residents are portrayed as solo players with few allies against a powerful alliance of business and real estate developers. This image also has been disputed. Arnold (1979) believed that the key protagonist of neighborhood associations is municipal government and, further, that their relationship to each other is becoming more cooperative over time as municipal officials realize that neighborhood associations are valuable for information and advice.

Similarly, Taub and Surgeon (1977) argued that neighborhood associations increasingly are created or supported by government agencies that need them as channels of communication, sources of legitimation, vehicles of social control, and a means to organize and direct resources. This need has grown as the ideology emphasizing local participation and control has become more widespread. Of course, cooperation may tend toward co-optation, and some researchers and community activists are concerned that "the supposed opening of government is only a technique for seducing citizen groups" (Thomas 1986, 5). But others (Ley and Mercer 1980) emphasize that local government itself is not a monolithic institution, and citizen groups may find supporters in some quarters while battling other city officials.

The relationship between neighborhood associations and land developers also may be complex. Logan and Molotch (1987, 139–46) pointed out that in gentrifying city neighborhoods, neighborhood associations representing more affluent residents may well play a double role in growth politics. On the one hand, they protect their turf against nonresidential development. On the other hand, they promote the continued conversion of the neighborhood. For example, Mollenkopf (1983, 175) reported close links between the Boston Redevelopment Authority and the leadership of the South End neighborhood in Boston. In another premutation of this pattern, the University of Chicago established and funded the Southeast Chicago Commission as a supposed community organization as part of its efforts to redevelop the Hyde Park-Kenwood neighborhood (Rossi and Dentler 1961).

Certainly these visions of local political alignments depend upon the kind of issues that analysts have in mind. Some, intent on exploring land-development questions, emphasize business and developers as opponents (or sometimes as manipulators) of neighborhood associations; others, thinking of the demand for public services, emphasize local government. A major research question for us is how neighborhood associations themselves define their issues and, in turn, whom they perceive to be either their key allies or opponents.

It is unnecessary to posit a unitary pattern across time and space. Neighborhood associations may vary according to the logic of their own evolution or the character of their environment or members (Henig 1982; Fisher 1984;

Thomas 1986). We will look specifically for differences between neighborhood associations in central-city and suburban locations. Suburbs are distinctive in the composition of their populations and housing stock. Further, a much narrower range of public services is provided in the suburbs than is provided in central cities (Dye 1970; Cox 1973, 30–48). Also, according to some political analysts, a particularly high level of community identity is enjoyed in the suburbs, and the means to enhance and perpetuate that identity are provided through public policy (Wood 1958; Greer 1962, 109). The continuing "close contact" of people to government in the suburbs makes the public's response to political decisions predictable and forces (or enables) local officials to adhere to public opinion (Crain and Rosenthal 1967). Therefore, one might expect to find relatively little emphasis on issues of service and public infrastructure in suburban neighborhoods and higher levels of cooperation with local government compared to that in city neighborhoods.

In sum, our purpose here is to examine the causes of the founding of neighborhood associations, the kinds of issues on which they focus their attention, and their understanding of the forces that support and oppose their goals. The analysis is as much historical and descriptive—generating hypotheses for future work—as it is statistical, although some specific hypotheses are tested. We adopt an implicit causal model here in which some objective characteristics of the larger political environment and of neighborhoods themselves are expected to affect creation of neighborhood associations and the relative salience of different types of issues, which in turn affect perceptions of cooperation and conflict.

RESEARCH DESIGN

This study is based upon survey research in 1986 among neighborhood associations in New York's Capital District (encompassing Albany, Schenectady, Troy, and surrounding suburbs). A list of 99 existing neighborhood associations was compiled in the following manner. First, we contacted every local (municipal or county) planning office to obtain names of organizations.

Second, in the city of Albany, we obtained a list of member organizations of the Council of Albany Neighborhood Associations. Third, we reviewed relevant newspaper articles from the *Albany Times Union*, which is indexed by the library staff at the State University of New York at Albany. Finally, in every interview, we asked respondents for names of other neighborhood associations in the area. Because this last method provided no new names we are confident that our list is comprehensive.

Most of these organizations explicitly refer to themselves as neighborhood associations; a small number refer to themselves as homeowner, home improvement, tenant, resident, and civic associations. The majority are formally incorporated. On average, they have a membership of 156 persons and an annual budget of under $1,000. Only four have any paid staff. Most are financed entirely by dues paid by members.

We acknowledge some ambiguity in the definition of neighborhood association as we use it here. As noted earlier, our emphasis is on the representation of collective interests of residents in a bounded community area. During interviews with local informants, we learned that in one city neighborhood, this function was for many years handled by lay organizations of a local church. Of course, the church drew parishioners from a wider area than the neighborhood, and its principal purpose was religious worship, but our research would be incomplete if we ignored the activities of the organization in this church prior to about 1970. Another illustration of definitional ambiguity is provided by merchants' associations. We know about one case in which residents of a neighborhood who also own small businesses in the same area are the dominant voice in what is formally designated as a neighborhood association, and this association is included in our sample. In another neighborhood, business proprietors along a single street have formed a merchants' association that often acts in concert with local residents to regulate new development; this merchants' association is not included in our sample.

A total of 74 personal interviews were completed; thus the response rate was about 74%. Of these, 72 included sufficient information to be used in this analysis. In fact, most refusals were from organizations that existed in name only, having ceased to function years before. In every case, we attempted to interview the current top elected representative of the association. In some organizations with an informal leadership structure, we were referred from one person to another until an appropriate and willing respondent was found. Interviewing leaders is a strategic choice, given their high levels of involvement and information. As Barber (1965) noted, "There exists in any given association, an active minority and inactive majority among the members" (see also Wood 1981; Mansbridge 1980).

In the following analysis, comparisons are made between neighborhood associations in central-city and suburban areas (39 in cities and 33 in suburbs). There are three central cities in this metropolitan area, each in a separate county, and for some purposes, it might be interesting to distinguish among them. However, we will not distinguish among them here because there are few cases in the smaller cities of Schenectady (9) and Troy (7) and because it is not meaningful to categorize suburbs in this area according to the city to which they are more closely connected. The City of Albany and Albany County contain the majority of neighborhood associations in this sample, and at some points, we give special attention to these cases.

THE FORMATION OF NEIGHBORHOOD ASSOCIATIONS

The Capital District's neighborhood association movement is relatively young (compare to Fisher 1984). Of the neighborhood associations in our sample, only 6 were founded before 1960. Another 10 date from the 1960s. By contrast, in the six years between 1980 and 1985, 26 neighborhood associations were established, and since we completed our interviews in mid-1986, several new neighborhood associations have come into existence. We searched carefully for evidence of associations from earlier periods that did not survive into the present. We found only 4, all in the City of Albany. More common in earlier years were settlement houses and other social service organizations oriented to specific neighborhoods.

The peak period of establishment differs slightly between city and suburban neighborhoods. The high point for new neighborhood associations in the city neighborhoods was 1975–1979, and the greatest number of new neigh-borhood associations in the suburbs were established between 1980 and 1985. It is tempting to interpret this difference as a demonstration effect; that is, perhaps this type of political activity in the central cities paved the way for such activity in the suburbs. Before adopting this view, however, one must look for the distinct sources of neighborhood association formation in both parts of the metropolitan area.

Regarding the city neighborhoods, the surprise is that Albany, Schenectady, and Troy were affected so little by the explosion of grassroots organizing that occurred elsewhere in the country during the 1960s and early 1970s primarily as a result of the civil rights movement and federal support of community organizations (Schoenberg and Rosenbaum 1980). Our discussion will focus on the Albany case, because nearly two-thirds of the city neighborhood associations are in Albany. In this case, the failure to organize more neighborhood associations may be attributable in part to the endurance of the county's Democratic political machine. Following 30 years of Republican party rule in Albany, the Democratic party, under Dan O'Connell, took control in 1921. O'Connell maintained a political monopoly until his death in 1977, when power passed to his handpicked mayor, Erastus Corning, who held office from 1941 until he died in 1983. This machine enjoyed the longest period of domination of any party apparatus in the country (Brown 1986, 69–70). Like many others, it operated through precinct leaders who were responsible for securing the Democratic vote and for keeping an eye on potential local issues. Mayor Corning maintained a reputation for responsiveness, and he actually encouraged people to approach him directly with their problems. This combination of political machine and political boss left little space for independent voluntary associations.

Nor did federal antipoverty programs of the 1960s have much lasting effect on community organizing in Albany County. As the novelist William Kennedy noted in his history of Albany, the party machine opposed federal antipoverty programs as "interference" in the local scene (Kennedy 1983, 278). Like New Orleans, where rejection of outsiders is notorious (Smith and Keller 1983), Albany was among the last major cities to take advantage of the federal programs. The Albany County Urban Renewal Agency was not established until 1960, and ground breaking for the first housing project did not take place until 1967. Curiously, then, it was the Republicans, not the Democrats, who promoted greater participation in the War on Poverty (an issue in the 1965 mayoral election). The first application for antipoverty funds for the city was denied because local officials failed to sign it; the next application was denied because the city's three-person "community representative" advisory board was understood even by the federal bureaucracy to be unrepresentative of the community.

In several city neighborhoods, independent community organizers backed by voluntary social service agencies attempted to promote local action groups in the mid-1960s. The most telling example is Albany's South End neighborhood, where a church-backed settlement house, the Trinity Institution, encouraged the formation of four small community-action organizations (the Progressive Community Betterment Association, the Catherine Street Civic Association, the Grand Community Association, and the Better Homes and Community Organization). But precisely at the time that these groups began to agitate vocally for improved city services, the city government retaliated by cutting off funding of the Trinity Institution (from a level of about $13,000 per year; see Kennedy 1983, 341). None of the four action groups survived beyond the 1960s.

By the late 1960s, however, the machine was beginning to weaken. From 1966 until 1970, a Republican represented the area in Congress; and in 1968, voters elected a Republican state senator, two Republicans to the state assembly, and a Republican to the critical position (for operation of a political machine) of County District Attorney (McEneny 1981). Although redistricting prevented the reelection of these Republican officials, a new level of competitiveness had been introduced into local politics (Swanstrom and Ward 1987). Then, in the early 1970s, large-scale redevelopment associated with the construction of a new state office complex (a $2 billion project completed in 1973) removed much of the downtown residential area and threatened what remained. These events created both the stimulus and the opportunity for grass-roots electoral challenges to the machine's hegemony. Mayor Corning, who had won reelection in 1969 by a landslide (37,896 to 15,212), won by his smallest margin ever in 1973 25,390 to 21,838). Also in 1973, an insurgent Democrat lost by only 14 votes in her bid to represent a downtown residential neighborhood in the city council.

Thus the surge in neighborhood association establishment in Albany after 1975 seems to have responded to the conjuncture of changes in the local political environment, but what accounts for the even later formation of neighborhood associations in the suburban ring? One obvious explanation would be that it is tied to the timing of suburban population growth. We have found, however, that Albany's suburbs grew most rapidly between 1950 and 1960, with a fairly steady growth rate since that time. No special surge in population or housing construction occurred around 1980. Nor did suburban job development accelerate at that time. A critical moment in that respect occurred in 1966, when the first major suburban shopping mall, anchored by Macy's and Sears Roebuck, opened in the suburban town of Colonie. Subsequently, as in most of the United States, retail, wholesale, and manufacturing employment have grown more rapidly in the Albany suburbs than in the central cities of Albany, Schenectady, or Troy. Again, however, no particular acceleration of this trend occurred around 1980 that would account for the rush to form neighborhood associations. If their founding was a response to suburban growth, it was

a delayed one and was, perhaps, a response to accumulated issues.

Such a delayed response is s curious phenomenon. We tend to think of growth politics in terms of local oppositions to plans for change in the immediate future—a proposed new highway, or landfill, or apartment complex. One analyst, Rudel (1989), painted quite a different picture for semirural areas in western Connecticut that only recently have experienced high-density growth. In these places, the notion of planning itself is new and, to some degree, has been imported by newcomers. Only after the subdivisions are in, Rudel suggested, do residents notice inadequate drainage or over-crowded roadways or other problems of development. Then, after the fact, residents become conscious of growth as a political question. We cannot test Rudel's interpretation here, but it represents an important hypothesis for future research.

FOUNDING ISSUES

We can gain a better sense of the origins of these neighborhood associations by looking into the issues that initially motivated their organization. By a large majority, the neighborhood associations were formed as a result of a specific issue (in 59 of 72 cases). We coded the founding issues into four categories, with a residual "other" category. The most common was a specific industrial or commercial development (23 cases). Specific residential developments (9 cases) also were common. Both of these typically involved disputes over the rezoning of land to a higher density or from residential to nonresidential use. Transportation issues were the concern in 10 cases, ranging from the establishment of "trackless trolley routes" (the McKownville Improvement Association, dating back to 1924!), to truck traffic in a residential area, to construction of a major highway. All transportation issues mentioned by respondents referred to "intrusions" into the neighborhood environment, rather than availability of transportation services. In 3 cases, the respondents cited simply a "general concern" with the neighborhood as their reason for forming, and the remaining 14 were formed for miscellaneous reasons.

These results reveal the central importance of land-development questions for neighborhood associations, as distinct from, for example, public services or social activities. By and large, neighborhood associations sprang up in response to specific land-use changes that concerned residents.

This generalization applies particularly to the suburban neighborhood associations. Of 28 suburban neighborhood associations that noted a specific issue, 16 listed industrial and commercial projects of various sorts. These included, for example, expansion of an industrial zone adjacent to a residential area and the placement of a neighborhood shopping center.

City neighborhood associations show a different pattern: Nearly half (19 of 39) of the city cases were formed based on "other" issues or on no specific issue. This trend was most apparent during the 1975–1979 period of rapid growth of city neighborhood associations, when 10 of 18 cases had "other" or no issues as the basis for their formation. We interpret this finding as an illustration of two sorts of processes. The first is the delayed response to federal redevelopment programs. The second is what can best be summarized as an epidemic of neighborhood organizing: neighborhood associations formed in response to the creation of other neighborhood associations.

Numerous examples reveal the importance that federal funding has had in stimulating neighborhood association formation since 1975. The neighborhood association may seek specifically to provide services using federal funds or to serve as a pressure group to influence how those funds are used in the city or simply to be the formal mechanism by which the community-participation requirements for funding are fulfilled. We note that the first funds from the Community Development Block Grant program were distributed in Albany in 1975 (at about $2 million per year, increasing to about $4 million per year in 1979). The South End Neighborhood Association was formed in 1978 to promote the construction of moderate-income housing in the neighborhood with federal community-development funding. In Schenectady, the Mont Pleasant Neighborhood Association was formed in 1975 to deal with community development funds; Troy's South Troy United Neighborhood Association was formed in 1978 for the same purpose.

The epidemic, or imitation effect, results from the activities of a central core of pioneer organizations. In Albany, several early organizations established a Neighborhood Resource Center in 1975 with the specific mission of encouraging new neighborhood associations. In the following year, they created a formal coalition, the Council of Albany Neighborhood Associations (CANA). Among respondents in our survey, the representatives of three neighborhood associations cited the importance of such support (Delaware Avenue, Krank Park, and Inner Brick Square). None of these reported a specific founding issue and the Inner Brick Square Neighborhood Association (established in 1981) specifically identified CANA as its principal stimulus. This concrete evidence of the process through which imitation may have occurred convinces us that this explanation should be taken seriously.

CURRENT ISSUES

However a neighborhood association was formed, a more important question is what issues it deals with on a continuing basis. For most neighborhood associations, the issue that stimulated its organization is long past, but after the initial issue is resolved, the neighborhood association may find new matters to confront. What are these issues?

To gain information on this question, our interviewers offered respondents a series of 18 different types of issues and asked how often these had been discussed at board meetings in the past year. Response categories ranged from 1 ("not at all") to 4 ("almost every meeting"). Because such striking differences appear between city and suburban issues, each geographic region will be discussed separately.

For city neighborhood associations, the top issues (in order) are "streets and sidewalks," "cleanliness of the area," and "traffic congestion and parking." Other very common issues are "parks and playgrounds," "condition of the area," and "police protection." Of these, only traffic congestion and parking was frequently discussed by a majority of suburban neighborhood associations (at the extreme, only 18.8% of suburban associations frequently discuss police protection). Clearly, most of these are specifically urban issues, responsive to the higher urban crime rate and shared responsibility for the immediate environment. City neighborhood associations are more likely than suburban associations to discuss frequently all of these issues.

By contrast, land developments—in the form of "residential land-use changes," "industrial-commercial encroachment on residential land use," and, perhaps, "traffic congestion and parking"—clearly is the central issue in suburban neighborhood associations, as posited in the growth-machine model. This does not mean that development questions are unimportant to the city neighborhood associations; two-thirds or more cited such issues. In some ways, indeed, every issue—whether noise or public safety or some other—may be associated with development. What is distinctive is that neighborhood association leaders in the suburbs are more likely to *describe* their issues as development issues. Moreover, development issues are the nearly exclusive concern in the suburbs, whereas they are among many issues of concern in the cities.

One also might have expected a strong emphasis on school issues, especially in the suburbs. However, school-related questions (such as class size or tax rates or school closings) were mentioned by only two respondents. This does not represent a disinterest in problems of public education but, rather, a very clear demarcation of responsibilities between neighborhood associations and other organizations that are concerned with schools (especially the parent-teacher organizations).

Working with 18 distinct issues is difficult. We inspected the Pearson correlations among them and also used exploratory factor analyses to determine which kinds of issues seem to come up together in neighborhood association meetings. Although these are not interval-scale variables, Pearson correlations commonly are applied to ordinal scales with as many as four response categories.

The 18 indicators have been combined into four indices, defined in the following list.

The conceptual distinctions among these four are not always obvious. For example, we have already intimated that traffic congestion may be a development issue, but it is listed here under the category of "collective consumption." The basis for our choice is the correlations of discussion of traffic cogestion with other issues.

1. *Safety* includes four issue areas: police protection, fire protection, personal safety, and street lighting. These are positively intercorrelated, especially police and fire protection, police and personal safety, and police and street lighting.
2. *Collective consumption* includes six kinds of services or facilities that affect the convenience of living in the neighborhood (although some are privately, rather than publicly, provided): parks and playgrounds, streets and sidewalks, garbage collection, traffic congestion, shopping facilities, and health care facilities.
3. *Life-style* includes six issues in which the amenities or quality of life in the neighborhood are emphasized: condition of the housing, reputation of the area, cleanliness of the area, noise level, visual aspects and architectural standards, and types of people who live in the area. Several of these issues are highly correlated with one another. Visual aspect is not much associated with noise level or types of people, but it has correlations above .30 with both condition of housing and reputation.
4. *Development* includes only two issues, though these are among the most consistently discussed by neighborhood associations: impact of commercial, industrial, institutional activities on residential land use, and residential land-use changes, such as construction of new housing developments and condominium conversion. These two issues are *negatively* correlated with the majority of other issues, making them quite a distinct pair.

We have used these categories to code responses to the question, "Which three issues have board members been most concerned about in the past year?" We proceed now to this item because for each of these three issues, we have additional information concerning the political process. In analyzing the distribution of these top three issues, note that there are potentially 216 cases (72 neighborhood associations times 3 issues). Issues that could not be classified clearly are combined into an "other" category. Thus development issues are especially important to the suburban associations (31.3% of suburban neighborhood associations listed development as one of their top three issues), and collective consumption, life-style, and safety issues are relatively more important in the cities. These differences are statistically significant (based upon standard t-tests) for both the development and life-style issues.

What accounts for this emphasis on development issues in the suburbs? One factor might be the higher income levels of suburban residents, which is related to the privatization of services and de-emphasis of collective services. Another factor might be the more recent development of suburban areas, making new construction a more potent issue. In principle, these two interpretations could be evaluated by multivariate analysis, in which the effects of suburban location are examined with controls for the median family income and age of the housing stock or other variables such as occupational composition or home ownership. We have chosen not to report more complete models because of the small number of independent observations (74 interviews) and the high correlations between suburban location, income, and age of housing.

OPPONENTS AND ALLIES

The final step in our analysis is to examine neighborhood associations' perception of their political situation on these issues. Who are the important actors on their side, and who are their main opponents? The interview question noted that

> neighborhood organizations often find themselves working together with other groups on some issues, while engaged in conflict at other times. Taking each of the three issues you have mentioned, please indicate the major groups

with which you have cooperated and with which you have been in conflict.

We provided no set response categories. Responses subsequently were coded into the following categories: state government (or specific state agencies or officials), local government (or specific local agencies or officials), businesses or land developers, other local voluntary organizations, and other individual residents in the neighborhood.

The distribution of responses was, cross-tabulated by the type of issue and city/suburban location. Within each panel, one for each major issue category, we report the number and proportion of neighborhood associations that noted a particular actor as cooperating or conflicting. For example, on only one life-style issue cited by a city neighborhood association (2.9% of life-style issues cited by city neighborhood associations) were state officials noted as a cooperating group. These data are provided separately for city, suburban, and all neighborhood associations.

By far the most important protagonist of neighborhood associations turns out to be local government. Local government was cited as a cooperating organization in more than half of the issues (53%) and as a conflicting organization in nearly half (43%). In 15 suburban cases and 26 central-city cases, local government was cited on both sides. For example, the neighborhood association may perceive a municipal agency as an opponent but perceive the city council or a particular council member as an ally. Local government was most likely to be considered cooperative on safety and life-style issues but was most likely to be considered an opponent on land-development issues. This pattern holds among both city and suburban neighborhood associations. However, partly because land-development issues are less predominant in the central city, local government is slightly more likely to be considered an ally for city neighborhood associations and less likely to be seen as an opponent.

The importance of local government is reinforced by responses to another question on the frequency of interaction with representatives of various other organizations. The highest frequency of interaction was reported with city government: 38% reported "much" interaction (the top category on a 5-point scale).

The next most common player, especially as a conflicting group, is businesses and land developers. This result certainly supports the growth-machine paradigm of local politics as business development versus the neighborhoods. Business is most commonly perceived as an adversary on land-development issues (47% of such issues) but also is cited on 33% of life-style issues as an adversary.

Perhaps the surprise here, given the literature's emphasis on conflicts, is the number of cases in which business and land developers are seen to be allies of neighborhood associations—in 14% of the cases, even including nine land-development issues. Seven of these land issues are in central-city areas, and they deserve more detailed attention. In two cases, the specific issue was historic preservation of buildings in the neighborhood, which was being pursued by private developers with the support of neighborhood association leaders. In two other cases, the issue was housing rehabilitation using public subsidies.

Again, we have complementary evidence from another question. Respondents were asked whether their organization tended more often to agree, to agree and disagree about equally, or more often to disagree with "realtors and property developers" in their areas. Although 48% reported that they more often disagree, an important minority of *15% said that they more often agree* with realtors and property developers.

One interesting example is a neighborhood association in downtown Schenectady in which the majority of the members were local business persons. This association sought to have vacant land developed for business uses, as well as to promote construction of low-income and senior citizen housing. In this process they worked closely with a large local construction company.

Sometimes, such relationships are initiated by real estate developers. For example, in one interview that we conducted, a representative of a firm that has large financial commitments to housing renovation in downtown Albany described a number of improvement activities in cooperation with neighborhood associations. These included support of renovation of a historic landmark, sponsorship of summer camps and youth employment programs, neighborhood cleanups, and the like. Clearly, these activities were directed at generating a positive public image, as well as influencing the reputation of gentrifying areas in which the firm was investing.

Such examples are a reminder that the business sector is a needed partner in neighborhoods in which the residents seek constructive changes. These cases may be more prevalent in central cities. When asked whether their orientation was more toward preserving the neighborhood pretty much as it is or toward making some major changes in the neighborhood, 20% of city neighborhood associations responded that they seek major changes, compared to only 3% of suburban associations.

Other groups are named much less frequently. Other local voluntary organizations are sometimes supporters (22% of issues), especially on land-development issues (32%); yet they rarely are viewed as opponents. State government officials and local residents are mentioned in fewer than 10% of the cases as either allies or opponents.

Multivariate analysis is a method to sort out the results of the survey. Overall, what is the effect of the type of issue on whether local government or developers are considered to be allies or opponents? Are there any independent city/suburban differences? Logistic regression is similar to ordinary least squares in that the direction and statistical significance of the coefficients allow one to weigh the relative effects of predictor variables. The difference is that the dependent variable is the log of the odds of being in one category versus the other category of a dichotomous dependent variable. . . .

First, local government is somewhat more likely to be considered an *ally* on life-style and collective consumption issues than on other issues. Location also has a significant effect: City neighborhood associations are less likely to see local government as an ally than are suburban associations. Local government is significantly more likely to be considered an *opponent* on development issues than on other issues. This effect is relevant to the assumption inherent in the growth-machine model that local officials are allied to prodevelopment forces.

Second, business and developers are more likely to be perceived as a cooperating group on collective consumption issues, which include some facilities (shopping and health care) that are privately provided. They are significantly more likely to be seen as opponents on development issues than on other issues. No city/suburban difference appears in perceptions of developers as allies or opponents.

CHALLENGES TO THE GROWTH-MACHINE PARADIGM

This study leads to some conclusions about neighborhood organizing in our specific case and to some implications for theories of growth politics in general.

In the Capital District, we find that neighborhood associations are a remarkably recent phenomenon: the great majority formed after 1975 in the central cities and after 1980 in the suburbs. A careful review of the city of Albany suggests a range of external and internal influences on the appearance of neighborhood associations. The major influence here probably was the strength of the local Democratic party machine, which was jealous of any independent political force. Eventually, federal antipoverty and community-development programs, offering new resources for neighborhoods to compete for and introducing requirements for grass-roots representation, became one foundation for neighborhood organizing. A second factor was gentrification and the commercial revitalization of downtown Albany following construction of Rockefeller's new government building complex in the heart of town. These events injected new issues and, in gentrifying neighborhoods, a new type of local activist, whose influence was magnified through the Neighborhood Resource Center.

We would argue that the *political machine* has been supplanted by a *growth machine*. Although we have not traced the history of neighborhood organizing in surrounding towns, we suspect that further research would reveal similar kinds of factors. The formation and character of neighborhood associations depend upon the local political context, the intervention of external agencies, the composition of the population, and the objective growth patterns that people experience.

We can conclude more definitely that these associations are formed to be single-issue political actors, most commonly in response to specific changes or proposals for change in land use. In their foundation, neighborhood associations are profoundly identified with the politics of growth.

We must distinguish, however, between city and suburban neighborhoods. In the heyday of 1975–1980, when most city neighborhood associations were formed, a large proportion had no particular founding issue. We cannot discount the role of fashion and learning in this process. Even in the suburbs, where respondents had no difficulty identifying a founding issue, the timing of new organizations (concentrated in a five-year period after most city associations had become active) hints at the role of imitation.

After the initial issue is resolved, neighborhood associations deal with quite a broad range of issues. In suburban communities, land-development questions remain uppermost, a result that we can attribute to the recency of development. In the cities, however, land use is only one of many issues; much attention is given to safety, public amenities, and services of various sorts. Suburban location is negatively related to life-style issues, even when controlling for income and age of housing effects.

We believe that in both suburban and city neighborhoods, the intention of neighborhood organizing is to protect the residential environment. In the suburbs, much of this environment is privately owned and controlled, and nonresidential activities are more spatially segregated. City residents deal with surroundings over which they have less personal control, so they experience a wider range of problems as collective issues. These observations indicate that questions that are only indirectly related to land development need to be addressed in the growth-politics model. Residents defend many dimensions of neighborhood, such as the land and buildings, the kinds of people who live there, their access to daily necessities, and personal safety.

In a more recent formulation (Logan and Molotch 1987), these are described as *use values*, in contrast to the *exchange values* that the rentier coalition seeks through more intensive land development. The issue is not simply the growth of the city but whether growth will favor one or the other set of values. This formulation has the advantage that it can encompass those situations in which residents advocate growth (particularly in declining neighborhoods, where people understand the issue not as growth but as abandonment). More research is needed on the range of values pursued by residents in different sorts of neighborhoods.

Complexity in the range of issues is matched by variation in the lineup of allies and opponents of neighborhood associations. Business interests and real estate developers typically are identified as opponents of neighborhood associations on issues of land use, and this statistically significant relationship provides good evidence for the basic model shared by Elkin (1985), Molotch (1976), Logan and Molotch (1987), Mollenkopf (1983), and Fainstein and Fainstein (1983). Yet some exceptional cases also are theoretically important. In some inner-city neighborhoods, developers are perceived as *allies* in promoting positive changes. This would be a surprising alliance: Most of the authors cited here believe, with Fainstein and Fainstein (1983, 257), that capitalists respond to working-class or minority concerns only when "confronted with a threat to the social relations of production." Our view is that depressed neighborhoods may embrace developers by default: The political system is closed to them, and their only apparent hope for change is through private investment.

Another provocative finding is that city government is perceived to be a more important political actor than real estate interests. Further, local government is seen as often as an ally (but especially on life-style and collective-consumption issues) as an opponent (especially on development questions). If these perceptions were accurate, they would undercut the growth-machine paradigm and lend more credence to a pluralist model of local politics. Perhaps the most important possibility in this respect is that city

governments are split, or at least are perceived to be split, on some of the issues important to neighborhood associations. This could take the form of a minority representation among elected officials—a voice, but not a decisive voice, in favor of neighborhood interests. Or structural divisions may occur. For example, Elkin (1985) argued that city bureaucracies often are more supportive of residents' interests than are elected officials and that in the current "federalist" period, these bureaucracies increasingly are autonomous. If so, there may be room for successful maneuvering in defense of use values—even in cities in which one has no difficulty in identifying a dominant progrowth coalition.

Our respondents were almost uniformly optimistic about their activity: Most of them (80%) asserted that their organizations had been "very" or "moderately" successful in achieving their goals over the past year, and even more (89%) believed that they had been very or moderately successful in dealing with the issue that stimulated their initial organization. One tends to discount such reports as image management by committed leaders; yet our data show a rapid expansion of this form of grass-roots organization, focused especially on land-development issues, in which the leaders perceive that they have important allies in local government. Is this a true gauge of political realities, or is it a reflection of regime strategies of negotiation, posturing, co-optation, and compromise?

Rather than thinking of residents as a single class of actors, it may be more useful to expect that the city government will protect *some* neighborhoods from *some* kinds of changes. More research should be directed toward identifying when and why this occurs. By stressing the middle-class electoral constituency that most local regimes rely on, both Elkin (1985) and Fainstein and Fainstein (1983) implied that middle-class neighborhoods will tend to be protected. We concur that there is likely to be a class bias in land-use politics. We would be cautious in interpreting this bias, however. Our fieldwork provided clear evidence that neighborhood association leaders do not take cooperation for granted. Middle-class residential leaders, especially those from gentrifying neighborhoods, approach city government most often as outsiders demanding a response, wary of the intentions of city officials and unwilling to rely on them to define the issues. In the era of the political machine, neighbors approached ward leaders as supplicants, expecting their protection. Today's neighborhood associations attempt to take a more active role, wielding power in their own right. In the Albany case, this is the most important change brought about by the movement.

REFERENCES

ARNOLD, J. L. 1979. The neighborhood and city hall: The origin of neighborhood associations in Baltimore, 1880–1910. *Journal of Urban History* 6 (November): 3–30.

BARBER, B. 1965. Participation and mass apathy in associations. In *Studies in leadership: Leadership and democratic action*, edited by A. Gouldner, 477–504. New York: Russell & Russell.

BOYTE, H. 1980. *The backyard revolution: Understanding the new citizen movement*. Philadelphia: Temple Univ. Press.

BROWN, C. 1986. Machine politics. In *Experiencing Albany*, edited by A. F. Roberts and J. A. Van Dyk, 67–73. Albany, NY: Nelson A. Rockefeller Institute of Government.

BURNETT, A. 1983. Neighborhood participation, political demand making, and local outputs in British and North American cities. In *Public service provision and urban development*, edited by A. Kirby, P. Knox, and S. Pinch, 316–62. New York: St. Martin's.

COX, K. R. 1973. *Conflicts, power and politics in the city*. New York: McGraw-Hill.

———. 1981. Capitalism and conflict around the communal living space. In *Urbanization and urban planning in capitalist society*, edited by M. Dear and A. J. Scott, 431–56. New York: Methuen.

CRAIN, R. L., and D. B. ROSENTHAL. 1967. Community status as a dimension of local decision making. *American Sociological Review* 32 (6): 970–84.

CRENSON, M. 1983. *Neighborhood politics*. Cambridge, MA: Harvard Univ. Press.

DAVIDSON, J. L. 1979. *Political partnerships: Neighborhood residents and their council members*. Beverly Hills, CA: Sage.

DYE, T. 1970. City-suburban social distance and public policy. In *Perspectives in urban politics*, edited by J. Goodman, 363–73. Boston: Allyn & Bacon.

ELKIN, S. L. 1985. Twentieth century urban regimes. *Journal of Urban Affairs* 7 (Spring): 11–28.

FAINSTEIN, N. I., and S. S. FAINSTEIN. 1983. Regime strategies, communal resistance, and economic forces. In *Restructuring the city: The political economy of urban development*, by S. Fainstein, N. Fainstein, R. Hill, D. Judd, and M. Smith, 245–82. New York: Longman.

FISHER, R. 1984. *Let the people decide: Neighborhood organizing in America*. Boston: Twayne.

FORM, W. 1954. The place of social structure in the determination of land use. *Social Forces* 32 (May): 317–23.

GOERING, J. M. 1979. The national neighborhood movement: A preliminary analysis and critique. *American Planners Association Journal* 45 (October): 506–14.

GREER, S. 1962. *The emerging city: Myth and reality*. New York: Free Press.

GUEST, A. M. 1985. The mediate community: The nature of local and extra-local ties within the metropolis. Paper presented to the American Sociological Association, Washington, DC, August.

GUEST, A. M., and S. OROPESA. 1984. Problem-solving strategies of local areas in the metropolis. *American Sociological Review* 49 (December): 828–40.

HENIG, J. R. 1982. *Neighborhood mobilization: Redevelopment and response*. New Brunswick, NJ: Rutgers Univ. Press.

JANELLE, D. G. 1977. Structural dimension in the geography of locational conflicts. *Canadian Geographer* 21 (4): 311–28.

KENNEDY, W. O. 1983. *O Albany*. Albany, NY: Viking.

LEY, D., and J. MERCER. 1980. Locational conflict and the politics of consumption. *Economic Geography* 56 (April): 89–109.

LOGAN, J. R., and H. MOLOTCH. 1987. *Urban fortunes: The political economy of place*. Berkeley: Univ. of California Press.

LONG, N. 1958. The local community as an ecology of games. *American Journal of Sociology* 64 (November): 251–61.

LOWE, P. D. 1977. Amenity and equity: A review of local environmental pressure groups in Britain. *Environment and Planning* 9 (1): 35–58.

MANSBRIDGE, J. J. 1980. *Beyond adversary democracy*. New York: Basic Books.

McENENY, J. J. 1981. *Albany: Capital city on the Hudson*. Woodland Hills, NY: Windsor.

MOLLENKOPF, J. H. 1983. *The contested city*. Princeton, NJ: Princeton Univ. Press.

MOLOTCH, H. 1976. The city as a growth machine. *American Journal of Sociology* 82 (February): 309–30.

ROSSI, P., and R. DENTLER. 1961. *The politics of urban renewal.* Glencoe, Il: Free Press.

RUDEL, T. 1989. *Situations and strategies in American land-use planning.* New York: Cambridge Univ. Press.

SCHOENBERG, S. P., and P. L. ROSENBAUM. 1980. *Neighborhoods that work: Sources for viability in the inner city.* New Brunswick, NJ: Rutgers Univ. Press.

SMITH, M. P., and M. KELLER. 1983. Managed growth and the politics of uneven development in New Orleans. In *Restructuring the city: The political economy of urban development,* by S. Fainstein, N. Fainstein, R. Hill, D. Judd, and M. Smith, 126–66. New York: Longman.

SWANSTROM, T., and S. WARD. 1987. Albany's O'Connell organization: The survival of an entrenched machine. Paper presented at the annual meeting of the American Political Science Association, Chicago, September.

TAUB, R. P., and G. P. SURGEON. 1977. Urban voluntary associations, locality based and externally induced. *American Journal of Sociology* 83 (March): 425–42.

THOMAS, C. J. 1986. *Between citizen and city: Neighborhood organizations and urban politics in Cincinnati.* Lawrence: Univ. Press of Kansas.

WOOD, J. 1981. *Leadership in voluntary organizations.* New Brunswick, NJ: Rutgers Univ. Press.

WOOD, R. 1958. *Suburbia: Its people and their politics.* Boston: Houghton Mifflin.

INSHOPPING BY RESIDENTS OF SMALL COMMUNITIES

James R. Pinkerton, Edward W. Hassinger, and David J. O'Brien
Department of Rural Sociology, University of Missouri–Columbia

With improvements in transportation and communication, rural consumers no longer are limited to their local trade center and personal factors become more important in shaping consumer patterns. With data from residents in two small rural communities in northwestern Missouri, this study examines the effects of consumers' socioeconomic characteristics, personal location situations, and community satisfaction on buying within the local community (inshopping) versus in other communities (outshopping) for selected goods and services. Age is the socioeconomic variable most strongly related to inshopping. Residing in the center versus open country, jobholders outside the community, and residing in the more viable community are related to shopping for certain of the goods and services as is satisfaction with the community. Location remains an important influence on shopping behavior but it needs to be conceptualized differently.

INTRODUCTION

Historically, the rural settlement pattern of the Midwest has consisted of population centers and open-country residents. The centers were established as locations of commercial and service enterprises that served not only townspeople but also open-country residents who were predominately farm families. The centers tended to claim a defined service area in the open country immediately surrounding them. Because of the time/distance limitations of transportation, residents obtained most of their goods and services within their trade area. The variety of the services provided by these relatively small centers was quite large and provided for most needs (Atherton 1954). The center with its trade area was identified by Galpin (1915) as the basis for the rural community and has been influential in rural sociologists' conceptualization of the structure of rural society.

From *Rural Sociology* 60, 3 (1995): 467–480. Copyright © 1995 by the Rural Sociological Society.

The pattern of settlement was disrupted by the improvements in transportation and communication technologies as well as by the rise in consumerism (Brown 1993). No longer confined to a small area for services and subject to advertising and changing consumption values, people ranged more widely in pursuit of goods and services. In the process, some trade centers declined as purveyors of goods and services while others gained. Now some centers offer only limited goods and services while other offer a larger number and a greater selection. The result is a greater differentiation among the centers in what they offer and a greater distance that customers travel for some services. This paper examines personal factors of residents of two small rural communities who shop for selected goods and services within their own trade centers (inshopping) versus other places (outshopping).

REVIEW OF CONCEPTS AND RESEARCH

A number of models define market areas for trade and service centers. Reilly's law of retail gravitation (1929), for example, defined the extent of a center's market area on the basis of the relative size of adjacent population centers. Building on the work of Huff (1963), Holden and Deller (1993) offered a model in which the customer drawing power of a center consists of probability contours based on size of the service center and size and distance of competing centers. Christaller's (1966) theory of central places was based on the range and threshold of individual goods and services, which yields a hierarchy of competing service centers.

As long as consumers were largely confined to local service areas, there was considerable regularity in location and patterns of goods and services used by them (Berry 1967). In a detailed analysis of current service relationships of American villages, however, Johansen and Fuguitt (1984) found irregularities in the hierarchy of services that suggested a dispersed city. They (1984:111) make the point that this "... places neighboring villages in a complementary position as opposed to the competitive situation posited by central place theory and thus differs sharply from the generally accepted model of retail location based on spatial compe-

tition." A version of the dispersed city is found in Fox and Kumar's (1966) conceptualization of functional economic areas. Collaboration among centers in the dispersed city mold is the basis for the conceptualization and research on "multicommunity collaboration" (Cigler et al. 1994).

HYPOTHESES
Market area models do not examine the variable behavior of consumers within the local area as they seek different goods and services. Given changes in service patterns such as those suggested by Johansen and Fuguitt (1984), individuals are assumed to have more options. Therefore, it is useful to identify personal factors related to inshopping and outshopping. In this study, socioeconomic characteristics of respondents or their households, location situations of respondents or their households, and general community satisfaction of respondents are related to shopping for selected goods and services in the community.

SOCIOECONOMIC VARIABLES
It is hypothesized that households headed by older members will be more likely to shop locally because of transportation problems (Coward and Lee 1985). Reduced mobility should lead to greater shopping in the local community. Furthermore, older respondents in rural communities are likely to be long-term residents with attending loyalties to the community. Several writers cite the positive effect of retired persons on local economic activity (Hoppe 1991; Summers and Hirschl 1985). For example, Hoppe (1991:31) noted that property and transfer income has a strong effect in rural areas because "... retired people spend a large share of their income in the local area." In the studies reviewed, age of household members was the personal variable most generally associated with shopping in the community (Leistritz et al. 1989; Papadopoulos 1980).

It is hypothesized that household income is negatively related to inshopping. Evidence on the relationship of household income to inshopping is mixed, however. In a study of shopping patterns in trade centers in Minnesota, Henderson and Hines (1990) found that an increase in income of families led to an increase in spending in the larger towns of the area. They reasoned that as incomes increase, consumers expanded the selection of goods they buy, some of which may be available only in larger communities. While shopping in a larger community, consumers may buy goods or obtain services previously obtained in their home community. In a review article, Papadopolous (1980) examined personal and other factors related to inshopping and outshopping in six studies of communities ranging from 1,500 to 80,000; there was general agreement that income was positively related to outshopping. Leistritz et al. (1989), however, reported different findings in a study of shopping patterns in six North Dakota towns that ranged in size from about 1,600 to 16,000 population. Household income was not related to shopping in or out of the community for convenience (food, hardware, banking) or other (furniture, automobiles, clothing) items.

Race has not been a consideration in studies of location of shopping. It is possible to examine the effect of race because each of the communities in this study had a small black population. It is hypothesized that because of their relatively small numbers, black households will be more likely than white households to extend their personal networks beyond the local community area and thus encourage shopping outside the community. In several studies, the relationship of gender to inshopping and outshopping was inconsistent (Leistritz et al. 1989; Samli and Uhr 1974). Gender is included among the independent variables without statement of expected direction of the relationship to inshopping.

LOCATION VARIABLES

The second set of hypotheses is based on location variables attached to respondents and individual households. It is predicted that employment outside of the community by the household's principal job holder is negatively related to inshopping. Commuting to work is common in rural communities. Johansen and Fuguitt (1984) reported from a survey of 100 mayors that in only 15 percent of the villages did most of the people who lived there also work there. Papadopolous (1980:57) commented that ". . . once a consumer reaches a larger trade center for whatever other reason, shopping appears to become a significant secondary activity." Therefore, it is expected that employment outside the community will be negatively related to inshopping.

It is hypothesized that residence in the community's center (as opposed to residence in the open country) will be positively related to inshopping. Families in the open country may not identify as closely with the community as families who live in the center. Furthermore, those on the outskirts of the area may find it convenient to shop in a neighboring center.

It is also hypothesized that members of households in a community judged to be more viable on objective criteria will be more likely to shop in the community. In this instance, the more viable community also has greater outshopping opportunities because it is closer to the area's larger regional shopping center. The question is whether the higher viability community, which should promote inshopping, will be overcome by its greater outshopping opportunity because of its proximity to the regional shopping center.

SATISFACTION WITH THE COMMUNITY

The final hypothesis is that community satisfaction is positively related to inshopping. The variable is in response on a seven-point scale (1 = dissatisfied, 7 = satisfied) to the question: "How satisfied are you in living in your community?" A general satisfaction question was given limited support as an indicator of shopping in North Dakota communities by Leistriz et al. (1989). Papadopoulos' (1980) review of six studies found positive relationships between more specific questions related to shopping satisfaction and shopping in the community.

RESEARCH METHODS
The Communities Studied

Data come from a study of two trade-centered communities in Missouri whose pseudonyms are Brian and Winder. The communities were incorporated places, each just over 1,000 population, and their respective open-country areas. Community boundaries were delineated by their school districts. Rural high school districts in the state are relatively small and are closely identified with the centers located in them. Both communities function as trade centers for agricultural areas. They are located in adjoining counties; neither is a county seat. Since size of community has been found to be related to inshopping and outshopping patterns (Papadopoulos 1980), the common size of the two trade centers establishes an important control in the analysis. Although the two communities are similar in many ways, they differ on selected structural attributes, including population change from 1970 to 1980 and from 1980 to 1990, changes in high school enrollment from 1977 to 1987, and on the availability of retail and health services. Winder has a more favorable position than Brian on all of these attributes and thus is considered to be the more viable community (O'Brien et al. 1991).

The two largest centers that draw trade from Winder and Brian number about 12,000 and 70,000 inhabitants respectively. The smaller of these centers is about equidistant (25 and 26 road miles) from the two study communities, but the larger center is close to Winder than Brian (36 and 66 road miles, respectively). Other proximate centers offering shopping opportunities are about equal for the two study communities.

Household Samples
A random sample of households was taken and personal interviews were conducted with household heads, which were systematically divided between males and females. Reference was to household purchases of goods and services; some of the independent variables (age, gender, race, satisfaction with the community) were respondent characteristics while the other independent variables (income, employment location, residential location) were household characteristics. The number of interviews was 311 (147 in Brian and 164 in Winder). The completion rate was 85 percent.

Goods and Services
A list of 29 goods and services was compiled. Respondents were asked if they or other household members bought each of these goods or services. If respondents reported buying a particular good or service, they were asked how often

they bought it in their community. The possible responses were never, once in a while, most of the time, and always. Those who reported shopping in their community for a given good or service once in a while or never were asked where they most often shopped for that item.

Responses of shopping for a good or service in the community always or most of the time were defined as inshopping, responses of once in a while or never as outshopping. Gasoline and oil were the products most often purchased within the community (83% of those using these products purchased them in the community). Forty percent or more of the households obtained 13 of the 29 goods or services in their community always or most of the time. The 13 items in order of inshopping were gasoline/oil products, auto repair, agricultural supplies, banking, appliance repair, lumber/hardware, food/groceries, construction supplies, legal services, beautician/barber, laundry/dry cleaning, major appliances, and lawn/garden supplies. At the other end of the distribution, less than 12 percent of the respondents obtained eight items in the community (infant supplies, sport supplies, adult shoes, adult clothes, shoe repair, maternity clothes, children's clothes, children's shoes).

There is a general correspondence between the two communities in which goods are obtained locally and which ones are not. If the 29 goods and services are ranked on the basis of the percentage of households inshopping for them, Spearman's rank order correlation between the two communities is 0.749. There are, however, some large differences in the rankings of specific goods and services that reflect the availability and quality of offerings in the two communities. Two examples illustrate these differences. Sixty-four percent of the households in Winder usually obtained prescription drugs in their community while virtually none did in Brian. Appliances and appliance repairs were much more likely to be obtained in Brian than in Winder. In the case of prescription drugs, the wide difference between Brian and Winder is simply explained by the fact that Winder has a well-established drug store while Brian does not have a pharmacy. The four respondents in Brian who said they obtained prescriptions drugs in the community may have obtained them from a local physician or may not have drawn a distinction between prescription and nonprescription drugs. In the second case, although appliance repairs and sales are not absent in Winder, Brian has a well-stocked service/sales appliance business whose reputation extends beyond the community's boundaries. If the cluster of health services (prescription drugs, nonprescription drugs, and other medical supplies) and buying appliances and appliance repair are removed from the rankings, then the rank order correlation of inshopping for the two communities become 0.904.

Most of the outshopping was done in relatively few places. A gross indication of outshopping is the sum of the responses of shopping in the community once in a while or never for the 29 goods and services. About half of the outshopping was done in 2 places, about 75 percent in 5 places, and more than 90 percent in 10 places.

TESTING HYPOTHESES
Selecting Goods and Services for Analysis
The first criterion was that the good or service must be available in the communities in a stable business. A second criterion was that goods and services commonly bought by household members were included in the analysis. Considered for selection were goods or services bought by at least 75 percent of the households. This eliminated 12 of the 29 listed. A third consideration was the variability among the community's inshoppers and outshoppers for particular goods or services. A good or service that almost all of the households bought in the community, such as gasoline/oil, would not show variation among households; the same was true for a good or service that was almost always purchased outside of the community, such as adult clothes. Six goods and services that were bought by at least 75 percent of the households and that were purchased by 40 to 75 percent of those households within the community always or most of the time were selected for analysis. These include three goods (food/groceries, lawn/garden supplies, major appliances) and three services (banking, beautician/barber, legal services).

Intercorrelation of Variables
The independent variables either are not significantly or are only moderately intercorrelated, thus reducing the problem of multicollinearity in the logistic regression analysis. Each independent variable, with the exception of household income, is significantly related to location of shopping for at least one good or service. Respondents' age (full range), location of the household in the center, and respondents' satisfaction with the community are positively related to inshopping. Respondents' race, gender and employment of the household's principal job holder outside the community tend to be negatively related to inshopping. The direction to inshopping is mixed for income (using midpoints of eight categories) and residence in the less viable community. The correlation matrix also shows substantial positive correlations among the six goods and services. Overall, inshoppers for one good or service are those who are likely to shop in the community for other goods or services.

Logistic Regression Analysis
In the logistic regressions the hypothesis that age is positively related to inshopping is supported for all the goods and services except banking and beautician/barber. No relationship was hypothesized between gender and inshopping and none is found. There is no support for the prediction that household income is negatively related to inshopping. The hypothesis that race is negatively associated with inshopping is supported only in the food/groceries equations.

The location variables, which were entered in the second equations, show the most consistent pattern of relationships to place of shopping. The hypothesis that employment outside the community is negatively associated with inshopping is found for all the goods and services except major appliances. The prediction that residents of the trade center are more likely than residents of the open country to shop locally is supported except for lawn and garden supplies. The hypothesis that residents in the less viable community are more likely than residents of the more viable community to be outshoppers is supported for banking and lawn/garden supplies, but the relationship for major appliances is in the opposite direction.

The final entry into the regression analysis is a measure of community satisfaction. The equations for three of the goods and services (food/groceries, lawn/garden supplies, major appliances) support the hypothesis that community satisfaction is positively related to inshopping.

Of the goods and services considered, food and groceries is most sensitive to the independent variables in the regression analysis. In the final food and grocery equation, five of the eight independent variables are significantly related to location of shopping. This is followed by four variables for lawn/garden supplies and major appliances, three for banking services and legal services.

DISCUSSION

The two communities examined each have about 1,000 residents. Centers of this size at one time provided a fairly complete range of goods and services to a population in the center and an adjacent trade area. Suppliers of goods and services can no longer depend on captive customers and clients, however, either in the center or its hinterland. Nonlocal competitors reach into the community for customers who respond in varying degrees.

Much of the research on location and use of goods and services has been based on bounded market areas. However, when customers are not bounded by trade areas, then socioeconomic characteristics, personal location situations, and community satisfaction become more important in explaining location of shopping.

The relation of age to shopping behavior is consistent with the general observation in the literature that older people spend a larger share of their resources in the local community than do younger people (Henderson and Hines 1990; Summers and Hirschl 1985). The only other socioeconomic characteristic related to location of shopping behavior is race. Blacks are more likely than whites to shop outside the community for groceries. This might be attributed to the non-local networks of blacks because of their small numbers in the communities studied.

Personal location variables are consistently related to shopping behavior. With the exception of purchasing major appliances, employment of the principal household employee outside the community is negatively related to inshopping for all of the goods and services. This suggests that the transportable location of employment competes with the permanent location of residence in affecting shopping location.

Among the personal location variables, there also is a relationship between center versus open-country residence and shopping location. Except for lawn and garden supplies, center residents are more likely than open-country residents to shop in their community. The open-country community boundaries were based on the high school district and, therefore, were somewhat arbitrary. More than that, however, personal mobility has nullified to some degree discrete open-country community boundaries.

Community viability is associated with shopping in the local community for three of the six goods and services. For two of these (banking, lawn and garden supplies), the relationships indicate greater inshopping for Winder thus supporting the expectation based on community viability. The third relationship indicates greater inshopping in Brian for major appliances, thus supporting the expectation based on more limited outshopping opportunities. However, shopping for major appliances in Brian seems more likely to illustrate that exceptional service and quality can retain local shoppers.

The idea of a community-bounded trade area, such as found in Reilly's law (1929) or later in Huff's (1963) or Holden and Deller's (1993) shopping probability contours that are based on the size and distance of competing trade centers, does not capture the reality of shopping behavior. The entire population of a trade-center community does not act in concert in shopping behavior. At the same time, these findings show that location factors continue to play a substantial role in shaping shopping patterns, although in a different way than was conceptualized by earlier writers. Being located in town versus the open country surrounding a town is an important variable in determining the likelihood of a household to shop in town. Furthermore, the impact of location factors is now substantially modified by the personal location of individuals during their daily routines. Households that have job holders who work outside of the local area are more likely to shop outside of the community for certain goods and services. Placement of plants and other employment opportunities may have a significant impact on shopping patterns in commuters' communities of residence. Location factors remain important but need to be conceptualized differently.

On a more general level, these findings add insight about the influence of place of residence versus personal situation on the day-to-day behavior of community members. Fischer's (1982) research indicated that informal relationships are not necessarily constrained by location of individuals. This study shows that certain situational and demographic factors encourage outshopping. An issue for further study is whether commuting and other kinds of transportation and communication linkages outside the community (e.g., routine health services in other communities) affect other activities besides shopping. A conceptual task for the future is to develop a framework that identifies key limiting or enabling characteristics of an individual's personal lifestyle and social networks that moderate or reinforce limitations imposed by place of residence.

REFERENCES

ATHERTON, LEWIS. 1954. *Main Street on the Middle Border*. Bloomington, IN: Indiana University Press.

BERRY, BRIAN J. L. 1967. *Geography of Market Centers and Retail Distribution*. Englewood Cliffs, NJ: Prentice Hall.

BROWN, RALPH B. 1993. "Rural community satisfaction and attachment in mass consumer society." *Rural Sociology* 58:387–403.

CHRISTALLER, WALTER. 1966. *Central Places in Southern Germany* (trans. C. Baskin). Englewood Cliffs, NJ: Prentice Hall.

CIGLER, BEVERLY A., ANICCA C. JANSEN, VERNON D. RYAN, and JACK C. STABLER. 1994. Toward an Understanding of Multicommunity Collaboration. Staff Report 9403, Agriculture and Rural Economic Division. Washington, DC: U.S. Department of Agriculture.

COWARD, RAYMOND T., and GARY R. LEE. 1985. *The Elderly in Rural Society*. New York: Springer.

FISCHER, CLAUDE S. 1982. *To Dwell Among Friends*. Chicago: University of Chicago Press.

FOX, KARL A., and KRISHNA T. KUMAR. 1966. Delineation of Functional Economic Areas. Iowa State University Center for Agricultural and Economic Development, Research and Education for Regional and Area Development. Ames, IA: Iowa State University Press.

GALPIN, CHARLES J. 1915. The Social Anatomy of an Agricultural Community. Agricultural Experiment Station Research Bulletin No. 34. Madison, WI: University of Wisconsin.

HENDERSON, DAVID A., and FRED K. HINES. 1990. "Increases in rural income may not help smalltown retailers." *Rural Development Perspectives* 6:31–36.

HOLDEN, JOHN P., and STEVEN C. DELLER. 1993. "Analysis of community retail market area delineation techniques: an application of GIS technologies," *Journal of the Community Development Society* 24: 141–58.

HOPPE, ROBERT A. 1991. "The elderly's income and rural development: some cautions." Rural *Development Perspectives* 7:27–32.

HUFF, DAVID L. 1963. "A probabilistic analysis of shopping center trade areas." *Land Economics* 40:81–90.

JOHANSEN, HARLEY E., and GLENN V. FUGUITT. 1984. *The Changing Rural Village in America*. Cambridge, MA: Ballinger.

LEISTRITZ, F. LARRY, HOLLY E. BASTOW-SHOOP, TIMOTHY L. MORTENSEN, and BRENDA L. EKSTROM. 1989. "Why do people leave town to buy goods and services?" *Small Town* 20(July–August):20–27.

O'BRIEN, DAVID J., EDWARD W. HASSINGER, RALPH B. BROWN, and JAMES R. PINKERTON. 1991. "The social networks of leaders in more and less viable rural communities." *Rural Sociology* 56:699–716.

PAPADOPOULOS, N.G. 1980. "Consumers outshopping research: review and extension." *Journal of Retailing* 56:41–58.

REILLY, WILLIAM J. 1929. Methods for the Study of Retail Relationships. Bulletin No. 2994. Austin, TX: University of Texas.

SAMLI, A. COSKUN, and ERNEST B. UHR. 1974. "The outshopping spectrum: key for analyzing intermarket leakage." *Journal of Retailing* 50:70–79.

SUMMERS, GENE F., and THOMAS A. HIRSCHL. 1985. "Retirees as a growth industry." *Rural Development Perspectives* 1:13–16.

COMMENTARY ON THE READINGS

In applying a survey methodology to their study of neighborhood associations, Logan and Rabrenovic (1990) are first faced with determining their population and the members of that population that will be selected. As they note in the research design section of the article, the authors chose to identify a specific area—Albany, Schenectady, and Troy, New York, and their surrounding suburbs—and then develop methods to identify all of the neighborhood associations that fall within their definition of the population. Based on the description of their methods, we can see that they did not draw a sample from their population but rather included all possible respondents. In this respect, this approach is similar to the survey administered by the U.S. Census Bureau. Yet by the number of steps they utilized to obtain a complete list, one can see that including all members of a designated population may not be as easy as it sounds.

In the article by Pinkerton and colleagues, the authors identified their population based on previous research, chose two communities that meet the previously determined criteria for the population they were interested in studying, and then sample households within those two communities. Their sample of households was a random sample. Thus the unit of analysis in these two survey articles differs. In the Logan and Rabrenovic study, the unit of analysis is the neighborhood association, whereas in the study by Pinkerton and colleagues the unit of analysis is the individual. Despite this difference, both sets of researchers had to identify a population and then determine how they would select the respondents of their survey instrument.

Logan and Rabrenovic chose to administer their survey using personal interviews. Within each neighborhood association the top elected representative of the association was interviewed, and in cases where the leadership was informal the individual to be interviewed was selected by speaking to association members until an appropriate and willing individual was identified. Those at the upper levels in the associations were selected to be interviewed because the authors believed that these members would have the information required to answer the questions based on their level of involvement in the association. Logan and Rabrenovic note that their response rate was 74 percent, or that 74 of the 99 associations in their population provided sufficient data to be included in their analysis. Their primary reason for nonresponse was that the association identified existed in name only.

Pinkerton and colleagues also used a personal interview method to administer their survey. They took a random sample of the households within each of the two communities they selected to study. Within the households selected, the head of the household was interviewed. The heads of households were divided between males and females. The number of interviews completed was 311—147 in one community and 164 in the other. Their stated response rate was 85 percent, and the reasons for nonresponse were not noted. Therefore, both of these studies utilize a personal interview method of administering their survey tools, and as a result each experiences a more than adequate response rate.

In the remainder of each article the authors describe their measures and note the responses they received to those measures. For the most part, the authors only report on those aspects of their interviews where the findings are significant to the phenomena the authors are interested in studying. For example, in discussing their question-naire, Pinkerton and colleagues noted that a list of 29 goods and services had been put together and respondents were first asked if they bought the items and then how often they bought the item in their community. The responses to the second question were provided—*never, once in a while, most of the time,* and *always*—and respondents who gave either of the first two responses were then asked where they most often shopped for that item. After collecting the data, the authors coded the responses. Coding is in-dicated in the text when the authors define inshopping and outshopping as corre-sponding to specific responses—*always* and *most of the time* and *once in a while* and *never,* respectively. They continue by discussing how their findings relate to their hy-pothesis. Their analysis includes not only the responses to the shopping questions, but demographic data all of which are utilized in a logistic regression.

Logan and Rabrenovic analyze the three issues they are most concerned with, as indicated by their section headings—the formation of neighborhood associations, founding issues, current issues, and opponents and allies—in their analysis of the data collected. They conclude by bringing their findings into a more general discussion of growth machines. Pinkerton and colleagues also relate their findings to those estab-lished previously.

CONCLUSION

Surveys are perhaps the social science research method best known to the general public. Every day we are bombarded with the results of new polls, opinion polls, and other surveys. Given the advantages of surveys, it seems likely that this popular prac-tice will continue.

CHAPTER 6

SECONDARY DATA ANALYSIS

After data are collected for one study, they need not go to waste. Data collected for one purpose are often recycled and used in other studies. In many cases, data are collected simply for the purpose of data collection and then released as a data set to researchers who utilize the data in their own research. The use of data for purposes other than for which they were collected is called secondary data analysis.

SECONDARY DATA

Secondary data includes documents, survey results and their other forms of data collected previously with goals that may differ from those of the current research analyst. Data sources often utilized include government reports or previously conducted surveys. One of the most commonly known sources used in secondary data analysis is the general social survey. The National Opinion Research Center, located at the University of Chicago, conducts a national survey sponsored by the federal government to gather information on a variety of social science variables. The results of this survey are placed in a data set and made available to researchers who analyze the data in accordance with their own research agendas.

In secondary data analysis the researcher obtains data from an existing source and then reorganizes it. This method often allows researchers to benefit from the work of established scholars in their field who have previously collected and established the reliability and validity of data. The researcher may combine segments of several existing sources into one data set or combine an existing source with newly collected data. In either case the researcher will need to restructure the data set to appropriately address her or his research questions. For example, survey data collected by the U.S. Census Bureau is collected to determine appropriate policies and programs—those that will best meet the needs of the American people based on their current circumstances. However, it is common for researchers to use the demographic data—age, race, income, education—collected by the Census Bureau to describe populations of people in studies that are not related to policies and programs.

ADVANTAGES AND DISADVANTAGES

As a research method, secondary data analysis presents a variety of advantages over other types of research. The collection of new data involves considerable amounts of time and money, both of which are saved in analyzing data previously collected. For example, it is faster, easier, and less costly to extract a set of variables from the U.S. Census Bureau than it is to develop and administer a survey. A researcher who was interested in studying the relationship between income, education and gender for the population over age 18 in the 50 largest metropolitan areas in the United States could either (1) establish an appropriate sampling frame, draw a sample, sample from within the sample to assure that it is representative, develop a survey tool, train interviewers, administer the survey, organize the data and finally analyze the data; or (2) simply download the desired variables for the desired year from the U.S. Census Bureau's web page and then complete the analysis.

At first glance, it appears that secondary data analysis is quick and easy, and one could question why other research methods are used at all. The answer to this question is quite simple: There are also several disadvantages to secondary data analysis. The most apparent issue is validity: The researcher cannot be sure that the data collected to address the goals of one researcher will be suitable for her or his purposes. Often the goals and research questions in the original study will be similar to those of the current study, but just as often the researcher attempting to use the previously collected data has additional questions or concerns that may not be fully addressed by the existing data. The critical issue is whether or not the existing data can be organized in such way that they are a valid measure of the variables the researcher wishes to analyze.

In addition to the issue of validity, there are other disadvantages a researcher utilizing existing statistics must consider. For one, all of the data a researcher will need to complete a study may not be available in an existing data set. Furthermore, the researcher cannot be sure that the data he or she is hoping to find exist at all, and searching for a meaningful source of data can be a very lengthy and time-consuming process. The original data set may not be accurate—it is possible that the data source includes a variety of errors. The researcher had no control over the data collection process, the sample, the coding (if any), or the transcription of the data from its original to its current format. In addition, existing data sources often consist of more variables than the researcher will need. Thus it is not simply a matter of downloading the variables needed for the study, but downloading a set of variables and then sorting through them. This process, which may be very time consuming, requires that the researcher become familiar with the codebook that explains the meaning of each variable. The researcher may also need to combine variables to obtain the variable he or she is actually seeking to explore. These issues must be resolved before the data are analyzed.

THE READINGS

The following article is an example of research that draws on existing statistics. "Economic Deprivation and AIDS Incidence in Massachusetts," by Sally Zierler and colleagues (2000), looks at the relationship between economic conditions and re-ported AIDS cases. Zierler and colleagues utilize 1990 census data as well as data from the Massachusetts Department of Public Health to analyze the relationship between socioeconomic status and reported AIDS cases.

ECONOMIC DEPRIVATION AND AIDS INCIDENCE IN MASSACHUSETTS

Sally Zierler
Brown University School of Medicine

Nancy Krieger
Harvard School of Public Health

Yuren Tang, William Coady, Erika Siegfried, and Alfred DeMaria
Bureau of Communicable Disease Control

John Auerbach
Massachusetts Department of Public Health

Objectives. This study quantified AIDS incidence in Massachusetts in relation to economic deprivation.

Methods. Using 1990 census block-group data, 1990 census population counts, and AIDS surveillance registry data for the years 1988 through 1994, we generated yearly and cumulative AIDS incidence data for the state of Massachusetts stratified by sex and by neighborhood measures of economic position for the total, Black, Hispanic, and White populations.

Results. Incidence of AIDS increased with economic deprivation, with the magnitude of these trends varying by both race/ethnicity and sex. The cumulative incidence of AIDS in the total population was nearly 7 times higher among persons in block-groups where 40% or more of the population was below the poverty line (362 per 100 000) than among persons in block-groups where less than 2% of the population was below poverty (53 per 100 000).

Conclusions. Observing patterns of disease burden in relation to neighborhood levels of economic well-being elucidates further the role of poverty as a population-level determinant of disease burden. Public health agencies and researchers can use readily available census data to describe neighborhood-level socioeconomic conditions. Such knowledge expands options for disease prevention and increases the visibility of economic inequality as an underlying cause of AIDS.

In the United States, public health agencies collect and report national and state AIDS surveillance data with reference to race/ethnicity, sex, age, and mode of transmission.[1,2] Conspicuously absent are data on economic conditions,[3] even though several US studies have reported that HIV infection occurs disproportionately and increasingly among the poor[4–10] and 4 studies have documented the incidence of AIDS or HIV in relation to economic deprivation.[11–14] Three of these studies provided AIDS incidence data stratified by economic level for 3 cities (Philadelphia, Pa,[11] Newark, NJ,[12] and Los Angeles, Calif[13]), while the fourth analyzed economic disparities in HIV seroprevalence among newborns in New York State.[14] Thus, 20 years into the AIDS epidemic, there exist few data in

From *American Journal of Public Health, 90,* 7 (2000): 1064–73. Copyright © American Public Health Association.

the United States empirically quantifying links between economic deprivation and incidence of AIDS. In light of research on causal links between poverty and risk of HIV infection, however, such data could have important ramifications for guiding and evaluating AIDS prevention initiatives and programs and allocation of resources.[1,3,6,8–10]

Building on the limited extant research, we sought to quantify AIDS incidence in relation to economic deprivation in the state of Massachusetts, which presently ranks midway in the quartile of states with the second-highest incidence of AIDS.[2] An additional objective was to extend this description by examining economic disparities in AIDS incidence in relation to both race/ethnicity and sex. To overcome the absence of socioeconomic data in AIDS surveillance records, we used the same strategy employed by the prior 3 studies on economic deprivation and AIDS incidence: that of categorizing AIDS cases and individuals in the total population in terms of the economic characteristics of each person's residential neighborhood.[11–13] This approach permits determining and comparing population-based incidence rates among persons residing in neighborhoods with greater and lesser economic deprivation.[3,15,16] Whereas the prior 3 studies used area-based socioeconomic measures at the zip code (average population = 25 000) and census tract (average population = 400) level, we used data from a smaller, more economically homogeneous level, the census block-group (average population = 1000).[15]

METHODS
Study Population
The study base comprised all 6.3 million people included in the 1990 US census as residents of Massachusetts, of whom 86.0% were designated as White, 4.7% as Black, 4.4% as Hispanic, 2.2% as Asian/Pacific Islander, 0.2% as American Indian, and 2.0% as "other." We assumed that all in-state Massachusetts AIDS reports included in this study originated from this at-risk population.

AIDS cases. We included all incident cases of AIDS reported to the Massachusetts Department of Public Health by the state HIV/AIDS Reporting System between January 1, 1988, and December 31, 1994. HIV/AIDS Reporting System uses the standard Centers for Disease Control and Prevention (CDC) case report form and defines an incident case of AIDS as a unique first report of diagnosis of an AIDS-defining condition, using the AIDS case definitions of the CDC.[11,12] In light of the CDC's 1987 revision of the AIDS case definition,[17] we restricted the study time period to include only cases diagnosed after December 31, 1987, and we extended the study to include all subsequent calendar years for which entry of AIDS data was complete (through 1994, as of the time our study was conducted). In addition to date of diagnosis, AIDS case records included information on age at diagnosis, sex, race/ethnicity, mode of transmission, and residential address at time of diagnosis.

Between January 1, 1988, and December 31, 1994, the surveillance system documented 8874 incident AIDS cases in Massachusetts. Of these cases, 13 of the persons resided in non-prison institutions, 335 were in prisons, 204 were homeless, and 9 lived out of state. Of the remaining 8313 persons with AIDS who were domiciled residents, we were able to geocode 8059 (96.9%) to the census block-group level, using MapInfo Pro version 4.0 (MapInfo Corporation, Troy, NY). The geocoded address was recorded at the time of diagnosis and/or at the time of the initial case report, or, if the address at diagnosis could not be established, an address from 5 years before or 2 years after diagnosis was used. Among geocoded cases, we restricted analyses to the Black non-Hispanic, Hispanic, and White non-Hispanic populations (n = 7994), since small numbers precluded meaningful analysis of data for other racial/ethnic groups.

Census block-group socioeconomic measures. To characterize neighborhood socioeconomic conditions, we employed census block-group socioeconomic measures.[15,16,18] We obtained census block-group data from Summary Tape File 3A for the 1990 US census.[18] In 1990, Massachusetts contained 5603 block-groups, with an average population size of 1074 people.

Using the census data, we constructed numerous measures of neighborhood socioeconomic conditions, assessed in relation to absolute and relative poverty and wealth, crowding, education, and occupational class.[15,16] Specific measures pertained to (1) poverty (percentage of people living below the poverty line, which was set at $12 674 for a family of 4 in the 1990 census; according to federal guidelines, a "poverty area" is one where 20% or more of residents live below the poverty line and an "extreme poverty area" is one where 40% or more of residents live below the poverty line[18,19]); (2) high income (percentage of households with an annual household income of at least $150 000, the highest income category reported by the US census[18]); (3) ratio of lower-income households (<$20 000) to higher-income households (≥$60 000); (4) population density (number of persons per square mile); (5) crowding (percentage of households with more than 1 person/room); (6) education (percentage of adults 25 years and older who had not completed high school); and (7) working class (percentage of persons employed in nonsupervisory occupations, as determined by a previously validated block-group class measure[15,16]). Because these diverse indicators revealed comparable patterns of AIDS incidence in relation to economic deprivation and advantage (data available upon request), we present results for only 3 indicators: (1) poverty, (2) population density, and (3) high income, conceptualized as a measure of wealth. Data on these indicators were available for 98% of the state's population.

Statistical Analysis

Constructing numerators and denominators stratified by block-group socioeconomic measures. Numerators consisted of geocoded AIDS cases whose individual records were linked to the selected block-group measures characterizing socioeconomic conditions in the cases's block-group. For each calendar year, we tallied the number of cases, stratified by race/ethnicity and sex, who lived in block-groups with the specified socioeconomic characteristics (e.g., White women who lived in block-groups where fewer than 2% of residents were below the poverty line).

Denominators of incidence rates reflected the combined number of person-years of residents in block-groups sharing a particular economic condition for each calendar year from 1988 to 1994. Block-group population counts by sex were directly available for Hispanics from Summary Tape File 3A.[18] For Blacks and Whites, counts by sex did not distinguish between persons of Hispanic and non-Hispanic origin[18]; we therefore estimated the number of non-Hispanic Blacks and Whites by (1) calculating, for each block-group, the proportion of White and Black persons of non-Hispanic origin and (2) multiplying these proportions by each group's sex and age distribution within the block-group.[16] We then summed across all block-groups in the catchment area within the same economic stratum to obtain denominator data stratified by race/ethnicity (Black non-Hispanic, Hispanic, White non-Hispanic), sex (women, men), and block-group economic position (measures pertaining to poverty, population density, and wealth).

Calculating incidence rates and cumulative incidence. For each calendar year 1988 through 1994, we estimated annual incidence rates. To estimate 7-year cumulative incidence (as an estimate of absolute risk), and to account for changes in incidence over the study period within each sex-racial/ethnic population and block-group level of economic deprivation, we used the formula[20]

$$1 - e \uparrow \left[- \sum_{1998}^{1994} IR \right].$$

where e is the base in the natural logarithm system and is approximately equal to the value 2.71828. *IR* represents the annual incidence rates. The ratios of estimates for cumulative incidence at the extremes of economic distributions and 95% confidence intervals are presented for the total Massachusetts population. We also present estimates of absolute difference in risk between extremes of the economic distributions. For these estimates, the standard errors were minute (approximately 0.0001 excess cases per 100 000 persons), and confidence intervals are therefore not presented.

Estimates of trend. We estimated trends in cumulative incidence (with interval estimation) across the social gradient constructed for each socioeconomic measure. To simplify comparisons of the public health impact of economic conditions across subpopulations in this and other studies, we visually depict these trends by using figures with untransformed scales.[21]

RESULTS

To assess the incidence of AIDS in relation to block-group socioeconomic conditions, we first describe the socioeconomic distribution of the AIDS cases and of the total Massachusetts population and then present annual and cumulative incidence rates stratified by the poverty, population density and wealth block-group measures, both for the total population and for the total population additionally stratified by race/ethnicity and sex.

Sociodemographic Characteristics of AIDS Cases and of Massachusetts Population

Among the 8059 geocoded and 815 non-geocoded AIDS cases as recorded in the AIDS surveillance system, persons with non-geocodable addresses were more likely to be men, to be Black or Hispanic, and to have "injection drug use" assigned as their mode of HIV acquisition. Socioeconomic characteristics of the AIDS cases and of the 1990 Massachusetts population differed considerably in terms of the block-group measures of poverty, population density, and wealth. Thus, most of the Massachusetts population resided in block-groups where less than 10% of the population was below the poverty line, population density was fewer than 5 000 people per square mile and at least 2% of the population had household incomes of $150 000 or more. By contrast, in most of the AIDS cases in the state the person lived in block-groups where at least 10% of the population was below the poverty line, population density exceeding 10 000 people per square mile, and fewer than 2% of households had incomes of $150 000 or more.

Cumulative Incidence of AIDS in Relation to Block-Group Socioeconomic Measures: Total Population

Overall, cumulative incidence of AIDS for the total Massachusetts population for 1988 to 1994 equaled 128 cases per 100 000 persons. During this time period, yearly incidence and cumulative incidence showed monotonic patterns of increasing AIDS occurrence with decreasing economic resources and increasing population density. Thus, the cumulative incidence of AIDS in the total population was nearly 7 times higher among persons in block-group where 40% or more of the population was below the poverty line (362 per 100 000) than among persons in block-groups where less than 2% of the population was below the poverty line (53 per 100 000). For population density, cumulative incidence rates ranged from 40 per 100 000 among persons in the least densely populated block-groups (<1 000 persons/square mile) to 373 per 100 000 among those in the most densely populated block-groups (≥25 000 persons/square mile). As a demonstration of a protective effect of neighborhood wealth, cumulative incidence was 69 cases per 100 000 among persons living in block-groups where at least 10% of households had annual incomes of $150 000 or more but was 175 per 100 000 among those in block-groups where fewer than 2% of households had incomes of $150 000 or more.

Combined Impact of Socioeconomic Position, Race/Ethnicity, and Sex on Cumulative Incidence of AIDS

Population patterns of socioeconomic gradients in cumulative incidence of AIDS were evident across racial/ethnic and sex subgroups, but they varied in both steepness and monotonicity. Among both women and men, monotonic patterns were most evident and consistent among the Black and White populations. Only for 1 block-group measure, high income, were economic inequalities in AIDS incidence greater among women than among men, a finding that may reflect elevated risk of AIDS in more affluent gay neighborhoods.

As evidence of the combined impact of socioeconomic position, sex, and race/ethnicity on risk of AIDS, the cumulative incidence among persons living in block-groups where 40% or more of the population was below the poverty line equaled 442 cases per 100 000 among non-Hispanic Black women and 352 per 100 000 among Hispanic women but only 13 per 100 000 among non-Hispanic White women; higher rates among men ranged from 936 per 100 000 among non-Hispanic Black men and 930 per 100 000 among Hispanic men to 411 per 100 000 among non-Hispanic White men. Moreover, the absolute excess risk of AIDS among persons living in these impoverished block-groups, compared with persons living in block-groups where less than 2% of the population was below the poverty line, was 309 cases per 100 000 for non-Hispanic Black women, 221 per 100 000 for Hispanic women, 13 per 100 000 for non-Hispanic White women, 375 per 100 000 for non-Hispanic Black men, 396 per 100 000 for Hispanic men, and 327 per 100 000 for non-Hispanic White men. Finally, cumulative incidence in categories of greatest poverty, greatest population density, and least wealth among White women was always lower than in categories of least poverty, least population density, and most wealth among both non-Hispanic Black and Hispanic women; the same pattern was apparent among the men.

DISCUSSION

Our study provides additional evidence, for the first time at the state level, that neighborhood levels of economic deprivation and population density are powerful determinants of AIDS incidence.[11–14] Between 1988 and 1994, both relative and absolute risk of AIDS increased among persons in Massachusetts living in economically deprived and densely populated block-groups. Compared with those residing in the least poor block-groups, persons residing in the poorest block-groups were burdened with an excess of 309 cases per 100 000; compared with those living in the least densely populated block-groups, those living in the most densely populated block-groups had an excess of 333 cases per 100 000; compared with those living in block-groups with the smallest percentage of high-income households, those living in block-groups with the largest percentage of high-income households had 106 fewer cases per 100 000.

Moreover, because we were able to stratify the data by sex and race/ethnicity, our results provide new evidence of the combined impact of economic deprivation, race/ethnicity, and sex on incidence of AIDS: the highest rates for the state occurred among non-Hispanic Black men living in block-groups with the greatest population density (1053 cases per 100 000), followed by non-Hispanic Black men and Hispanic men living in the most impoverished block-groups (more than 900 cases per 100 000), while the lowest rates occurred among White women in the least impoverished block-groups (0 cases per 100 000). Whereas government surveillance reports as well as published studies of AIDS incidence typically describe risk in relation to sociodemographic categories of sex and race/ethnicity, our results indicate that these social categories are insufficient to describe the population burden of AIDS; data must additionally be stratified by measures of adverse living conditions.

Possible Sources of Error Affecting Study Results

Interpretation of our findings rests on several assumptions about validity of measures, especially pertaining to block-group measures of socioeconomic position and race/ethnicity. As we discuss below, however, it is unlikely that these study results are exaggerated by measurement error.

First, an unknown proportion of people may have changed residence in the interval between HIV infection and diagnosis of AIDS. Some researchers have suggested that AIDS cases are greater among the poor because deterioration of health leads to poverty,[4] with loss of assets causing relocation to poorer block-groups. Misclassification introduced by using residential address at the time of AIDS report rather than of HIV infection, however, would introduce error in the direction of overestimating economic gradients only among people at risk of losing substantial income or other assets. Among the chronically poor, no such misclassification would occur. Nor would misclassification occur if AIDS cases emerged from neighborhoods with economic conditions similar to those of neighborhoods where HIV infection was first acquired in those cases. Further countering these concerns about the likely direction of causal pathways between economic deprivation and AIDS are (1) a recent Massachusetts study demonstrating that positive HIV tests among persons seeking HIV testing at public clinic were 4 times more frequent among persons living in lower-income zip codes than among persons living in higher-income zip codes[22] and (2) additional US studies documenting newly diagnosed HIV infection disproportionately among the poor, with excess risk linked to poverty most profoundly among women.[4,5,7]

Second, reliance on census block-group socioeconomic measures is unlikely to have inflated estimates of socioeconomic gradients in the incidence of AIDS. In fact, underestimation of these gradients is the more likely bias, for several reasons. First, lack of residential address resulted in exclusion of prisoners and homeless persons, 2 populations known to be at high risk of HIV infection and AIDS.[8,23] Underascertainment of AIDS among medically underserved populations would likewise deflate estimates of relative and absolute risk among the poorest populations. Prior non-AIDS studies have shown that disparities in individuals' health identified via area-based measures resemble or are underestimates of health disparities identified via gradients based on individual- or household-level economic data.[15,16,24,25] Additional contextual research likewise demonstrates that block-group socioeconomic measures are far more than simply proxies for unavailable individual-level economic data; instead, they provide data on how neighborhood conditions themselves affect health, independent of and in conjunction with individual- and household-level socioeconomic resources.[15,16,26]

Third, validity of estimates could be affected by factors differentially compromising classification of and enumeration by race/ethnicity, among numerators and/or denominators. Misclassification by race/ethnicity, documented to occur in AIDS surveillance systems,[27,28] would affect validity most seriously if it had occurred differentially in numerator and denominator data (i.e., AIDS case reporting and US census self-identification) and differentially within social class categories. Regarding the numerator data, a recent reliability study of AIDS surveillance data in Massachusetts noted 99% agreement for sex and 94%, 94%, and 91% agreement

for Black, White, and Hispanic race/ethnicity, respectively, comparing surveillance data with information in medical records.[29] A related form of misclassification is use of racial/ethnic categories that are heterogeneous with respect to social meaning, because among the persons in each category there are differences in historical experience of conquest and enslavement, in current refugee and immigrant status, and in country of origin.[8-10,30,31] Heterogeneity pertaining to country of origin and immigrant status, for example, may explain why economic gradients in AIDS incidence were least pronounced among the Hispanic population. Finally, undercounting of populations of color (estimated nationally in the 1990 census to have been between 2% and 12%, depending on race/ethnicity, sex, and age) could lead to overestimation of incidence rates among these populations.[32–34] This marginal inflation of rates due to an undercounted denominator, however, is insufficient to explain the magnitudes of excess AIDS incidence by race/ethnicity that we observed. Notably, however, racial/ethnic disparities apparent within our block-group socioeconomic strata are likely to reflect residual confounding, since Black residents of a wealthy block-group, for example, are likely to be less wealthy than their White counterparts, while White residents in a poor block-group are less likely to be as impoverished as their Black counterparts.[15, 35]

Including Socioeconomic Data in AIDS Surveillance Systems

Despite possible biases, our results are compatible with and extend the finding of the 4 published US studies[11–14] and 3 non-US studies (1 Australian,[36] 1 Spanish,[37] and 1 Canadian[38]) quantifying AIDS or HIV incidence in relation to economic resources. Although none of these prior studies reported results stratified by sex, 1 US study, like ours, reported that incidence of AIDS was inversely associated with income in each of 4 racial ethnic groups: Asian/Pacific Islander, Black, Hispanic, and White.[13] Together, these results indicate that our findings may be generalizable to other states, especially those containing urban populations; future research, however, should address this issue by quantifying AIDS incidence in relation to economic deprivation in additional states, taking into account both rural and urban areas.

In conclusion, our results suggest that public health agencies can feasibly expand AIDS and other disease surveillance systems to include neighborhood-level economic data. When rich descriptions of neighborhood conditions are linked at the block-group level to residential address of HIV/AIDS cases dynamics of the epidemic in relation to neighborhood economic resources become more visible. Such knowledge can inform HIV prevention initiatives that emphasize social and economic harm reduction at the neighborhood level.[6,8–10] At a time of disturbing trends of increasing geographic concentrations of poverty within the United States,[39] coupled with increasing evidence of poverty as a causal determinant of risk of HIV infection,[8–10] data on AIDS incidence in relation to neighborhood economic conditions strongly suggest that reducing the incidence of AIDS will depend vitally on approaches that promote the growth of social and economic resources in neighborhoods where AIDS is endemic.

REFERENCES

1. NATIONAL CENTER FOR HEALTH STATISTICS. *Health, United States, 1998, With Socioeconomic Status and Health Chartbook.* Hyattsville, Md: National Center for Health Statistics; 1998. DHHS publication PHS 98-1232.

2. CENTERS FOR DISEASE CONTROL AND PREVENTION. HIV/AIDS Surveillance Report, 1998. Vol 10, No. 2.

3. KRIEGER N, CHEN JT, EBEL G. Can we monitor socioeconomic inequalities in health? A survey of US health departments' data collection and reporting practices. *Public Health Rep.* 1997; 112:481–491.

4. DIAZ T, CHU SY, BUCHLER JW, BOYD D, CHECKO PJ. Socioeconomic differences among people with AIDS: results from a multistate surveillance project. *Am J. Prev Med.* 1994; 10:217–222.

5. BROWN VB, MELCHIOR CR, HUBA GJ. Mandatory partner notification of HIV test results: psychological and social issues for women. *AIDS Public Policy J.* 1994; 9:86–92.

6. WALLACE R, WALLACE D. US apartheid and the spread of AIDS to the suburbs: a multicity analysis of the political economy of spatial epidemic threshold. *Soc Sci Med.* 1995; 41:333–345.

7. BARKAN SE, PRESTON-MARTIN S, KALISH L, et al. The WIHS—characteristics and comparisons with AIDS cases in United States women. Paper presented at: XI International Conference on AIDS; July 7–12, 1996; Vancouver, British Columbia.

8. ZIERLER S, KRIEGER N. Reframing women's risk: social inequalities and HIV infection. *Annu Rev Public Health.* 1997; 18:401–436.

9. FRIEDMAN SR, DES JARLAIS DC, STERK CE, et al. AIDS and the social relations of intravenous drug users. *Milbank Q.* 1990; 68(suppl 1):85–110.

10. FARMER P, CONNORS M, SIMMONS J. eds. *Women, Poverty; and AIDS: Sex, Drugs, and Structural Violence.* Monroe, Me: Common Courage Press; 1996.

11. FIFE D, MODE C. AIDS incidence and income. *J Acquir Immun Defic Syndr.* 1992; 5:1105–1110.

12. HU DJ, FREY R, COSTA SJ, et al. Geographical AIDS rates and sociodemographic variables in Newark, New Jersey, metropolitan area. *AIDS Public Policy J.* 1994; 9:20–25.

13. SIMON PA, HU DJ, DIAZ T, KERNDT PR. Income and AIDS rates in Los Angeles County. *AIDS.* 1995; 9:281–284.

14. MORSE DL, LESSNER L, MEDVESKY MG, GLEBATIS DM, NOVICK LF. Geographic distribution of newborn HIV seroprevalence in relation to four sociodemographic variables. *Am J Public Health.* 1991; 81(suppl):25–29.

15. KRIEGER N, WILLIAMS D, MOSS N. Measuring social class in US public health research: concept, methodologies and guidelines. *Annu Rev Public Health.* 1997; 18:341–378.

16. KRIEGER N. Overcoming the absence of socioeconomic data in medical records: validation and application of a census-based methodology. *Am J Public Health.* 1992; 82:703–710.

17. CENTERS FOR DISEASE CONTROL. Revision of the CDC surveillance case definition of acquired immunodeficiency syndrome. *MMWR Morb Mortal Wkly Rep.* 1987; 36(suppl 1):1S–15S.

18. U.S. *Census of Population and Housing, 1990. Summary Tape File 3 Technical Documentation, Prepared by the Bureau of the Census.* Washington, DC: US Bureau of the Census; 1991.

19. US BUREAU OF THE CENSUS. Poverty areas in large cities: 1980 Census of population, Vol 2, Subject Report. Washington, DC: US Bureau of the Census; 1985. Publication PC 208D.

20. BRESLOW NE, DAY NE. *The Analysis of Case-Control Studies.* Lyons, France: International Agency for Research on Cancer; 1980. *Statistical Methods in Cancer Research;* vol 1. IARC Scientific Publication 32.

21. ROTHMAN KJ, GREENLAND S. *Modern Epidemiology.* 2nd ed. Philadelphia, Pa: Lippincott-Raven; 1998.

22. MURRAIN M, BARKER T. Investigating the relationship between economic status and HIV risk. *J Health Care Poor Underserved.* 1997; 8:416–423.

23. VLAHOV D, TF BREWER, KG CASTRO, et al. Prevalence of antibody to HIV-1 among entrants to US correctional facilities. *JAMA.* 1991; 265:1129–1132.

24. GREENWALD JP, POLISSAR NL, BORGATTA EF, MCCORKLE R. Detecting survival effects of socioeconomic status: problems in the use of aggregate data. *J Clin Epidemiol.* 1994; 47:903–909.

25. GERONIMUS AT, BOUND J, NEIDERT LJ. On the validity of using census geocode data to proxy individual socioeconomic characteristics. *J Am Stat Assoc.* 1996; 91:529–537.

26. DIEZ-ROUX AV. Bringing context back into epidemiology: variables and fallacies in multilevel analysis. *Am J Public Health.* 1998; 88:216–222.

27. LINDAN C, HEARST N, SINGLETON J, et al. Underreporting of minority AIDS deaths in the San Francisco Bay Area. 1985–86. *Public Health Rep.* 1990; 105:400–404.

28. KELLY J, CHU S, DIAZ T, et al. Race/ethnicity misclassification of persons reported with AIDS. *Ethn Health.* 1996; 1:87–94.

29. GALLAGHER K. *The Reliability of AIDS Surveillance Data* [dissertation]. Boston, Mass: Boston University School of Public Health; May 1998.

30. WILLIAMS DR, COLLINS C. US socioeconomic and racial differences in health: patterns and explanations. *Annu Rev Sociol.* 1995; 21:349–386.

31. DIAZ T, KLEVENS M. Differences by ancestry in sociodemographics and risk behaviors among Latinos with AIDS. The Supplement to HIV and AIDS Surveillance Project Group. *Ethn Dis.* 1997; 7:200–206.

32. Census undercount and the quality of health data for racial and ethnic populations. *Ethn Dis.* 1994; 4:98–100.

33. ROBINSON JG, BASHIR A, PRITHWIS DG, WOODROW KA. Estimation of population coverage in the 1990 United States Census based on demographic coverage. *J Am Stat Assoc.* 1993; 88:1061–1071.

34. HOGAN H. The 1990 Post-enumeration Survey: operations and results. *J Am Stat Assoc.* 1993; 8:1047–1057.

35. KAUFMAN JS, COOPER RS, MCGEE DL. Socioeconomic status and health in Blacks and Whites: the problem of residual confounding and the resiliency of race. *Epidemiology.* 1997; 8:621–628.

36. HOLMAN CDJ, CAMERON PV, BUCENS MR, et al. Population-based epidemiology of human immunodeficiency virus infection in Western Australia. *Med J Aust.* 1989; 150:362–370.

37. BORRELL C, PLASCENCIA A, PASARIN I, ORTUN V. Widening social inequalities in mortality: the case of Barcelona, a southern European city. *J Epidemiol Community Health.* 1997; 51:659–667.

38. HANKINS C, TRAN T, HUM L, et al. Socioeconomic geographical links to human immunodeficiency virus seroprevalence among childbearing women in Montreal, 1989–1993. *Int J Epidemiol.* 1998; 27:691–697.

39. MASSEY DS. The age of extremes: concentrations of affluence and poverty in the twenty-first century. *Demography.* 1996; 33:395–412.

COMMENTARY ON THE READINGS

It is also important to note that the data in this study were obtained from the U.S. Census Bureau. The data were collected to provide information to the government and other organizations responsible for providing programs and developing policies that will adequately meet the needs of the American people. Even more basic, the data were collected for the purpose of reapportioning congressional House of Representative districts. As indicated previously, secondary data analysis often requires combing sources and reorganizing the data to fit the research agenda of the current researchers. Zierler and colleagues used this data to construct "numerous measures of neighborhood socioeconomic conditions." This statement, coupled with the description that follows in the text of the article, indicates that the authors had to reorganize the census data they selected to form variables that were appropriate measures of the social phenomena the researchers were seeking to analyze.

The study was also limited not so much by the data provided to the Massachusetts Department of Health by the HIV/AIDS Reporting System as by the definition incident case of AIDS provided by the Centers for Disease Control and Prevention. This organization changed its definition in 1987, making cases before this time and after noncomparable. In scientific studies, it is important in making comparisons of some occurrence over time to be sure that the two items being compared are exactly the same. The authors were able to include subsequent years (after 1987) when data were available, so data entry on the desired variables was complete. In addition to the desired variable—date of diagnosis—the data set obtained also provided age at diagnosis, sex, race/ethnicity, mode of transmission, and residential address at time of diagnosis. In this case several of these variables were utilized by the researchers, but if these variables had not been useful to the researchers, they would have had to filter them out and once again reorganize the data before beginning their analysis.

From this example of secondary data analysis it is apparent that researchers who choose to utilize this method of research are not taking the easy route, but rather have got their work cut out for them. Before they can begin their study, they must search for appropriate measures, which may not be found in one but many different sources. They must also be willing to reorganize the data obtained, which requires that the researchers know what variables could be combined or manipulated to create measures that could be utilized in their analysis. Secondary data analysis is thus convenient if the variables and measures being sought are commonly used within the field of research. Starting from the ground up to create such measures compiled from a variety of sources, however, may be quite challenging.

CONCLUSION

Secondary data analysis is widespread in the social sciences for a very basic reason: It makes research more efficient. Recycling data sets again and again allows researchers to generate research without the additional investment of time and money that other research methods often require.

CHAPTER 7

CONTENT ANALYSIS

As humans pass through time, they leave a plethora of data to mark their presence. Written records, poetry, art, even garbage all carry with them the meanings and values of the people who created them. It thus makes sense that social researchers can learn so much from the study of these artifacts. Content analysis is the analysis of data recorded by a target population on cultural artifacts.

UNOBTRUSIVE MEASURES

Content analysis relies upon *unobtrusive measures*—data gathered through mechanisms that do not interfere in the ordinary patterns of the life of the subjects (see also the discussion of historical comparative methods in Chapter 8).

The researcher is able to do this by analyzing the data found on *artifacts*, or physical remnants of a social group. Artifacts include anything physical produced by a social group and are measures of the culture and technology of the group. A book, for example, carries meaning besides what is written in its pages: The presence of a book denotes that a group had access to such technology, for most societies have not produced books. Some have produced scrolls, but most did not even do this! The mere presence of a book suggests other clues about a society as well: that there is some symbolic form of communication that can be presented in a book (e.g., words or drawings), that at least some members of the group wish to preserve information, and that some member of the group has enough free time to produce the book. Of course, the true meaning of a book is found in its content.

The major source of information in an artifact is contained in its *text*, the conceptual information conveyed by the artifact. The first image that comes to mind by text is probably words on a page, but text can take other forms as well. The audiovisual information presented in a movie or the hieroglyphics in an Egyptian tomb are also examples of text. The text may contain a statement, or a narrative (story), or a pronouncement by its producer. A Shakespeare play, for instance, contains a narrative. The text was written hundreds of years ago, and its meaning reflects the norms and values of the author's time. Reading the text thus allows the researcher several layers for analysis: There is the narrative itself, the story that Shakespeare wished to present. There is also a glimpse of life in his time. From many of his plays, the image of strong monarchies, wealthy families, and political maneuvering reflect conditions in his time. Shakespeare did not write about nomadic tribesmen or about Wall Street stockbrokers because he knew nothing of them. He wrote about feudalistic societies because he was a member of one.

In most cases researchers use content analysis to examine the text of an artifact. Given the multiple levels of meaning often found in a text, it is not surprising that content analysis can be very challenging. However, since the information has already been recorded, the researcher cannot influence its content. Yet previously existing data still present challenges of their own.

ORGANIZING THE DATA

Collecting data in a content analysis requires that the researcher has a clear notion of what to look for. *Content analysis* is understood as a quantitative technique because of its attempt to quantify what seems to be unquantifiable—that is, meanings. Like other research methods, this technique requires a very precise definition of what is to be measured. For instance, if one wishes to measure the level of racist thought found in a text, one needs a clear definition of what is meant by racism.

Based on a definition of the concept, the researcher doing content analysis can then choose indicators for the concept. For instance, a researcher studying racism on television may examine the roles assigned to different individuals on particular shows. The researcher can code each character on the show by race and role (doctor, bar owner, criminal, etc.) and then search for a statistical relationship between the two variables.

One concern with this method is determining the unit of analysis. The unit of analysis consists of the particular items we seek to explain. To make a statement about racism on television, the researcher needs to choose the unit of analysis and comment only on that unit of analysis. For instance, do we want to study commercial ads, individual shows, or the news? Network programming or local programming? To comment about television as a totality, the researcher needs to study all of these elements. To comment on only shows, the researcher needs to study only shows.

When the units of analysis and the indicators have been chosen, the actual methods of collecting the data need to be developed. This process starts with a coding sheet. The coding sheet contains the indicators and variables one is studying in a format that allows for the data to be easily collected. Coding sheets can be as simple or as complicated as the study requires. One study might require a simple counting mechanism whereas another may call for an elaborate sheet that resembles in some ways a survey, such as that in Figure 7.1. In a study of racism on network television shows, each show, all of its characters, and their respective roles need to be coded. In this case, there will likely be one coding sheet per episode. The data from the coding sheets will be entered into a computer and analyzed when data collection is completed.

FIGURE 7.1   **Coding Sheet** A coding sheet for a study examining the portrayal of race on television might look something like this.

Name of Show: The College Years

Episode ID: 42189
Date: May 8
Network: CBS

CHARACTER	ROLE	RACE	VIOLENT*	COMICAL*	INTELLECT*	CENTRALITY*
Jan	Teacher	2	1	3	5	4
John	Teacher's friend	3	2	3	5	3
Steve	Boss	1	4	2	1	1

*Rate on scale from 1 to 5, 1 lowest to 5 highest.

Like other research methods, content analysis often relies on sampling for collecting data. In sampling, the individual units of analysis are chosen for the study. The ideal way to conduct a study of racism on network television shows would be to collect data on all the shows during a particular time period, such as fall 2002 between the hours of 8:00 p.m. and 11:00 p.m. There may be constraints on such a design, however. There are six commercial public broadcast networks (NBC, ABC, CBS, Fox, WB, and UPN), public broadcasting (PBS), and a seemingly endless array of cable-only channels. Even if the scope of the study is narrowed to the six commercial broadcast networks, the cost of videotapes and the staff needed to watch and analyze the shows might be prohibitive for the average researcher. A sample would allow the researcher to analyze a more manageable number of shows and still have generalizable results. One might randomly sample for the shows to be analyzed, with a second random sample to select certain episodes of each show.

CODING

Coding refers to the collection of data and its classification as belonging to one or another variable attribute. As stated earlier, precise definitions are very important in content analysis. Consider the variable *race*. How do we code race? Social scientists have struggled with this same question for decades, and the result has been an expanding array of differing racial categories. In addition, how do we code for someone whose parents are of different races? Even with precise definitions, coding can be difficult. With poor definitions, coding is impossible.

There are two types of coding: manifest and semantic coding. Manifest coding is best understood as simple counts of an item, such as the number of instances of the word *cool* in a magazine. By counting the number of times the term *cool* appears in magazines, one can study the apparent visible content of a unit of analysis. By adding the term *cool* to a list of other terms, the researcher may study the overall age orientation of various magazines or study the use of such terms over a long period of time. One limitation to this approach is that the meaning of the term *cool* may change depending on the context of the article; a surfing article may comment that some surfers do not like to surf when it is cool outside. Or, in other cases, the definition of the term itself may change over time. Semantic coding is useful in picking up on such subtle variations.

Semantic coding concentrates on the latent content of a text. The researcher may read an entire magazine or article, for instance, and then code the article based on the overall impression on the reader. Semantic coding analyzes the meaning of a word or symbol within the differing contexts in which words or symbols are found. A study of the age orientation of various magazines would thus look not only at individual words (e.g., *cool*), but at the overall context in which the articles takes place. This allows for an article about the financial prospects of a company called Cool Dude Industries to be placed in proper perspective.

Manifest and semantic coding can be used together. For instance, a study of the use of the term *gay* in major newspapers from 1950 to 2000 would greatly benefit from such an approach. The definition of the term *gay* has changed during the past fifty years. After World War II, *gay* implied "happy-go-lucky" or simply fun. My grandmother would remark that she had gone dancing and had "a gay old time," for instance. By the 1970s, *gay* was used to refer to homosexual men and women by both gay and straight people. A content analysis utilizing both manifest and semantic coding can be useful in understanding this change over time.

Manifest coding can be useful by measuring the number of times the term was used in a sample of articles. Because the coding is manifest, a very large number of articles can be analyzed. If the data are electronic, a computer can search for the word throughout thousands of individual articles and report the result. The result will be highly reliable: either the word *gay* is there, or it is not. The data can then be presented as a line chart in order to show the years in which the term was used the most and the years when it was not used.

A subsample of the thousands utilized in the manifest coding can be subjected to semantic coding. For each year, the overall context of the use of the term can be coded by article. The usage of the term over time could thus be analyzed. Although the more subjective nature of semantic coding makes it less reliable than manifest coding, it is a more valid measure because it can discern the nuances that manifest coding cannot.

One crucial aspect of coding is intercoder reliability. Coding by one person is normally reasonably reliable, but coding by more than one person can become a serious issue. Because each person perceives the data differently, different coders could potentially code the same data differently. Researchers can improve intercoder reliability by insuring the definitions are very precise. Even with the most precise definitions, however, it is wise to ask coders to code the same data together and separately in order to identify potential problems and correct them.

THE READINGS

In our first example of content analysis, "Images of Rosie: A Content Analysis of Women Workers in American Magazine Advertising 1940–1946," by Charles Lewis and John Neville (1995), the authors analyze World War II advertising in order to understand representation of gender during a time of record female participation in the workplace. In the second example, "The Color of Crime and the Court: A Content Analysis of Minority Representation on Television," by Ron Tamborini and colleagues (2000), the authors seek to determine the depiction of whites, African Americans, and Latinos in the criminal justice system—both as representatives of the court and as criminals.

■ ■ ■ ■ ■

IMAGES OF ROSIE: A CONTENT ANALYSIS OF WOMEN WORKERS IN AMERICAN MAGAZINE ADVERTISING, 1940–1946

Charles Lewis
Mankato State University
John Neville

This study, based on a content analysis of magazine advertising images of women during the World War II era, has two purposes. One is to help determine whether advertisers made a concerted change in their shaping of women's images during and after World War II. The other purpose is to indicate further research on the topic of women and advertising during the war years. This examination is an initial attempt to better explain the relationship between the advertising industry, the actual "reality" of working women, and sociocultural constructions of female gender identity immediately before, during, and immediately following World War II.

INTRODUCTION

Women's images in American advertising have undergone rich but sporadic changes since the late nineteenth century, when pictures of women began to appear on biscuit packages and flour sacks. While scholars have produced varied historical works about women in relation to American advertising in the nineteenth and twentieth centuries, one historical era of the past two centuries has been relatively overlooked. For decades, historians of advertising neglected the World War II period. This state of affairs began to change in the early 1970s when interest in the advertising industry's often uncertain relationship with the federal government during World War II triggered a modest stream of scholarship. More recently, there has been a surge of interest in mass media portrayals of women during the period of American involvement in the war, as the following literature review indicates.

Still, the topic of women in advertising during World War II bears further scrutiny. No analysis has focused on the war period and changes in how women were depicted in advertising. Because the war era bridged two very different historical experiences—the 1930s Depression and the post-war era of prosperity—this oversight seems particularly acute. For instance, as Friedan noted, the 1930s witnessed a noticeable emphasis on career-women characters in magazine fiction, a phenomenon that changed drastically in the late 1940s when suburban America's sociocultural boundaries

From *Journalism & Mass Communication Quarterly*, 72, 1 (Spring 1995): 216–27. Copyright © AEJMC.

swelled to accommodate the burgeoning postwar middle classes.[1] But what of the war period? How did advertisers adjust to what was then nothing less than an unprecedented, unplanned, and badly needed influx of women into the nation's coal mines, warehouses, automobile plants, railroads, aircraft assembly plants, and other business operations? Also, how did advertisers react after the final victory of September 1945?

This study has two purposes. One is to help determine whether advertisers made a concerted change in their shaping of women's images during and after World War II. The other purpose is to indicate further research on the topic of women and advertising during the war years. This examination is an initial attempt to better explain the relationship between the advertising industry, the actual "reality" of working women, and sociocultural constructions of female gender identity immediately before, during, and immediately following World War II.

BACKGROUND

Between 1940 and 1943, more than fifteen million men and women had either joined the American armed forces or entered the domestic labor force. The unemployment rate in the United States plummeted from 13% in 1937 to 1.3% in 1943.[2] Because so many men had volunteered or been drafted into the military, the country faced a serious "manpower" shortage by late 1942. After Pearl Harbor, the nation's unemployed breached the employment gap for a time, but with the almost immediate need for new factories, retooled auto plants, and enlarged aircraft production factories and shipyards, it rapidly became apparent that women would have to be used as a means of filling the wartime labor shortage. President Roosevelt declared in an October 1942 speech that societal prejudices about women performing industrial work would have to be forgotten.[3]

In 1940, about 25% of white adult American women and about 38% of black women worked in manufacturing, clerical, or domestic service jobs. To put this in historical perspective, just five million women worked in the American labor force in 1920. By 1940 the number was at eleven million, and by 1944 more

than nineteen million women worked in the United States. By this time fully 37% of adult American women were in the civilian work force. Most of this crushing influx came in manufacturing and heavy industry, which were then almost exclusively retooled and reconfigured for the defense effort. According to the U.S. Department of Labor, this explosion of female workers increased the number of women working in durable goods production from 8% before the war to 25% in 1944.[4] Moreover, the flood of female workers into the aircraft, ammunition, and shipping industries helped to account for this surge in numbers. At the beginning of 1944, women constituted 34.2% of all ammunition workers, 10% of ship production workers, 10.6% of steel workers, 8% of railroad employees, and fully 40% of aircraft industry workers.[5]

However, if the entrance of women into the workplace was rushed, their exit in 1945 and 1946 was just as hasty. With millions of demobilized men discharged from the armed services into the workplace in 1946, most of the major defense industries "permanently" reassigned women back to the home. Women, many claimed, would be only too happy to escape their unpleasant interlude of grime, noise, and long hours of riveting, soldering, and welding.[6]

But it is also interesting to note that government surveys taken in 1944 revealed that up to 80% of women workers in war production plants expressed a desire to work after the war in "comparable" positions at similar wage scales.[7] Still, not all of the "laid off" women marched off into suburban domestic bliss. Many single or divorced women had to relocate into positions as domestic or clerical workers or waitresses—occupations that paid far less in wages and provided few benefits.

LITERATURE REVIEW

A growing body of literature exists that explores women's images in advertising, but the topic of women's images during the historical context of World War II remains quite unexplored.[8] Most histories of American advertising either fail to address or barely note the World War II period, much less the topic of women and advertising during the war. Many of the histories of advertising in the twentieth century end before World War II, skip the war, or begin after the war.[9] Fox provides the only lengthy treatment of advertising during World War II.[10] In an insightful monograph, Fox concludes that the war likely saved the advertising industry from repressive consumer-protection legislation because the prewar consumer movement was especially strong and quite critical of advertising. Fox determines that the War Advertising Council was formed with the cooperation of an initially unsympathetic Roosevelt Administration as a way to help advertisers survive during the dislocations of wartime. According to Fox, many traditional advertising messages were thus replaced, with the government's blessing, by institutional advertising—in other words, patriotic propaganda and public service messages. Thus, government agencies were better able to publicize certain messages, and, by sponsoring these patriotic appeals, big business was able to not only keep its name in the public's eye during the war period when fewer consumer goods were sold, but reinforce ideas of postwar prosperity as well.

While most histories of advertising skirt World War II, histories of the war period that focus in some way on women in American society have led to provocative conclusions about women's contributions to the war effort as well as gender relationships in political and economic spheres during the war. Chafe documents how during World War II for the first time in American history married women came to outnumber single women in the workforce. He also disparages the myth that most working women during this period were barely out of their teens. He shows that by 1945 half of all women employees in the United States had reached age thirty-five.[11] In contrast, Hartmann and Anderson each present the argument that instead of establishing a pattern of work-oriented independence for women, World War II reinforced more traditional gender identities.[12]

Blum provides one of the most detailed cultural and political histories of the war years. He establishes President Roosevelt's initial reluctance to trust any propaganda effort, given his fear of unleashing domestic political forces he could not directly control. Blum explains that Roosevelt's Office of War Information, which lacked the personnel or organization for propaganda dissemination, settled on the recently dispossessed advertising industry to handle the chore of constructing images calculated to arouse patriotism but not Republicans.[13] Rupp compares German and American propaganda in women's magazines of both countries during the war for thematic contrasts and similarities. She asserts that both propaganda machines tactically compared wartime defense work, no matter how difficult or dangerous, to household chores.[14]

Honey deflates the enduring myth that women defense workers were overwhelmingly white, young, and middle-class, and wanted nothing more than to become full-time housewives after the war. She describes the "Womanpower Campaign," launched by the Magazine Bureau and the War Manpower Commission in September 1943 to encourage women to disregard cultural prejudices about working outside the home. To this end the "Magazine War Guide" was developed so that thousands of magazine editors nationwide could be put in touch with writers experienced in producing "acceptable" wartime fiction—fiction loaded with heroines with great aplomb for work and capturing spies. Honey notes that the Bureau regularly flooded publishers with photographs and background information on women workers who excelled at making the transition from home to defense work.[15] Gluck provides an oral history of ten women defense workers who worked in a variety of defense jobs in southern California during the war. Lastly, Campbell contends that the tendency of scholars to focus on "Rosie the Riveter" obscures the fact that most wartime housewives did remain in the home and did not receive credit for their role in keeping families intact.[16]

Another important body of writings concerning women and advertising during the war era is the advertising trade journals from 1940 to 1946. Discourse during the war years within the two most popular advertising trade journals, *Printer's Ink* and *Advertising & Selling*, indicates how the advertising community reacted to women in the workplace. The number and focus of articles dealing with women and advertising before, during, and after the war indicate how those in advertising were certainly aware of the new social reality of women as wage-earners. Immediately before and after the war, women were rarely discussed at length in the two trade journals. But during the war, women—primarily working women—were an important journal topic. However, the advertising-trade people usually focused on certain market-oriented aspects of working women, asking such questions as: "How can we target this new group of consumers?"

In the prewar period of 1940 and 1941, the few journal articles about women and advertising focused on the mechanics of understanding and reaching female consumers. For example, in one May 1940 issue of *Printer's Ink*, the average female consumer is described as a "wholesome-looking woman with clear, blue eyes . . . to be seen at the market any day picking over fresh fruits or snaring bargains in a department store." An August 1940 *Printer's Ink* article detailed a readership study indicating how women would pay closer attention to food ads if recipes and products were displayed together.[17]

During the war, however, the number of articles devoted to women and advertising increased substantially. Most of the articles focused on two topics: (1) how to reach the new group of working women; (2) the postwar future of women in the workplace and how that would affect advertising strategies. Articles devoted to the problem of reaching the new social group of working women were published mostly in the first two years of the war. But even before the war started, *Printer's Ink* had begun to take steps to address the potential social situation of women in the workforce during a "military" economy. For example, an August 1941 article reported that working women would have a "profound effect on merchandising." The general message was that "women at work have more money to spend, and, being out in the world every day, more incentive to improve their dress. They wear out clothes faster, particularly shoes and hosiery."[18]

In 1942, several articles in both journals dealt with reaching blue-collar women workers. For example, a March 1942 *Advertising & Selling*

article called for more images of women factory workers because they were becoming a group of consumers with greatly increased purchasing power: "Miss Factory never sees her counterparts in advertising illustrations . . . she feels rudely neglected." An August 1942 *Advertising & Selling* article detailed how women controlled most consumer purchasing and also called for more ads directed toward women workers: "So far, little has been done to make a heroine of the lady on the assembly line." Another article in the August 1942 issue described how to get good action photographs in industrial plants for wartime ads. The key was not to photograph in the plant but to create a plant setting in the studio. In the photographs depicting women factory workers, "office girls" were used "instead of professional models because models do not look like factory girls."[19]

After 1942, few articles in the two journals dealt with the topic of reaching women workers. However, articles continued to be published throughout the war about whether women would work after the war. Views on each postwar scenario were published. For example, Jean Austin, editor of *The American Home* magazine, wrote in an October 1942 isssue of *Printer's Ink* that "a woman doing war work in slacks is a woman right now dreaming of going back to her life as a woman at home." Carmel Snow, editor of *Harper's Bazaar* magazine, wrote in an April 1943 issue of *Printer's Ink* how "many women will refuse to go back to the kitchen when the war is over but will continue to maintain their places in a man-sized world to do a man-sized job."[20] In any case, a common discussion was how to reach women in the postwar years, no matter what their work status at the time. The underlying assumption of this discussion was that the war was changing the perceptions of the consuming public, men and women. Concerning women, the question for advertisers was always similar to the following: "Will the girl who has learned how to be . . . a welder or a worker in an airplane plant be quite so responsive to the good old "you-won't-get-your-man-if-you-don't-watch-out" technique?"[21]

But the answer to this question was not presented in the journals during the first year after the war. In 1946, no articles in the two journals dealt at length with the topic of women and advertising. Apparently, the new social reality of working women was no longer considered a pressing issue.

THEORETICAL FRAMEWORK

Central to this study are two theoretical concepts. The first springs largely from feminist social theory and postulates that certain traditional notions of gender such as "females are more nurturant than males" are not based on intrinsic or essential elements like biological structure. Rather, such notions of gender are considered to be social and cultural *constructions* of meaning.[22] The second central concept of this article, developed largely by critical scholars of mass media, concerns how advertising images feed into the constructive process of gender meanings. Jhally claims the debate on whether gender images are true or false is a misleading argument. Following Goffman, Jhally stresses advertising gender displays are "hyper-ritualizations" that emphasize some aspects of real-life gender displays while de-emphasizing others.[23] Thus, in American capitalist culture, advertising-oriented gender displays in various conventionalized forms have become a pervasive and powerful part of the process of how notions of gender are constructed and maintained. These potent gender displays of capitalist image makers influence notions of gender among the populace—perhaps even as much or more than the day-to-day gender displays of interpersonal relations.

Jhally's thinking about gender displays helps place in perspective the rather unusual World War II experience of women's images in advertising. Although women had been portrayed as independent and career-minded in the magazine literature of the 1930s, seldom before World War II had advertisers presented women as anything other than traditional sexual ornamentation, homemakers, or mothers.[24] However, the aftermath of Pearl Harbor presented a barrage of new political, economic, and social issues for the American woman, and the advertising community was forced to reconfigure its imagery much as factories had to retool assembly lines for the war.

Indeed, patriotism was used as a major recruiting device to lure women into the industrial workforce. The "Women's Bureau" of the "War Manpower Commission" had to work hard to combat initial reluctance among employers to hire women.[25] These initial objections were, in part, overcome by advertising gender constructions that presented images of women at work while respecting the traditional separation of sex roles. Honey claims this was accomplished by presenting women in magazine advertisements as self-sacrificing soldiers and martyrs—not feminist pioneers.[26] Lears' discussion of "therapeutic ethos," the desire to reach psychic fulfillment through consumption, also applies here, for advertisers had to appeal to women not only as consumers, but also as patriots and working-class pioneers.[27] Thus, the war prompted an odd, prolonged, topsy-turvy state of advertising siege—one which has no historical precedent.

But how did women's images of advertising change from 1940 to the height of the war, and then after the war? How closely did advertising images correspond to the rapid-fire social, economic, and political developments taking place in women's lives and the larger culture? Did, in advertising magnate's Raymond Rubicam's words, women have to be convinced through propaganda to take less than "socially desirable" jobs?[28] Or is that interpretation a myth the advertising community has advanced since Norman Rockwell's image of Rosie first graced the cover of the *Saturday Evening Post*?[29]

METHOD

The research design of this study is a content analysis of women's images in advertisements from three magazines—two general-circulation lifestyle magazines and one general-circulation women's magazine. The magazines are the *Saturday Evening Post*, *Life*, and *Ladies Home Journal*. These popular-press magazines were chosen because of their strong, sweeping middle-class readerships. The years selected for this study are 1940, 1943, and 1946. These years were selected because they represent the years immediately before, during, and immediately after World War II. The months selected for this study are January and October. January was selected because it is traditionally a slow advertising month; October was selected because it is traditionally a heavy advertising month. Because of the extremely large number of ads in the magazine issues of the sample group, only full-page ads were analyzed for content.

Despite the focus on only full-page ads, the number of ads in the sample remains quite large. The sample contains a total of 1,957 full-page advertisements from 54 magazine issues: 519 from 1940; 576 from 1943; and 864 from 1946. The subsample of full-page advertisements portraying women contains a total of 1,071: 332 from 1940; 256 from 1943; and 483 from 1946.

A "focus group" approach was used in the coding process. Instead of separate coders coding all or parts of the content and later checking the reliability of the separate coding, the authors chose to consult with one another in the coding of all content. An intra-coder retest of 200 randomly chosen advertisements—10% of the sample—was conducted by the authors six months after the initial coding. The agreement coefficients of the four coding categories averaged .945 in this retest.[30]

The content of each full-page advertisement in the sample group was examined according to the following coding categories: (1) general depictions of men and women as well as gender relations; (2) rhetorical form; (3) depictions of settings; and (4) depictions of occupational (work-related) roles. Each of these categories included numerous subcategories, many of which were collapsed for purposes of analysis.[31] The first category was used to examine the presence or absence of men and women in ads. Ads depicting children or just products were coded as having no adults portrayed. The second category was used to discern the rhetorical form of an ad—whether it appealed to women in general, homemakers or mothers, had no specific appeal to women indicated, or was institutional- or duty-oriented. The third category indicated whether the setting women were depicted in was in a wage-earning work environment, a home-work environment, a leisure setting, or some "other" setting, which was usually no environment at all. The fourth category was used to determine whether women depicted in ads were homemakers and/or mothers,

wage-earning workers, members of volunteer organizations or the military, or had no discernible occupational role.[32]

RESULTS
To increase clarity, the major findings are here reduced to two areas—depictions of occupational roles and settings.[33] In 1940, women appeared as homemakers and/or mothers in 36% of all ads containing images of women. In 59% of these ads, women did not appear in occupational roles. No women appeared as members of the armed forces or volunteer organizations, and only 5% appeared as wage-earning workers.[34] In 1943, images of women as wage-earners increased substantially to 19%, while images of women in no discernible occupational role decreased substantially to 38%. While images of women as homemakers and/or mothers remained relatively stable at 30%, images of women as members of the armed forces or volunteer organizations increased to 13%. In 1946, images of women reverted to roughly the same level of prewar displays. Images of women as wage-earners decreased to 7%. Women appeared in no discernible occupational role in 60% of the ads. Images of women as homemakers and/or mothers remained relatively constant at 33%. No women appeared as members of the armed forces or volunteer organizations. The differences between these frequencies are significant.[35]

Concerning depictions of settings, images of women in a workplace setting other than the home went from 5% in 1940 to 24% in 1943, and then declined to 6% in 1946. Images of women in a setting other than a workplace, home, or leisure went from 43% in 1940 to 15% in 1943, and then increased to 39% in 1946. Images of women working in a home setting remained constant in 1940 and 1943 at 22%, but declined to 13% in 1946. Images of women in a leisure setting increased from 30% in 1940 to 39% in 1943 to 42% in 1946.

DISCUSSION
Advertisers in the magazines analyzed did adjust substantially to the tremendous social, political, and economic transformations of the war years. In particular, images of wage-earning, working

women increased significantly from 1940 to 1943, while images of women without an occupational role decreased substantially from 1940 to 1943. And images of women working in a setting other than the home increased dramatically from 1940 to 1943. Advertising imagery during the war years clearly reflected the altered social context created by worldwide struggle.

However, the statistical analysis can be misleading. While the changes in the depictions of women were considerable, they did not parallel the scope nor the reality of the rather radical changes that took place in society at large. It appears traditional female gender constructions in advertising based on a social and cultural system of male dominance persisted during the war. Apparently advertisers—at least those with ads in the magazines sampled—were restrained in their use of portrayals of women's new roles in the workplace. This caution existed despite two important factors: (1) government agencies clearly made repeated appeals to the advertising community to target women for job recruitment; (2) working women were a new group of consumers with considerable purchasing power—a seemingly important group for advertisers to target, as the trade journals *Printer's Ink* and *Advertising & Selling* often pointed out in the early years of the war.

This reaffirms Honey's point that gender construction in World War II advertising did not threaten traditional notions of sex role division. The images of women in the work place might have been new and surprising, but the social position of the woman worker was qualified by connotations of her new role being that of a patriotic martyr who will work only while the nation was at war.

For example, an advertising image typifying women's stereotypical images in the prewar period is a 1940 Campbell's Soup ad in which the mother serves a handsome executive-type father and a Jack-Armstrongish son. The woman depicted is the idealized homemaker and mother, whose hair is attractively coiffed even as she prepares lunch.[36] Such traditional, prewar female gender stereotyping was apparent even in many of the 1943 advertisements depicting wage-earning female workers. Whereas the 1940 ads rarely showed a woman at work outside the

home, the 1943 ads did depict women outside the home—but often in ways that seemingly patronized the women figures at work. For example, a Pond's Cold Creme ad from October 1943 tells the stories of five female war workers whose fiances were overseas in the armed forces. All of the women are young and pretty, the wartime version of beauty queens giving testimony for cosmetic products. The copy reads that "these girls have given up personal ambition" in order to work, but they are "none the less feminine for all their efficiency."[37]

Women's images quickly underwent a drastic retransformation after the war. In advertisers' schemes, women returned en masse to the kitchens of home nests with a song on their lips and uniformly cheerful smiles. The White Motor Company, for example, features an ad with an immaculately dressed mother and grandmother cooking and cleaning in a postwar house while grandchildren study. Juxtaposed with the image of the homemakers is an image of working men in a utility company truck ready to supply the power necessary for home appliances. It appears the message of the ad is indeed about power, not only electric power but power relations between men and women—the underlying meaning indicates that men should provide and women should nurture.[38]

CONCLUSION AND RESEARCH SUGGESTIONS

As Jhally notes, advertising is seldom an accurate reflection of reality, but it does contain elements of social reality and is itself part of social reality. This study establishes that changes in depictions of women in wartime advertising were significant. However, it appears that advertisers during the war never quite relinquished their version of the prewar social reality. Even during the turbulent years of the war, advertisers did not abandon to any great extent the traditional prewar images of women. And as soon as the war was over, prewar images of women once again filled the pages of the mass magazines. Except for images of homemakers and mothers, images of working women were largely abandoned by advertisers soon after the Allied victory. Women in a male-dominated society were abruptly thrust into new, traditionally male work roles during the war, and then cast out of these work roles after the war. Advertising helped to smooth over the uncertainty that accompanied these changes. The trade literature of the day indicates advertisers knew the war would not last forever. Thus, it appears the wartime advertising industry performed the slippery task of presenting women in new gender roles while figuring out a way not to depart too far from its prewar formulas. The result was a curious farrago of wartime social realism, patriotic imagery, and traditional gender stereotyping.

This content analysis indicates the general nature of certain mass magazine advertising images of women during the World War II era, but it could be built upon in several ways. For example, one could code for specific companies or types of products in conjunction with types of women's images. Questions concerning the nature of women's images in advertisements for automobile manufacturing companies or home-appliance companies could be answered through such coding. Coding for depictions of men's work roles could be quite useful—images of men's work roles could be compared to images of women's work roles.

One could explore the gender displays of children before, during and after the war. One could more closely examine images of nuclear families during the war years. Why did some advertisements of working women trivialize them while other advertisements showed respect for them? More elaborate coding categories that would differentiate among types of working-women images could help answer this question. In addition, the reader should bear in mind that the results of this study might not generalize to other mass media of the same period. Therefore, future research on this topic might focus on the differences of depictions of women among various mass media.

NOTES

1. BETTY FRIEDAN, *The Feminine Mystique* (NY, London: W.W. Norton and Co., 1983), 71–84.
2. ALAN WINKLER, *America During World War II* (Arlington Heights, Illinois: Harlan Davidson, 1986), 49–57.
3. SHERNA BERGER GLUCK, *Rosie the Riveter Revisited: The War and Social Change* (Boston: Wayne Publishers, 1987), 10.
4. U.S. DEPARTMENT OF LABOR, BUREAU OF LABOR STATISTICS, *Handbook of Labor Statistics*, bulletin 916 (Washington, DC: Govern-ment Printing Office, 1947).
5. CHESTER GREGORY, *Women in Defense Work During World War II* (NY: Exposition Press, 1974), 81, 95, 114, 130.
6. JEAN AUSTIN, "Women People?" *Printer's Ink* 201, 23 October 1942, 21.
7. U.S. DEPARTMENT OF LABOR, WOMEN'S BUREAU, *Women Workers in Ten Production Areas and Their Post-War Employment Plans*, bulletin 209 (Washington, DC: Government Printing Office, 1946).
8. Examples of the body of literature that explores women's images in advertising include seminal critical explorations such as JUDITH WILLIAMSON, *Decoding Advertisements* (London: Marion Boyars, 1978); and TREVOR MILLUM, *Images of Women: Advertising in Women's Magazines* (London: Chatto & Windus, 1975). Both use critical theory and semiological analysis to show how advertising imagery exploits women. During the last two decades numerous articles have provided detailed, critical explorations of women's advertising images. Examples include B. KAITE and S. THOMAS, "The Body and Femininity in Feminine Hygiene Advertising," *Studies in Communication* 10, no. 2 (1987); G. L. SULLIVAN and P. J. O'CONNOR, "Women's Role Portrayals in Magazine Advertising: 1958–1983," *Sex Roles* 11, no. 4 (1988); and L. KRUSE, E. WEIMER and F. WAGNER, "What Women and Men Are Said To Be: Social Representation and Language," *Journal of Language and Social Psychology* 12, no. 5 (1988).
9. See, for example, ROLAND MARCHAND, *Advertising and the American Dream: Making Way for Modernity, 1920–1940* (Berkeley, Los Angeles, London: University of California Press, 1986); STUART EWEN, *Captains of Consciousness: Advertising and the Special Roots of the Consumer Culture* (NY, Toronto: McGraw-Hill Book Co., 1976); WILLIAM LEISS, STEPHEN KLINE, and SUT JHALLY, *Social Communication in Advertising: Persons, Products and Images of Well Being* (Toronto,

NY, and London: Methune, 1986); Michael Schudson, *Advertising, the Uneasy Persuasion* (NY: Basic Books, 1984); Stephen Fox, *The Mirror Makers: A History of American Advertising and Its Creators* (NY: Vintage Books, 1985); and Vance Packard, *The Hidden Persuaders* (NY: D. McKay, 1957).

10. Frank W. Fox, *Madison Avenue Goes to War: The Strange Military Career of American Advertising, 1941–45*, Charles E. Merrill Monograph Series in the Humanities and Social Sciences, vol. 4, no. 1 (Salt Lake City, UT: Brigham Young University, June 1975).

11. William Chafe, *The American Woman: Her Changing Social, Economic and Political Roles, 1920–1970* (NY: Oxford University Press, 1972). For a similar interpretation, see Margaret Mead, "The Women in the War," in *While You Were Gone: A Report on Wartime Life in the United States*, ed. Jack Goodman (NY: Simon and Schuster, 1946), 274–289. Mead argues that World War II merely accelerated a trend of women entering the workforce that had long been developing in the United States.

12. Susan M. Hartmann, *The Home Front and Beyond: American Women in the 1940s* (Boston: Twayne Publishers, 1982); Karen Anderson, *Wartime Women: Sex Roles, Family Relations and the Status of Women During World War II* (Westport, CT: Greenwood Press, 1981).

13. John Morton Blum, *V Was For Victory: Politics and Culture During World War II* (NY and London: Harcourt Brace Jovanovich, 1986). Another important cultural and social history of the war years is Richard Polenberg's *War and Society: The U. S., 1941–45* (NY: Lippincott, 1972). Also see Studs Terkel, *The Good War: An Oral History of World War II* (NY: Pantheon Books, 1984). See Cluck, *Rosie the Riveter Revisited*, 108–134.

14. Leila J. Rupp, *Mobilizing Women for War: German and American Propaganda 1939–1945* (Princeton, NJ: Princeton University Press, 1978).

15. Maureen Honey, *Creating Rosie the Riveter: Class, Gender and Propaganda During World War II* (Amherst: University of Massachusetts Press, 1984), pp. 47–53.

16. D'Ann Campbell, *Women at War with America: Private Lives in a Patriotic Era* (Cambridge: Harvard University Press, 1984).

17. Anna Richardson, "American Women Are Friends of Advertising," *Printer's Ink* 191, 31 May 1940, 14; and C. B. Larabee, "Women Read Service Copy more Eagerly than Hot War News," *Printer's Ink* 192, 2 August 1940, 13–15.

18. P. H. Erbes, "The Women Take Over," *Printer's Ink* 196, 15 August 1941, 9, 71.

19. Lawrence Karp, "Selling the Female Industrial Group," *Advertising & Selling* 35 (March 1942): 26; Sylvia Carewe, "Where's the Woman's Angle in This War?" *Advertising & Selling* 35 (August 1942): 23; John Murphy, "How to Get Action Photos in Wartime Advertising," *Advertising & Selling* 35 (August 1942): 30.

20. Austin, "Women People?"; Carmel Snow, "Woman War Worker Today—Executive Tomorrow!" *Printer's Ink* 203, 2 April 1943, 38.

21. William Day, "Copy Themes-194?" *Advertising & Selling* 35 (December 1942): 13.

22. There are numerous works detailing this theoretical position. For general discussions of gender construction in feminist theory, see Jane Flax, "Postmodernism and Gender Relations in Feminist Theory," *Signs* 12 (1987): 621–43; and Evelyn Fox Keller, "Feminist Perspectives on Science Studies," *Barnard Occasional Papers on Women's Issues* 3 (Spring 1988): 10–36.

23. Sut Jhally, *The Codes of Advertising: Fetishism and the Political Economy of Meaning in the Consumer Society* (NY: St. Martin's Press, 1987), 135. In addition, see Erving Goffman, *Gender Advertisements* (NY: Harper and Row, 1979).

24. This is not to suggest that significant numbers of women did not work outside the home before World War II. Louise Lamphere records in her history of New England working women how "participa-

tion of women in wage labor began in the early years of the industrial revolution." LAMPHERE, *From Working Daughters to Working Mothers: Immigrant Women in a New England Industrial Community* (Ithaca, NY: Cornell University Press, 1987), 43.

25. ANDERSON, *Wartime Women*, 27–28.

26. HONEY, *Creating Rosie*, 6.

27. T. JACKSON LEARS, "Salvation to Self-Realization: Advertising and the Therapeutic Roots of the Consumer Culture," in *The Culture of Consumption*, ed. Richard Fox and T. Jackson Lears (NY: Pantheon Books, 1983), 27.

28. See RAYMOND RUBICAM, "Advertising" in *While You Were Gone*, ed. Jack Goodman, 421–446.

29. "Rosie" first appeared on the cover of the 29 May 1943 issue of *Saturday Evening Post*.

30. In content analysis, an agreement coefficient above .8 is considered extremely reliable. An agreement coefficient of .945 indicates the intra-coder reliability is 94.5% above the level of chance agreement.

31. Because of the complexity of visual communication, the authors tried to be as comprehensive as possible in devising semiological-oriented coding categories. Thus, more information was coded for than was found to be needed in the analysis offered in this article. A complete explanation of the coding scheme may be obtained from the authors by mail.

32. The agreement coefficients of each category are as follows: Category one: .97; category two: .97; category three: .95; and category four: .89.

33. In order to increase clarity, all percentages are rounded to the nearest whole number.

34. "Wage-earners" include blue- and white-collar workers, although nearly all women models were depicted in blue-collar roles such as waitresses or industrial workers.

35. Because some cells in the category variable "Armed Forces/Volunteers" were empty, this category was excluded from the test of significance because its empty cells would skew results.

36. *Saturday Evening Post*, 13 January 1940, 29.

37. *Ladies Home Journal*, October 1943, 45.

38. *Saturday Evening Post*, 9 January 1946, 5.

■ ■ ■ ■ ■

THE COLOR OF CRIME AND THE COURT: A CONTENT ANALYSIS OF MINORITY REPRESENTATION ON TELEVISION

Ron Tamborini
Michigan State University

Dana E. Mastro
Boston College

Rebecca M. Chory-Assad
West Virginia University

Ren He Huang
Michigan State University

This content analysis examines portrayals of Whites, African Americans, and Latinos in the criminal justice system as representatives of the court and as criminals. Results indicate that African Americans and Latinos were similar to White characters in their roles, personalities, and aggressive behaviors. Most African Americans and Latinos were depicted as representatives of the court, and the attributes associated with these characterizations were positive. Mass media's depictions and viewers' perceptions of raical/ethnic issues concerning law enforcement and criminal tendencies also are discussed.

From *Journalism & Mass Communication Quarterly*, 77, 3 (Autumn 2000): 639–53. Copyright © 2000 AEJMC.

The cultivation hypothesis posited by Gerbner[1] remains one of the best documented and most investigated theories of media's effects on beliefs and attitudes.[2] The framework originated from national concern regarding the effects of televised violence in the 1960s and 1970s. Early cultivation research revealed that heavy viewers were more likely to give the "television answer" than were light viewers when asked their perceptions and opinions of social reality.[3] This mild but persistent cultivation effect becomes salient when TV's systematic, but very selective, portrait of the world leads its audience to develop stereotyped and distorted perceptions of reality.

Cultivation theorists hold that television, among modem mass media, has acquired a central place in our daily lives and has become the primary source of socialization and everyday information. Its (distorted) messages about reality may be substituted for personal experience and other means of knowing about the social world.[4] After continuous, heavy television exposure, audiences gradually adopt the "symbolic reality" created by television and incorporate its images into their living environment. This symbolic reality may potentially contain both stereotypical and imprecise images.

In order to identify the implications of such exposure, the present study focuses on representations of African Americans and Latinos in the criminal justice system, both as representatives of the court and as criminals. More specifically, this study assesses these groups' character roles and personalities, and the behavioral tendencies associated with them. Finally, mass media's depictions of racial/ethnic issues are discussed in order to form a basis for understanding the role of the media in shaping perceptions of law enforcement and criminal tendencies among African Americans and Latinos.

BACKGROUND
Distorted Images
Historically, television has been said to over-represent certain aspects of social life while under-representing others. For example, in their content analysis of network television drama from 1969 to 1984, Gerbner and colleagues found that television's presentation of societal demo-graphics was greatly skewed. Men outnumbered women three to one. People under 18 years old comprised only one-third of their true population proportion, while people over sixty-five years old constituted only one-fifth of their actual proportion of the population. Similarly, African Americans on television represented three-fourths and Hispanics only one-third of their true representation in the U.S. population. During that period of time, the television world was also much more crime-ridden than the real world. Crime was ten times as rampant on prime-time television as in the real world. The typical viewer of an average week's programming would encounter the portrayal of thirty police officers, seven lawyers, and three judges, but only one engineer or scientist and very few blue-collar workers. Lifestyle and socioeconomic status portrayals showed that nearly 70 percent of television characters were middle class, while only 25 percent were employed as blue-collar or service workers. In reality, blue-collar and service jobs employed 67 percent of all Americans during that period.[5]

The rationalization for the depiction of these repetitive and stereotypical images is often defined in terms of the audience. Sprafkin and Liebert explain the reason for the media's promulgation of stereotypes as a narrative convention through which such images provide the lowest common denominator upon which to develop storylines. They suggest that general audience members will find it easier to accept such characterizations as credible because the portraits are consistent with their conventional expectations.[6]

Stereotypes
Stereotype formation is one of the major consequences of media cultivation. American journalist Walter Lippmann introduced the term in 1922 to refer to the "pictures in our heads" of various social groups. It has become one of the most frequently mentioned terms in the study of social issues related to ethnic attitudes, prejudice, and intergroup perception and conflict.[7]

Stereotypes originate from perceptions and designate a belief or opinion about the attributes associated with a target. Early researchers defined stereotypes as generalizations concerning an out-group member made from prior experience or learning. While these over-simplifications may be unjustified by the observer, they are not necessarily inaccurate.[8] Stereotypes have also been defined as beliefs about a cluster of traits attributed indiscriminately to all members of a group or to a given situation or event.[9] Such perceptions may be held for racial/ethnic out-group members as well as for individuals with varying social, organizational, and socioeconomic affiliations.

Although stereotypes have been conceptualized as resulting from personal interaction, this does not imply that they are necessarily based on people's first-hand experiences with members of the stereotyped group. Stereotypes may be learned indirectly from the descriptions of others or through images found in the mass media.[10] While the use and reliance on stereotypes is an unavoidable cognitive action taken to deal with the complexity of modern life, the process may become harmful when it is based on inaccurate information provided by institutional forces like the dominant mass media.

In order to provide a more comprehensive understanding of stereotype use, Berg, in his examination of stereotypes in the media, investigated the implications of media stereotypes of Latinos from contemporary sociological, psychological, psychoanalytical, and ideological perspectives.[11] In reviewing these frameworks, he presents the foundation both for analyzing such imagery in the media as well as for assessing the system that propagates them. From a sociological perspective, then, he suggests that media images may serve to reinforce and validate learned stereotypes, thereby indicating norms for the treatment of certain groups. When negative stereotypes are used as indicators of ways in which groups should interact, then media images that stratify groups create power relationships that lead to problematic social relationships. Conversely, a psychological approach to understanding media stereotypes would suggest that stereotypes allow individuals to reject negative characteristics of the self and project them onto others. The result is the repression of one's own disagreeable tendencies by way of disassociation with negative qualities and internalization of positive qualities. Accordingly, negative media images of racial/ethnic groups simultaneously provide individuals with a cultural other alongside a representation of his/her internal fears.

From a psychoanalytical perspective, media stereotypes supply a social "other" to both idealize and deny.[12] The other is inextricably bound to the individual, as it is the basis of oppositional definition as well as the idealized fulfillment of one's unattainable wholeness. Berg, therefore, suggests that media stereotypes (of Latinos in particular) have persevered in the media because they fulfill a need for wholeness among the dominant culture. Last, from an ideological framework, stereotypes are considered a negative counterpoint to the mainstream value system. In presenting other racial/ethnic groups as inferior, dishonest, corrupt, and/or immoral, in the media, the superiority, honesty, integrity, and morality of the mainstream is reinforced. Media stereotypes maintain the status quo and reinforce the existing hegemony.

Ethnicity in the Media

It has long been a concern that the mass media, especially television, have repeatedly portrayed certain social groups unfavorably, resulting in the acquisition of negative attitudes and the solidification of racial/ethnic stereotypes by members of the audience.[13] For some time, the media have been criticized for underrepresenting racial/ethnic minorities. Moreover, when these infrequent images have appeared, they have been largely disparaging in nature.

Images of African Americans in Entertainment Television. Many scholars have focused content analyses on the images of African Americans offered by the mass media. In their review of previous studies, Poindexter and Stroman indicate that although there has been a trend toward increased visibility, African Americans have been under-represented and stereotyped in their portrayals and have typically appeared in minor roles and in low-status occupations.[14] Additional research on the portrayal of African Americans in prime-time television from 1955 to 1986 found that only 6 percent of the characters were African American, while 89 percent of the TV population was White. Among these African-American characters, 49 percent lacked a high school diploma and 47 percent were low in economic status.[15]

Over the past few decades, a trend toward increased visibility of African Americans on television is apparent. Of characters in comedies and dramas, African-American males increased from 6 percent in 1971 to 9 percent in 1980, while African-American females fluctuated from 5 to 6 percent across the decade.[16] For the 1991–1992 season, African Americans constituted 11 percent of prime-time program characters,[17] which nearly matched their 1992 actual population proportion of 13 percent.[18] Current assessments of depictions of African Americans support the suggestion that this group has achieved equality in terms of frequency of portrayals compared to the real-world population, however, the types of images remain somewhat controversial.[19] Research suggests that this parity on a numerical basis is limited to roles in predominately African-American sitcoms.[20]

Portrayals of African Americans on television have gone through several periods of change. During the 1940s and 1950s, African Americans were rarely presented on television. When they were included, it was either in minor roles or in highly stereotypic characterizations.[21] Such representations were usually consistent with pre-Civil Rights Movement images including overweight domestic servants (e.g., *Beulah*) and lazy simpletons (e.g., *Amos 'n Andy*).[22]

Following the Civil Rights Movement, from the middle of the 1960s to the early 1970s, African Americans appeared in more professional and intellectual roles. These portrayals appeared in television programs such as *Star Trek*, *The Mod Squad*, *Peyton Place*, and the first all-Black drama, *Julia*. While the 1970s were the decade of the prime-time Black situation comedy, this era marked a shift in the portrayals of African Americans toward more realistic and personal stories of individual characters.[23] Nonetheless, the findings of content analyses suggested that distorted and stereotyped representations still remained. Several studies noted that television over-represented African Americans as overweight, and others found that African Americans were less likely to be portrayed in prestigious roles.[24] By the early 1980s, fictional entertainment television began featuring more successful African-American professionals and authority figures. Alongside this trend emerged an upscale version of Black situation comedies.[25]

Images of Latinos in Entertainment Television. Analyses of the portrayals of Latinos on television suggest that these images are infrequent and largely characterized by a narrow assortment of roles.[26] A few principal stereotypes of Latinos and Latinas, often adopted from the film industry, have served as the basic formula from which decades of images in television continue to be derived. A case in point is that of El Bandito (the Mexican Bandit). This image was established during the silent film era with representations of Latinos as violent and unintelligent scoundrels.[27] Such depictions were common throughout a variety of TV westerns and can be seen today in roles of Latino drug-dealers and gangsters in police crime dramas.[28] A second recurring image is that of the Buffoon. These characters are often the object of humor due to their lack of intelligence and inability to speak English. This type of personification can be seen in characterizations from Pancho on the *Cisco Kid* and Ricky Ricardo on *I Love Lucy* to more current portrayals on programs such as *a.k.a. Pablo*. What's more, when considering portrayals of women, even fewer roles exist.[29] The scarce number of Latinas that have been found predominately include secondary characters as mothers, girlfriends, and sassy spitfires.

Although early representations of Latinos were limited primarily to subordinate, objectified characters,[30] content analyses have revealed some exceptions to these negative stereotypes, principally with regard to images of Latino criminality.[31] In particular, Edward James Olmos' character in *Miami Vice* and Jimmy Smits' roles, in both *LA Law* and *NYPD Blue* presented Latinos as respected officers of the legal system. As such, by the 1980s, roles for Latinos in the legal system became much more common, both as criminals and as officers. Current portrayals have deviated little from this tendency. A content analysis of 1996 prime-time television programming reported that 77 percent of the depictions of Latinos appeared on crime/drama programs, which comprised only 28 percent of prime-time shows.[32]

The Color of Crime. Early content analyses reveal that although African Americans were found more often in less significant roles than Caucasians, they were portrayed somewhat more favorably than whites regarding aggression. Analyses of early 1970s television comedies and dramas indicated that Caucasians were more likely than non-Caucasians to be seen as violent, hostile, illegal, or immoral.[33] Non-Caucasians, however, were more likely to be the victims of crime and violence.[34] Additional research revealed that African-American male characters, in particular, were less aggressive than their Caucasian counterparts.[35]

Content analyses of fictional programs have also demonstrated that television depicts Caucasians as criminal suspects more often than it depicts other racial/ethnic groups as criminal suspects.[36] These depictions are inaccurate compared to real-world statistics indicating that 48.9 percent of those arrested for serious crimes are African American. In contrast, African Americans represent less than 10 percent of all perpetrators on television.[37] It has been suggested that this underrepresentation demonstrates a variation of tokenism in that the small roles do not have much impact in changing the "White-Black" status quo. Hinton and colleagues posit that the favorable portrayal of Blacks in these minor roles poses no threat to the world of the White man on television.[38]

In contrast to fictional programming, analyses of more realistic content, including televised news and reality-based police shows, suggest that portrayals of African Americans in such genres are far more negative. Research on the news media in New Orleans indicated that African Americans accounted for 93 percent of the robbery suspects featured in a local newspaper and more than 80 percent of robbery suspects shown on local television newscasts.[39] In Chicago, almost half of all news stories broadcast on local television news featured African Americans involved in violent crime.[40]

Furthermore, research has shown that 77 percent of crime stories reported on network news were related to African-American suspects, compared to only 42 percent of stories featuring Caucasian criminal suspects.[41]

Not only are African Americans more often shown as criminal suspects, but television news is also more likely to represent those African-American suspects hand-cuffed, poorly dressed, and nameless, compared to Caucasian suspects.[42] In a sample of national news portraying alleged criminals from 1985 to 1989, African-American characters appeared more frequently than Whites as criminal suspects and were more likely to be depicted as physically threatening.[43] It has been suggested that these news portrayals may encourage racial/ethnic hostility, fear of African Americans, and the proliferation of racial/ethnic stereotypes.[44]

Like television news, reality-based police programs, such as *Cops*, also demonstrate more negative portrayals of African Americans than Caucasians. In her analysis of reality-based police shows, Oliver reported that African-American characters were more likely to be portrayed as criminal suspects, whereas Caucasians were cast more frequently as police officers. Seventy-seven percent of African-American characters appeared as criminal suspects compared to only 38 percent of Caucasian characters. The probability of being cast as a criminal suspect was even higher (86 percent) for Latino characters in these shows.[45] Regardless of the numbers' consistency with actual criminal activity, these news and reality-based police shows present a very negative image of African Americans and Latinos.

In an attempt to replicate and extend research on the portrayal of African Americans and Latinos, depictions concerning crime, violence, and the criminal court were coded in content analytic research. To date, many studies have researched the ethnicity of criminals on television, but few have focused on behavioral representations of criminals of different ethnicities. Further, very little is known about attributes of minorities who appear as representatives of the court. This study assesses racial/ethnic stereotypes concerning the representation of African

Americans and Latinos in the criminal justice system, both as officers of the court and as criminals. The behavioral tendencies of Whites, African Americans, and Latinos in these roles, and differences in these portrayals observed across varying genres in primetime television, are also investigated.

METHOD
Sample
A one-week, representative sample was reconstructed to include prime-time TV programming that aired on ABC, CBS, NBC, and FOX during the fall of 1997. All programs included in the sample were randomly selected over a three-week period and aired from 8 p.m. to 11 p.m. Eastern Standard Time (EST). The total sample consisted of 103 programs, constituting 84 hours of programming.

Units of Analysis. The units of analysis in the present study were: (1) all programs in the sample, (2) speaking characters who appeared as officers/representatives of the court, and (3) speaking characters who appeared as criminal suspects. Note that every speaking character that appeared as an officer of the court or as a criminal suspect, regardless of the context, storyline, or genre of the show, was coded in this study.

Program. The *genre* of every program contained in the sample was also coded. The programs were coded as belonging to one of the following genres: (1) action adventure (storyline revolves around physical/high-risk activities within a variety of settings), (2) cartoon (animated program), (3) courtroom drama (a serious presentation surrounding a courthouse, legal, or similar setting), (4) crime drama (a serious presentation surrounding a police or law enforcement setting), (5) family drama (a serious presentation of problems within the context of a family), (6) medical drama (presentation of non-comic problems surrounding a hospital or medical setting), (7) news magazine/public affairs (presentation of in-depth news-type stories in an entertaining manner), (8) reality-based (presentation of real-life footage or recreations of dramatic events), (9) science fiction (storyline

involves settings or characters of an extraterrestrial, paranormal, or outerspace nature), (10) sitcom (humorous presentation of content within a variety of settings), (11) soap opera (storyline revolves around the melodramatic lives, relationships, and lifestyles of the characters), or (12) other.

Officers/Representatives of the Court. Officers/representatives of the court were coded for their role, ethnicity, personality, and their use and receiving of aggression. *Role* consisted of the following: police (any state or federal law enforcement agent), attorney (defense or prosecuting/plaintiff), judge/arbitrator, witness (eye witness to a crime, expert witness, or other witness called to testify at a trial), military (any member of the armed forces), and crime victim. *Ethnicity* was coded as White (Caucasian, of European descent, or individual with white skin), Black (African American, Jamaican American, or individual with black skin), Latino (Mexican American, Central American living in the United States, Puerto Rican, Cuban American, or any other individual of Hispanic origin), Asian American (Japanese American, Chinese American, Korean American, Vietnamese American, Pacific Islander, or Indian American/individual from India), or Native American (American Indian, Eskimo, Aleut). Because only one Asian American (a doctor who was a witness on *Law and Order*) and one Native American (a sheriff on *Murder, She Wrote*) appeared as representatives of the court, they were dropped from further analyses.

Representatives of the court were also coded for the following personality characteristics: *competency* (ability to meet the needs of the job/role, qualifications to serve in that position), *honesty* (truth-telling, uprightness, scrupulousness, decency), *unbiasness* (objectivity, fairness, impartiality), *knowledge* about the incident (familiarity with the facts, awareness of the circumstances surrounding the incident), and *verbal aggression* (verbally hostile, loud, combative, offensive). Each of these personality characteristics were coded on a three-point scale ranging from possessing a great deal of the attribute (e.g., taking extra precautions to remain objective or stating one's intentions to remain objective), through being neutral on the attribute (not going out of one's way to remain impartial, nor taking steps to remain impartial, but not showing or expressing prejudice), to possessing very little of the attribute (e.g., being prejudiced). Representatives of the court were also coded for their *use of physical aggression* (yes/no), *receiving of physical aggression* (yes/no), and *receiving of verbal aggression* (yes/no).

Criminal Suspects. Criminal suspects were coded for their ethnicity, the crime they committed/were arrested for, whether or not they were guilty of this crime, whether or not they were brought to trial, and their use of aggression. *Ethnicity* for the criminal suspects was classified into the same categories as those used for the representatives of the court. Again, as with representatives of the court, Asian Americans and Native Americans were dropped from further analyses due to their lack of representation (one Asian American and no Native Americans). *Crime* committed or arrested for was coded into one of two categories: murder/attempted murder (successful or unsuccessful attempts to kill another person, including manslaughter, homicide, and murder) or all other crimes. Criminal suspects' *guilt status* (suspect really committed the crime, regardless of what any character said vs. suspect really did not commit the crime, regardless of what any character said) was also coded. Characters shown committing the crime were coded as guilty. Those characters who were not shown actually committing a crime, but were arrested for one, were coded guilty or not guilty, depending on information revealed throughout the show. Criminal suspects' *trial status* was also coded into one of two categories: character was brought to trial (criminal suspect appeared in a court trial as a defendant—conveyed either visually or verbally) or not brought to trial (criminal suspect did not appear in a court trial as a defendant—conveyed either visually or verbally).

Criminal suspects' use of physical aggression involved in committing the crime and apart from the crime was also assessed. *Use of physical aggression involved in the crime* was defined as the level of violence, cruelty, and bodily exertion in-

volved in executing the crime. This variable was coded as high physical aggression (e.g., beating a person to death with a baseball bat), some physical aggression (e.g., shooting an individual from a distance), or no physical aggression/crime was not visually portrayed in the program. Criminal suspects' *overall use of physical aggression not including the crime* was defined as the level of violence, cruelty, and bodily exertion involved in harming another person aside from the crime the suspect was arrested for/committed. This variable was coded as physically aggressive (high to moderate degrees of physical aggression) or not physically aggressive (low degrees of physical aggression or no physical aggression). Finally, criminal suspects' *overall verbal aggressiveness not including the crime* was defined as the suspect's level of cruelty, meanness, or attempt to hurt others through speech. This variable was coded as verbally aggressive (high to moderate degrees of verbal aggression) or not verbally aggressive (low degrees of verbal aggression or no verbal aggression).

Coders

Two undergraduate students majoring in communication, one male and one female, served as coders for the present study. These individuals were trained in coding procedures for approximately 10 hours each. Intercoder reliability was assessed by calculating Scott's pi. Programs used for training were not part of the final sample. Reliabilities for each officer/representative of the court variable follow: role (.85), race (.85), competence (.92), honesty (.85), unbiasness (.77), knowledge (.85), verbal aggression (.84), use of physical aggression (.85), receiving physical aggression (.86), and receiving verbal aggression (.61). Reliabilities for criminal suspect variables follow: ethnicity (.85), crime (1.0), guilt status (.78), trial status (.78), physical aggression in the crime (.69), overall physical aggression (1.0), and overall verbal aggression (1.0). The reliability for program genre was 1.0.

RESULTS

Within this sample of 103 prime-time television programs, 349 characters were classified as either officers/representatives of the court or criminal suspects. Seventy-five percent of these characters were identified as officers/representatives of the court ($n = 261$) and 25% were deemed criminal suspects ($n = 88$). When assessed by ethnicity, the percent distribution of criminals and court representatives was nearly equivalent. Eighty-three percent of the portrayals of officers/representatives of the court were White ($n = 216$), 13% were Black ($n = 35$), and 4% were Latino ($n = 10$). For criminal suspects, 82% were White ($n = 72$), 11% were Black ($n = 10$), and 7% were Latino ($n = 6$).

Portrayal of Characters by Program

Racial portrayals in the sample differed by genre, although these findings were not statistically significant either for officer/representatives of the court, or for criminal suspects. The majority of White (37%) and Black (60%) criminal suspects appeared on fictional crime dramas. Fifty percent of Latinos, however, appeared in reality-based programs such as *Cops.*

Portrayal of Officers/Representatives of the Court

The ethnicity of the court representative was significantly related to the role of the character. White characters predominately portrayed police officers (52%). Their second most common depiction was that of attorney (15%). Similarly, the most frequently occurring role for Blacks was police officer (86%). Following second was attorney at 9%. The primary roles for Latinos included police officers (60%) and victims (40%). No significant differences emerged for ethnicity by program genre; the majority of Whites (56%), Blacks (71%), and Latinos (56%) appeared on courtroom or crime dramas.

Differences in the representation of characters by ethnicity did not emerge for most attribute variables assessing personality traits and characteristics of officers/representatives of the court. Only one variable, bias, showed significant differences. The data suggest that White officers/representatives were shown as less biased than other minority officers/representatives. White officers/representatives were considered neutral on bias most often (60%),

followed by unbiased (39%) and biased (1%). For Black officers/representatives, 67% were depicted as neutral on bias, and the remaining 33% were considered unbiased. For Latinos, 50% were classified as neutral on bias, 30% were recognized as unbiased, and 20% were seen as biased. The remaining attribute measures identified Whites, Blacks, and Latinos as very competent (63%, 64%, and 90%, respectively); as equally neutral in honesty (63%, 61%, and 60%, respectively); and equitably high in knowledge (71%, 67%, and 80%, respectively).

Among aggression measures for representatives of the court, Whites were judged neutral on expressions of verbal aggression (54%) as were Blacks (49%). The majority of Latinos were identified as not verbally aggressive (70%). Ethnicity of officer was not related to receipt of verbal aggression, with the majority of White (84%), Black (88%) and Latino (89%) officers/ representatives of the court receiving no verbal aggression. On measures of the use of physical aggression, 95% of Whites used no physical aggression, 91% of Blacks did not use physical aggression, and 89% of Latinos used no physical aggression. Few officers/representatives were recipients of physical aggression. In 89% of the cases, Whites experienced no physical aggression. Ninety-one percent of Black officers/representatives received no physical aggression, and 78% of Latinos received no physical aggression. However, these differences were not statistically significant.

Portrayal of Criminal Suspects

Examinations of the attributes of criminal suspects across this sample yielded no significant findings by ethnicity. Regardless of ethnicity, suspects were most frequently arrested for murder/attempted murder. Fifty-three percent of White criminal suspects, 90% of Black suspects, and 60% of Latino suspects were arrested for or committed murder/attempted murder. In addition, most suspects were not brought to trial. Only 20% of White suspects and 25% of Black suspects were brought to trial. No Latinos went to trial for their suspected crime. Further, the vast majority of White (94%), Black (78%), and Latino (80%) criminal suspects were identified as guilty of the crime for which they were arrested.

Measurements of the level of physical aggression in committing the crime, while not significant, indicate that the majority of Whites (64%) and Blacks (80%) utilized high levels of physical aggression. In only 33% of the cases were Latinos identified as highly aggressive in committing the crime. The overall physical aggressiveness of the criminal suspect, not including the crime, suggested that White (62%) and Black (56%) suspects were low on aggression. Latino suspects were portrayed equally across the levels of aggression with 50% of the depictions high on aggression and 50% low. The criminal suspect's overall verbal aggression, not including the crime, suggests that the majority of White (63%), Black (67%), and Latino (67%) suspects rated low on verbal aggression.

DISCUSSION

On both a comparative and an absolute basis, the portrayals of Blacks and Latinos were found to be very similar to those of their White counterparts in the roles they held and the attributes associated with those roles. The vast majority of depictions were of representatives of the court (75%), and the attributes associated with these characterizations were, in the main, highly positive. Court representatives were equally competent, honest, and knowledgeable across all ethnicities. What then should be expected to result from exposure to media's representation of minority characters in the criminal justice system? Perhaps consideration of the portrayal patterns can provide some indication of this.

In general, representations of minority characters involved with the justice system were on par with depictions of Whites with regard to the characteristics examined. If these portrayals are expected to impact perceptions, it follows that the resulting stereotypes should be highly positive. Because stereotypes often assist in perceiving and predicting human behaviors, such television images may favorably influence social interaction at the interpersonal and societal levels. Yet, while the existing images are positive, the relative scarcity of images, particularly with regard to Latinos, may impact stereotype formation in a more subversive manner. Rather than aiding in the formation of positive perceptions, the limited number of portrayals of Latinos on television may instead further a perception that Latinos, in fact, are inconsequential.[46] Future research would benefit from examinations of this issue.

Latino advocacy groups such as the National Hispanic Foundation for the Arts and the National Council of La Raza have also responded to the relative absence of Latinos on TV. For example, these groups recently urged Hispanic viewers not to watch ABC, CBS, NBC, or Fox for a one-week period in September in protest against the networks for their failure to feature minority stars on their twenty-six new programs for 1999. Efforts such as this boycott suggest the beginning of a campaign to pressure TV executives to better represent the Latino population. At the same time, these network executives claim they are working toward the goal of better representations of Latinos on TV.[47]

Media Exposure and Perceptions of Ethnic Minorities

Several studies exploring the relationships between media exposure and beliefs about African Americans show support for some aspects of media's impact on perception. From the standpoint of social stereotyping and social-role learning,[48] evidence indicates that relevant broadcast-media content significantly influences the formation and reinforcement of audience beliefs about racial characteristics and behaviors.[49] Evidence also suggests that media's impact on social perceptions goes beyond its relationship with stereotypes of racial socioeconomic status, and extends to racial stereotypes of criminality as well. For example, Oliver and Armstrong[50] showed that reality-based police programs represent African Americans as criminal suspects and that exposure to reality-based police television programs is associated with significantly higher estimates of criminality among African Americans.

Limitations

While the results of this investigation contribute to our understanding of the intersections of ethnicity and the legal system on television, several limitations warrant consideration. First, it is important to note that differences in the amount of time the characters appeared on screen, the number of lines/amount of time they spoke, and/or the centrality of the characters to the storylines also are likely to contribute to TV's overall representation of ethnic groups. In the present study, for example, a Latino police officer that spoke five lines and a White police officer that spoke twenty lines may have received equally positive ratings, although the representation of both clearly would not have been the same. Future investigations should study the proportion of characters' time on screen and the length of their spoken parts to assess the relationships among screen time and portrayals.

Second, representations of African Americans, Latinos and other ethnic minorities in the United States in other roles (e.g., as medical professionals, teachers, or parents) compared to Whites in these same roles should be addressed in future research. It may be that when examining additional roles, or the complete population of ethnic minority TV characters, and comparing these portrayals to those of White characters, an entirely different picture of the TV world appears. If this were the case, the potentially positive effects of exposure to the portrayals examined in the present study may be limited.

Finally, given the small population of ethnic minorities present on TV, the composite week of programming analyzed in this study is somewhat limited in scope. The present sample contained only forty-five African-Americans and sixteen Latinos. While this small number does not seriously restrict the generalizability of the results, future studies should collect more extensive samples of programming to better understand the depictions of these ethnic groups on TV.

Based on the present data showing that portrayals of Blacks and Latinos were equivalent to depictions of Whites, one would expect the associated perceptions to be equally positive. What is missing, however, is evidence of the relationship between these positive portrayals and social perceptions. Of equal import is the question: how does the minimal representation of African Americans and Latinos on television, as well as the more conspicuously overlooked groups such as Native Americans and Asian Americans, influence Whites' social perceptions of racial minorities and racial minorities' perceptions of self? Clearly, the frequency and quality of minority portrayals on television warrant further consideration.

NOTES

1. GEORGE GERBNER, "Cultural Indicators: The Third Voice," in *Communication Technology and Social Policy*, ed. George Gerbner, Larry Gross, and William H. Melody (NY: Wiley, 1973), 553–73.
2. GEORGE GERBNER, LARRY GROSS, MICHAEL MORGAN, and NANCY SIGNORIELLI, "Growing up with Television: The Cultivation Perspective," in *Media Effects: Advances in Theory and Research*, ed. Jennings Bryant and Dolf Zillmann (NJ: Lawrence Erlbaum, 1994); NANCY SIGNORIELLI and MICHAEL MORGAN, eds., *Cultivation Analysis* (CA: Sage, 1990).
3. GEORGE GERBNER and LARRY GROSS, "Living with Television: The Violence Profile," *Journal of Communication* 26 (spring 1976): 172–99.
4. GEORGE GERBNER, LARRY GROSS, MICHAEL MORGAN, and NANCY SIGNORIELLI, "Living with Television: The Dynamics of the Cultivation Process," in *Perspectives on Media Effects*, ed. Jennings Bryant and Dolf Zillmann (NJ: Lawrence Erlbaum Associates, 1986), 17–40.
5. GERBNER et al., "Living with Television."
6. JOYCE N. SPRAFKIN and ROBERT M. LIEBERT, "Sex-typing and Children's Television Preference," in *Hearth and Home: Image of Women in the Mass Media*, ed. Gaye Tuchman, Arlene K. Daniels, and James Benét (NY: Oxford University Press, 1978), 228–39.
7. WALTER LIPPMANN, *Public Opinion* (NY: Macmillan, 1922).
8. JERRY C. BRIGHAM, "Ethnic Stereotypes," *Psychological Bulletin* 76 (July 1971): 15–38.
9. JAMES T. TEDESCHI and SVENN LINDSKOLD, eds., *Social Psychology* (NY: Wiley, 1976).

10. ELISHA Y. BABAD, MAX BIRNBAUM, and KENNETH D. BENNE, *The Social Self: Group Influences on Personal Identity* (CA: Sage, 1983).

11. CHARLES RAMIREZ-BERG, "Stereotyping in Films in General and of the Hispanic in Particular," *Howard Journal of Communication* 2 (summer 1990): 286–300.

12. RAMIREZ-BERG, "Stereotyping in Films."

13. STEPHEN SCHUETZ and JOYCE N. SPRAFKIN, "Spot Messages Appearing within Saturday Morning Television Programs," in *Hearth and Home*, ed. Tuchman, Daniels, and Benét, 69–77.

14. PAULA M. POINDEXTER and CAROLYN STROMAN, "Blacks and Television: A Review of the Research Literature," *Journal of Broadcasting* 25 (winter 1981): 103–122.

15. S. ROBERT LICHTER, LINDA S. LICHTER, STANLEY ROTHMAN, and DANIEL AMUNDSON, "Prime-time Prejudice: TV's Images of Blacks and Hispanics," *Public Opinion* 10 (1987): 13–16.

16. JOHN F. SEGGAR, JEFFREY HAFEN, and HELENA HANNONEN-GLADDEN, "Television's Portrayals of Minorities and Women in Drama and Comedy Drama, 1971–80," *Journal of Broadcasting* 25 (spring 1981): 277–88.

17. GEORGE GERBNER, *Women and Minorities on Television (a Report to the Screen Actors Guild and the American Federation of Radio and Television Artists)* (PA: Annenberg School, University of Pennsylvania, 1993).

18. BUREAU OF THE CENSUS, *Blacks in America—1992* (U.S. Department of Commerce, May 1994).

19. GERBNER, *Women and Minorities*; BRADLEY S. GREENBERG and JEFF BRAND, "Minorities and the Mass Media: 1970s to 1990s," in *Media Effects*, ed. Bryant and Zillmann, 273–314; THOMAS FORD, "Effects of stereotypical television portrayals of African-Americans on person perception," *Social Psychology Quarterly* 60 (September 1997): 266–78.

20. RUSSEL WEIGEL, ELANOR KIM, and JILL FROST, "Race relations of prime time television reconsidered: Patterns of continuity and change," *Journal of Applied Social Psychology* 25 (1995): 223–36.

21. DALLAS W. SMYTHE, "Reality as Presented by Television," *Public Opinion Quarterly* 18 (summer 1954):143–56.

22. GORDON L. BERRY, "Television and Afro-Americans: Past Legacy and Present Portrayals," in *Television and Social Behavior: Beyond Violence and Children*, ed. Stephen B. Withey and Ronald P. Abeles (NJ: Lawrence Erlbaum Associates, 1980), 231–48.

23. BERRY, "Television and Afro-Americans.[77]"

24. PILAR BAPTISTA-FERNANDEZ and BRADLEY S. GREENBERG, "The Content, Characteristics, and Communication Behaviors of Blacks on Television," in *Life on Television*, ed. Bradley S. Greenberg (NJ: Ablex, 1980), 13–22; GEORGE GERBNER, LARRY GROSS, and NANCY SIGNORIELLI, *The Role of Television Entertainment in Public Education about Science* (PA: Annenberg School of Communication, University of Pennsylvania, 1985); LOIS KAUFMAN, "Prime Time Nutrition," *Journal of Communication* 30 (summer 1980): 37–46; GEORGE W. SWEEPER, "The Image of the Black Family and the White Family in American Prime Time Television Programming 1970 to 1980" (Ph.D. diss., New York University, 1984); OSCAR H. GANDY and PAULA W. MATABANE, "Television and Social Perceptions among African-American and Hispanics," in *Handbook of International and Intercultural Communica-tion*, ed. Molefi Kete Asante and William B. Gudykunst (CA: Sage, 1989), 318–48.

25. see *The Cosby Show* [citation omitted from original article].

26. DANA E. MASTRO and BRADLEY S. GREENBERG, "The Portrayal of Racial Minorities on Prime Time Television," *Journal of Broadcasting and Electronic Media* (in press); NCLR, "Out of the Picture: Hispanics in the Media, "*National Council of La Raza* (August 1994), 1–30; FEDERICA SUBERVI-VELEZ, "Mass Communication and Hispanics," in *Handbook of Hispanic Cultures in the United States: Sociology*, ed.

Felix Padilla (TX: Arte Publico Press, 1994), 304–357.

27. RAMIREZ-BERG, "Stereotyping in Films"; SUBERVI-VELEZ, "Mass Communication and Hispanics."

28. RAMIREZ-BERG, "Stereotyping in Films."

29. SUBERVI-VELEZ, "Mass Communication and Hispanics."

30. BAPTISTA-FERNANDEZ and GREENBERG, "The Content, Characteristics"; AIDA BARRERA and FREDERICK P. CLOSE, "Minority Role Models: Hispanics," in *TV and Teens: Experts Look at the Issues*, ed. Meg Schwartz (Addison-Wesley Publication, 1982), 88–95; BRADLEY S. GREENBERG, CARRIE HEETER, DAVID GRAEF, KURT DOCTOR, JUDEE BURGOON, MICHAEL BURGOON, and FELIPE KORZENNY, *Mass Communication and Mexican Americans*, ed. BRADLEY S. GREENBERG, MICHAEL BURGOON, JUDEE BURGOON, and FELIPE KORZENNY (NJ: Ablex Publishing, 1983), 7–34; CLINT WILSON and FELIX GUTIERREZ, *Race Multiculturalism, and the Media: From Mass to Class Communication* (CA: Sage, 1995), 61–105.

31. SUBERVI-VELEZ, "Mass Communication and Hispanics."

32. MASTRO and GREENBERG, "The Portrayal of Racial Minorities."

33. JAMES L. HINTON, JOHN F. SEGGAR, HERBERT C. NORTHCOTT, and BRIAN F. FONTES, "Tokenism and Improving the Imagery of Blacks in TV Drama and Comedy: 1973," *Journal of Broadcasting* 18 (fall 1974): 423–32.

34. GEORGE GERBNER, "Cultural Indicators: The Case of Violence in Television Drama," *The Annual of the American Academy of Political and Social Science* 388 (1970): 69–81.

35. PATRICIA C. DONAGHER, RITA WICKS POULOS, ROBERT M. LIEBERT, and EMILY S. DAVIDSON, "Race, Sex, and Social Example: An Analysis of Character Portrayals on Interracial Television Entertainment," *Psychological Reports* 37 (December 1975): 1023–1034; SUSAN E. HARVEY, JOYCE N. SPRAFKIN, and ELI RUBINSTEIN, "Prime-time TV: A Profile of Aggressive and Prosocial Behaviors," *Journal of Broadcasting* 23 (spring 1979): 179–89.

36. JOSEPH R. DOMINICK, "Crime and Law Enforcement on Prime time Television," *Public Opinion Quarterly* 37 (summer 1973): 241–50; RHODA ESTEP and PATRICK T. MACDONALD, "How Prime Time Crime Evolved on TV, 1976–1981," *Journalism Quarterly* 60 (summer 1983): 293–300; W. JAMES POTTER and WILLIAM WARE, "Traits of Perpetrators and Receivers of Antisocial and Prosocial Acts on TV," *Journalism Quarterly* 64 (summer–autumn 1987): 382–91.

37. W. JAMES POTTER, MISKA VAUGHAN, RON WARREN, KEVIN HOWLEY, ART LAND, and JEREMY HAGEMEYER, "How Real Is the Portrayal of Aggression in Television Entertainment Programming," *Journal of Broadcasting & Electronic Media* 39 (fall 1995): 496–516.

38. HINTON et al., "Tokenism and Improving."

39. JOSEPH F. SHELEY and CINDY D. ASHKINS, "Crime, Crime News, and Crime Views," *Public Opinion Quarterly* 45 (winter 1981): 492–506.

40. ROBERT M. ENTMAN, "Modem Racism and the Images of Blacks in Local Television News," *Critical Studies in Mass Communication* 7 (December 1990): 332–45; ROBERT M. ENTMAN, "Blacks in the News: Television, Modern Racism and Cultural Change," *Journalism Quarterly* 69 (summer 1992): 341–61.

41. ROBERT M. ENTMAN, "Representation and Reality in the Portrayal of Blacks on Network Television News," *Journalism Quarterly* 71 (autumn 1994): 509–520.

42. ENTMAN, "Blacks in the News."

43. KATHLEEN H. JAMIESON, *Dirty Politics* (NY: Oxford University Press, 1992).

44. ROBERT M. ENTMAN, "African Americans according to TV News," *Media Studies Journal* 8 (1994): 29–38.

45. MARY BETH OLIVER, "Portrayals of Crime, Race, and Aggression in 'Reality-based' Police Shows: A Content Analysis," *Journal of Broadcasting & Electronic Media* 38 (spring

1994): 179–92.

46. NCLR, "Out of the Picture."

47. JOSEPH HANANIA, "White Out: Latinos on TV," *TV Guide*, 21 August 1999, 31–39.

48. BRADLEY S. GREENBERG, "Minorities and the Mass Media," in *Perspectives on Media Effects*, ed. Jennings Bryant and Dolf Zillmann (NJ: Lawrence Erlbaum, 1986), 165–88.

49. BRADLEY S. GREENBERG and CHARLES K. ATKIN, "Learning about Minorities from Television," in *Television and the Socialization of the Minority Child*, ed. Gordon L. Berry and Claudia Mitchell-Kernan (NY:

Academic Press, 1982), 215-43; GEORGE B. ARMSTRONG, KIMBERLY A. NEUENDORF, and JAMES E. BRENTAR, "TV Entertainment, News, and Racial Perceptions of College Students," *Journal of Communication* 42 (summer 1992): 153–76.

50. MARY BETH OLIVER and GEORGE B. ARMSTRONG, "The Color of Crime: Perceptions of Caucasians' and African Americans' Involvement in Crime," in *Entertaining Crime: Television Reality Programs*, ed. Mark Fishman and Gray Gavender (NY: Aldine de Gruyter, 1998).

COMMENTARY ON THE READINGS

As in other research methods, the first issue the researcher using content analysis must consider after the research question has been developed is the sample. In their study of the representation of different races in the criminal justice system on television, Tamborini and colleagues selected a one-week time frame, including a representative sample of the television shows airing on the ABC, CBS, NBC, and Fox networks between the hours of 8:00 p.m. and 11:00 p.m. Eastern Standard Time. Their total sample consisted of 103 television shows, which represented 84 hours of programming and the analysis of 349 characters. Rather than taking a representative sample of all popular magazines during World War II, Lewis and Neville selected the three for their analysis: the *Saturday Evening Post, Life*, and the *Ladies Home Journal*.

The next step in both of these studies was to identify which portions of the television programs or magazines would be analyzed. Lewis and Neville decided to analyze magazines in January and October during the years 1940, 1943, and 1946. The authors created an instrument to code the representation of gender and work in the magazines. Tamborini and colleagues coded each of the programs into a series of genres and then further coded officers/representatives of the court for their role, ethnicity, personality, and use and receiving of aggression; they coded criminal suspects for their ethnicity, the crime they committed/were arrested for, guilt status, trial status, and use of physical aggression involved in the crime as well as overall use. Representatives were further coded for selected personality.

The issue of intercoder reliability would be the next aspect of the study to gain the attention of the researchers. Tamborini and colleagues controlled for intercoder reliability by training their two undergraduate student research assistants for 10 hours. Lewis and Neville used a "focus group" approach in which members of the teams were assembled and coded all of the advertisements together at the same time. The data accumulated were analyzed and the results reported in both articles.

CONCLUSION

Content analysis is an important method in the social sciences. It is one of the few methods that enable the researcher to study a phenomenon without interfering and possibly altering the results. To a point, historical comparative methods also have this advantage, but they also involve even more subjectivity during analysis than content analysis does.

CHAPTER 8

HISTORICAL
COMPARATIVE METHODS

Historical comparative research is most often considered to be qualitative, but it contains elements of both quantitative and qualitative methods. In fact, historical comparative research is not so much a method as an umbrella term to describe several related research traditions that compare social processes among different units of analysis.

RESEARCH ORIENTATION

Historical comparative research can be oriented in different ways. Some research is historically oriented, concentrating on historical trends or patterns. Historically oriented research normally analyzes the similarities and differences between different past phenomena or between past and present phenomena. Research can also have a comparative orientation in which the emphasis of the research is a comparison between different units of analysis in the present.

Units of analysis in historical comparative research vary according to the study. Some historical comparative research compares two or more units, such as two nations, cities, or blocs of nations. In some cases, however, the research may seek to compare historical practice to the present, normally by tracing the development of a particular phenomenon over time. In other cases, historical comparative studies may compare national or global trends to a more local phenomenon. Such comparisons can be helpful in understanding cases where national trends do not appear to apply.

Historical comparative research often relies on ideal types. Max Weber first used the term *ideal types* to describe the essential element of a given phenomenon. To Weber, there was an ideal type of bureaucracy, consisting of a hierarchy of authority, a specialized division of labor, and a formal set of rules that guides the behavior of the organization. Weber used the ideal type as a basis of comparison for real organizations. The ideal type is a concept based on empirical research, however, and thus is a part of a research cycle. Research is conducted that generates the data from which the ideal type is created, and the ideal type is then used as the basis of comparative research.

The units of analysis can vary considerably. In general, historical comparative research seeks to compare social phenomena across cultures. The classic sociological theorists—Karl Marx, Max Weber, and Emile Durkheim—all strove to base their assertions by utilizing evidence from numerous societies. For instance, Emile Durkheim's (1997 [1897]) study *Suicide* compared suicide rates in numerous European countries in order to understand the nature of social integration. By comparing countries, Durkheim concluded that the nations with higher levels of integration among their populations had lower suicide rates than more individualistic societies.

Many social researchers immediately think of studies based on the nation-state as the unit of analysis, but historical comparative methods can utilize other units of analysis as well. Immanuel Wallerstein (1979) has studied economic relationships among and between blocs of countries. Wallerstein divided blocs of nations into three categories. Core countries are those nation-states that, through their economic, political, and military power are able to dominate the global economy, such as the United States, Great Britain, and Japan. Countries of the periphery are those in the developing world with little economic, political, and military power, such as Bangladesh and Cambodia. Semiperipheral nations, such as Mexico and Saudi Arabia, are often powerful in their own regions but have comparatively less power than core countries. By using blocs of nations as the unit of analysis, Wallerstein was able to discuss the global economy in a way that transcended notions of the nation-state.

Historical comparative methods can utilize smaller units of analysis as well. Molotch and colleagues (2000) compared two cities in California: Santa Barbara and Ventura. They sought to understand how tradition in a community affects the character of a community. They chose the two cities because they were near each other, were approximately the same size, and had similar origins. They could thus be confident that any differences were the result of traditions developed in each city after their early histories. Obviously, they needed very precise definitions of both tradition and character in order to conduct the study. Molotch and colleagues then compared the development of each city over time, exploring how past decisions had influenced the appearance and economic development opportunities in each city. In this case, the unit of analysis was the individual metropolitan area.

ASPECTS OF HISTORICAL COMPARATIVE RESEARCH

Historical comparative research includes a broad range of techniques, but there are several steps and components of the research method that most studies have in common.

Conceptualization

Conceptualization is the process of formulating the data that is to be compared. Historical comparative research requires very precise research questions. Often, research is conducted specifically to test theories about how social processes work. Max Webers' (1930) *The Protestant Ethic and the Spirit of Capitalism* compared the development of Capitalism in protestant countries as a way of arguing against the economic determinism of Marxism at the time. Whereas many Marxists at the turn of the century in Europe believed the development of capitalism to be the result of macro-level political and economic forces, Weber argued that the ideology of certain forms of Protestantism, specifically Calvinist sects, encouraged believers to work, save, and invest in their businesses. Weber's research was important because it specifically focused on the role of ideology in economic and social change.

Data Collection

Once the research question has been fully conceptualized, data collection can commence. Finding data, especially of an historical nature, can be a complicated task. In general, data become more sparse the further back in time one wishes to study. For instance, a researcher studying the United States in the late twentieth century would have access to extensive data sets, including the U.S. Census Bureau, numerous private polling companies such as the Gallup Poll and Zogby International, and newspaper reports from all over the country. Trying to find similar information about the United States in 1750, in contrast, would require the researcher to find alternate forms of data since none of these resources existed 250 years ago.

The researcher needs to read sources with a skeptical eye because the quality of data can vary widely. U.S. Census Bureau data, for instance, are collected with the utmost care; the bureau takes years preparing for each census. The result is high-quality data. Some opinion polls, in contrast, offer little quality. Consider the "reader poll" found in some magazines. Here, readers are encouraged to mail in a completed questionnaire and the results are published in a later issue. Consider the problems with these data: Only readers of that one issue of the magazine are asked, and only those who wish to share their opinion or have nothing better to do will send in the questionnaire. The results are not only not generalizable to the population, but they do not even adequately reflect all readers of the magazine. Does this mean that such research is useless? No, but the researcher needs to recognize the limitation of the data and use them appropriately.

Another factor to consider in data collection is equivalence. Equivalence refers to the ability to compare data between units of analysis. For instance, unemployment rates are figured differently in the United States and France. Although both figures are called unemployment rates, the method used to calculate the unemployment rate in France normally results in a higher number than the unemployment rate in the Untied States. The unemployment rates in the two countries are not equivalent and thus are not good benchmarks for comparison. Similarly, the buying power of one U.S. dollar was different in 1995 than it was in 1975, and thus dollar amounts from these two years is not equivalent. In order to make a valid comparison of buying power, the effect of inflation needs to be considered and the comparison made in constant dollars.

Synthesis

The total of all the data is synthesized into a final product after it has been collected. Often, this includes a mixture of quantitative and qualitative sources. Brought together, the combined data can often tell the story of the phenomenon under study.

Types of Data

Although historical comparative research is considered qualitative, it typically uses a combination of quantitative and qualitative data from a variety of sources. In general, comparative research is more likely to use quantitative data than historical research. This emphasis is dependent upon the overall nature of the study.

In historically oriented research, the emphasis is on the collection of historical data. Historical data comes as primary and secondary data, running records and recollections. Primary data are data that were recorded by an individual or group that reflect their interests at that time. For instance, a collection of letters written by a Civil War soldier to his wife, the orders of General George Washington to his troops during the American Revolution, and maps drawn to show the location of sewers and storm pipes in a city are all examples of primary data. These data were created for a particular purpose other than the historical record. In the same way, a newspaper provides information to those who read it, a movie entertains. Such data are helpful because they are unobtrusive, but they also reflect the views of their creator.

Secondary data are data that were not recorded at the time of an event, but rather were written by historians years after an event. Although working with primary data adds a level of realism, it may be difficult to obtain. In such circumstances, the researcher must rely upon secondary data.

Historical research is greatly aided by running records. Running records are documents and statistics recorded on a continual basis over a period of time. Hospital records, education records, and church records are useful in research where a time series is necessary. Hospital records, for instance, can be used to track an infection years after an epidemic started. Similarly, church records can be used to track the births, deaths, and marriages of members of its congregation.

Oral Histories

Recollections of participants can be useful in historical research as well. Interviews about a particular event can help clarify official views and indicate new avenues of research about an event. In studies examining questions about more general topics, oral histories are useful. In oral history, the subject is asked to recount how life was during a particular time period or in a particular institution. For instance, Kathleen Blee (1991), in her work on women in the Ku Klux Klan, asked former members of the Ku Klux Klan to recount their experiences within the organization. She then verified certain aspects of their stories with other sources of data in order to ensure accuracy.

In comparative studies, the use of such quantitative techniques as surveys and secondary data analysis is also possible, especially if the study is focused on the present time. Equivalence is important in this kind of study. As stated earlier, nations tend to record or compute statistics in different ways, and even survey questions may mean different things to different people in different cultures.

THE READINGS

The two readings for historical comparative methods can be understood as two poles of a continuum between historical and comparative research. Many historical comparative studies resemble these two, and most share elements of both. In "The Great War and Ethnic Nationalism in Utica, 1914–1920," Philip Bean (1993) compares the experience of immigrants in Utica, New York, to wider trends found in the United States during World War I. In "A Comparison of Confidence in the Police in China and in the United States," Liqun Cao and Charles Hou (2001) use statistical models to compare citizens' feelings of trust toward the police in China and the United States.

■ ■ ■ ■ ■

THE GREAT WAR AND ETHNIC NATIONALISM IN UTICA, NEW YORK, 1914–1920

Philip A. Bean
Hamilton College

For many immigrants and their children it was difficult to be impartial about the European conflict. For too many other Americans it was difficult to understand the bonds between immigrants and their homelands. In Utica, NY, during World War I, the experience of immigrants depended on what group you were part of.

A generation of intensifying rivalry among the Great Powers had succeeded by 1914 in dividing Europe into two camps, later known as the Allies (consisting of Great Britain, France and Russia) and the Central Powers (Germany and Austria-Hungary). The members of each of these camps were committed in varying degrees to assist one another in the event of war. The assassination of the Austrian Archduke Franz Ferdinand by a Bosnian terrorist in June 1914 set off an international crisis that resulted in the outbreak of war in August 1914 between the Allies and Central Powers. Other Powers followed suit with relative rapidity: Japan declared war on the Central Powers at the end of that summer; Turkey entered the war on the side of the Central Powers in the fall of 1914; Italy turned her back on her onetime German and Austrian friends and intervened on the Allied side in May 1915.

Although the American general public had mixed and increasingly negative feelings about involvement in the war in Europe, we should remember that since the late nineteenth century America's urban areas—especially in the populous industrial Northeast—had been dominated by European immigrants and their children. For these "ethnic" Americans, the war started not in April 1917 with Woodrow Wilson's appeal to Congress for a declaration of war on Germany, but in the summer of 1914, when the Powers of Europe unleashed the "Great War." For many

From *New York History* (October 1993): 383–413. Copyright © 1993 by the New York State Historical Association.

immigrants and their children, the First World War was therefore no mere foreign conflict, but was instead a contest that would decide the fate of their ancestral homelands.

In 1914, Utica, New York, was a growing manufacturing city of about 80,000 people. Nearly two-thirds of Utica's gainfully employed worked in several dozen textile and knit-goods factories, which dominated the local economy. Utica was virtually a one-industry town, a fact that its citizens would one day regret, but the city was ethnically diverse. Nearly one-third of Utica's population was foreign-born; over one-third more were the children of immigrants. Heading the list of foreign-born Uticans were the Italians, about 7,000 of whom had settled in the city; they were followed in numerical terms by approximately 4,000 Poles, over 3,000 Germans, over 2,000 from Ireland, almost 1,400 from England, over 1,000 from Wales and perhaps as many as 500 "Syrians." By 1914, Utica was also home to about 1,500 Jews, whose ancestors had lived in either Germany, Russia or the Austro-Hungarian Empire. This diverse population brought distinctive traditions to Utica, making it, like so many other American cities, a colorful and lively mixture of ethnic cultures. Many immigrants—and, in time, their children—also developed patriotic feelings toward their ancestral homelands.[1]

In the opening days of August 1914 civic groups in Utica sponsored "Old Home Week," an elaborate series of public events designed to celebrate local pride and ethnic unity. The central event of Old Home Week was the "Pageant of Utica," which traced the history of the city and of its major ethnic groups. The pageant, which took place in Roscoe Conkling Park daily between August 5 and August 8, ended with a parade of scores of representatives of the various local ethnic groups. The pageant program wrote approvingly that "the Germans, Welsh, Dutch, English, Irish, Scotch, Italians, Polish, Syrians and Negroes" had brought "to Utica that which they consider the best thing their Nation has given to the world." The Germans were given a particularly important role in the pageant because Palatine Germans had been among the earliest settlers of the Mohawk Valley and had

played a major role in the Battle of Oriskany, a Revolutionary War battle that took place on the outskirts of what became the city of Utica.[2]

In fact, aside from the Pageant of Utica, the other key event of Old Home Week was the tenth annual Utica German Day, which was held on August 3, 1914. The high point of the day's festivities was a massive parade, reviewed by New York State Governor Martin Glynn, which ended with the unveiling of an imposing monument to Baron Friedrich von Steuben, the Prussian aristocrat who helped transform the American Continental Army into a disciplined fighting force in the 1770s. After the war, von Steuben settled in Central New York and was buried a few miles from Utica. By the late nineteenth century, von Steuben had become a symbol to local German-Americans of their cultural ties to Germany and of their historic political loyalty to the United States. As a sign of the considerable approval that the German-American community then enjoyed, President Woodrow Wilson himself was scheduled to attend the festivities. Utica's German-American Alliance (an umbrella organization of local German organizations) also informed Kaiser Wilhelm II that the von Steuben monument would be dedicated; in the stead of His Imperial Majesty, the unveiling ceremony was to have been attended by the German Ambassador to the United States, Count Johann von Bernstorff.[3]

For reasons that would ultimately transform the attitude of the general public throughout the United States toward the kind of ethnic diversity and ethnic pride that was celebrated during Old Home Week, however, neither Count Bernstorff nor President Wilson attended Utica's German Day. While local Germans enjoyed perhaps the greatest ethnic celebration in the history of their community, events were unfolding in Europe that would lead to considerable political tension in Utica. Indeed, on August 3, 1914, the day the von Steuben monument was unveiled, Germany declared war on France; on the following day, Great Britain declared war on Germany. The homelands of many of those represented in the finale of the Pageant of Utica— the Germans, English, Scots, Welsh, Poles and Syrian-Lebanese in particular—would soon be embroiled in a bloody conflict that would topple seemingly mighty empires and rearrange the map of Europe.

Although there is little evidence that the war created overt hostility between Uticans who came from countries that were at war with one another, the patriotic efforts of the Germans and the British in Utica, not to mention those of other groups, were dedicated to goals that were fundamentally in opposition. While hundreds of Uticans of British parentage volunteered to defend the British Empire against German aggression, German-Americans raised money to help their *Vaterland* defeat "Perfidious Albion." In the meantime, the general public became increasingly alarmed by what they considered Germany's aggressive policies toward the United States. In time, this concern led to the tragic persecution of German-Americans in Utica.

Although American wartime propaganda emphasized that all Americans should be united in their pursuit of a "world safe for democracy," such unity was often either coerced or was the outgrowth of immigrant loyalties toward countries that happened to be allied with the United States. Most ethnic groups could appeal to American concepts ("self-determination," "freedom" and "democracy") to cast their ethnic nationalist aspirations in an American patriotic light. In addition, ethnic histories sometimes emphasize the role played by members of particular groups in the American armed forces during the war, as if to suggest that the process of assimilation had blunted the ethnic nationalist sentiment of such people by 1917. Even the local press went so far as to advance the rather strange argument that immigrants who fought in the Polish Army did so to "show their patriotism and love" for the United States.[4] But to say that they were "good Americans"—which, in many ways, is to be granted—overlooks the reality that many immigrants and even their children still thought in terms that were very much foreign to the majority of Americans.

The outbreak of war in Europe was greeted with particular enthusiasm by two of Utica's ethnic communities: the German-Americans and Irish-Americans. Like their counterparts in Germany, many Utica Germans had long thought that Britain was jealous of Germany's economic success and wanted therefore to destroy Germany. Utica's German-language newspaper, the *Deutsche Zeitung*, declared soon after the outbreak of the war that "England's goal is the destruction of Germany" and that it was "the duty of every German-American to . . . [uphold] the power and honor of the Reich." Harvard professor and eminent German-American Hugo Muensterberg told an audience of 20,000 gathered in Utica for the dedication of the local monument to Baron von Steuben on August 3, 1914 that the statue of the Prussian aristocrat was "a symbol of war's romanticism and idealism . . . an appeal to the world never to forget the ties which bind the United States and Germany." Amidst great applause, Muensterberg blamed the Russians, abetted by Britain and France, for starting the war, and wished that Kaiser Wilhelm's "sword be blessed like his great ancestor, Frederick the Great."[5]

The German-American community sponsored several fundraisers for the relief of German and Austrian war sufferers in 1914–17 and expressed considerable criticism of the apparently pro-British policies of the Wilson Administration. The sinking of the British passenger ship *Lusitania* (in which 127 Americans died) in May 1915 was enormously unpopular among the American general public. But German-Americans in Utica expressed support for the sinking of the *Lusitania* on the grounds that the ship had been carrying munitions for Britain. A local German protest meeting in June 1915 sent a telegram to a rally being held in Madison Square Garden:

> Twenty thousand citizens of German ancestry of Utica and the Mohawk Valley . . . emphatically and unequivocally condemn without reservation any and all attempts to enmesh this, our beloved country whatsoever [in the war] . . . it is either an insane or an asinine law that allows that shipment of explosives on a passenger-carrying vessel.[6]

In addition, German-American critics of the Wilson Administration contended that the

British blockade of Germany was causing hardship in Germany that was not noted by the American general public. The *Deutsche Zeitung* stated that as "unfortunate as an attack on a passenger ship may seem, one must not forget that it has occurred because a people has been forced to struggle for its existence."[7]

In the meantime, efforts in Utica to raise funds for Germany continued apace, as did declarations of German patriotism. Rings sold by the local Relief Fund on German Day in 1915 bore the following expression of devotion to Germany:

> As a token of my loyalty to the old fatherland,
> In time of crisis I gave gold for this iron band.[8]

A one-week bazaar sponsored by Utica's German and Austro-Hungarian Relief Association in February 1916 netted over $8,000, a contribution to the well-being of the Central Powers which (the officers of the local Relief Association were proud to announce in the *Utica Daily Press*) was hailed by the German Ambassador as a "beautiful testimonial of the liberality and patriotic spirit of Utica's German-American community."[9]

Before the outbreak of the war, many Irish-Americans had hoped that if England became embroiled in a conflict with Germany, German-Americans and Irish-Americans could create an anti-English coalition that would keep America out of the war. Such Irish-Americans hoped that with England engaged alone in a life-or-death struggle with Germany, people in Ireland would be able to rebel successfully against their British "oppressors." Efforts to establish such an anti-British "alliance" in Utica stemmed back as far as 1911, when Irish nationalist leader Judge James K. O'Connor (a native Utican who served as mayor in 1919–21) called for violent revolution against English rule in Ireland and for cooperation between the Irish and German communities in America to prevent the United States from allying with England. O'Connor told Utica's Division 2 of the Ancient Order of Hibernians on March 20, 1911:

> I know that I am and have been all my life an enthusiastic Irish nationalist . . . because of the plain and simple tales told me in boyhood days . . . of the famine days. . . . [An] alliance between America and England [has] been prevented by an American Teuton-Celt federation. . . . For many years to come these sons of 48', Teuton and Celt, shall stand with arms intertwined. . . .[10]

Hatred of Germany's enemy, England, was still so strong in the local Irish-American community that a local Catholic priest inspired thunderous applause when he stated in a Saint Patrick's Day sermon in Utica in 1911 that "nowhere in the annals of pagan or sacred history can you find worse persecution or more inhuman fiendishness than were inflicted upon the Irish people" during the eight centuries of English rule.[11]

Shared hostility toward Britain therefore provided a basis for cooperation between the German and Irish communities in Utica. This wartime cooperation was most evident during the bazaar held in February 1916 by the Utica German and Austro-Hungarian Relief Association. The president of the Association at that time was an Irish-American, William F. Dowling, and several nights of entertainment during the course of the bazaar featured popular Irish music, as well as German songs. In addition, Judge O'Connor often played the part of the regional German-American revolutionary hero, Nicholas Herkimer, in local parades before 1917, despite the fact that the Judge's celebrated girth was a striking contrast to the evidently svelte Herkimer.[12]

While members of the Irish and the German communities promoted the fortunes of Imperial Germany, those of British parentage in Utica rallied to the defense of their own ancestral homeland. Although the activities of British immigrants and their children on behalf of the United Kingdom during the conflict are often overlooked, the history of Utica during the Great War suggests that "British ethnics" were no less active in the defense of their ancestral homeland than any other immigrant group during the war. Nearly 350 Uticans served in the British and Canadian armed forces during the First World War. Many volunteered for duty shortly after the outbreak of war in 1914 even though there was no British recruiting station in

Utica until February 1918. Among the Uticans of British parentage who helped to defend the Empire was Dr. William Hale, a medical officer who was awarded the British Military Cross for heroism in the face of the enemy, Stella Jenkins, a nurse who was awarded the Royal Red Cross by King George V for "valuable services with the armies in France and Flanders," and Reginald Heath, who boasted that he had flown thirty-two different types of aircraft during his career in the Royal Air Force. In September 1916, British-born women in Utica also attempted to contribute to the war effort of their homeland by establishing a chapter of the "Daughters of the British Empire."[13]

Initially, Utica's Welsh-American bi-weekly, the *Cambrian* (which had thousands of subscribers throughout the United States), was somewhat ambivalent toward the war. The *Cambrian* had a Christian-Socialist slant and was moderately Welsh nationalist. Consequently, in the opening weeks of the war, it published articles which condemned the fact that "it is working people that bear the brunt of the sorrows and suffering of every war." But the *Cambrian* soon had to admit that although "England in the past has not been free from faults and crimes," the British government had tried in earnest to prevent the war. When Britain realized that Germany was bent on destroying her power, "she joined hands with France and Russia against the voracity and rapaciousness of the Kaiser and the greed of his clique."[14] By November 1914, the *Cambrian* was publishing poems that celebrated the role of Welshmen in the British armed forces:

> English! Irish! Welsh and Scot! . . .
>   Greater Britons of the race,
> Who for righteousness and peace,
>   Till the reign of law they place
> Never in their efforts to cease![15]

Another poem, entitled "Wales's Response," declared:

> Through the city's din we heard the call
>   That Britain needed her men,
> For Britain's honor and Britain's fame,
>   We'll prove her valour again.[16]

Although it had at first expressed reservations about war, by the winter of 1915–16 the *Cambrian* was criticizing pacifists, whom it characterized as "the most impractical of Christians." "Militarism must be met and crushed by militarism," it declared, "right is helpless and hopeless against might."[17]

The *Cambrian* and the Welsh-American community increasingly supported the British war effort for a number of reasons. The *Cambrian* argued that however much England could be criticized, "Germany's anger and jealousy of Great Britain have led [Germany] on a career of violence and lies." In addition, from the outset of the war many Welshmen who had not emigrated to America had volunteered to serve in the British armed forces, thus giving their relatives in Utica a greater emotional stake in the outcome of the war. Many of the letters these Welsh soldiers sent to their parents, brothers, sisters and cousins in Utica (and which were published in the *Cambrian*) emphasized the justice of the Allied cause and the sacrifices being made by citizens of Wales for the British Empire. "I am very sorry to know that parcels intended for me went down on the *Lusitania*," wrote one Welshman to his cousin in Utica, "but the parcels are little compared with the enormous loss of life that took place on that sad day. I cannot explain my feelings when I read about it."[18]

Welsh-Americans also took pride in the increasingly prominent role played by their fellow Welshman, David Lloyd George, in the direction of the British war effort. Lloyd George, who served as Chancellor of the Exchequer and then as Prime Minister during the conflict, was quoted liberally by the *Cambrian*, which boasted that "in the darkest hour of the war, when the deficiencies of British organization and equipment seemed to threaten the success of the Allies . . . the empire turned to the great little democrat from the home of the Druids."[19]

In the early years of the war many British and Canadian immigrants were employees at Utica's Savage Arms Company, producer of the Lewis Gun, 13,000 of which were made for Great Britain and Canada during the war. An air-cooled machine gun that could fire 700 rounds a minute, the Lewis Gun was the most distinctive contribution of industrial Utica to the Allied war effort. In addition to those produced for British Imperial forces during the war, 57,000 of these guns were made in Utica for the United States Army in 1917–18. In fact, the Lewis Gun became the standard machine gun of the United States armed forces. Many of these weapons were mounted on bipods and used by Allied infantry, but over 90 percent were installed on British and American airplanes. Although only 700 employees were involved in the production of the weapon at the time of the American declaration of war on Germany in 1917, by the end of the war nearly 6,500 Uticans worked at Savage Arms, which by that point was able to produce up to 100,000 Lewis Guns per year.[20]

While the German-American community promoted its efforts on behalf of their *Vaterland* and British ethnics flocked to the aid of their Mother Country, Uticans of other ethnicities also strove to assist their respective homelands. Local Syrian and Lebanese immigrants (all of whom were commonly referred to simply as "Syrians" at the time) staged several events before the American declaration of war to assist their homeland and fellow Lebanese who were in the American armed forces. The lands which now comprise Syria and Lebanon were parts of the Turkish Ottoman Empire until the end of the First World War. Both lands had sizeable Christian minorities which had periodically resisted Turkish rule. The decision of Turkey to enter the war in 1914 as the ally of Germany intensified the desire of local Lebanese and Syrian immigrants to support the Allied war effort.

Even before the outbreak of the war, local Lebanese and Syrians were renewing their efforts to promote the cause of their homeland. In February 1914, local "Syrians" had established a branch of the Mount Lebanon League of Progress, which hoped to compel the Turks at least to honor their 1863 undertaking to give autonomy to Christian-dominated Mount Lebanon. Members of this group resolved to hold an annual Lebanese "Independence Day" observance until their people had "wrest[ed] from Turkey the privileges which belong to the Mt. Lebanon people." As the United States

moved closer to intervention, Utica Lebanese also sponsored fundraisers to assist the families of those who had been dispatched by the National Guard to protect a New York reservoir. It must be emphasized, however, that although they spoke of themselves as simple American patriots, Utica's Lebanese and Syrian immigrants decided to patronize this particular National Guard unit because so many of their relatives and ethnic brothers were on duty in it.[21]

The aspect of the First World War that made the most profound impression on many local Lebanese, however, was the cruel genocide perpetrated on their relatives still in Lebanon by Germany's ally, Turkey, in 1916–17; $700 was raised for Lebanese famine victims at a single protest meeting in January 1917. So powerful and lasting was the impression created by this Turkish-engineered famine—as a result of which every Lebanese family in Utica was said to have lost a relative—that later, in 1930, Saint Louis of Gonzaga Maronite Church sponsored *Jemal Pasha in Mount Lebanon*, a play written by the parish priest which focused on the cruel treatment of inhabitants of Mount Lebanon by the Turks.[22]

The local Jewish community—1,500 strong—also assisted their suffering religious brothers and sisters in Europe during the war. This group, like other ethnic groups in Utica, had periodically been plagued by divisions, but now united in a common ethnic cause. Inspired by the example of other ethnic groups that were raising funds to assist their homelands and by reports of the hardship that European Jews were experiencing—primarily as a result of the campaigns being waged in Central and Eastern Europe by Germany, Austria and Russia—local Jews organized the Jewish Relief Fund on January 6, 1916. Each of the Fund's four drives (which raised a total of $80,000 in 1916–20) enjoyed the enthusiastic support of the *Utica Daily Press*, which printed special Jewish Relief Issues. The proceeds from these sales were donated to the Fund; $1,600 of the $10,000 raised in 1916 was garnered through sales of special issues of the *Press* by "Hebrew women."[23]

Although the Jewish Relief Fund enjoyed the patronage of many Uticans who were not

Jews, the effort was significant chiefly in that it had an almost cathartic effect on many local Jews. Meetings held for the benefit of the Fund were evidently very moving events for the Jews who attended them. The *Press* described one of the first such meetings to be held in Utica:

> As Mr. [Samuel] Reichler swung into his peroration his voice rose to the wail of the mourners, and [with] the words "zeduka tazil mimoves," the cry of the "holy ones" at the funeral, so laden with sorrowful and familiar memories to the Jewish mind, sobs broke out among the audience. At the second wailing cry the big audience rocked to the fresh outburst of weeping. It was a dramatic scene.[24]

Another speaker indicated that the war and the Jewish relief drive were reforging the identity of at least some local Jews:

> Three and a half millions of Jews are being offered up to preserve royalty in the old world. When the war is over the countries will care for their own—all will have their own countries to return to, but the Jews will have no country.[25]

World War I helped therefore to intensify the devotion of many Jews in Utica to Zionism (the movement for the creation of a Jewish State), a cause later given a seemingly strong boost by the pledge of British Foreign Secretary Arthur Balfour in November 1917 to create "a national home" in Palestine for the Jews.

Utica's largest ethnic group, the Italians, had a lively Italian-language press which kept its readers in contact with the events in Italy and in Europe that would lead to the somewhat belated Italian intervention in the war in May 1915. For decades Italy had been associated with Austria-Hungary and Germany in a loose alliance. Although it was convenient for Italian diplomacy (because it insured that Austria would not suddenly attack Italy), this alliance antagonized Italian nationalists who resented past Austrian domination of northern Italy and the continued Austrian occupation of lands that contained Italian minorities. After the outbreak of the war in August 1914, Italy entered into negotiations with Britain and France which resulted in the Treaty of London. Under the terms of this treaty, Italy was to be given generous territorial concessions after the defeat of the Central Powers in return for her intervention on the Allied side.

Much of the Italian-American community was galvanized by the Italian declaration of war on Italy's "historic oppressor," Austria, in May 1915. The local Italian-language press accused the Kaiser of conducting a "vendetta against Italy," because the German Emperor had delivered an undiplomatic speech (one of many!) in which he predicted that Venice would be reconquered for Austria-Hungary.[26] Utica's generally left-of-center Italian-language newspaper, *La Luce*, exclaimed after the Italian declaration of war:

> To arms, then, oh sons of Italy, against the eternal and barbaric enemy, to again enhance the glory of our radiant tricolor. Victory will be ours, because of the holiness of our cause and the fervor of our spirit![27]

The more conservative nationalist *Pensiero Italiano* was, for a change, entirely in agreement with its competitor, *La Luce*, in calling upon readers to heed the "ancient battlecry of our forefathers" to create "a new Roman empire" by destroying the Austro-Hungarian empire. In particular, local Italians looked forward to the "liberation" of northeastern Italy, especially the cities of Trieste and Trent, from Austrian domination. "The ghost of Garibaldi is leading us to liberate our brothers in Trent and Trieste," wrote Utica's *La Sentinella* shortly before Italy's declaration of war on Austria.[28]

On June 16, 1915 the first 300 local Italians to report for duty in the Italian Army departed from Utica. The local English-language press reported that in addition to this large company of recruits, "reservists are leaving in small parties from day to day." The local Italian consular agent told the press that "considerable numbers" of draft-age Utica Italians— who could have chosen to ignore their government's call to arms since the United States was still neutral—were reporting for duty every day. So many local Italians were returning to their homeland to fight the "alien barbarians" that the organizers of the local drive for the Italian Red Cross reported in June 1915 that two-thirds of the funds raised would remain in Utica to assist the families of local Italians who were serving in the Italian armed forces. At least four Utica Italians died while fighting the Austrians and the Germans in the Alps in 1915–18.[29]

Utica's Italian-Americans followed battle reports with great eagerness, especially when local Italian-language newspapers published letters from former Utica Italians serving in the Italian army. In the summer of 1915, for example, the local Italian-language press published a letter in which an Italian soldier wrote hopefully to his brother in Utica: "We are forty kilometers from Trieste and hope to arrive there with as great a victory as the Italian army has reported hitherto. . . . *Viva l'Italia!*" When the Italian army defeated the Austrians at the Battle of Gorizia in the summer of 1916, Utica's Italian district was electrified. Over 3,000 Italian-Americans marched in a "purely impromptu" victory parade that was so raucous that local officials actually launched an investigation to discover who was responsible for starting such a disturbance of the peace. A local Italian bookseller reported that sales of Italian newspapers and of phonograph records of Italian patriotic music increased noticeably "due to great enthusiasm over the Italian successes."[30]

How many German-Americans from Utica served in the German armed forces during the war is not clear—it was not the sort of thing about which many people boasted after America's declaration of war on Germany in April 1917. It may be that the number was not extremely high simply because the German immigrant population was much older on average than were the members of other immigrant communities in Utica. In any case, at least some Utica German-Americans are known to have served under the German tricolor during World War I. In November 1916, the *Utica Deutsche Zeitung* announced that Arthur Aprath, a young German immigrant who had lived in Utica for several years, had been killed on the Russian front while serving as a *Landsturmmann* in the

One Hundred and Seventy-first Infantry Regiment of the German Army. Aprath, who was evidently quite popular among local German-Americans, happened to be visiting relatives in Germany when the war broke out. The twenty-six year old Utican reported for duty when his reserve unit was then called to arms. An obituary placed in the *Deutsche Zeitung* by Aprath's former co-workers at the Utica Cutlery Company (the employees of which were almost exclusively German) praised him for having "fought for the honor and defense of his fatherland."[31]

A more fascinating case was August Essel, who joined the German Army even though he had been born and raised in America. Essel's father was a baker who had emigrated from Alsace-Lorraine in 1886. Why the younger Essel decided to volunteer for service in the Kaiser's army is unknown. The fact that he had served in the German Army was disclosed nonchalantly in the spring of 1919 by the *Utica Deutsche Zeitung*, which reported that two of the Essel brothers were serving in the American Army, while August and his uncle had served in the German Army. The *Zeitung*'s report had little to do with these facts; the newspaper merely wanted to tell its readers that one of the two Essels serving in the American Army had written a letter to his mother "in good German."[32]

German-Americans resented the fact that their efforts to help Germany in 1914–16 were increasingly seen by many Americans as violations of American neutrality and even as slightly treasonous, while efforts made by other Americans to support the Allied cause before the United States declaration of war on Germany were considered acceptable, if not patriotic. Particularly annoying to local Germans were President Wilson's attacks in 1915–16 on "hyphenated" Americans—that is, the German- and Irish-American communities—who seemed to interfere continually in the formulation of American policy toward England. The program of the 1916 Utica German Day angrily denounced this apparent double standard by saying that "the Germans, whenever assembled, never sing 'God Save the Kaiser,' but always 'My country 'tis of Thee.' " In contrast, the program argued snidely, the "so-called 'real Americans' in

Boston" sang the British national anthem, "God Save the King," at a memorial service for British Field Marshal Kitchener, who met his death when his ship was sunk in the North Sea in 1916. "If this is 'real Americanism,' " the program defiantly concluded, "the 'hyphenates' beg to be excused from adopting it."[33]

Unable to fathom how honest people could identify American interests with the well-being of the British (the historic enemies of American independence) while considering the "enlightened" German Empire a threat to the United States, German-Americans tended to dismiss pro-British forces in American society as hypocrites and as un-American. In a last-ditch effort to prevent the United States from intervening on the Allied side, the *Utica Deutsche Zeitung* and other German-American forces in Utica attempted to block Woodrow Wilson's re-election to the presidency in 1916. As in many other communities, Wilson's re-election slogan, "He Kept us out of War," elicited scoffs from the German-language press in Utica. "How Mr. Wilson can be hailed as a man of peace is incomprehensible," wrote the *Deutsche Zeitung* in October 1916, "he has wanted war, but has not been able to get it."[34]

Unfortunately for the German-American community, President Wilson was re-elected, thus setting the stage for the diplomatic clashes that would bring Germany and the United States to war in April 1917. Although many German-Americans had become increasingly apprehensive about the deterioration of relations between Germany and the United States, the *Deutsche Zeitung* and many local Germans continued after the election of 1916 to proclaim their support for Germany's war against England, France and Russia.

Shortly after Wilson's victory, the local German-American Alliance sponsored a military farce entitled *Der Feldgraue Sepp'l* (the "Field-Grey Fool") for the benefit of "thousands of our countrymen who today languish in Siberia," presumably in Russian prisoner of war camps. The secretary of the local branch of the German-American Alliance asserted that "it should be a *sacred duty* for us to lighten the burden of these unfortunate *heroes*." In February 1917—less than

two months before the American declaration of war—a play entitled *O Wir Barbaren* ("Oh We Barbarians") was presented at the Utica Maennerchor-Halle. The play evidently mocked the stories of German war atrocities that so enraged much of the American general public. The *Deutsche Zeitung* dismissed the Allied coalition against Germany as a "menagerie" and even after the American declaration of war on Germany continued to denounce England's blockade of Germany as inhumane.[35]

These attitudes did not help the German-American community in the atmosphere of rising American impatience with the German government and with German-American outspokenness. On April 3, 1917, President Wilson went before Congress to request a declaration of war against Germany. While he stated in his address that "most" German-Americans were loyal citizens, he mixed this conciliatory gesture with intimations that coercion might be used against German-Americans. "If there should be disloyalty," he told Congress, "it will be dealt with with a firm hand of stern repression." The tone of Wilson's address was echoed by the Sheriff of Oneida County who, in public announcements placed in the local English- and German-language newspapers, assured Uticans from Austria-Hungary and Germany that he would do his utmost to protect them from any attempts to infringe on their rights; at the same time, though, he warned them to "keep their mouths shut" and that "any act, however slight, tending to give aid or comfort to the enemy is TREASON, and for any such act severe penalties are provided, and will be enforced in every case. . . ."[36]

To German-Americans, many of whom had dismissed as absurd the changing attitude toward Germany of the American public in 1914–17, the outburst of anti-German sentiment that occurred in 1917–18 was astounding. To them it seemed that overnight the American conception of Germans as the descendants of such American patriots as Baron von Steuben, Nicholas Herkimer and Carl Schurz had been transformed; the American press and government propaganda now portrayed Germans as blood-thirsty, fiendish "Huns" who threatened to destroy American democracy. As late as June

1917 the *Zeitung* took the local English-language press to task for using "repeatedly such expressions as 'Huns' and 'Bosches' when speaking of people of our ancestry." The *Deutsche Zeitung* complained that German-Americans were "trying their very best to prove good and loyal citizens, although their hearts ache and cry out often under the vile slander and attacks upon everything of German origin."[37]

One of the first signs of growing intolerance toward the local German community was an editorial cartoon published in the popular *Utica Saturday Globe* in November 1917. Bearing the caption "Forbearance has Ceased to be a Virtue," the cartoon depicted the stereotypical German-American (a short, pudgy man with tiny glasses and a bushy mustache), who was labelled "Seditious Editor" and was shown to be in a rather defiant mood while being whipped into jail by the long arm of the law. On the ground was a German-American newspaper with the seditious headline *Gott Strafe Wilson* ("God punish Wilson"). In February 1918, the German-American caricature was again in a front-page cartoon in the *Globe*. Identified this time as the "German Propagandist" and surrounded by the instruments of sabotage (bombs, kerosene, dynamite), the German-American was being introduced to a noose by a rather angry-looking Uncle Sam.[38]

President Wilson promised that the "firm hand of stern repression" would fall on all who seemed to oppose the American war effort. In the spirit of that warning, local "super-patriots" went out of their way—especially in 1918—to root out the disloyalty they assumed was rampant in the German-American community. In April 1918 a local German who was being harassed to purchase American war bonds told bond salesmen that he did not want to support anything that might "kill his kin in Germany." When the salesmen pressed him to prove whether he was a "true American" or a German, the man, who had been a naturalized citizen of the United States for forty-one years, commented in exasperation to his aggressive visitors that he was a German and promptly threw them out of his house. Shortly thereafter, he was arrested by the federal marshal on charges of sedition.[39]

The "assault on all things German" came to a climax in July 1918 when the Utica Board of Education voted to abolish German-language instruction. As early as December 1917, the *Utica Saturday Globe* had argued that German-language textbooks were being used to "poison the minds of children with pernicious German propaganda, injected with the use of German gold." To no small extent, the almost bizarre notion that German-language instruction constituted a form of brain-washing was inspired by *Im Vaterland* ("In the Fatherland"), the textbook used in the public schools in Utica and many other communities. The frontispiece of *Im Vaterland*, which was first published in 1910, bore the visage of the Kaiser himself. In addition, the widely-used text had laudatory readings on the Imperial family and the German Army, as well as the lyrics of such German nationalist favorites as *Die Wacht am Rhein*. *Im Vaterland*, in short, confirmed the worst fears of alarmed patriots, who were already predisposed to think that anything German would have an insidious effect on impressionable American youth. On June 28, 1918, the School Board voted unanimously to remove this "pernicious propaganda" from the public schools; German-language instruction was not reintroduced in Utica's public schools until 1927. Shortly after the decision of the School Board to abolish German-language instruction, the *Utica Deutsche Zeitung* stated that there were many reasons to continue to teach German, but concluded with a tone of resignation that it was "completely useless" to try to discuss the subject intelligently in the atmosphere created by the war.[40]

While German-Americans were thus being subjected to the assaults of American patriots, their erstwhile Irish-American nationalist allies beat a strategic retreat. Judge James K. O'Connor, the leading local pre-war advocate of cooperation between Germans and Irish in America to prevent an alliance between the United States and Great Britain, soon began to denounce the Kaiser with the enthusiasm that one would expect from a good American patriot in 1917–18. In what one suspects was almost an ironic vein, O'Connor wrote in the *Globe* in March 1918:

No more hyphen. No more second loves. I feel grateful to England that it drove my grandparents across the Atlantic and gave me a chance to be born under the starry flag.[41]

As a measure of the disingenuousness of such statements, soon after the end of the First World War O'Connor was once again active in the movement to promote armed revolution against British rule in Ireland.[42]

But such fulsome patriotic declarations as O'Connor made during 1917–18 helped, to some extent, to save the local Irish-American community from suffering the fate that befell their German-American neighbors. Of course, the other factor which protected local Irish-Americans was the fact that they (in contrast to local German-Americans) exercised political power far in excess of their numbers. The mayor, half the Common Counsel, the chief of police, most of the police and fire departments, and a large part of the local judiciary in 1917–18 were Irish-American—a rather tall persecution order for even the most intrepid of Nativists!

While Utica's German-American community was being subjected to persecution for the enthusiasm it had previously exhibited for Germany's war against what were now America's allies, other ethnic groups found that the political causes of their brethren overseas were now very much in favor with the American public. Although there was nothing qualitatively different between what the Poles, Italians and other groups now did on behalf of their respective homelands and what the German-Americans had done for Germany in 1914–17, the fact that the former were all anti-German sat well with the general public after the American declaration of war.

Utica's tiny Armenian community sponsored efforts to help Armenians who had survived Turkish genocide. In April 1918, local Armenians held a protest meeting on Bleecker Street to kick off a campaign to collect $1,200, the local quota for the national campaign to raise $1,000,000 for Armenian relief. Aram Kazanjian, who came to Utica in 1908 and who had volunteered for service in the American Army in April

1917, was identified by the local press as the "president of the Armenian residents of Utica and vicinity in this campaign" despite the fact that he was at that point stationed at Fort Dix, New Jersey. At least one Utican is known to have served in an "Armenian Army," evidently a force which fought in the name of the Czar against the Central Powers and their Turkish allies.[43]

The most impressive ethnic nationalist movement in Utica was the Polish-American campaign to relieve the suffering of their fellow countrymen in Europe and to create an independent Poland. Between May 1914 and July 1919 Utica's approximately 4,000 Polish immigrants raised an astounding $113,000 for the Polish nationalist movement. The bulk of this money was donated in the form of individual contributions from local Poles; of $91,316 in individual donations by name, only $3,711 was donated by "Americans." Given that the Polish-American community was hardly the largest or the most affluent ethnic group in Utica and consisted largely of modest, hard-working families, its ability to raise such a large sum was a measure of Polish-American devotion to the struggle for the independence of their homeland and their determination to secure the defeat of the oppressors of Poland.[44]

Many Polish-Americans also volunteered for service in the Polish Army which fought side-by-side with the Allies in France after June 1917. Although Polish territory was occupied by the Germans and the Austrians by 1917 and, in fact, an independent Poland had not existed since the eighteenth century, the Allies agreed to allow Polish volunteers to fight under their own colors against the Germans in Western Europe. By so doing, Polish nationalists hoped to earn the right for an independent Poland to be created at the end of the war.

A total of 22,000 Polish-Americans from throughout the United States volunteered to serve in the Polish Army in France. Although this response cannot be compared to the approximately 300,000 who served in the American armed forces during the war, it should be kept in mind that the United States instituted conscription only a few days after the establishment of the Polish "Blue Army" and that the American government did not permit recruiting for the Polish force to be conducted in the United States until October 6, 1917. In addition, of the first 100,000 volunteers for the American armed forces, at least 40,000 are believed to have been Poles.[45] This response might suggest a Polish love of America that was for some reason unique among immigrant groups; it might also (and more plausibly) suggest that many Poles were convinced that the United States would champion the Polish cause. After all, Woodrow Wilson had stated in his January 22, 1917 "Peace Without Victory" speech: "I take for granted that statesmen everywhere are agreed that there should be a united, independent and autonomous Poland."

Believing that America was fighting for the independence of Poland, the Falcons, a Polish nationalist fraternal organization, played a key role throughout America in encouraging Polish immigrants to volunteer for service in the American armed forces. Within three months of the American declaration of war on Germany, 38,000 members of the Falcons' paramilitary forces, which had trained for years in preparation for the liberation of Poland, volunteered for service in the United States Army.[46] In September 1917, after the United States had been at war for nearly six months, the Falcons held a regional convention in Utica at which hundreds of delegates from throughout Central New York expressed the desire that President Wilson permit Poles to cross into Canada, where a training camp for the Polish Army had been established. The first twenty Utica Poles volunteered for duty under the Polish flag at a Liberty Loan rally held in Utica in October 1917, only days after President Wilson's decision to allow recruiting for the Polish Army to be permitted in the United States. By March 1918, a Polish recruiting station had been established in Utica which served as the headquarters for the Polish Army recruiting effort in a district stretching from Poughkeepsie to Syracuse.[47]

During 1917–18, nearly 170 local Poles served in the Polish Army, which was actually more than the number of local Polish-Americans who fought in the American armed forces during the war. Once again, although Americans considered the willingness of Poles to fight in the United States armed forces a sign of their American patriotism, it would appear that many, if not most Utica Poles considered the war primarily a struggle for Polish independence, not a crusade for America. While the war ended in November 1918 for the 135 local Polish-Americans who fought under the Stars and Stripes, those who volunteered for the Polish Army served until the summer of 1920, helping to repel the invasion of the newly-independent Poland by the Red Army. The first of the volunteers returned to Utica on April 29, 1920. By September 1920, the bulk of the volunteers were once again in Utica, having fought, in effect, two wars: one against the Central Powers, another against the Russian Communists.[48]

While the Polish-American community clearly had mixed motives for supporting the Allied war effort and did not do so simply out of a sense of loyalty or gratitude to the United States, much the same can be said of other ethnic groups in Utica. Although hundreds of Italians left Utica between the Italian declaration of war on Austria in May 1915 and America's intervention in the conflict in April 1917, nearly 800 more served in the American armed forces during 1917–18; 23 local Italians were killed and 78 were wounded while fighting under the Stars and Stripes.[49] The total number of Utica Italians who served during 1915–18 in the Italian Army is not known, but it should suffice to say that the 300 local Italians who answered the Italian call to arms on a single day in June 1915 alone were equal to about one half of all Utica Italians fighting for the United States during the entire war. In other words, it does not seem unlikely that as many of them served in the Italian Army as in the American armed forces.

As with the local Poles, one should not underestimate the extent to which Italians in Utica thought of the war as a struggle for Italian unification rather than as a war for the defense of America from Kaiserism. After the American declaration of war on Germany, Utica's *La Luce* referred to America as a "second fatherland." An "America First" issue of another local Italian publication referred to the United States as merely the "ally" of millions of Italian immigrants. The United States government also encouraged Italians to think in this fashion.

Advertisements placed by the American Food Administration in local Italian newspapers encouraged immigrants to conserve food because Italy, not America, needed it.[50]

Still, the Italians and Poles alone accounted for perhaps as many as one-fourth of those from Utica who served under the colors of the United States during the war—this at a time when all of the members of those two immigrant groups constituted only about one-seventh of the population of Utica. If one also takes into account the fact that other immigrant groups—the Lebanese, Syrians, Armenians, British, etc.—played a role in the American armed forces, that workers in Utica's industries were predominantly immigrants and that well over 1,000 more immigrants served in the British Imperial, Italian and Polish armed forces during the war, it becomes clear that the bulk of Utica's contribution to the Allied victory was made by the immigrants and their children whom Nativists would attack as dangerous foreigners after the war.

Similarly, although they were subjected to persecution during the war, the local German-American community nonetheless made significant contributions to the American war effort. Hundreds of Uticans of German descent served in the American armed forces; at least 110 young men from Saint Joseph's Parish alone served under the American flag in 1917–18. In July 1918, it was announced that local German-American organizations alone had contributed $87,000 to the Liberty Loan drive, approximately 18 percent of the total even though German immigrants and their children accounted for less than 10 percent of Utica's population at that time. Therefore, in an attempt to demonstrate that they were "100 percent Americans," Utica's German-Americans made a contribution to the local bond drive in 1918 that was twice as large as could have been expected from a group of their size.[51] Unfortunately, such efforts could not keep anti-German patriots entirely at bay during the war.

The post-war period brought much upheaval: economic downturn, labor unrest, prohibition. But the most significant of the disturbances of life in Utica and elsewhere was "Nativism," the belief that immigrants constituted a political danger to the United States. The contribution of immigrants to the Allied victory in 1917–18 was forgotten as a generation of anxieties about cultural and economic change, combined with fears promoted by the Russian Revolution, came to a head in an outburst of anti-foreign hysteria (the "Red Scare") in 1919–20.

In Utica, as in many other industrial communities throughout America, the year 1919 witnessed considerable labor unrest which many alarmed residents interpreted as the first acts of a Bolshevik revolution. Following a successful strike staged by Italian and Eastern European immigrants against the copper mills in nearby Rome, New York, textile workers in Utica's largely Italian East End went on strike in July 1919. Joined by hundreds of their neighbors who lived in a tiny Polish enclave in East Utica, thousands of Utica Italians, perhaps as many as half of whom were women, picketed several factories for over four months seeking an increase in wages and the recognition of their unions.[52]

Every effort was made by strikers to remind Uticans that foreigners had played a significant role in the American war effort. Protest parades and picket lines were headed by bemedalled veterans in American Army uniforms. Spokesmen for the strikers emphasized that low wages and high unemployment were the only rewards that immigrant veterans had received for having risked their lives for the Allied cause. But in the atmosphere created by the war and by the Russian Revolution, the general public was uneasy.

When Utica police fired on rioting picketers (wounding five Italian-Americans) outside the Oneita knitting plant on October 28, 1919, forces opposed to the strike published full-page advertisements in local newspapers which played on fears that immigrant strikers were attempting to bring an evil foreign ideology—Bolshevism—to Utica. Bearing headlines reading "The Red Flag of Revolution Waved in Utica," these advertisements argued that the strike was not a simple dispute over wages but part of an effort by immigrant "Reds" to destabilize American institutions.[53] The Utica *Observer* left no doubt as to what it would do with immigrants who participated in the strike:

Many of them are ignorant. . . . These must be convinced that we do not tolerate such things in America, and as most of them are aliens, they must come to an understanding that they must conduct themselves after the manner we have adopted *or take their ways back to the countries whence they came.*[54]

Under pressure from the police and faced by the intransigence of mill owners, the strike fell apart in November–December 1919.

In 1919–20, the coercive pattern established in 1917–18 was reversed. German-Americans were no longer the subject of patriotic abuse, but Italian-Americans and Polish-Americans, who had been praised during the war, were now viewed as dangers to American democracy. An irony of this nativistic, anti-Communist backlash against the immigrants who had provided much of the backbone of the local Allied war effort was that while Polish strikers were being condemned as Bolshevik revolutionaries in Utica, almost 200 other Utica Poles were still fighting to throw the Red Army out of Poland. Indeed, at least one local Pole, Aleksander Pupek, was killed in action against Communist forces on June 9, 1919, while workers in Utica were preparing to strike for better wages.[55]

In the meantime, local Italian-Americans were dismayed to find that many Americans were not only branding them Bolshevik revolutionaries, but were also denigrating the Italian war effort and labelling Italy an incompetent and avaricious ally. In November 1918 Utica's Italian east side had greeted with wild enthusiasm the news of the disintegration of the Austro-Hungarian and German forces at Vittorio Veneto in the face of the final Italian offensive of the war. Concerts of Italian patriotic music took place throughout East Utica after the announcement of the Austro-Italian armistice on November 4, 1918. "Without much preparation," the *Daily Press* reported in astonishment, "spontaneously the Italian residents of the city marched out in demonstration." Victory parades criss-crossed the East End until late at night on November 5, despite inclement weather. The next day, the celebration continued with "band

music, impromptu parades, flag-waving and cheering."[56]

A few months later, local Italian-Americans were disappointed to find that at the peace conference, which opened at Paris in January 1919, the Allies took a dim view of Italy's territorial ambitions and had decided instead to incorporate territories such as Dalmatia—which Italy had been promised by the Allies in the 1915 Treaty of London—into the newly established "Jugoslavia." Worst of all, President Wilson himself played a leading role in rebuffing Italian aspirations. The *Pensiero Italiano* angrily condemned the Versailles Treaty as a "pyrrhic peace" and concluded:

Germany's bitterness toward the Allies is not something to be neglected; if simmering Italian irritation with France, England *and the United States* should be added to this, no League of Nations would be able to avoid . . . the inevitable.[57]

The injury to Italian pride was compounded by lingering embarrassment over the earlier Italian military debacle at Caporetto in October–November 1917, when Austrian and German forces broke through Italian lines and drove nearly eighty miles into Italian territory. Although the Italians eventually halted the enemy advance, Caporetto was perhaps the most ignominious military setback inflicted on any of the Allied Powers during the war, a fact that the American press would not let Italian-Americans forget. So embarrassing was Caporetto to many Italian-Americans that the initial response of Utica's *Pensiero Italiano* to Vittorio Veneto was to say: "The disgrace of Caporetto, which a few cowardly traitors [in Italy] had wanted and obtained, is completely canceled, and Italy has resurrected its warrior spirit. . . ."[58]

The war therefore left discontent and disillusionment in its wake. Admittedly, some of Utica's ethnic groups emerged from the war at least temporarily satisfied. The Lebanese were pleased that their homeland was now released from Turkish oppression, albeit under French supervision. Local Jews could derive satisfaction from the fact that the British seemed to be fulfilling their promise to establish a Jewish "homeland" in Palestine. Irish-Americans renewed their efforts to free Ireland (local Irish-Americans raised over $20,000 for Irish freedom in three months in 1921), which were finally rewarded with the withdrawal of British forces from most of Ireland and the establishment of the Irish Free State in 1922. Local Poles could well be proud that their efforts played an important role in securing Polish independence. British immigrants could be equally proud that they had contributed to the defense and apparent strengthening of the Empire.

But these seemingly felicitous consequences of the Great War were outweighed for many immigrants by other considerations. During the interwar period, local Jews were to become disillusioned with Britain's administration of Palestine, particularly the British decision to curtail Jewish immigration after the Nazis had begun to persecute German Jews. As in Italy, Italian-American disappointment with the peace settlement helped to lay the foundation for popular enthusiasm for the aggressive foreign policy of Italian dictator Benito Mussolini, particularly the conquest of Ethiopia in 1935–36, which inspired mass Italian nationalist demonstrations, the likes of which had not been seen since the Great War. Utica Italians, for instance, collected thirty-four pounds of gold in 1936 to help Mussolini defeat the Ethiopians and, in so doing, to defy the Powers (chiefly Great Britain) which had frustrated Italy's ambitions in 1919. The local German-American community was permanently damaged by the outburst of anti-German sentiment in 1917–18; once-strong German ethnic organizations went into decline, while societies that had been weak before 1917 soon disappeared altogether. Once hailed as patriots, Italians, Poles and other Southern and Eastern European immigrants were reviled as un-American "Reds" in 1919–20. Although the Great War resulted in apparent victories for the ancestral homelands of many immigrants, for many of Utica's ethnics the war's aftermath was bitterly disappointing indeed.[59]

NOTES

1. *Thirteenth Census of the United States*, Washington: United States Government Printing Office, 1913, 3:262–63; S. Joshua Kohn, *The Jewish Community of Utica, New York, 1847–1948* (New York: American Jewish Historical Society, 1959), 3. Regarding "Syrians": There were in Utica a number of Syrians from Aleppo and a number of Lebanese. Today, of course, the two are distinctly labelled, but at one time, because Lebanon was part of the Turkish province of Syria, the two groups were commonly referred to (even among Lebanese until the 1930s) as "Syrians."

2. Margaret MacLaren Eager, *Official Program and Book of Words of the Pageant of Utica* (Utica: Childs Print, 1914).

3. *Utica Deutsche Zeitung*, July 31, Aug. 7, 1914; *Utica Herald Dispatch*, Aug. 3, 1914; *New York Times*, Aug. 4, 1914, p. 10.

4. *Utica Sunday Tribune*, Oct. 28, 1917, p. 6. Italian-Americans seem to be especially prone to this tendency to downplay the intensity of ethnic nationalist sentiment during World War I. While historians of Polish-America are proud to recount the role played by "Polonia" in helping to liberate their fatherland, Italian-American histories have little to say about Italian nationalist agitation in Italian-America during World War I; if anything, they are quick to stress the role played by Italians in the American armed forces. See, for example, George Schiro, *Americans by Choice* (Utica: Thomas Griffiths Sons, 1940), 157; Luciano Iorizzo and Salvatore Mondello, *The Italian Americans* (Boston: Twayne Publishers, 1980), 132; Jerre Mangione and Ben Morreale, *La Storia: Five Centuries of the Italian American Experience* (New York: Harper Collins, 1992), 340. John W. Briggs's *An Italian Passage: Immigrants to Three American Cities, 1890–1930* (New Haven: Yale University Press, 1978), which also studied Utica, had nothing at all to say about World War I or nationalism despite the fact that it examined the period 1890–1930. For my criticisms of Briggs, see

"Fascism and Italian-American Identity. A Case Study: Utica, New York," *The Journal of Ethnic Studies*, 17 (1989), 101–19. In contrast to many Italian-American histories, one might consult Joseph A. Wytrwal, *Behold! The Polish-Americans* (Detroit: Endurance Press, 1977), 197–232 and Andrzej Brozek, *Polish Americans, 1854–1939* (Warsaw: Interpress, 1985), 135–47.

5. *New York Times*, Aug. 4, 1914, p. 10. See also *Utica Deutsche Zeitung*, March 9, 1917.
6. *Utica Deutsche Zeitung*, July 9, 1915.
7. Ibid., May 14, 1915.
8. "Fest Programm, Deutscher Tag. 26 Juli 1915. Veranstaltet von dem Utica'er Deutsch-Amerikanischer Bund." The translation of the inscription is mine.
9. *Utica Daily Press*, March 25, 1916, p. 5.
10. MARGARET M. O'CONNOR, ed., *James K. O'Connor—His Voice and Pen* (New York: Davis' Union Printery, 1913), 115–21.
11. *Utica Daily Observer*, March 18, 1911, p. 4.
12. *Utica Herald-Dispatch*, Feb. 1, 1916, p. 5; *Utica Daily Press*, March 25, 1916, p. 5.
13. *Utica Saturday Globe*, Sept. 21, 1918, p. 4; "Utica Home Defense Committee," (typescript, Oneida County Historical Society, Utica, 267–74 and 431). I would like to express my gratitude to Douglas Preston, director of the Oneida County Historical Society and to the staff of the society (particularly George and Beatrice White) for the generous help they have given me in this and other research projects over the years.
14. *The Cambrian*, Sept. 1, 1914, Oct. 1, 1914.
15. Ibid., Nov. 1, 1914.
16. Ibid., Jan. 15, 1915.
17. Ibid., Feb. 15, 1916.
18. Ibid., Sept. 15, 1914; Feb. 15, April 15, July 15, Nov. 15, Sept. 13, Nov. 9, 1915; May 15, 1916.
19. Ibid., Oct. 15, Dec. 1, 1914; Jan. 15, Sept. 1, 1915.
20. *Utica Saturday Globe*, March 30, 1918, p. 2 and May 4, 1918, p. 1; "Savage Arms Corporation: Utica Plant" (typescript in the Utica Home Defense Committee Papers, Oneida County Historical Society, Utica).
21. *Utica Saturday Globe*, Sept. 15, 1917, p. 2 and Jan. 5, 1918, section 2, p. 3.
22. "Jemal Pasha in Lebanon," playbill (1930).
23. *Utica Daily Press*, Jan. 25, 1916, p. 3; "Utica Home Defense Committee," 321.
24. *Utica Daily Press*, Jan. 24, 1916, pp. 3, 9.
25. Ibid., p. 9.
26. *La Luce*, April 10, 1915.
27. Ibid., May 29, 1915.
28. *Il Pensiero Italiano*, Dec. 26, 1914, May 29, 1915; *La Sentinella*, March 27, 1915.
29. *Utica Daily Press*, June 16, 1915, p. 6 and June 17, 1915, p. 3; *La Luce*, June 5, 19, 1915. Utica's experience was similar to that of other communities. By August 1915, 1,500 recruits had departed for Italy from Providence, Rhode Island, which was home to 27,000 Italians. About 1,700 Italians from Rochester (in which 11,000 Italians had settled) served in the Italian Army during World War I, which was almost equivalent to the 2,000 Rochester Italians who served in the United States armed forces in 1817–18. It has been estimated that approximately 90,000 Italians from the United States served in the Italian armed forces during World War I. See *La Luce*, Aug. 21, 1915; *Stampa Unita*, Oct. 15, 1926; Michael Musmanno, *The Story of the Italians in America* (Garden City, N.Y.: Doubleday and Company, Inc., 1965), 141.
30. *Utica Daily Press*, Aug. 11, 1916, p. 3; *Il Pensiero Italiano*, July 17, 1915; *Utica Saturday Globe*, July 10, 1915, p. 6.
31. *Utica Deutsche Zeitung*, Nov. 24, 1916.
32. Ibid., April 25, 1919.
33. "Fest Programm, Deutscher Tag, Juli 1916, Veranstaltet von dem Utica'er Deutsch-Amerikanischer Bund."
34. *Utica Deutsche Zeitung*, Oct. 13, 1916.
35. Ibid., Dec. 8, 1916; Feb. 9, 16, April 6, 1917.
36. *Utica Saturday Globe*, April 1, 1917, p. 2.
37. *Utica Deutsche Zeitung*, June 22, 1917.
38. *Utica Saturday Globe*, Nov. 17, 1918, p. 1, Feb. 9, 1918, p. 1.
39. *Utica Deutsche Zeitung*, Feb. 22, April 26, July 5, 1918. See also *Utica Observer*, Dec. 13, 1917, p. 16.

40. Paul Valentine Bacon. *Im Vaterland* (Boston: Allyn and Bacon, 1910): *Utica Saturday Globe*, Dec. 15, 1917, p. 3: *Utica Herald Dispatch*, June 29, 1918, p. 5: *Utica Deutsche Zeitung*, July 5, 1918, p. 2. Authorities in Mount Vernon, New York, voted not only to abolish German-language instruction in this period but to destroy all copies of *Im Vaterland*. See *New York Times*, July 5, 1918, p. 7. The reason for the intensification of anti-German sentiment in the summer of 1918 was probably that Americans had just witnessed Germany's frightening offensives which, we now know, were to be the last enemy offensives of the war.

41. *Utica Saturday Globe*, March 16, 1918, p. 3.

42. "Entertainment and Dance for the Benefit of the Commodore John Barry Branch of the Friends of Irish Freedom" (1920). Oneida County Historical Society, Utica.

43. *Utica Saturday Globe*, April 20, 1918, p. 3: "Utica Home Defense Committee," 279.

44. *Zlota Ksiega Czyli Piec Lat Pracy Dla Polski W Utica, N.Y.* (Utica: Utica Polish Relief Committee, 1920), 73; "Utica Home Defense Committee," 322.

45. Wytrwal, *Polish-Americans*, 217–18, 223.

46. Ibid., p. 223.

47. *Utica Observer*, Sept. 1, 1917, p. 6; *Utica Daily Press*, Sept. 3, 1917, p. 6, Oct. 22, 1917, p. 6; *Utica Saturday Globe*, March 16, 1918, section 2, p. 2.

48. *Zlota Ksiega*, 23–24; *Pamietnik Zlotego Jubileuszu Paraffi Sw. Trojcy, 1896–1946* (Utica: Parafji Sw. Trojcy, 1946); "Utica Home Defense Committee," 258–63.

49. *Utica Observer*, Aug. 12, 1919, p. 12.

50. *Il Pensiero Italiano*, Feb. 16, 1918: *La Luce e Il Pensiero Italiano*, July 21, 1917. The two rival publications. *La Luce* and the *Pensiero*, merged in 1917, but ideological differences between the editors soon destroyed this Italian patriotic cooperation.

51. *Utica Deutsche Zeitung*, July 12, 1918, Nov. 7, 1919.

52. For more details concerning the Utica strike see Philip A. Bean, "The Role of Community in the Unionization of Italian Immigrants: The Utica Textile Strike of 1919," *Ethnic Forum* 12 (1992), 36–55.

53. *Utica Observer*, Oct. 29, 1919, p. 12.

54. Ibid., Sept. 2, 1919, p. 8. *Underlining* added.

55. "Utica Home Defense Committee," 263.

56. *Utica Daily Press*, Nov. 5, 1918, p. 3; *Utica Observer*, Nov. 5, 1918, p. 4.

57. *Il Pensiero Italiano*, July 19, 1919. *Underlining* added.

58. Ibid., Nov. 9, 1918.

59. S. Joshua Kohn, *The Jewish Community of Utica, New York, 1847–1948* (New York: American Jewish Historical Society, 1959), 102; Bean, "Fascism and Italian-American identity," 101–19; Philip A. Bean, *Germans in Utica* (Utica: Utica College of Syracuse University, 1990).

■ ■ ■ ■ ■ ▬▬▬▬▬▬▬▬▬▬▬▬▬▬▬▬▬▬▬▬▬▬▬▬▬▬

A COMPARISON OF CONFIDENCE IN THE POLICE IN CHINA AND IN THE UNITED STATES

Liqun Cao
Eastern Michigan University, Ypsilanti
Charles Hou
National Taipei University, Taipei, Taiwan

Few studies, either qualitative or quantitative, have been done on public attitudes toward the police in the People's Republic of China. The "bamboo curtain" still covers China, which since 1979 has launched ambitious economic reforms but has continued to maintain restrictions on public opinion surveys on key political issues. This study analyzed a rare data set that contains information about public confidence in the police in China as well as in the

From *Journal of Criminal Justice*, 29 (2001): 87–99. Copyright © Elsevier Science Ltd. All rights reserved.

United States. The data show that the public in the U.S. has greater confidence in the police than do their Chinese counterparts. The Tiananmen incident has undoubtedly attributed to this gap, although how much is directly attributable to it cannot be determined. The study also indicated that a universal pattern of evaluating the police is emerging despite the cultural, economical, and political differences.

INTRODUCTION

Two decades of economic reforms in the People's Republic of China have transformed an internally oriented economy and underdeveloped nation into an outreaching and growing regional economic power. Despite sweeping economic changes, however, political reform has stagnated, and the Communist Party of China has maintained its monopoly over the government. The bamboo curtain, although much looser than twenty years ago, is still hanging. Surveys on public opinion were reintroduced during the reform, but sensitive information within surveys remained censored by the Communist Party. The unique data analyzed in this study offer a rare chance to examine comparative public opinion about policing and its social determinants in China and in the United States.

China was selected as the research target for this comparison mainly because of the distinct ways in which China differs from the United States. First, China is a developing country with more than half of its population working in the agricultural sector, while the U.S. is the leading developed country with less than 3 percent of its population engaging in agricultural-related work. Second, China is an East Asian culture with the religious heritages of Buddhism, Confucianism, and Taoism. In contrast, the U.S. is a Western country with a Judeo-Christian religious tradition. Third, China has a one-party political system, a tradition of centralized government, and a highly politicized and centralized police structure while the U.S. has a predominantly two-party political system, a tradition of federal government, and a multilevel and often fragmented police structure. These differences may result in public attitudes towards police in China that differ from what scholars know pertaining to Western societies.

Despite the huge differences between the two societies, the two nations also have much in common. Criminal justice systems, for example, are set up for the purpose of crime control, crime prevention being a dominant theme of the two societies. Minimizing crime and lowering crime rates are standard objectives of both police agencies. Among contemporary societies of the world, Chinese police and administration are similar to the European and Japanese styles with a centralized structure. In its bid for modernization, China has abandoned its socialist economy and has moved toward a market economy. One byproduct of the current economic reform is the increased criminal activity (Curran, 1998; Deng, Zhang, & Cordilia, 1998; Dutton, 1992; Dutton & Lee, 1993; Friday, 1998; Ren, 1997; Situ & Liu, 1996; Zhang, Messner, Lu, & Deng, 1997). To deal with a problem similar to that of the U.S., a corresponding change in crime control strategy has also occurred. The similarities in the objectives of policing and in dealing with problems they both face have provided a solid basis for a meaningful comparison.

Analyzing public opinion toward police is important because people are the consumers of police services, because positive images of the police are necessary for them to function effectively, and because public opinion has the potential to serve as the barometer of a culture's contemporary outlook on governmental institutions as a whole (Cao, Stack, & Sun, 1998). As a result, public opinion about police has been monitored closely in the United States among academia and policymakers (Benson, 1981; Brandl, Frank, Worden, & Bynum, 1994; Cao, Frank, & Cullen, 1996; Correia, Reisig, & Lovrich, 1996; Cullen et al., 1996; Dean, 1980; Decker, 1981; Dunham & Alpert, 1988; Flanagan, 1985; Scaglion & Condon, 1980; Skogan, 1978; Webb & Marshall, 1995; White & Menke, 1978; Zamble & Annesley, 1987). Whatever it is called—confidence toward the police, satisfaction with the police and trust in the police—this concept taps the public's global attitude toward the police as an institution in society. They represent a generalized support for the institution, and they constitute a reservoir of goodwill normally directed toward the institution rather than particular incumbents (Cao et al., 1998; Dennis, 1976).

Little systematic attention in criminology and criminal justice, however, has been given to *comparative* public opinions (Cao et al., 1998). Since they use functionally equivalent instruments, the results of recent surveys may provide insight into the attitudes of the public with regard to the police as an institution and into the responses of different segments of a society. The expressed attitudes may also foreshadow popular changes within a society toward the police.

Furthermore, little research has been published on Chinese public attitudes toward police, and little attention has been paid in the academic literature to the relationship between the Chinese police and the public from the viewpoint of the police clientele. Most scholars of China focus on testing Western criminological theories in China (Friday, 1998; Liu, 1996; Liu et al., 1998; Sheu, 1988; Yang & Hoffman, 1998; Zhang & Messner, 1995) or on the operation of the criminal justice system rather than on its clientele—the public (Bracey, 1989; Dutton, 1992; Jiao, 1995; Johnson, 1983; Ma, 1997; Ren, 1997; Wang, 1996). The limited English information that exists concerning the relationship between the police and the public in China is largely based on government-controlled media, observational and nonrandom data, or secondary sources.

Chinese public confidence in the police is pertinent to study because it is difficult to obtain the public's opinion about the Chinese government these days. Public confidence in the police indirectly taps the general confidence in the political apparatus as a whole (Stack & Cao, 1998). Furthermore, Chinese data from 1990 are particularly valuable because a legitimacy crisis was introduced into the Chinese political system, of which the police were a part, in the aftermath of the student movement of 1989.

The aim of this study was thus twofold. First, it addressed the research gap in comparative literature on criminology and criminal jus-

tice by quantitatively testing the hypothesis that the American public has higher confidence in their police than do the Chinese. Second, it explored whether, and if so to what extent, the social determinants of public attitudes differ in the two nations.

The hypothesis that the American public has a *higher* confidence in their police than do the Chinese is based on three considerations. First, China is a nondemocratic society based on the Soviet socialist model and Confucianist tradition. The government has made a series of mistakes since it came into power in 1949. Since it controls the media, however, it can afford to pay less attention to public opinion. In contrast, the U.S. government is a popularly elected one, based on democratic principles, and it has a long tradition of heeding grass-roots politics and public opinions. Second, the prestige of police as an occupation was rated significantly lower by residents of Beijing in China than populations of the U.S., Japan, and Taiwan according to Lin and Xie's (1988) study. Third, the 1989 Tiananmen incident, which created a legitimacy crisis in the Chinese government, may have lowered the public's evaluation of the police. Based on these considerations, this study tested this hypothesis in the multivariate analysis and control for twelve variables. These twelve variables were selected based on the previous empirical studies on attitudes toward the police (Cao et al., 1996, 1998; Carter, 1985; Correia et al., 1996; Percy, 1980; Scaglion & Condon, 1980; Stack & Cao, 1998) and on availability of current data. They were used to explore whether, and if so to what extent, the social determinants of attitudes differ in the two nations. The following section reviews the literature about the public attitudes toward the police in the two societies.

PUBLIC ATTITUDES TOWARD THE POLICE IN THE U.S.

Since the U.S. is one of the leading democratic societies in the world, a substantial body of research exists resulting from studies that have examined the dynamics of the public's satisfaction, trust, and confidence in the police. With American culture centering on the values of freedom, individualism, decentralization of authority, and "original sin" (Bellah, Madsen, Sulivan, Swidler, & Tipton, 1985; Cao et al., 1998; Rojek, 1989), the institutionalization of the police was accepted reluctantly according to a utilitarian philosophy: the police could prevent greater harm to the society than the harm they might cause. In other words, police are regarded as a "necessary evil." The responsibility of police for crime control in the U.S. is, however, constrained by law and potential liability. Their task is thus described as an "impossible mandate" (Manning, 1978). Although American citizens have deep suspicions about state power (Bayley, 1976; Lipset & Schneider, 1983), studies have shown that the public generally holds positive attitudes toward the police (Cao et al., 1996; Dean, 1980; Stack & Cao, 1998; White & Menke, 1978; Zamble & Annesley, 1987). It is also known, however, that these sentiments are not displayed equally across all sectors of the social order.

From the literature, it appears that age and conservative political ideology are generally positively related to confidence in and satisfaction with the police (Benson, 1981; Brandl et al., 1994; Cao et al., 1998; Correia et al., 1996; Percy, 1980; Stack & Cao, 1998; Zamble & Annesley, 1987). The effects of education, gender, and income on confidence in the police are mixed, however. Some have found that females, the rich, and the better educated rate the police higher than males, the poor, and the less educated; others have found that males, the less educated, and people with higher incomes are more confident than their counterparts towards the police (Benson, 1981; Brandl et al., 1994; Cao et al., 1996; Correia et al., 1996; Percy, 1980; Scaglion & Condon, 1980; Stack & Cao, 1998). Minorities in the U.S. appear to evaluate law enforcement less favorably than their majority White counterparts[1] (Albrecht & Green, 1977; Carter, 1985; Peek, Lowe, & Alston, 1981; Webb & Marshall, 1995).

PUBLIC ATTITUDES TOWARD THE POLICE IN CHINA

In contrast to the U.S., Chinese culture emphasizes collectivism, family, shame, informal codes of conduct, and respect for authority (Anderson & Gil, 1998; Grant, 1989; Ren, 1997; Troyer &

Rojek, 1989; Zhang & Messner, 1995). Under this cultural framework, law enforcement in China is sometimes perceived as repressive to the people in the West (Biddulph, 1993; Curran & Cook, 1993a; Simon, 1985). The 1989 Tiananmen incident greatly reenforced this image. Despite the impression that China is a police state, it has one of the lowest reported police-to-population ratios (Dutton & Lee, 1993; Ma, 1997). Social control is achieved largely through forced population stability and a form of culturally based "community policing." This practice of community-based social control through the use of household registration is not new to the Communist regime. The old system, called *baojia*, dates back to the Qin Dynasty (221–206 BC). The current registration called *hukou* was established in 1949. Together with Ren Shi Dang An (labor-personnel dossiers), it was very effective in controlling the static population until the current economic reform brought change (Bian, 1994; Curran, 1998; Dutton, 1992; Falkenheim, 1987; Li, 1996; Shaw, 1996; Whyte & Parish, 1984).

Chinese police rely heavily on mini-stations in urban and rural areas to control criminal activities in an area. The basic idea is similar to that of Japanese practice, but because of its socialist nature, Western scholars are more critical of it. These mini-stations are geographically arranged to coexist with the neighborhood committees and are coordinated with public security committees in the work-units within their jurisdiction. Since police officers actually live and work in a neighborhood for a long time, they become familiar with the residents (Bracey, 1989; Johnson, 1983). Police officers generally travel by foot or by bicycle. American-style motorized patrol was introduced only in the late 1980s (Jiang & Dai, 1990; Wang, 1996). The emergency number 110, equivalent to the American 911, was introduced in large cities in the same time period. After the Tiananmen incident in 1989, the police adopted the new policy of "comprehensive improvement of public order" through selectively targeting "floating populations"[2] in an effort to regain trust from the urban residents (Curran, 1998; Dutton & Lee, 1993; Jiang & Dai, 1990; Situ & Liu, 1996).

The Chinese police follow the "mass-line" in policing: they rely on work-unit security forces and neighborhood committees (Bian, 1994; Johnson, 1983; Li, 1996; Shaw, 1996; Situ & Liu, 1996; Wang, 1996; Ward, 1985; Zhang et al., 1996). As a result, police penetration into people's daily life occurs much more routinely in China than in the U.S. For example, the police are more active in service-oriented activities that are unrelated to law enforcement, such as providing legal education, counseling in mediation committees, and doing census registration. This penetration has not negatively affected the public's satisfaction with the police because neighborhood committees—duly elected neighbors and co-workers—seem to intrude more into residents' privacy than do the police. The committees seem to act as a buffer between the police and the public (Bracey, 1989). The public–police relationship is often described as harmonious and cooperative in the government-controlled media. Many scholars attribute the low crime rate in China partially to the perceived close working relationship among the police, neighborhood committees, and residents.

Compared with American police, Chinese police have greater authority and power over ordinary citizens (Biddulph, 1993; Ma, 1997; Wang, 1996). In addition to crime control functions, the police are responsible for supervising probationers and parolees. They enjoy discretionary power to apply sanctions in dealing with minor crime and public order crime without court approval. They also are entitled to confiscate property without court approval. China's reputation as a "police state" thus rests more on its greater police power than on the number of officers on the street. It seems that such police power has seldom been questioned, nor has it been reported as a source negatively affecting public satisfaction with police. Indeed, there is evidence that police flexibility in detention, although sometimes a structural form of the abuse of human rights, appeals greatly to fearful urban dwellers (Dutton & Lee, 1993).

The literature in English on the Chinese attitude toward police is scarce, unspecific, observational, and secondary. From the limited sources, it is known, for example, that the public–police relationship seems to be dubiously harmonious and cooperative (Bracey, 1989; Troyer & Rojek, 1989). There is organized support for the police in China through semi-official neighborhood committees in the urban areas. Since the police institution in China is national in design, the police carry with them the legitimatizing influence of the national government. Moreover, respect for authority is ingrained in Chinese culture. The literature seems to suggest that, as in the U.S., social support for the police in China also differs according to such social variables as age. For example, citing Wang's original study in Chinese, Curran and Cook (1993b) reported that a significantly larger percentage of the young have less confidence in the police than do their elders. Leaders of the omnipresent neighborhood committees across the country tend to be elderly, male, and supportive of the status quo, and thus of the police. More rigorous testing of these ideas is needed, however.

METHODOLOGY
The Sample
The current study employs data from China and the U.S. covered in the World Values Survey of 1991. This data collection is designed to facilitate cross-national comparisons of basic values in a wide range of concerns. The survey is based on national representative samples of the adult population in more than forty-two countries. For the current purpose, a total of 2,839 persons were selected for the analysis (1,839 Americans and 1,000 Chinese). Excluding those who were not born in the United States or China and who lived fewer than fifteen years in the U.S. or China, the final sample contains information on 998 Chinese and 1,791 Americans. The American survey was conducted by Gallup Poll during May and June 1990 while the Chinese data were collected by Jiang Xingrong and Xiang Zongde of the China Statistical Information Center during July and December 1990.[3] For a further discussion of the survey, see World Values Study Group (1994).

This data collection was designed for comparative studies. The wording of the questions, answer categories, and sequencing are identical in all languages, including English and Chinese. The survey is one of the most cross-culturally comparable datasets on values and attitudes in existence. Schafer's (1997) Norm was used to handle the missing data[4] of all the independent variables. With the largest missing data being education (about 11 percent), the Norm generated all missing data for the regression analyses. Further checkup analyses without including these missing data did not seem to alter significantly the currently reported results.[5]

The Dependent Variable
The dependent variable, confidence in the police, was measured by the item: "How much confidence do you have in the police: Is it a great deal, quite a lot, not very much, or none at all?" Respondents could choose from 1 = a lot, 2 = quite a lot, 3 = not very much, 4 = not at all. The order of the answers was reversed in this study so that the higher score would indicate the higher confidence in the police: 4 = a lot, 3 = quite a lot, 2 = not very much, and 1 = not at all. Thus, the original scale was subtracted from 5 to form a new scale where 1 = low confidence to 4 = high confidence in the police. A limitation was that the dependent variable is measured in terms of a single item of a global attitude. The global attitudes, however, have been reported to be highly correlated with and predictive of specific attitudes (Frank et al., 1996).

The Independent Variables
The major independent variable, nation, was a binary variable with 0 = China and 1 = the United States. In addition, variables that could confound the relationship between the global attitude toward the police and the effect of the nation were included as control variables in the multivariate analyses. These variables were classified into three groups: demographic variables, social bond variables, and a group of attitudinal variables thought to be predictive of confidence in the police.

Demographic Variables
Four demographic controls were included in the analysis. Age was measured as the respondent's actual age in years at the time of the survey. Aging is generally a process that promotes conservatism and integration into the institutional

order. Ethnicity was coded as 1 = Whites in the U.S. and Han nationality in China, and 0 = all other minority groups in both countries. Education was assessed with the available data in the survey as an ordinal variable, where 1 = low (did not complete high school), and 10 = high (graduate degree or more). Gender was measured using a dummy variable where female = 0 and male = 1. It was expected that the younger, the more educated, males, and minorities are less confident in the police.

Social Bond Variables
Bonds to existing social institutions that might support the status quo were measured in the following manner: (1) employment status was measured as a binary variable where 1 = employed full-time and the retired; 0 = all others; (2) income as an ordinal variable, where 1 = low in local currency and 10 = high in local currency; (3) marriage as a dummy variable where 1 = married and widowed; 0 = all other nonmarital statuses; and (4) parenting, as a binary variable where 1 = reports having had at least one child and 0 = no children. Cao et al. (1998) noticed that the relationship between social bonds and attitudes toward the police has been largely neglected in the literature. Zhang and Messner (1995) and Ren (1997) found that family is a key in understanding juvenile delinquency in China. This study further tested this linkage with the Chinese audience. It was expected that those being employed, those with higher income, those being married, and those with children are more confident in the police.

Attitudinal Variables
Four attitudinal variables were included in the analysis. First, deviant subculture, which is an index of the acceptance of criminal behavior, was formed from seven attitudinal measures in the survey. It was contended that persons who are less willing to accept the legal order will tend to have a negative view of its enforcers, the police, as well. The seven items all have the same lead-in question: "Please tell me for each of the following statements whether you think it can always be justified, never be justified, or something in between: (1) claiming government ben-

efits which you are not entitled to, (2) avoiding a fare on public transport, (3) cheating on tax if you have the chance, (4) buying something you knew was stolen, (5) someone accepting a bribe in the course of their duties, (6) fighting with the police, (7) failing to report damage you've done accidentally to a parked vehicle." The responses range from 1 = never through 10 = always. The index of the deviant subculture was calculated as the sum of the seven items. The reliability of this index was .77. The distribution of the index variable is marked by a problem of skewness. It was treated with a log transformation to address this problem accordingly.[6]

Second, alienation was measured as: "During the past few weeks, did you ever feel (1) very lonely or remote from other people, (2) bored, (3) depressed or very unhappy?" The respondent's options are from 1 = no to 2 = yes. The index of alienation was calculated as the sum of the three items.[7] The Cronbach alpha of the measure was .61. Third, belief in the social system was assessed with three items tapping the respondents' trust in education, in the legal system, and in the social security system: how much confidence you have in each of the institutions?[8] The responses ranged from 4 = a great deal to 1 = not at all. The index of belief was calculated as the sum of the three items. The Cronbach alpha of the index was .60.

Finally, an index of personal satisfaction was created with three items on general satisfaction and happiness in life through a principal components analysis. (1) Happiness: (reverse coded): "Taking all things considered, would you say you are 1 = not at all happy, 2 = not very happy, 3 = quite happy, 4 = very happy." (2) Financial satisfaction: "How satisfied are you with the financial situation of your household?" 1 = dissatisfied through 10 = satisfied; (3) overall satisfaction: "All things considered, how satisfied are you with your life as a whole these days?" 1 = dissatisfied through 10 = satisfied. Since the scales of these three items were not the same, the standardized scores of each item were used to form the index variable. The Cronbach alpha of the measure was .59. It was argued that persons' responses to confidence with such social institutions as the police may be a function of a more

basic personal satisfaction with their lives as a whole. It was thus expected that confidence in the police is negatively associated with deviant subculture and alienation, and positively associated with belief and satisfaction.

ANALYSIS

The mean score of confidence in the police is 2.93 in America, a figure higher than that for China, 2.80. As expected, this difference in mean scores is statistically significant.

In addition, the two nations differ significantly in four demographic variables, with China being higher in the percentage of male respondents (66 percent in China vs. 50 percent in the U.S.) and of the majority ethnic group (92 percent vs. 85 percent), and with Americans being older (47 vs. 39) and having more years of education (7.79 vs. 7.03). The two nations also differ in two of the social bond variables, with more Chinese in marriage and with more Americans having relatively higher income. There is, however, no statistically significant difference between the two nations in terms of percentages having at least one child and of employment status.

It is also interesting to note the differences in the patterns of missing data. It seems that Chinese are more reluctant to reveal their attitudes toward the police than are their American counterparts, while Americans are more unwilling to report their age and income, and more ambiguous about their gender and ethnicity than Chinese. None of these differences seems to be surprising, and they may be only the tips of the iceberg due to the political, cultural, and developmental factors expected from the two countries. The categories in marital statuses have no missing data in either society.

Using multiple regression analyses, the results for the pooled sample include both American and Chinese respondents. Controlling for the other variables in the equation, Chinese respondents continue to show less confidence in the police than Americans. In addition, the older they are, the more confident people in both countries are toward the police. Ethnic dominating groups in both nations have greater confidence in the police. The less educated and married persons have more confidence in the police than do the better educated and unmarried people. The rest of the demographic and social-bonding variables are not significant. The finding that the Chinese people have less confidence in the police than American people could still be spurious. In order to test this possibility, more controls for the attitudinal variables are added to the equation.

Controlling for the other independent variables, Chinese respondents still have significantly less confidence in the police than do Americans. The coefficient is eleven times its standard errors. Ethnicity and marriage continue to be significant with the majority groups and the married in both nations showing more confidence towards the police, while the effects of age and education become insignificant. Higher scores in the deviant subculture index and in alienation reduce significantly confidence in the police, while higher scores in belief and in satisfaction in life increase it significantly. From the standardized coefficients, belief, nation, and deviant subculture are the three variables most closely associated with the variance of confidence in the police. The complete model explains 21.5 percent of the variance in confidence in the police.

Finally, two equations were developed to analyze data separately for the two nations. Controlling for the other variables in the equation, the leading correlate of confidence in the police is belief. As expected, the more confidence one has in the social institutions, the greater the confidence he/she has in the police. Deviant subculture is the second most important determinant, and satisfaction in life trails at the end. Alienation is not significantly associated with confidence in the police. None of the demographic and social bonding variables is significantly related to the attitudes towards the police in China. The model as a whole explains approximately 28 percent of the variance in Chinese confidence in the police.

As in the case of China, respondents' belief and satisfaction in life are positively related to confidence in the police, and subculture is negatively related to the confidence in the police, and alienation is not significantly associated

with attitudes towards the police. Unlike in China, however, ethnicity and marriage in the U.S. are also significantly related to attitudes toward the police. Whites in America show greater confidence in the police than other ethnic and racial groups, and so do married as compared to unmarried people. The rest of the demographic and social-bonding variables in the equation are not statistically significant. The model explains 18 percent of the variance in American confidence in the police.

DISCUSSION

Public confidence in the police is not a simple attitudinal issue. It is a political matter concerning the public image and political legitimacy of a leading governmental institution. This is much more so in China than in the United States. A ruling political party like the Chinese Communist Party has claimed its legitimacy to rule on the basis of ideological infallibility and behavioral rectitude. This party would not allow itself to be tarred with the "lost mandate" to rule or even with an implication of diminishing legitimacy to rule.

Previous research on the police–public relationship in China has been based largely within China. This work has generally built an image of popular support and confidence of the Chinese people in their police. There has been a dearth of survey research to test this general assertion cross-nationally, however. The present study helps to fill this gap in the research. An analysis of data taken from the 1990 World Values Survey suggests that indeed the Chinese have less confidence in their police than do Americans. This effect holds true even after introducing a number of controls in the multiple regression analyses.

This study represents an initial effort in exploring the quantitative differences in attitudes toward the police between the Chinese and Americans. As such, the finding must be viewed as preliminary, and as constrained by a particular timing. The World Values Survey itself was not specifically designed for criminologists to investigate public confidence in the police. Consequently, the unidimensional item of the global attitude toward the police may not be specific enough given the complex nature of public attitude toward the police in cross-national comparison. At the same time, many salient variables that might have been controlled are not in the survey. For example, the key cultural differences between the two nations in the area of crime control—shame and collectivism—are not well captured. Future studies need to address these issues more rigorously.

Timing is another consideration, since public opinion is highly sensitive to big events (Rae, 1940). The survey in China was done a little more than one year after the Tiananmen incident, and it is not clear to what extent the observed confidence gap between the U.S. and China is directly attributable to this event. It seems that a gap may have always been there, as Lin and Xie's (1988) occupational prestige study indicated before the incident. Although the Chinese police showed great restraint during the student movement and were not directly involved in the crackdown on demonstrations, they certainly played a critical role in hunting the popular student leaders afterwards. The relatively low level of public confidence in the police may well be the extension of the low level of public confidence in the regime in general. The effect of significant events on public opinion is well documented in the U.S. According to Maguire, Pastore, and Flanagan 1993, p. 173, there was a fourfold increase in perception of police brutality after the televised videotaped beating of motorist Rodney King on March 3, 1991, in comparison to the number of affirmative responses to the same survey item in 1965. "Do you think there is any police brutality in your area, or not?"

The fact that the survey in China passed the censorship and was permitted, however, is a sign of renewed openness and progress on the part of the Chinese government after the 1989 incident. It may also indicate a degree of confidence from the government in its ability to regain its legitimacy. There is some evidence indeed that urban dwellers have recovered some of their confidence in the police with respect to controlling crime (Dutton & Lee, 1993).

In spite of these limitations, the current data do have an advantage: data in both countries are comparable, and the survey instrument is the same internationally. Since the World Values Survey has been translated into at least two dozen different languages and has been used for years to compare the core values in different languages and cultures, it is reasonable to accept its functional validity in Chinese and in English. At the least, some evidence exists to conclude that the difference in the level of confidence in the police is not an artifact of translation. Additional results from this analysis, such as deviant subculture and belief, enhance confidence in the validity of the findings in this domain.

The present analyses offered some other thought-provoking findings. First, the huge differences between the two nations in terms of political and legal systems, economic structures, and cultures have not translated into a difference in social determinants of confidence in the police. Three commonalities—deviant subculture, belief, and satisfaction in life—are found to be significant predictors of confidence in the police in both nations. Those who are deeply involved with the subculture of deviance show less confidence in the police, and those who show confidence in other social institutions and who are satisfied with their lives demonstrate higher confidence in the police. These findings provide evidence that confidence in the police is a derivative of the status quo and of a larger value system and reflects the political orientation in these two very different societies. They add one more piece of documentation that a trend toward a universal pattern of public opinion is emerging in various contemporary societies (Cao et al., 1998; Stack & Cao, 1998), transcending the cultural, economic, and political boundaries.

Second, this study also revealed that some specific determinants of attitudes toward the police differ in the two societies. Ethnicity predicts confidence in the police in America, but not in China. The findings that ethnic minorities in the U.S. have lower confidence in the police than do whites is consistent with previous findings in the U.S. on the relationship (Albrecht & Green, 1977; Carter, 1985; Correia et al., 1996; Peek et al., 1981; Webb & Marshall, 1995). In contrast, the same relationship is not significant in China, and even the sign points in the opposite direction. China consists of fifty-five officially recognized nationalities, and these nationalities do not share the same language or culture. Tension between the dominant group Han and other nationalities and among different nationalities is not new or latent. It is obvious that the Survey was not translated into any other ethnic-minority languages in China. It is therefore possible to conclude that the observed relationship in China may only reflect minority and majority relationships in the Han-dominated areas.

Furthermore, married people in the U.S. are more confident in the police than are those in other household arrangements, while the effect of marriage is not significant and in the opposite direction. Interestingly, the insignificant and negative effect of marriage found in the Chinese sample is consistent with the results in Cao et al.'s 1998 research on Japanese attitudes toward the police. It is possible that social bonds might influence a person's attitudes in a different way in a communitarian society like China and Japan (Anderson & Gil, 1998; Zhang et al., 1996). Future studies are needed to investigate these effects of the differentiation.

China has been undertaking a rapid economic transformation, which, in turn, affects changes in every aspect of social life. Despite the Communist Party's resistance to political change, and despite the impatience of the political dissidents, there is evidence that slow but steady changes have been introduced into the political system, of which the legal system is a part. Legal reform, which has arisen less out of system need, has emerged from a reluctant recognition from the government that greater foreign business and commerce would be stymied without it. The situation is adequately described as "the structural strains of China's socio-legal system" (Li, 1996). The interplay of developmental, cultural, and ideological factors has significantly complicated the understanding of the Chinese criminal justice system. Any effort that overemphasize one factor over the other or ignore any one of the factors are doomed to produce shallow scholarship.

The public-opinion literature that emerged in China since 1980 is beginning to mature and provide greater details and insights into public attitudes behind the "bamboo curtain." Although this study was exploratory in nature and the conclusions were tentative, it helps build a quantitative literature on the police in China and set a quantitative baseline for future comparison in this area. Hopefully, it will also stimulate more research in the future.

NOTES

1. A recent study, however, found that in Detroit African Americans are more satisfied with the police than Whites (Frank, Brandl, Cullen, & Stichman, 1996).
2. "Floating populations" or "transient populations" refer to surplus rural laborers who have moved into urban areas since 1979 in search of better opportunities, violating the household registration that a person cannot change their place of residence without prior government approval.
3. Although both national random and quota sampling were used, it was acknowledged that the populations of India, China, and Nigeria, as well as rural areas and the illiterate population, were undersampled.
4. Multiple imputation is a simulation-based approach to the statistical analysis of incomplete data (Schafer, 1997). In multiple imputation, each missing datum is replaced by $m > 1$ simulated values. The resulting m versions of the complete data can then be analyzed by standard complete-data methods, and the results combined to produce inferential statements (e.g., interval estimates or P-values) that incorporate missing-data uncertainty.
5. All directions of correlation coefficients have the same signs, and all variables, significant or insignificant, remain the same. The magnitude of some coefficients changes, however. The results of these analyses are available upon request.
6. After log transformation, the skewness for the index of the deviant subculture is .63 for the sample. Elsewhere this measure was labeled as anomie (Cao, 1999).
7. The item tapping directly the concept of alienation was dropped from the 1990

Survey and the newly created index of emotional alienation substitutes for the original concept of alienation.

8. The 1990 Survey in China did not ask the question about the political ideology among Chinese. The general trust in the existing social institutions is supposed to tap the similar concept of the respondents' ideology in support of the status quo.

REFERENCES

ALBRECHT, S. L., & GREEN, M. (1977). Attitudes toward the police and the larger attitude complex: implications for police—community relationships. *Criminology, 15,* 67–86.

ANDERSON, A. F., & GIL, V. E. (1998). China's modernization and the decline of communitarianism: the control of sex crimes and implications for the fate of informal social control. *Journal of Contemporary Criminal Justice, 14,* 248–261.

BAYLEY, D. H. (1976). *Forces of order: policing modern Japan.* Berkeley, CA: Univ. California Press.

BELLAH, R., MADSEN, R., SULLIVAN, W. M., SWIDLER, A., & TIPTON, S. M. (1985). *Habits of the heart.* New York: Harper & Row.

BENSON, P. R. (1981). Political alienation and public satisfaction with police services. *Pacific Sociological Review, 24,* 45–64.

BIAN, Y. (1994). *Work and inequality in urban China.* Berkeley: State University of California.

BIDDULPH, S. (1993). Review of police powers of administrative detention in the People's Republic of China. *Crime and Delinquency, 39* (3), 337–354.

BRACEY, D. H. (1989). Policing the People's Republic. In: R. J. Troy, J. P. Clark, & D. G. Rojek (Eds.), *Social control in the People's Republic of China* (pp. 131–140). New York: Praeger.

BRANDL, S. G., FRANK, J., WORDEN, R., & BYNUM, T. (1994). Global and specific attitudes toward the police. *Justice Quarterly, 11,* 119–134.

CAO, L. (1999). A test of anomie theory with cross-national data. Paper presented at the 1999 Annual Meeting of American Society of Criminology, Toronto, Canada.

CAO, L., FRANK, J., & CULLEN, F. T. (1996). Race, community context, and confidence in the police. *American Journal of Police, 15* (1), 3–22.

CAO, L., STACK, S. J., & SUN, Y. (1998). Public confidence in the police: a comparative study between Japan and America. *Journal of Criminal Justice, 26* (4), 279–289.

CARTER, D. L. (1985). Hispanic perception of police performance: an empirical assessment. *Journal of Criminal Justice, 13,* 487–500.

CORREIA, M. E., REISIG, M. D., & LOVRICH, N. P. (1996). Public perceptions of state police: an analysis of individual-level and contextual variables. *Journal of Criminal Justice, 24,* 17–28.

CULLEN, F. T., CAO, L., FRANK, J., LANGWORTHY, R.H., BROWNING, S. L., KOPACHE, R., & STEVENSON, S. (1996). "Stop or I'll shoot": racial differences in support for police use of deadly force. *American Behavioral Scientist, 39,* 449–460.

CURRAN, D. J. (1998). Economic reform, the floating population, and crime: the transformation of social control in China. *Journal of Contemporary Criminal Justice, 14,* 262–280.

CURRAN, D. J., & COOK, S. (1993a). Introduction. *Crime and Delinquency, 39,* 275–276.

CURRAN, D. J., & COOK, S. (1993b). Growing fears, rising crime: juvenile and China's justice system. *Crime and Delinquency, 39,* 296–315.

DEAN, D. (1980). Citizen ratings of the police: the difference police contact makes. *Law and Policy Quarterly, 2,* 445–471.

DECKER, S. H. (1981). Citizen attitudes toward the police. *Journal of Police Science and Administration, 9* (1), 80–87.

DENG, X., ZHANG, L., & CORDILIA, A. (1998). Social control and recidivism in China. *Journal of Contemporary Criminal Justice, 14,* 281–295.

DENNIS, J. (1976). Who supports the presidency? *Society, 13* (5), 48–53.

DUNHAM, R., & ALPERT, G. (1988). Neighborhood differences in attitudes toward policing: evidence for a mixed-strategy model of policing in a multi-ethnic setting. *The Journal of Criminal Law and Criminology, 79,* 504–521.

DUTTON, M. R. (1992). *Policing and punishment in China.* London: Cambridge Univ. Press.

DUTTON, M. R., & LEE, T. (1993). Missing the target? Police strategies in the period of economic reform. *Crime and Delinquency, 39* (3), 316–336.

FALKENHEIM, V. C. (1987). *Citizens and groups in contemporary China.* Ann Arbor: Univ. Michigan Press.

FLANAGAN, T. J. (1985). Consumer perspectives on police operational strategy. *Journal of Police Science and Administration, 13,* 10–21.

FRANK, J., BRANDL, S., CULLEN, F. T., & STICHMAN, A. (1996). Reassessing the impact of race on citizens' attitudes toward the police: a research note. *Justice Quarterly, 13,* 321–334.

FRIDAY, P. (1998). Crime and crime prevention in China: a challenge to the development-crime nexus. *Contemporary Criminal Justice, 14,* 296–314.

GRANT, G. (1989). The family and social control: traditional and modern. In: R. J. Troy, J. P. Clark, & D. G. Rojek (Eds.), *Social control in the People's Republic of China* (pp. 17–25). New York: Praeger.

JIANG, B., & DAI, Y. (1990). Mobilize all possible social forces to strengthen public security—a must for crime prevention. *Police Studies, 13* (1), 1–9.

JIAO, A. Y. (1995). Community policing and community mutuality: a comparative analysis of American and Chinese police reforms. *Police Studies, 18* (3/4), 69–91.

JOHNSON, E. H. (1983). Neighborhood police in the People's Republic of China. *Police Studies, 6,* 8–21.

LI, J. (1996). The structural strains of China's socio-legal system: a transition to formal legalism. *International Journal of the Sociology of Law, 24,* 41–59.

LIN, N., & XIE, W. (1988). Occupational prestige in urban China. *American Journal of Sociology, 93,* 793–832.

LIPSET, S. M., & SCHNEIDER, W. (1983). *The confidence gap: business, labor, and government in the public mind.* New York: The Free Press.

LIU, J., ZHOU, D., LISKA, A. E., MESSNER, S. F., KROHN, M. D., ZHANG, L., & LU, Z. (1998). Status, power, and sentencing in China. *Justice Quarterly, 15,* 289–300.

LIU, W. (1996). Delinquency potentiality among Chinese high school students: a control theory perspective. In: J. Hu, Z. Hong, & E. Stavrou (Eds.), *In search of a Chinese road towards modernization* (pp. 270–293). Lewiston, NY: The Edwin Mellen Press.

MA, Y. (1997). The police law 1995; organization, functions, powers and accountability of the Chinese police. *Policing, 20* (1), 113–135.

MANNING, P. (1978). The police: mandate, strategies, and appearances. In: P. Manning, & J. Van Maanen (Eds.), *Policing: a view from the street* (pp. 7–31). Santa Monica, CA: Goodyear Publishing.

MAGUIRE, K., PASTORE, A. L., & FLANAGAN T. J. (Eds.) (1993). *Bureau of Justice Statistics Sourcebook of Criminal Justice Statistics—1992.* Washington, DC: U.S. Government Printing Office.

PEEK, C. W., LOWE, G. D., & ALSTON, J. P. (1981). Race and attitudes toward local police. *Journal of Black Studies, 11,* 361–374.

PERCY, S. L. (1980). Response time and citizen evaluation of police. *Journal of Police Science and Administration, 8,* 75–86.

RAE, S. F. (1940). Public opinion survey. *Public Opinion Quarterly,* 75–76 (March).

REN, X. (1997). *Tradition of the law and law of the tradition: law, state and social control in China.* Westport, CT: Greenwood.

ROJEK, D. G. (1989). Confucianism, Maoism and the coming of delinquency to China. In: R.J. Troy, J. P. Clark, & D. G. Rojek (Eds.), *Social control in the People's Republic of China* (pp. 84–96). New York: Praeger.

SCAGLION, R., & CONDON, R. G. (1980). Determinants of attitudes toward city police. *Criminology, 17,* 485–494.

SCHAFER, J. L. (1997). *Analysis of incomplete multivariate data.* New York: Chapman & Hall.

SHAW, V. (1996). *Social control in China: a study of Chinese work units.* Westport, CT: Praeger.

SHEU, C. (1988). Juvenile delinquency in the Republic of China: a Chinese empirical study of social control theory. *International Journal of Comparative and Applied Criminal Justice, 12,* 59–72.

SIMON, R. J. (1985). A trip to China. *Justice Quarterly, 2,* 99–101.

SITU, Y., & LIU, W. (1996). Restoring the neighborhood, fighting against crime: a case study in Guangzhou city, PRC. *International Criminal Justice Review, 6,* 89–102.

SKOGAN, W. G. (1978). Citizen satisfaction with police services: individual and contextual effects. *Police Studies Journal,* 469–479 (special issue).

STACK, S. J., & CAO, L. (1998). Political conservatism and confidence in the police: a comparative analysis. *Journal of Crime and Justice, XXI* (1), 71–76.

TROYER, R. J., & ROJEK, D. G. (1989). Introduction. In: R.J. Troy, J. P. Clark, & D. G. Rojek (Eds.), *Social control in the People's Republic of China* (pp. 3–10). New York: Praeger.

WANG, Z. (1996). The police system in the People's Republic of China. In: O. N. I. Ebbe (Ed.), *Comparative and international criminal justice systems* (pp. 155–167). Boston: Butterworth.

WARD, R. H. (1985). The police in China. *Justice Quarterly, 2,* 111–115.

WEBB, V. J., & MARSHALL, C. E. (1995). The relative importance of race and ethnicity on citizen attitudes toward the police. *American Journal of Police, 14* (2), 45–66.

WHITE, M. F., & MENKE, B. A. (1978). A critical analysis of surveys on public opinions toward police agencies. *Journal of Police Science and Administration, 6,* 204–218.

WHYTE, M. K., & PARISH, W. L. (1984). *Urban life in contemporary China.* Chicago: Univ. Chicago Press.

World Values Study Group. (1994). *World values surveys 1991.* Ann Arbor: ICPSR.

YANG, S., & HOFFMAN, J. P. (1998). A multilevel assessment of social disorganization theory in Taipei, Taiwan. *Journal of Contemporary Criminal Justice, 14,* 222–247.

ZAMBIE, E., & ANNESLEY, P. (1987). Some determinants of pubic attitudes toward the police. *Journal of Police Science and Administration, 15,* 285–290.

ZHANG, L., & MESSNER, S. F. (1995). Family deviance and delinquency in China. *Criminology, 33,* 359–387.

ZHANG, L., MESSNER, S. F., LU, Z., & DENG, X. (1997). Gang crime and its punishment in China. *Journal of Criminal Justice, 25,* 289–302.

ZHANG, L., ZHOU, D., MESSNER, S. F., LISKA, A., KHRON, M., LIU, J., & LU, Z. (1996). Strategies of community crime prevention in a communitarian society: 'Bang-Jiao' and 'Tiao-Jie' in the People's Republic of China. *Justice Quarterly, 13,* 199–222.

COMMENTARY ON THE READINGS

These two articles are very different in several ways, and show the great diversity found in historical comparative research methods.

Philip Bean examines the reaction of different immigrant groups in Utica to World War I by discussing the historical context leading up to the war. In this way, Bean places the local community into a wider global context. He also discusses the fact that Utica was similar to many other industrial cities in the United States at that time, especially in having a large immigrant population from countries all over Europe. Bean's account of the experiences of nationalism in Utica is thus meant to illuminate not only nationalism in Utica itself, but in American cities more generally. The specific comparison that he is making is between the various ethnic groups within the city.

As in all case studies, the specifics of "The Great War and Ethnic Nationalism in Utica, 1914–1920" cannot be generalized to all American cities. For instance, not all American cities had large Polish-American or ethnic Welsh populations like the proportions found in Utica. However, the inability to generalize specific aspects of the study is also a testimony to the detail that Bean is able to convey. A more general study would not have been able to capture the specific dynamics found in Utica, New York. In this sense, an historical case study is a tradeoff: in exchange for detail, generalizability is sacrificed. However, the case of Utica does bring out trends that were likely found in other northeastern cities despite the fact that the exact manifestation of those trends is not generalizable.

Liqun Cao and Charles Hou have written a very different study. In most respects, this comparison of confidence in the police between the United States and China resembles any other example of secondary data analysis. The researchers utilize data collected from the World Values Survey of 1991 because it uses "functionally equivalent instruments." The purpose of the research was to use the public's confidence in the police as an indicator of the public's confidence in the political system as a whole. The major concern in the survey was to construct a survey that could collect data on a variety of cultures and ensure that the measures are valid and reliable across each culture. The survey itself, however, was conducted specifically to collect comparative data so that researchers like Cao and Hou could analyze the data at a later time. The actual comparative analysis is highly statistical, and there is little historical context to the study. This is typical of research with a purely comparative orientation.

An interesting feature of "A Comparison of Confidence in the Police in China and in the United States" is its use of perception of the police as an indicator for wider social perceptions of the governments of the two countries. While not all comparative studies use their findings as indicators of broader trends, it is a feature of many such studies.

CONCLUSION

Historical comparative research is a big tent that houses many diverse approaches to research. What they all share is the intent to compare the experiences of various units of analysis to others, whether they be individual cities, ethnic groups within a city, or different nations.

CHAPTER 9

FIELDWORK

Fieldwork is a collection of purely qualitative methods. It involves an active engagement with the research subjects and relies on social interaction between the researcher and those who are being researched. This process gives fieldwork advantages and disadvantages when compared to other methods. It also raises unique practical and ethical issues.

PARTICIPANT OBSERVATION

Fieldwork is sometimes called participant observation, and for good reason. The researcher is certainly a participant in the social life of those studied, and much of the work is conducted through observation. In general, a fieldwork project will include both interviews and immersion in the group being studied. Most researchers also triangulate the results with other sources of data in order to place the research in the wider context of the community, world, and time period.

Early examples of fieldwork in American sociology were conducted by the faculty and students at the University of Chicago. During the early twentieth century, researchers went into city neighborhoods conducting interviews, collecting life histories, and participating in group activities. The result was a series of detailed descriptions of social life in such early classics as *The Hobo* (Anderson, 1923), which described life among migrant men. Early Chicago School research was also limited by this approach—there was little theoretical development and little attempt to analyze what was found.

After World War II, the Chicago School refined participant observation as a sophisticated technique informed by interactionist theories. Researchers would study people in their own environments by interacting directly with them. For instance, when Howard Becker (1991 [1963]) sought to study marijuana users during the 1950s, he did not survey anyone or read police reports. He hung out in jazz clubs in Chicago, interviewing participants and observing users in a natural setting. What emerged was *Outsiders*, the book in which Becker outlined the foundation of labeling theory and the social learning model—and revolutionized the study of deviant behavior.

What has developed during the past fifty years are two distinct traditions of fieldwork: ethnography and ethnomethodology.

Ethnography is the tradition that developed out of the work of the Chicago School sociologists and researchers in anthropology. Ethnography is informed by the interactionist paradigm but has a philosophy of its own. The goal is to understand the behaviors and attitudes of people from the perspective of those studied. Ethnographers recognize that there are multiple levels of meaning in an interaction or symbol and that research requires not only a sound description but also an analysis of data that seeks to understand the meaning behind people's actions.

The knowledge of the meaning of particular behaviors falls into two categories: explicit and tacit (Neuman, 2000). Explicit knowledge is that which is known to the participants. A high school swim meet, for instance, includes a number of known facts: that swimmers will race the freestyle, back, breast, and butterfly strokes, for instance. But the swim meet also includes tacit knowledge, knowledge that is not obvious to participants. Knowledge of how close to stand to other swimmers in between races, for instance, is known to meet participants but is most often not acknowledged. Violation of such a norm would elicit a negative response, but most participants would not recognize the existence of such a norm without being specifically asked.

In order to convey the layers of meaning and knowledge found in a social setting, ethnographers employ what anthropologist Clifford Geertz (1973) referred to as "thick description." Behaviors and events are discussed in amazing detail; even a seemingly trivial event in a local diner might warrant several pages of description. The appearance of the diner's interior, the history of certain artifacts, the personalities of the patrons, the relationships among them, the wider context of the event—all of these elements and more may be relevant to understanding the social setting.

Ethnomethodology, in contrast, focuses instead on how meaning is created by the participants in social interaction. Compared to ethnography, ethnomethodologists are more concerned with micro data—recordings of short conversations, social interactions, and the like. Ethnomethodology assumes that meaning is shaped and constructed through social interaction and thus the goal can be said to be the quest of the social construction of common sense. For all the times we have heard of one sports team "killing" another, we can be thankful that the literal words are not the actual meaning of the phrase. Herbert Garfinkel (1967), for example, would question the meaning of everyday expressions. He found that people use numerous terms that impart a meaning only distantly related to the literal meaning of the words spoken. Consider the following statement made to a man's wife:

> Dana succeeded in putting a penny in a parking meter today without being picked up (25).

Garfinkel revealed the hidden meanings and assumptions in the preceding statement, and translated it as:

> This afternoon as I was bringing Dana, our four-year-old son, home from nursery school, he succeeded in reaching high enough to put a penny in a parking meter when

we parked in a meter zone, whereas he had always had to be picked up to reach that high (25).

Like Garfinkel, ethnomethodologists seek out these other levels of meaning and the processes that produce them.

STEPS IN FIELDWORK

Fieldwork requires a considerable amount of preparation. Contrary to the image of Hollywood movies such as *Raiders of the Lost Ark*, a fieldworker needs to take several steps before and during data collection.

Preparation

Like most research techniques the researcher begins by conducting a thorough literature review. This enables the researcher to begin research with an idea of what others have found. Much fieldwork is conducted as grounded theory. Although other theories are reviewed, it is important to keep an open mind in the unique setting of a fieldwork study. Fieldwork also requires a considerable amount of additional preparation prior to entering the field. The site of the fieldwork needs to be chosen and any relevant background information needs to be collected. For instance, fieldwork in a rural town would require not just the choice of an appropriate community, but a complete background check of basic demographic variables (age, race, income, etc.), the history of the town, and its relationship to other communities both locally and globally.

Entrance

Entrance to a site is perhaps the most crucial component of fieldwork. A good impression in the beginning can open doors months later by helping the researcher to gain the trust of those being studied. Of course, a negative impression can also have lasting effects, possibly even making it impossible for the research to continue.

The researcher needs to be conscious of the fact that he or she is as much of an actor in the social setting as everybody else. In order to understand those in the field, the researcher needs to develop a deep understanding of his or her own social status. One's race, social class, institutional affiliations, even the status of "researcher" influences how the researcher perceives herself or himself. It is important to be sensitive to these issues because (1) they are potential sources of bias, (2) they influence how the researcher interacts with others, and (3) they influence how others perceive the researcher.

The role the researcher is to take during fieldwork needs to be understood prior to collecting data. The objectivist approach requires that the researcher attempt to be an impartial observer of events. Although it is not possible to avoid influencing events, objectivist researchers attempt to minimize the impact of their presence on those being studied. For instance, Janet Fitchen (1991) studied communities in upstate New

York by conducting interviews over a period of years but was careful to try not to significantly alter the events she was studying.

The objectivist model has been criticized on the basis that the people being studied are "objects" of study, and as such their humanity has been minimized. An alternative to the objectivist approach is participatory action research, where the researcher actively participates in the social lives of the research subjects by acting as a resource for social change. Such research is typically conducted with the researcher taking on the role of a resource to the people being studied. Often, research subjects help to craft the research goals as they and the researcher attempt to change their circumstances. Linda Ames and Jeanne Ellsworth (1997) studied women's participation in Head Start programs in upstate New York. In contrast to Janet Fitchen, the researchers took an active role in trying to give rural women a greater voice in the administration of Head Start programs.

The two approaches differ significantly in their approach to the issue of *disclosure*, the practice of informing research subjects of the research project. The level of disclosure ranges from *covert*, research in which the subjects are unaware that they are being studied, to *overt*, research in which all subjects are aware of the purpose and aims of the research. The level of disclosure varies by the nature of the project. In a study of drug dealers, for instance, the researcher may be more covert because subjects may be wary of researchers in their midst. Full disclosure of the research may jeopardize the research either by directly endangering the researcher or by subjects censoring themselves in the researcher's presence. It is fair to say, however, that most field researchers agree that some level of disclosure is warranted, even if it does create some early setbacks. Discovery of the research by subjects could destroy the project. Disclosure is also an ethical issue (see Chapter 3): Research subjects are people and as such have the right to know the intentions of the researcher. The level of disclosure is of particular concern in objectivist research, since participatory action research is by its nature fully overt. To take an active role in changing peoples' lives, the researcher must disclose every aspect of the fieldwork project.

Relationships

Entrance and subsequent access to a group of people is dependent upon gatekeepers. Gatekeepers are people who control access to segments of the group, such as an educational institution or a gang. In some cases, gatekeepers have formal positions. In a business, for instance, a manager may control files or access to information on people to talk with about particular topics. Gatekeepers may also have informal positions, such as a charismatic leader in a religious cult or a popular leader in a gang. In these cases, the gatekeeper functions in this role because other individuals respect her or his opinion.

Field researchers develop a network of informants. Informants are members of the group being studied who play a special role introducing the researcher to new contacts and explaining various aspects of the culture: power relationships, customs, and the like. Researchers often develop exchange relationships with members of the group being studied, and this is especially true with informants. The researcher may buy the informant a cup of coffee or perform small favors. These small acts help to develop trust in the relationship between the two and serve as an incentive for the informant to continue to help the researcher. Objectivist researchers develop exchange relationships with informants and others, but participatory action researchers base much of their research program on providing reciprocal services, such as technical assistance or acting as an advocate.

One important aspect of fieldwork is that the researcher needs to learn to control body language and facial gestures and adapt them to the cultural setting. Localized meanings are referred to as argot and include a range of cultural meanings specific to the group or culture to which the subjects belong. It is important to understand the argot of a group because it helps the researcher decipher the meaning behind what is being said. In addition, it is important to appear interested in all aspects of subjects' lives. Not doing so can offend people and damage the relationship between the researcher and the subjects. Needless to say, this hurts the research.

Data Collection

Data collection is based on qualitative interviews and observation. Qualitative interviewing is different from the structured interviews of survey research in that they tend to be nonstructured. Questions or talking points are arranged in a list, but the actual order of the questions is subject to change. Interviews are typically conducted a number of times with the same individual during the research period and are much more like conversations than those conducted in survey research. Often, questions will be asked as events warrant. The overall process is iterative—"each time you repeat the basic process of gathering information you come closer to a clear and convincing model of the phenomenon." (Rubin and Rubin, 1995, 46). Although the researcher may have specific topics to discuss, the interview itself is driven by what the subject wishes to discuss.

Life History

Observation is also an important aspect of data collection. Researchers need to take notes on everything they experience, no matter how seemingly insignificant. The sights, behaviors, and argot that may seem to be minor early in a project may turn out to be quite important upon later analysis. A good researcher wants to ensure complete notes from the earliest stages of the work. In addition, the early phase of fieldwork represents the researchers' last opportunity to perceive norms and values as a true outsider. Over time, the researcher becomes familiar with the phenomenon and may not pick up on it later in the project.

THE READINGS

The two fieldwork readings are quite different. In "Shifts and Oscillations in Deviant Careers," Patricia and Peter Adler (1983) discuss their six years of fieldwork experience conducting research on smugglers of illegal drugs. In "Illusions of Excellence and the Selling of the University," Janet Atkinson-Grosjean (1998) uses fieldwork methods in conjunction with content analysis as an inductive phase of a larger research project about marketing a Canadian university.

■ ■ ■ ■ ■ ▬▬▬▬▬▬▬▬▬▬▬▬▬▬▬▬▬▬▬▬▬▬▬

SHIFTS AND OSCILLATIONS IN DEVIANT CAREERS: THE CASE OF UPPER-LEVEL DRUG DEALERS AND SMUGGLERS*

Patricia A. Adler
University of Tulsa
Peter Adler

This is the first study of drug trafficking in the United States to penetrate the upper echelons of the marijuana and cocaine business—the smugglers and their primary dealers. We spent six years observing and interviewing these traffickers and their associates in southwestern California and examining their typical career paths. We show how drug traffickers enter the business and rise to the top, how they become disenchanted due to the rising social and legal costs of upper-level drug trafficking, how and why they either voluntarily or involuntarily leave the business, and why so many end up returning to their deviant careers, or to other careers within the drug world.

The upper echelons of the marijuana and cocaine trade constitute a world which has never before been researched and analyzed by sociologists. Importing and distributing tons of marijuana and kilos of cocaine at a time, successful operators can earn upwards of a half million dollars per year. Their traffic in these so-called "soft"[1] drugs constitutes a potentially lucrative occupation, yet few participants manage to accumulate any substantial sums of money, and most people envision their involvement in drug trafficking as only temporary. In this study we focus on the career paths followed by members of one upper-level drug dealing and smuggling community. We discuss the various modes of entry into trafficking at these upper levels, contrasting these with entry into middle- and low-level trafficking. We then describe the pattern of shifts

and oscillations these dealers and smugglers experience. Once they reach the top rungs of their occupation, they begin periodically quitting and re-entering the field, often changing their degree and type of involvement upon their return. Their careers, therefore, offer insights into the problems involved in leaving deviance.

Previous research on soft drug trafficking has only addressed the low and middle levels of this occupation, portraying people who purchase no more than 100 kilos of marijuana or single ounces of cocaine at a time (Anonymous, 1969; Atkyns and Hanneman, 1974; Blum *et al.*, 1972; Carey, 1968; Goode, 1970; Langer, 1977; Lieb and Olson, 1976; Mouledoux, 1972; Waldorf *et al.*, 1977). Of these, only Lieb and Olson (1976) have examined dealing and/or smuggling as an occupation, investigating participants' career developments. But their work, like several of the others, focuses on a population of student dealers who may have been too young to strive for and attain the upper levels of drug trafficking. Our study fills this gap at the top by describing and analyzing an elite community of upper-level dealers and smugglers and their careers.

We begin by describing where our research took place, the people and activities we studied, and the methods we used. Second, we outline the process of becoming a drug trafficker, from initial recruitment through learning the trade. Third, we look at the different types of upward mobility displayed by dealers and smugglers. Fourth, we examine the career shifts and

From *Social Problems, 31, 2 (December 1983): 195–207.*

oscillations which veteran dealers and smugglers display, outlining the multiple, conflicting forces which lure them both into and out of drug trafficking. We conclude by suggesting a variety of paths which dealers and smugglers pursue out of drug trafficking and discuss the problems inherent in leaving this deviant world.

SETTING AND METHOD

We based our study in "Southwest County," one section of a large metropolitan area in southwestern California near the Mexican border. Southwest County consisted of a handful of beach towns dotting the Pacific Ocean, a location offering a strategic advantage for wholesale drug trafficking.

Southwest County smugglers obtained their marijuana in Mexico by the ton and their cocaine in Colombia, Bolivia, and Peru, purchasing between 10 and 40 kilos at a time. These drugs were imported into the United States along a variety of land, sea, and air routes by organized smuggling crews. Southwest County dealers then purchased these products and either "middled" them directly to another buyer for a small but immediate profit of approximately $2 to $5 per kilo of marijuana and $5,000 per kilo of cocaine, or engaged in "straight dealing." As opposed to middling, straight dealing usually entailed adulterating the cocaine with such "cuts" as manitol, procaine, or inositol, and then dividing the marijuana and cocaine into smaller quantities to sell them to the next-lower level of dealers. Although dealers frequently varied the amounts they bought and sold, a hierarchy of transacting levels could be roughly discerned. "Wholesale" marijuana dealers bought directly from the smugglers, purchasing anywhere from 300 to 1,000 "bricks" (averaging a kilo in weight) at a time and selling in lots of 100 to 300 bricks. "Multi-kilo" dealers, while not the smugglers' first connections, also engaged in upper-level trafficking, buying between 100 to 300 bricks and selling them in 25 to 100 brick quantities. These were then purchased by middle-level dealers who filtered the marijuana through low-level and "ounce" dealers before it reached the ultimate consumer. Each time the marijuana changed hands its price increase was dependent on a number of factors: purchase cost; the distance it was transported (including such transportation costs as packaging, transportation equipment, and payments to employees); the amount of risk assumed; the quality of the marijuana; and the prevailing prices in each local drug market. Prices in the cocaine trade were much more predictable. After purchasing kilos of cocaine in South America for $10,000 each, smugglers sold them to Southwest County "pound" dealers in quantities of one to 10 kilos for $60,000 per kilo. These pound dealers usually cut the cocaine and sold pounds ($30,000) and half-pounds ($15,000) to "ounce" dealers, who in turn cut it again and sold ounces for $2,000 each to middle-level cocaine dealers known as "cut-ounce" dealers. In this fashion the drug was middled, dealt, divided and cut—sometimes as many as five or six times—until it was finally purchased by consumers as grams or half-grams.

Unlike low-level operators, the upper-level dealers and smugglers we studied pursued drug trafficking as a full-time occupation. If they were involved in other businesses, these were usually maintained to provide them with a legitimate front for security purposes. The profits to be made at the upper levels depended on an individual's style of operation, reliability, security, and the amount of product he or she consumed. About half of the 65 smugglers and dealers we observed were successful, some earning up to three-quarters of a million dollars per year.[2] The other half continually struggled in the business, either breaking even or losing money.

Although dealers' and smugglers' business activities varied, they clustered together for business and social relations, forming a moderately well-integrated community whose members pursued a "fast" lifestyle, which emphasized intensive partying, casual sex, extensive travel, abundant drug consumption, and lavish spending on consumer goods. The exact size of Southwest County's upper-level dealing and smuggling community was impossible to estimate due to the secrecy of its members. At these levels, the drug world was quite homogeneous. Participants were predominantly white, came from middle-class backgrounds, and had little previous criminal involvement. While the dealers' and smugglers' social world contained both men and women, most of the serious business was conducted by the men, ranging in age from 25 to 40 years old.

We gained entry to Southwest County's upper-level drug community largely by accident. We had become friendly with a group of our neighbors who turned out to be heavily involved in smuggling marijuana. Opportunistically (Riemer, 1977), we seized the chance to gather data on this unexplored activity. Using key informants who helped us gain the trust of other members of the community, we drew upon snowball sampling techniques (Biernacki and Waldorf, 1981) and a combination of overt and covert roles to widen our network of contacts. We supplemented intensive participant-observation, between 1974 and 1980,[3] with unstructured, taped interviews. Throughout, we employed extensive measures to cross-check the reliability of our data, whenever possible (Douglas, 1976). In all, we were able to closely observe 65 dealers and smugglers as well as numerous other drug world members, including dealers' "old ladies" (girlfriends or wives), friends, and family members.

BECOMING A DRUG TRAFFICKER

There are three routes into the upper levels of drug dealing and smuggling. First, some drug users become low-level dealers, gradually working their way up to middle-level dealing. It is rare, however, for upper-level dealers to have such meager origins. Second, there are people who enter directly into drug dealing at the middle level, usually from another occupation. Many of these do extremely well right away. Third, a number of individuals are invited into smuggling because of a special skill or character, sometimes from middle-level drug trafficking careers and other times from outside the drug world entirely. We discuss each of these in turn.

Low-Level Entry

People who began dealing at the bottom followed the classic path into dealing portrayed in the literature (Anonymous, 1969; Blum *et al.*, 1972; Carey, 1968; Goode, 1970; Johnson, 1973). They came from among the ranks of reg-

ular drug users, since, in practice, using drugs heavily and dealing for "stash" (one's personal supply) are nearly inseparable. Out of this multitude of low-level dealers, however, most abandoned the practice after they encountered their first legal or financial bust, lasting in the business for only a fairly short period (Anonymous, 1969; Carey, 1968; Lieb and Olson, 1976; Mandel, 1967). Those who sought bigger profits gradually drifted into a full-time career in drug trafficking, usually between the ages of 15 and 22. Because of this early recruitment into dealing as an occupation, low-level entrants generally developed few, if any, occupational skills other than dealing. One dealer described his early phase of involvement:

> I had dealt a limited amount of lids [ounces of marijuana] and psychedelics in my early college days without hardly taking it seriously. But after awhile something changed in me and I decided to try to work myself up. I probably was a classic case—started out buying a kilo for $150 and selling pounds for $100 each. I did that twice, then I took the money and bought two bricks, then three, then five, then seven.

This type of gradual rise through the ranks was characteristic of low-level dealers; however, few reached the upper levels of dealing from these humble beginnings. Only 20 percent of the dealers we observed in Southwest County got their start in this fashion. Two factors combined to make it less likely for low-level entrants to rise to the top. The first was psychological. People who started small, thought small; most had neither the motivation nor vision to move large quantities of drugs. The second, and more critical factor, was social. People who started at the bottom and tried to work their way up the ladder often had a hard time finding connections at the upper levels.[4] Dealers were suspicious of new customers, preferring, for security reasons, to deal with established outlets or trusted friends. The few people who did rise through the ranks generally began dealing in another part of the country, moving to Southwest County only after they had progressed to the middle levels. These people were lured to southwestern

California by its reputation within drug circles as an importation and wholesale dealing market.

Middle-Level Entry

About 75 percent of the smugglers and dealers in Southwest County entered at the middle level. Future big dealers usually jumped into transacting in substantial quantities from the outset, buying 50 kilos of "commercial" (low-grade) marijuana or one to two ounces of cocaine. One dealer explained this phenomenon:

> Someone who thinks of himself as an executive or an entrepreneur is not going to get into the dope business on a small level. The average executive just jumps right into the middle. Or else he's not going to jump.

This was the route taken by Southwest County residents with little or no previous involvement in drug trafficking. For them, entry into dealing followed the establishment of social relationships with local dealers and smugglers. (Naturally, this implies a self-selecting sample of outsiders who become accepted and trusted by these upper-level traffickers, based on their mutual interests, orientation, and values.) Through their friendships with dealers, these individuals were introduced to other members of the dealing scene and to their "fast" lifestyle. Individuals who found this lifestyle attractive became increasingly drawn to the subculture, building networks of social associations within it. Eventually, some of these people decided to participate more actively. This step was usually motivated both by money and lifestyle. One dealer recounted how he fell in with the drug world set:

> I used to be into real estate making good money. I was the only person at my firm renting to longhairs and dealing with their money. I slowly started getting friendly with them, although I didn't realize how heavy they were. I knew ways of buying real estate and putting it under fictitious names, laundering money so that it went in as hot cash and came out as spendable income. I slowly got more and more involved with this one guy until I was neglecting my real estate business and just partying with him all the time. My spending

went up but my income went down, and suddenly I had to look around for another way to make money fast. I took the money I was laundering for him, bought some bricks from another dealer friend of his, and sold them out of state before I gave him back the cash. Within six months I was turning [selling] 100 bricks at a time.

People who entered drug dealing at these middle levels were usually between the ages of 25 and 35 and had been engaged in some other occupation prior to dealing seriously. They came from a wide range of occupational backgrounds. Many drifted into the lifestyle from jobs already concentrated in the night hours, such as bartender, waiter, and nightclub bouncer. Still others came from fields where the working hours were irregular and adaptable to their special schedules, such as acting, real estate, inventing, graduate school, construction, and creative "entrepreneurship" (more aptly called hand-to-mouth survival, for many). The smallest group was tempted into the drug world from structured occupations and the professions.

Middle-level entrants had to learn the trade of drug trafficking. They received "on-the-job training" (Miller and Ritzer, 1977:89) in such skills as how to establish business connections, organize profitable transactions, avoid arrest, transport illegal goods, and coordinate participants and equipment. Dealers trained on the job refined their knowledge and skills by learning from their mistakes. One dealer recalled how he got "burned" with inferior quality marijuana on his first major "cop" [purchase] because of his inexperience:

> I had borrowed around $7,000 from this friend to do a dope deal. I had never bought in that kind of quantity before but I knew three or four guys who I got it from. I was nervous so I got really stoned before I shopped around and I ended up being hardly able to tell about the quality. Turned out you just couldn't get high off the stuff. I ended up having to sell it below cost.

Once they had gotten in and taught themselves the trade, most middle-level entrants strove for upward mobility. About 80 percent of these Southwest County dealers jumped to the upper levels of trafficking. One dealer described her mode of escalation:

> When I started to deal I was mostly looking for a quick buck here or there, something to pay some pressing bill. I was middling 50 or 100 bricks at a time. But then I was introduced to a guy who said he would front me half a pound of coke, and if I turned it fast I could have more, and on a regular basis. Pretty soon I was turning six, seven, eight, nine, 10 pounds a week—they were passing through real fast. I was clearing at least 10 grand a month. It was too much money too fast. I didn't know what to do with it. It got ridiculous, I wasn't relating to anyone anymore, I was never home, always gone. . . . The biggest ego trip for me came when all of a sudden I turned around and was selling to the people I had been buying from. I skipped their level of doing business entirely and stage-jumped right past them.

Southwest County's social milieu, with its concentration of upper-level dealers and smugglers, thus facilitated forming connections and doing business at the upper levels of the drug world.

Smuggling

Only 10 percent of Southwest County drug smugglers were formerly upper-level dealers who made the leap to smuggling on their own; the rest were invited to become smugglers by established operators. About half of those recruited came directly from the drug world's social scene, with no prior involvement in drug dealing. This implies, like middle-level entry into dealing, both an attraction to the drug crowd and its lifestyle, and prior acquaintance with dealers and smugglers. The other half of the recruits were solicited from among the ranks of middle-level Southwest County dealers.

The complex task of importing illegal drugs required more knowledge, experience, equipment, and connections than most non-smugglers possessed. Recruits had some skill or asset which the experienced smuggler needed to put his operation together. This included piloting or navigating ability, equipment, money, or the willingness to handle drugs while they were being transported. One smuggler described some of the criteria he used to screen potential recruits for suitability as employees in smuggling crews:

> Pilots are really at a premium. They burn out so fast that I have to replace them every six months to a year. But I'm also looking for people who are cool: people who will carry out their jobs according to the plan, who won't panic if the load arrives late or something goes wrong, 'cause this happens a lot. . . . And I try not to get people who've been to prison before, because they'll be more likely to take foolish risks, the kind that I don't want to have to.

Most novice smugglers were recruited and trained by a sponsor with whom they forged an apprentice-mentor relationship. Those who had been dealers previously knew the rudiments of drug trafficking. What they learned from the smuggler was how to fill a particular role in his or her highly specialized operation.

One smuggler we interviewed had a slightly larger than average crew. Ben's commercial marijuana smuggling organization was composed of seven members, not including himself. Two were drivers who transported the marijuana from the landing strip to its point of destination. One was a pilot. The dual roles of driver and co-pilot were filled by a fourth man. Another pilot, who operated both as a smuggler with his own makeshift crew and as a wholesale marijuana dealer who was supplied by Ben, flew runs for Ben when he wasn't otherwise occupied. The sixth member was Ben's enforcer and "stash house" man; he lived in the place where the marijuana was stored, distributed it to customers, and forcibly extracted payments when Ben deemed it necessary. The seventh member handled the financial and legal aspects of the business. He arranged for lawyers and bail bondsmen when needed, laundered Ben's money, and provided him with a legitimate-looking business front. Most of these family members also dealt drugs on the side, having the choice of taking their payment in cash ($10,000 for pilots; $4,000 for drivers) or in kind. Ben arranged the buying and selling connections, financed the operation, provided the heavy equipment (planes, vans, radios) and recruited, supervised, and replaced his crew.

Relationships between smugglers and their recruits were generally characterized by a benign paternalism, leading apprentices to form an enduring loyalty to their sponsor. Once established in a smuggling crew, recruits gained familiarity with the many other roles, the scope of the whole operation, and began to meet suppliers and customers. Eventually they branched out on their own. To do so, employees of a smuggling crew had to develop the expertise and connections necessary to begin running their own operations. Several things were required to make this move. Acquiring the technical knowledge of equipment, air routes, stopovers, and how to coordinate personnel was relatively easy; this could be picked up after working in a smuggling crew for six months to a year. Putting together one's own crew was more difficult because skilled employees, especially pilots, were hard to find. Most new smugglers borrowed people from other crews until they became sufficiently established to recruit and train their own personnel. Finally, connections to buy from and sell to were needed. Buyers were plentiful, but securing a foreign supplier required special breaks or networks.

Another way for employees to become heads of their own smuggling operations was to take over when their boss retired. This had the advantage of keeping the crew and style of operation intact. Various financial arrangements could be worked out for such a transfer of authority, from straight cash purchases to deals involving residual payments. One marijuana smuggler described how he acquired his operation:

> I had been Jake's main pilot for a year and, after him, I knew the most about his operation. We were really tight, and he had taken me all up and down the coast with him, meeting his connections. Naturally I knew the Mexican end of the operation and his supplier since I used to make the runs, flying down the money and picking up the dope. So when he told me he wanted to get out of the business, we made a deal. I took over the set-up and gave him a residual for every run I made. I kept all the drivers, all the connections—everything the guy had—but I found myself a new pilot.

In sum, most dealers and smugglers reached the upper levels not so much as a result of their individual entrepreneurial initiative, but through the social networks they formed in the drug subculture. Their ability to remain in these strata was largely tied to the way they treated these drug world relationships.[5]

SHIFTS AND OSCILLATIONS

We have discussed dealers and smugglers separately up to this point because they display distinct career patterns. But once individuals entered the drug trafficking field and rose to its upper levels, they became part of a social world, the Southwest County drug scene, and faced common problems and experiences. Therefore, we discuss them together from here on.

Despite the gratifications which dealers and smugglers originally derived from the easy money, material comfort, freedom, prestige, and power associated with their careers, 90 percent of those we observed decided, at some point, to quit the business. This stemmed, in part, from their initial perceptions of the career as temporary ("Hell, nobody wants to be a drug dealer all their life"). Adding to these early intentions was a process of rapid aging in the career: dealers and smugglers became increasingly aware of the restrictions and sacrifices their occupations required and tired of living the fugitive life. They thought about, talked about, and in many cases took steps toward getting out of the drug business. But as with entering, disengaging from drug trafficking was rarely an abrupt act (Lieb and Olson, 1976:364). Instead, it more often resembled a series of transitions, or oscillations,[6] out of and back into the business. For once out of the drug world, dealers and smugglers were rarely successful in making it in the legitimate world because they failed to cut down on their extravagant lifestyle and drug consumption. Many abandoned their efforts to reform and returned to deviance, sometimes picking up where they left off and other times shifting to a new mode of operating. For example, some shifted from dealing cocaine to dealing marijuana, some dropped to a lower level of dealing, and others shifted their role within the same group of traffickers. This series of phase-outs and re-entries, combined with career shifts, endured for years, dominating the pattern of their remaining involvement with the business. But it also represented the method by which many eventually broke away from drug trafficking, for each phase-out had the potential to be an individual's final departure.

Aging in the Career

Once recruited and established in the drug world, dealers and smugglers entered into a middle phase of aging in the career. This phase was characterized by a progressive loss of enchantment with their occupation. While novice dealers and smugglers found that participation in the drug world brought them thrills and status, the novelty gradually faded. Initial feelings of exhilaration and awe began to dull as individuals became increasingly jaded. This was the result of both an extended exposure to the mundane, everyday business aspects of drug trafficking and to an exorbitant consumption of drugs (especially cocaine). One smuggler described how he eventually came to feel:

> It was fun, those three or four years. I never worried about money or anything. But after awhile it got real boring. There was no feeling or emotion or anything about it. I wasn't even hardly relating to my old lady anymore. Everything was just one big rush.

This frenzy of overstimulation and resulting exhaustion hastened the process of "burnout" which nearly all individuals experienced. As dealers and smugglers aged in the career they became more sensitized to the extreme risks they faced. Cases of friends and associates who were arrested, imprisoned, or killed began to mount. Many individuals became convinced that continued drug trafficking would inevitably lead to arrest ("It's only a matter of time before you get caught"). While dealers and smugglers generally repressed their awareness of danger, treating it as a taken-for-granted part of their daily existence, periodic crises shattered their casual attitudes, evoking strong feelings of fear. They temporarily intensified security precautions and retreated into near-isolation until they felt the "heat" was off.

As a result of these accumulating "scares," dealers and smugglers increasingly integrated feelings of "paranoia"[7] into their everyday lives. One dealer talked about his feelings of paranoia:

> You're always on the line. You don't lead a normal life. You're always looking over your shoulder, wondering who's at the door, having to hide everything. You learn to look behind you so well you could probably bend over and look up your ass. That's paranoia. It's a really scary, hard feeling. That's what makes you get out.

Drug world members also grew progressively weary of their exclusion from the legitimate world and the deceptions they had to manage to sustain that separation. Initially, this separation was surrounded by an alluring mystique. But as they aged in the career, this mystique became replaced by the reality of everyday boundary maintenance and the feeling of being an "expatriated citizen within one's own country." One smuggler who was contemplating quitting described the effects of this separation:

> I'm so sick of looking over my shoulder, having to sit in my house and worry about one of my non-drug world friends stopping in when I'm doing business. Do you know how awful that is? It's like leading a double life. It's ridiculous. That's what makes it not worth it. It'll be a lot less money [to quit], but a lot less pressure.

Thus, while the drug world was somewhat restricted, it was not an encapsulated community, and dealers' and smugglers' continuous involvement with the straight world made the temptation to adhere to normative standards and "go straight" omnipresent. With the occupation's novelty worn off and the "fast life" taken-for-granted, most dealers and smugglers felt that the occupation no longer resembled their early impressions of it. Once they reached the upper levels of the occupation, their experience began to change. Eventually, the rewards of trafficking no longer seemed to justify the strain and risk involved. It was at this point that the straight world's formerly dull ambiance became transformed (at least in theory) into a potential haven.

Phasing-Out

Three factors inhibited dealers and smugglers from leaving the drug world. Primary among these factors were the hedonistic and materialistic satisfactions the drug world provided. Once accustomed to earning vast quantities of money quickly and easily, individuals found it exceedingly difficult to return to the income scale of the straight world. They also were reluctant to abandon the pleasures of the "fast life" and its accompanying drugs, casual sex, and power. Second, dealers and smugglers identified with, and developed a commitment to, the occupation of drug trafficking (Adler and Adler, 1982). Their self-images were tied to that role and could not be easily disengaged. The years invested in their careers (learning the trade, forming connections, building reputations) strengthened their involvement with both the occupation and the drug community. And since their relationships were social as well as business, friendship ties bound individuals to dealing. As one dealer in the midst of struggling to phase-out explained:

> The biggest threat to me is to get caught up sitting around the house with friends that are into dealing. I'm trying to stay away from them, change my habits.

Third, dealers and smugglers hesitated to voluntarily quit the field because of the difficulty involved in finding another way to earn a living. Their years spent in illicit activity made it unlikely for any legitimate organizations to hire them. This narrowed their occupational choices considerably, leaving self-employment as one of the few remaining avenues open.

Dealers and smugglers who tried to leave the drug world generally fell into one of four patterns.[8] The first and most frequent pattern was to postpone quitting until after they could execute one last "big deal." While the intention was sincere, individuals who chose this route rarely succeeded; the "big deal" too often remained elusive. One marijuana smuggler offered a variation of this theme:

> My plan is to make a quarter of a million dollars in four months during the prime smuggling season and get the hell out of the business.

A second pattern we observed was individuals who planned to change immediately, but never did. They announced they were quitting, yet their outward actions never varied. One dealer described his involvement with this syndrome:

> When I wake up I'll say, "Hey, I'm going to quit this cycle and just run my other business." But when you're dealing you constantly have people dropping by ounces and asking, "Can you move this?" What's your first response? Always, "Sure, for a toot."

In the third pattern of phasing-out, individuals actually suspended their dealing and smuggling activities, but did not replace them with an alternative source of income. Such withdrawals were usually spontaneous and prompted by exhaustion, the influence of a person from outside the drug world, or problems with the police or other associates. These kinds of phaseouts usually lasted only until the individual's money ran out, as one dealer explained:

> I got into legal trouble with the FBI a while back and I was forced to quit dealing. Everybody just cut me off completely, and I saw the danger in continuing, myself. But my

high-class tastes never dwindled. Before I knew it I was in hock over $30,000. Even though I was hot, I was forced to get back into dealing to relieve some of my debts.

In the fourth pattern of phasing-out, dealers and smugglers tried to move into another line of work. Alternative occupations included: (1) those they had previously pursued; (2) front businesses maintained on the side while dealing or smuggling; and (3) new occupations altogether. While some people accomplished this transition successfully, there were problems inherent in all three alternatives.

(1) Most people who tried resuming their former occupations found that these had changed too much while they were away. In addition, they themselves had changed: they enjoyed the self-directed freedom and spontaneity associated with dealing and smuggling, and were unwilling to relinquish it.

(2) Those who turned to their legitimate front business often found that these businesses were unable to support them. Designed to launder rather than earn money, most of these ventures were retail outlets with a heavy cash flow (restaurants, movie theaters, automobile dealerships, small stores) that had become accustomed to operating under a continuous subsidy from illegal funds. Once their drug funding was cut off they could not survive for long.

(3) Many dealers and smugglers utilized the skills and connections they had developed in the drug business to create a new occupation. They exchanged their illegal commodity for a legal one and went into import/export, manufacturing, wholesaling, or retailing other merchandise. For some, the decision to prepare a legitimate career for their future retirement from the drug world followed an unsuccessful attempt to phase-out into a "front" business. One husband-and-wife dealing team explained how these legitimate side businesses differed from front businesses:

We always had a little legitimate "scam" [scheme] going, like mail-order shirts, wallets, jewelry, and the kids were always involved in

that. We made a little bit of money on them. Their main purpose was for a cover. But [this business] was different; right from the start this was going to be a legal thing to push us out of the drug business.

About 10 percent of the dealers and smugglers we observed began tapering off their drug world involvement gradually, transferring their time and money into a selected legitimate endeavor. They did not try to quit drug trafficking altogether until they felt confident that their legitimate business could support them. Like spontaneous phase-outs, many of these planned withdrawals into legitimate endeavors failed to generate enough money to keep individuals from being lured into the drug world.

In addition to voluntary phase-outs caused by burnout, about 40 percent of the Southwest County dealers and smugglers we observed experienced a "bustout" at some point in their careers.[9] Forced withdrawals from dealing or smuggling were usually sudden and motivated by external factors, either financial, legal, or reputational. Financial bustouts generally occurred when dealers or smugglers were either "burned" or "ripped-off" by others, leaving them in too much debt to rebuild their base of operation. Legal bustouts followed arrest and possibly incarceration: arrested individuals were so "hot" that few of their former associates would deal with them. Reputational bustouts occurred when individuals "burned" or "ripped-off" others (regardless of whether they intended to do so) and were banned from business by their former circle of associates. One smuggler gave his opinion on the pervasive nature of forced phase-outs:

Some people are smart enough to get out of it because they realize, physically, they have to. Others realize, monetarily, that they want to get out of this world before this world gets them. Those are the lucky ones. Then there are the ones who have to get out because they're hot or someone else close to them is so hot that they'd better get out. But in the end when you get out of it, nobody gets out of it out of free choice; you do it because you have to.

Death, of course, was the ultimate bustout. Some pilots met this fate because of the dangerous routes they navigated (hugging mountains, treetops, other aircrafts) and the sometimes ill-maintained and overloaded planes they flew. However, despite much talk of violence, few Southwest County drug traffickers died at the hands of fellow dealers.

Re-Entry

Phasing-out of the drug world was more often than not temporary. For many dealers and smugglers, it represented but another stage of their drug careers (although this may not have been their original intention), to be followed by a period of reinvolvement. Depending on the individual's perspective, re-entry into the drug world could be viewed as either a comeback (from a forced withdrawal) or a relapse (from a voluntary withdrawal).

Most people forced out of drug trafficking were anxious to return. The decision to phase-out was never theirs, and the desire to get back into dealing or smuggling was based on many of the same reasons which drew them into the field originally. Coming back from financial, legal, and reputational bustouts was possible but difficult and was not always successfully accomplished. They had to re-establish contacts, rebuild their organization and fronting arrangements, and raise the operating capital to resume dealing. More difficult was the problem of overcoming the circumstances surrounding their departure. Once smugglers and dealers resumed operating, they often found their former colleagues suspicious of them. One frustrated dealer described the effects of his prison experience:

> When I first got out of the joint [jail], none of my old friends would have anything to do with me. Finally, one guy who had been my partner told me it was because everyone was suspicious of my getting out early and thought I made a deal [with police to inform on his colleagues].

Dealers and smugglers who returned from bustouts were thus informally subjected to a trial period in which they had to re-establish their trustworthiness and reliability before they could once again move in the drug world with ease.

Re-entry from voluntary withdrawal involved a more difficult decision-making process, but was easier to implement. The factors enticing individuals to re-enter the drug world were not the same as those which motivated their original entry. As we noted above, experienced dealers and smugglers often privately weighed their reasons for wanting to quit and wanting to stay in. Once they left, their images of and hopes for the straight world failed to materialize. They could not make the shift to the norms, values, and lifestyle of the straight society and could not earn a living within it. Thus, dealers and smugglers decided to re-enter the drug business for basic reasons: the material perquisites, the hedonistic gratifications, the social ties, and the fact that they had nowhere else to go.

Once this decision was made, the actual process of re-entry was relatively easy. One dealer described how the door back into dealing remained open for those who left voluntarily:

> I still see my dealer friends, I can still buy grams from them when I want to. It's the respect they have for me because I stepped out of it without being busted or burning someone. I'm coming out with a good reputation, and even though the scene is a whirlwind—people moving up, moving down, in, out—if I didn't see anybody for a year I could call them up and get right back in that day.

People who relapsed thus had little problem obtaining fronts, re-establishing their reputations, or readjusting to the scene.

Career Shifts

Dealers and smugglers who re-entered the drug world, whether from a voluntary or forced phase-out, did not always return to the same level of transacting or commodity which characterized their previous style of operation. Many individuals underwent a "career shift" (Luckenbill and Best, 1981) and became involved in some new segment of the drug world. These shifts were sometimes lateral, as when a member of a smuggling crew took on a new specialization, switching from piloting to operating a stash house, for example. One dealer described how he utilized friendship networks upon his re-entry to shift from cocaine to marijuana trafficking:

> Before, when I was dealing cocaine, I was too caught up in using the drug and people around me were starting to go under from getting into "base" [another form of cocaine]. That's why I got out. But now I think I've got myself together and even though I'm dealing again I'm staying away from coke. I've switched over to dealing grass. It's a whole different circle of people. I got into it through a close friend I used to know before, but I never did business with him because he did grass and I did coke.

Vertical shifts moved operators to different levels. For example, one former smuggler returned and began dealing; another top-level marijuana dealer came back to find that the smugglers he knew had disappeared and he was forced to buy in smaller quantities from other dealers.

Another type of shift relocated drug traffickers in different styles of operation. One dealer described how, after being arrested, he tightened his security measures:

> I just had to cut back after I went through those changes. Hell, I'm not getting any younger and the idea of going to prison bothers me a lot more than it did 10 years ago. The risks are no longer worth it when I can have a comfortable income with less risk. So I only sell to four people now. I don't care if they buy a pound or a gram.

A former smuggler who sold his operation and lost all his money during phase-out returned as a consultant to the industry, selling his expertise to those with new money and fresh manpower:

> What I've been doing lately is setting up deals for people. I've got foolproof plans for smug-

gling cocaine up here from Colombia; I tell them how to modify their airplanes to add on extra fuel tanks and to fit in more weed, coke, or whatever they bring up. Then I set them up with refueling points all up and down Central America, tell them how to bring it up here, what points to come in at, and what kind of receiving unit to use. Then they do it all and I get 10 percent of what they make.

Re-entry did not always involve a shift to a new niche, however. Some dealers and smugglers returned to the same circle of associates, trafficking activity, and commodity they worked with prior to their departure. Thus, drug dealers' careers often peaked early and then displayed a variety of shifts, from lateral mobility, to decline, to holding fairly steady.

A final alternative involved neither completely leaving nor remaining within the deviant world. Many individuals straddled the deviant and respectable worlds forever by continuing to dabble in drug trafficking. As a result of their experiences in the drug world they developed a deviant self-identity and a deviant *modus operandi*. They might not have wanted to bear the social and legal burden of full-time deviant work but neither were they willing to assume the perceived confines and limitations of the straight world. They therefore moved into the entrepreneurial realm, where their daily activities involved some kind of hustling or "wheeling and dealing" in an assortment of legitimate, quasi-legitimate, and deviant ventures, and where they could be their own boss. This enabled them to retain certain elements of the deviant lifestyle, and to socialize on the fringes of the drug community. For these individuals, drug dealing shifted from a primary occupation to a sideline, though they never abandoned it altogether.

LEAVING DRUG TRAFFICKING

This career pattern of oscillation into and out of active drug trafficking makes it difficult to speak of leaving drug trafficking in the sense of a final retirement. Clearly, some people succeeded in voluntarily retiring. Of these, a few managed to prepare a post-deviant career for themselves by transferring their drug money into a legitimate enterprise. A larger group was forced out of dealing and either didn't or couldn't return; their bustouts were sufficiently damaging that they never attempted re-entry, or they abandoned efforts after a series of unsuccessful attempts. But there was no way of structurally determining in advance whether an exit from the business would be temporary or permanent. The vacillations in dealers' intentions were compounded by the complexity of operating successfully in the drug world. For many, then, no phase-out could ever be definitely assessed as permanent. As long as individuals had the skills, knowledge, and connections to deal they retained the potential to re-enter the occupation at any time. Leaving drug trafficking may thus be a relative phenomenon, characterized by a trailing-off process where spurts of involvement appear with decreasing frequency and intensity.

SUMMARY

Drug dealing and smuggling careers are temporary and fraught with multiple attempts at retirement. Veteran drug traffickers quit their occupation because of the ambivalent feelings they develop toward their deviant life. As they age in the career their experience changes, shifting from a work life that is exhilarating and free to one that becomes increasingly dangerous and confining. But just as their deviant careers are temporary, so too are their retirements. Potential recruits are lured into the drug business by materialism, hedonism, glamor, and excitement. Established dealers are lured away from the deviant life and back into the mainstream by the attractions of security and social case. Retired dealers and smugglers are lured back in by their expertise, and by their ability to make money quickly and easily. People who have been exposed to the upper levels of drug trafficking therefore find it extremely difficult to quit their deviant occupation permanently. This stems, in part, from their difficulty in moving from the illegitimate to the legitimate business sector. Even more significant is the affinity they form for their deviant values and lifestyle. Thus few, if any, of our subjects were successful in leaving deviance entirely. What dealers

and smugglers intend, at the time, to be a permanent withdrawal from drug trafficking can be seen in retrospect as a pervasive occupational pattern of mid-career shifts and oscillations. More research is needed into the complex process of how people get out of deviance and enter the world of legitimate work.

NOTES

1. The term "soft" drugs generally refers to marijuana, cocaine and such psychedelics as LSD and mescaline (Carey, 1968). In this paper we do not address trafficking in psychedelics because, since they are manufactured in the United States, they are neither imported nor distributed by the group we studied.

2. This is an idealized figure representing the profit a dealer or smuggler could potentially earn and does not include deductions for such miscellaneous and hard-to-calculate costs as: time or money spent in arranging deals (some of which never materialize); lost, stolen, or unrepaid money or drugs; and the personal drug consumption of a drug trafficker and his or her entourage. Of these, the single largest expense is the last one, accounting for the bulk of most Southwest County dealers' and smugglers' earnings.

3. We continued to conduct follow-up interviews with key informants through 1983.

4. The exception to this was where low-level dealers rose on the "coattails" of their suppliers: as one dealer increased the volume of his or her purchases or sales, some of his or her customers followed suit.

5. For a more thorough discussion of the social networks and relationships in Southwest County's drug world see Adler and Adler (1983).

6. While other studies of drug dealing have also noted that participants did not maintain an uninterrupted stream of career involvement (Blum *et al.*, 1972; Carey, 1968; Lieb and Olson, 1976; Waldorf *et al.*, 1977), none have isolated or described the oscillating nature of this pattern.

7. In the dealers' vernacular, this term is not used in the clinical sense of an individual psychopathology rooted in early childhood traumas. Instead, it resembles Lemert's (1962) more sociological definition which focuses on such behavioral dynamics as suspicion, hostility, aggressiveness, and even delusion. Not only Lemert, but also Waldorf *et al.* (1977) and Wedow (1979) assert that feelings of paranoia can have a sound basis in reality, and are therefore readily comprehended and even empathized with others.

8. At this point, a limitation to our data must be noted. Many of the dealers and smugglers we observed simply "disappeared" from the scene and were never heard from again. We therefore have no way of knowing if they phased-out (voluntarily or involuntarily), shifted to another scene, or were killed in some remote place. We cannot, therefore, estimate the numbers of people who left the Southwest County drug scene via each of the routes discussed here.

9. It is impossible to determine the exact percentage of people falling into the different phase-out categories: due to oscillation, people could experience several types and thus appear in multiple categories.

REFERENCES

ADLER, PATRICIA A., and PETER ADLER. 1982. "Criminal commitment among drug dealers." Deviant Behavior 3:117–135. 1983. "Relations between dealers: The social organization of illicit drug transactions." Sociology and Social Research 67(3):260–278.

Anonymous. 1969. "On selling marijuana." Pp. 92–102 in Erich Goode (ed.), Marijuana. New York: Atherton.

ATKYNS, ROBERT L., and GERHARD J. HANNEMAN. 1974. "Illicit drug distribution and dealer communication behavior." Journal of Health and Social Behavior 15(March):36–43.

BIERNACKI, PATRICK, and DAN WALDORF. 1981. "Snowball sampling." Sociological Methods and Research 10(2):141–163.

BLUM, RICHARD H., and ASSOCIATES. 1972. The Dream Sellers. San Francisco: Jossey-Bass.

CAREY, JAMES T. 1968. The College Drug Scene. Englewood Cliffs, NJ: Prentice-Hall.

DOUGLAS, JACK D. 1976. Investigative Social Research. Beverly Hills, CA: Sage.

GOODE, ERICH. 1970. The Marijuana Smokers. New York: Basic.

JOHNSON, BRUCE D. 1973. Marijuana Users and Drug Subcultures. New York: Wiley.

LANGER, JOHN. 1977. "Drug entrepreneurs and dealing culture." Social Problems 24(3):377–385.

LEMERT, EDWIN. 1962. "Paranoia and the dynamics of exclusion." Sociometry 25(March): 2–20.

LIEB, JOHN, and SHELDON OLSON. 1976. "Prestige, paranoia, and profit: On becoming a dealer of illicit drugs in a university community." Journal of Drug Issues 6(Fall):356–369.

LUCKENBILL, DAVID F., and JOEL BEST. 1981. "Careers in deviance and respectability: The analogy's limitations." Social Problems 29(2):197–206.

MANDEL, JERRY. 1967. "Myths and realities of marijuana pushing." Pp. 58–110 in Jerry L. Simmons (ed.), Marijuana: Myths and Realities. North Hollywood, CA: Brandon.

MILLER, GALE, and GEORGE RITZER. 1977. "Informal socialization: Deviant occupations." Pp. 83–94 in George Ritzer, Working: Conflict and Change. 2nd edition. Englewood Cliffs, NJ: Prentice-Hall.

MOULEDOUX, JAMES. 1972. "Ideological aspects of drug dealership." Pp. 110–122 in Ken Westhues (ed.), Society's Shadow: Studies in the Sociology of Countercultures. Toronto: McGraw-Hill, Ryerson.

REDLINGER, LAWRENCE J. 1975. "Marketing and distributing heroin." Journal of Psychedelic Drugs 7(4):331–353.

RIEMER, JEFFREY W. 1977. "Varieties of opportunistic research." Urban Life 5(4):467–477.

WALDORF, DAN, SHEIGLA MURPHY, CRAIG REINARMAN, and BRIDGET JOYCE. 1977. Doing Coke: An Ethnography of Cocaine Users and Sellers. Washington, DC: Drug Abuse Council.

WEDOW, SUZANNE. 1979. "Feeling paranoid: The organization of an ideology." Urban Life 8(1):72–93.

ILLUSIONS OF EXCELLENCE AND THE SELLING OF THE UNIVERSITY: A MICRO-STUDY

Janet Atkinson-Grosjean
University of British Columbia

The article describes a preliminary study of a western Canadian university's "research awareness campaign" and links it to the parallel appointment of a new president with a strong "public affairs" focus. Both campaign and appointment are viewed as contributing to the commodification of knowledge. The rhetoric is seen as paradigmatic of the penetration of "market" discourse into the academy. The key problems seem to be (1) the administration's uncritical and unreflective pursuit of the economic at the expense of the intellectual, (2) the professoriate's passive acceptance of the new status quo, and (3) selective interpretation of market doctrines by university administrations in general, allowing them to attack the "front line" while preserving "management." A larger study will pursue the issues raised.

INTRODUCTION

Said (1994), after Orwell, says that clichés are evidence of the decay of language. Like background music in a supermarket, they seduce the mind into "passive acceptance of unexamined ideas and sentiments" (p. 28). Why would universities—supposed citadels of critical thought—unquestioningly adopt an outmoded and clichéd form of corporate discourse?[1] Long after the wave has passed in the business world, why have words like "vision," "mission," and "excellence" become omnipresent in the rhetoric of university presidents and administrators? And why are mission statements, vision documents, and research planning exercises so empty and instrumental?

Corporate thinking is dangerous for intellectuals, warns Said. It is antithetical to the questioning and skepticism we expect from those privileged to work in universities. But corporate thinking, according to Readings (1996: 11), is part of a trend towards universities as "consumer-oriented corporations," dominated not by academics but by administrators and their logics of accountability and excellence. "It is no longer clear what the place of the university is within society," says Readings, "nor what the exact nature of that society is" (Readings, 1996: 2).

The adoption of corporate discourse on campus is one facet of a pervasive new market-driven ethos which commodifies the products of knowledge, and knowledge itself, and offers them for sale in the marketplace of ideas. Left unchecked, it valorises application over enquiry, research over teaching, and science and technology over all other forms of knowledge. In doing so, it neglects traditional areas of scholarship which produce ideas rather than outcomes, and therefore potentially undermines the university's wider social role. The purpose of this paper is to offer an example of this commodification in action by following a western Canadian (hereafter WCU) university's campaign to promote public awareness of its research. The campaign is structured around the explicit understanding that knowledge can be promoted and sold using appropriate technologies of consumption. For clarity, it should be noted that there are only a handful of small private universities in Canada. It is knowledge produced in public institutions that is being commodified.

NATURE OF THE STUDY

The study was an informal seed enquiry into the penetration of WCU by the market. Its purpose was to establish a preliminary framework for a later, more comprehensive, case study of commodification of public sector research in Canada. While I used documentary analysis and

From *Electronic Journal of Sociology*, 3, 3 (1998). www.icaap.org/iuicode?100.3.3.1. Copyright © 1998 Electronic Journal of Sociology.

ethnographic techniques to examine the campaign's structure and underlying purpose, the limited scope of the enquiry restricts the amount of analysis that can usefully be undertaken. Thus, the discussion of the campaign itself is largely descriptive. To conduct the study, I attended a workshop with WCU's new president on "The Changing Role of the Research-Intensive[2] University" and discussed the topic informally with several students and members of faculty. I examined newspaper stories and WCU's public affairs publications and downloaded material from the websites of several other Canadian universities. I read widely in the associated literatures. And I conducted two in-depth interviews, a solo one with the campaign co-ordinator (hereafter CC) and the other with the Vice-President, Research (hereafter VPR) with CC "sitting-in" at VPR's request.

The administrators did not question the rightness of commodification (a term they did not know) or the appropriateness of importing market values into the university. Their insouciance reinforced my scepticism. I do not take the position that commodification of knowledge is undesirable by definition. After all, commodification and universities are old friends. This is not a new phenomenon, as reference to Veblen (1918) and Noble (1977) would demonstrate. But I am concerned that the universe of discourse appears closed to other elements—like culture, the arts, and humanities—when the promotion of research in science and technology dominates the agenda so completely (cf. Marcuse, 1964).

I am troubled that the administration's pursuit of commodification, in one university at least, seems largely unreflective and based on the unquestioned assumption that the trend cannot be resisted because there is no real alternative. As VPR put it, "if someone did [resist] they'd be all alone." In view of such attitudes, it seems almost inevitable—as Lyotard (1979) predicted—that the university will abandon its traditional role in favour of isomorphism with private-sector interests.

COMMODIFICATION IN
THE UNIVERSITY

Two decades ago, Lyotard's was a lonely voice warning of an impending legitimation crisis and a qualitative alteration in the status of universities and knowledge. In the Canadian context, recent work by Readings (1996), Emberley (1996), Bercuson et al. (1997), and others, indicates Lyotard is lonely no longer. The legitimation crisis seems to be upon us.

When defined as a commodity, knowledge tends to be valued in political and economic terms, rather than for its social or cultural significance (Shumar, 1997). And, as a political and economic question, it is clearly implicated in power. Particularly in the domain of science, research tends to be funding-driven. If money controls research does it thereby effectively control knowledge? Is Lyotard overly cynical or merely realistic when he says "whoever is the wealthiest has the best chance of being right" (p. 44)? Is his assessment of *performativity über alles* correct? That is, when knowledge is judged instrumentally, in terms of its efficiency and utility, does education become reduced to marketable technologies and work skills? (Noble, 1997; Shumar, 1997).

According to Webster (1995), in Britain granting councils judge university research on the basis of performativity. Proposals are assessed according to their market potential and competitive advantage—no potential, no funding; no funding, no research. Projects lacking commercial capacity—many of them in the arts and humanities—get sidelined. Similar principles of "new public management" operate in most OECD jurisdictions, although to different degrees. In Canada, for a variety of reasons, public service reform has been less draconian than elsewhere. The funding councils have been able to maintain somewhat more flexibility. Nevertheless, throughout the research community, the emphasis—and the lion's share of funding—falls on commercially viable applications. At the same time, performativity measures the influence of how education is being delivered in universities. In knowledge societies, professional schools and practical disciplines are burgeoning—some at full-cost recovery—while more traditional areas of scholarship are in retreat.[3]

Commodification is a process where the economic comes to dominate social institutions and social life. To borrow Bourdieu's terms, cultural, symbolic, academic, and human capital become subordinated to economic capital. Noble's (1997)[4] reading of knowledge commodification is that universities have become sites of capital accumulation, where research converts knowledge into market-tradeable, commercially viable products and processes. Over the last two decades, intellectual activity has been systematically converted into intellectual capital, he says, offering patents as a prime example.

Noble believes knowledge-based industries—like space, electronics, and bioengineering—pursued a deliberate strategy, beginning with the oil and economic crises of the seventies, of converting university research into corporate intellectual capital. He says, "within a decade [of the crises] there was a proliferation of industrial partnerships and new proprietary arrangements, as industrialists and their campus counterparts invented ways to socialise the risks and costs of creating this knowledge while privatising the benefits."

In the early '80s, and probably not coincidentally, granting bodies in OECD countries like the US, UK, and Canada reformed their patent policies, giving universities the right *and responsibility* to commercially exploit discoveries funded by government grants. Soon after, University-Industry Liaison (Technology Transfer) Offices appeared on most campuses to cultivate corporate ties and develop the administrative infrastructure for the commercial exploitation of research. The result, according to Noble, was "a wholesale reallocation of a university's resources towards its research function at the expense of its educational function." Newsom (1994) confirms the changes in institutional arrangements and practices that evolved to support corporate linkages. She describes some—like Centres of Excellence, spin-off companies, and research institutes with special funding arrangements—as parasitic on their host institutions (Newsom, 1994: 146–7).

Noble paints universities as impatient virgins, anxious to sell their innocence to the highest bidder. But the stampede to commodify research and secure corporate funding was prompted, in part, by the generalised retreat of government funding in most OECD jurisdictions. This retreat is characteristic of neoliberal economies, where the state tends to move away from supporting and regulating institutions, and delegates these responsibilities to the mediation of the market (Slater, 1997). Late 20th century commodification of university knowledge can be better understood when placed in this wider political-economic context.

Thus, while the motivation of the campaign I will discuss is ostensibly to raise public awareness of university research, it is ultimately about money. It is about winning public support and thereby political support, in order to reverse the decline in state funding.[5] As VPR says,

> Governments have a responsibility to fund research. When funding doesn't come through we whine . . . or else we go to Ottawa and lobby politicians and bureaucrats. And they say, "we understand what you're saying, but our constituents don't understand. You're not on the radar screen. You need to get there. You need to tell people what you do."

Consider this statement in the context of latter-day "flexible" economies, where increasingly differentiated products—often composed of non-material elements like culture, information, or knowledge—are marketed to increasingly differentiated consumers. "Telling people what you do" sounds more simple than it is. Reaching fragmented consumers in fragmented markets demands deployment of sophisticated marketing technologies. Under flexible accumulation, commodification is a semiotic process and the marketing of the university and its products is no exception (Shumar, 1997). As well, in a liberal-democratic society, "telling people what you do" is a key element of securing their consent for what you are doing.

PUBLIC RELATIONS, PUBLIC AWARENESS, AND THE PUBLIC SPHERE

Public relations (PR) is one way of securing popular consent and is an essential component, with advertising, of most marketing strategies; PR and advertising are integral parts of contemporary culture (Webster, 1995; Tumber, 1993). The techniques have colonised all social groups and major public-sector institutions, notably in the form of "image improvement" and advocacy advertising. Public awareness campaigns by universities are excellent examples. In fact, "public awareness campaign" is the preferred euphemism for public-sector PR. Euphemisms are ubiquitous in this industry. Practitioners prefer to "improve communications," or "get the message across," rather than "persuade the public about a particular position for payment"—a more accurate description of PR's rationale.

PR was viewed by initiators like Lippman and Bernays, as a necessary element of liberal democracy. Perhaps they envisioned a more balanced public arena than the one we currently inhabit. Habermas sees PR as undermining the public sphere and contributing to its decline. He considers it culpable of perpetuating disinformation and irrationality in public debate. Many would agree. The escalation of advertising and information management, and the emphasis on persuasion and commodification, is self-evident. It is hard to see how spin-doctored speeches by image-engineered politicians might *benefit* public institutions. Even so, Habermas's vision of a declining public sphere is problematic. There is more than one way to look at the situation, as Webster (1995) points out. On one hand, we can agree with Habermas that PR and advertising practices subvert democracy by corrupting the *quality* of information. On the other hand, we may consider civil society enhanced by the *quantity* of information available today, the diversity of its sources, and the better-educated citizenry interpreting it.

Notwithstanding the larger debates, "public awareness campaigns"—often crafted with cookie-cutter rhetoric—are increasingly in evidence in educational institutions. Shumar (1997) points to the discursive impact on rules, procedures and regulations. People's conversations about what they are doing and achieving are articulated differently. Thus when public institutions are drawn into the circuit of commodity production, "the force of the signifiers produced is to ultimately see all meaning in terms of what can be bought, sold, or made profitable. Education has increasingly little meaning outside a system of market relations" (Shumar, 1997: 5).

The system of market relations is emphatically at play in WCU's public awareness campaign, but it is difficult to tease apart those elements structuring the campaign and those related to the appointment of a new president (hereafter NP). The two are separate but intertwined aspects of the same phenomenon. Both the campaign, and the appointment of this particular president, illustrates several key aspects of the commodification trends outlined above.

NOT NEW, BUT DIFFERENT

Commodification and the adoption of commercial values are not in themselves new. NP exemplifies—in all respects except gender—those "captains of erudition" of the past who conceived the university as "a business house dealing in merchantable knowledge" and used publicity and "marketable illusions" to promote it (Veblen, 1918: 85, 137). It is probably fair to speculate that the Board approved the nomination of NP for precisely these attributes. The press release announcing the appointment emphasised her "demonstrated strengths" in "difficult financial times." Her former university's 25% increase in external research funding was attributed to her efforts.

But if commercial considerations are not new, the contemporary discourse of commodification is different in degree. It is overt, demanding, and unapologetic. And NP's "feisty" combative style matches the contemporary *zeitgeist* well. NP sells knowledge. It is her stock-in-trade. And she sells to the highest bidder. Her media interviews, workshops, and speeches hammer home the same themes:

- Knowledge is the most important commodity.
- There is a knowledge revolution.
- We live in a knowledge-based society.
- We need clearly enunciated visions: targeted markets, targeted performance, and accountability.
- We must "think" collaborations, development of excellence, strategic linkages.

The tensions of late capitalism enforce increasing isomorphism in institutional fields (DiMaggio and Powell, 1983). In other words, there is a tendency to conformity. Not only can we observe the increasing penetration *of* the university *by* the market, and the resulting homologies of structure, but also an increasing sameness in the response *by* universities *to* the penetration.

This is not the place to explore institutional theory in any detail. But two boundary-spanning elements of isomorphism are worth mentioning: the development of relational networks, and the interconnectedness of institutional elites. These foster mutual awareness and the recognition of involvement in a common enterprise, especially in times of uncertainty and change (Meyer and Rowan, 1977). In turn, these factors promote mimesis—imitation—fostered in part by the transfer of employees among institutions and the sharing of information through membership in "trade" associations (DiMaggio and Powell, 1983).

Thus, prior to her appointment, NP occupied a senior administrative position at another western Canadian university (hereafter UNP), where she was VP Research *and* Public Affairs—the conjunction seems significant. UNP had earlier initiated a highly successful public awareness campaign of its own, many elements of which were imported wholesale into subsequent similar efforts by other institutions, including the campaign studied here. The new president is also a key player, at the national level, in AUCC—the "trade association" of Canadian universities.

VPR acknowledges that isomorphism through mimesis was at work in the design and structure of WCU's public awareness campaign.

> We looked at UNP's campaign and decided it was conceptually what we wanted. . . . And [three of us] went to UNP for a session with NP and her crew. To learn about it, right? And, um, we really loved it . . . But we felt we were going to put a different "look" on our campaign. For one thing, if you do it's better. It's better to have different ones that are sending the same message.

To the uninitiated, any difference in look is dwarfed by the similarities: three-word slogans; downloadable screen-savers; buttons, bookmarks, and banners; mugs and mousepads; and lots of exclamation marks!!

Notwithstanding the forces structuring conformity, there is competition among universities. The publicity surrounding the annual Maclean's rankings confirms this. VPR would like to have co-operated with the other provincial universities on the awareness campaign, but:

> NP is pretty competitive you know. Every time I say I want things to happen *wit* [them] she says, "w-e-l-l no, let's do it ourselves." Like I wanted to launch the campaign with [the other local] university. I even wanted one slogan for all the universities in the province. But . . . NP wasn't keen.

THE GRAND NARRATIVE

Like VPR and her immediate predecessor, NP comes from the sciences. It is a commonplace that science is the dominant narrative of modernity (see Lyotard, 1979 among others). But together with technology, from which it can no longer be functionally separated, "hard" science—physical, medical, biological, and the interdisciplinary derivatives—is the commodity in question here. It is science and technology that drives most academy-industry partnerships. And it is science and technology that universities are exploiting with patents and spin-off enterprises.

Often, for scientists, research and science are synonymous. It takes intellectual effort to recall that research happens in other fields, even when such acknowledgement is the diplomatic course. Thus VPR mentioned his relief that of the 71 companies listed in WCU's new spin-off companies report, two were from the social sciences.[6] But he added:

> . . . let's be realistic. What research in the English department can produce a company? Versus someone discovering a new drug, or a new process, or a new car engine. I mean, let's be realistic.

So although the campaign is said to promote research in general, it is hard to escape the suspicion that such campaigns consciously or unconsciously devalue contributions from the arts and humanities. Meanwhile, the social sciences occupy their traditional ambivalent position of "dominated dominant" (Bourdieu, 1992).

It seems clear that those areas which deliver products (science and medicine) rather than ideas (arts, social sciences, and humanities) will continue to be favoured in this way, and will divert funding from other activities of a socially critical nature.

WHAT ABOUT TEACHING?

In the emphasis on research, teaching—and students—seem forgotten elements. Yet the public opinion poll conducted in July 1997 showed 65% of residents view teaching and research as equally important, while 26% place teaching ahead of research. There is a lot of lip service to teaching—especially undergraduate teaching—in NP's public pronouncements. But the reality seems to be that in an era of escalating class sizes and tuition fees, and reduced course offerings and access to professors, students are paying more and getting less (Noble, 1997).

CC admits that concerns were expressed about downplaying teaching when the campaign was being planned.

> The whole business of faculty morale was definitely brought up as a danger. I mean this could trigger a fair amount of resentment.

> Presumably, one of the criteria we had for the slogan and the campaign was that it would be versatile enough to incorporate [those] concerns.

> I haven't heard any concerns. Now whether they're simmering beneath the surface waiting to explode I don't know.

In some jurisdictions, there is systemic discrimination against those committed to teaching, rather than research. (For example, the "new public management" performance criteria and "research assessment exercises" in Britain) Of course, the publish or perish mentality is traditional in research universities and arguments can be made that teaching is epiphenomenal to research. It can be argued also, as Veblen (1918) did, that "Higher Learning" and teaching are inimical. Veblen believed that research universities should be graduate schools with no taught component—a not unattractive idea. Nevertheless, the fact remains that the state pays WCU an

enormous amount of money—about $300 million a year in block funding—to educate the province's students. And in a sense, WCU is reneging on that contractual obligation by shifting resources away from teaching to research, its spin-offs, and pay-offs.

VPR says he'd entertain a discussion on the differentiation of roles at WCU. He believes, he says, that two professorial streams—teaching and research—could be accommodated.

> I think it's possible to have people go through the professorial ranks, right to full professor, and be evaluated entirely on their teaching skills and then others entirely on their research skills . . . That might be naïve, but I think the discussion needs to take place. I think there's room for both and that both should be celebrated. But [pause] that's a big shift.

Despite protestations to the contrary, and at the risk of overstating the case, I suggest teaching is undervalued at WCU. And I believe a line can be drawn from this to the campaign's subtext. Research is an elite activity, teaching is not. Teaching is processing students through the classroom and into the general population. The general population is not smart enough to understand complex messages, so the campaign has to be "dumbed down" to something they can understand: a three-word slogan on a baseball cap.

Shouldn't universities—our principal cultural assets—be striving to *elevate* the general level of discourse? Why are they stooping to sloganeering? CC says, "You have to make it appealing. You have to grab them and shake them up a bit." VPR adds, "You can't get people's attention otherwise." He lays the blame on technology. Computers, cell phones, and television have reduced people's attention span and increased their appetite for instant gratification. He thinks the erosion is irreversible, and says, "not all progress is progress." Noble (1997) believes this élitist attitude finds its way into the commodification of instructional materials.

QUANDARIES OF COMMODIFICATION

The culture of commodification pervades WCU. The administration is strongly committed to strategic alliances, business-education partnerships, and industry-sponsored chairs and research.

A recent poll of the WCU community (n = 800) showed majority support (78%) for strategic partnerships with business, seeing such arrangements as preferable to alternatives such as higher tuition and user fees, or reduced services. However, the campus community's approval was hedged by strong concerns about restricting the involvement of business in teaching and research. The poll identified such restrictions as a trigger issue; that is, failure to address the concerns would "likely ignite strong opposition to strategic business partnerships." Significant reserve was also expressed about the types of partners selected—the preference being for good corporate citizens.

Responses like these highlight the potential ethical dilemmas of accepting money from corporate sponsors—whether for the exclusive right to market products on campus, a funded chair, or the $30 million a year WCU derives from sponsored research. The pragmatic question is: how many strings are attached to such arrangements? Does sponsorship potentially compromise academic integrity? In other words, would sponsorship influence choice of research topics and questions? Or, more importantly, would a researcher pull her punches if her results reflected negatively on her funding sponsor? VPR's first response of "absolutely not!" was modified somewhat on reflection.

> The answer to that is [pause] I would hope not. The answer to that is [pause] you can't control it. But the reality of it is . . . sponsorships are everywhere in society. . . . The university isn't protected from that and the question is should we be?
>
> What I feel is [pause] we have certain protective things in place which guarantee that at least for the majority of the [sponsors], which is 99% of them, they won't cheat. There are barriers against them cheating, and we can work in this sort of partnership and not feel compromised. But I won't deny you can't protect yourself from it completely.

VPR's confidence is not justified by studies of the corporate influence on scientific re-search. For example, a 1997 study of potential conflicts of interest by Sheldon Krimsky and colleagues indicated that in one of every three scientific papers examined, at least one of the chief authors had a financial interest connected to the research. In April 1998, a study of research-related gifts by Campbell and colleagues showed that restrictions on gifts by donors created potential ethical conflicts for recipients. Restrictions include reviewing articles and reports prior to publication—with resultant delays, and expected ownership of patentable results—with attendant secrecy and in contravention of most universities' intellectual property policies.

ANATOMY OF A CAMPAIGN

Having established the surrounding circumstances, and having attempted to place the campaign in a wider social and theoretical context, I will now turn to the details of the campaign itself: its structure, organisation, and format. As stated earlier, because this was a seed study it would be inappropriate to overanalyse or attach too much weight to the description that follows.

Original credit for the campaign belongs to VPR. VPR is a man committed to planning. When he took office in January 1996, he wanted a plan for what "WCU research *means*." The research plan and the public awareness campaign evolved together. In preparation for the change in the presidency, he brought together communications staff-members to brainstorm ideas. Subsequently, one person was seconded from his regular post in public affairs to act as campaign coordinator; a public opinion poll[7] was commissioned; an advertising/PR firm was contracted, at a cost of $10,000, to develop a concept and a soon-abandoned slogan; and a committee of 22 faculty was added to the core communications group.

After several months work, VPR took the idea to his academic colleagues.

> I presented it to all the Deans at a special meeting and they, as expected, hearing it for the first time . . . said, "What about me? I don't see me in there. I don't see my faculty in there." Especially the Dean of Arts, the Dean of Law—I mean the social science and hu-

manities Deans . . . but not a single Dean said, "You can't do this."

VPR is aware that the campaign privileges the natural and applied sciences but he takes the silence of the non-science deans—or the absence of specific prohibition—as acquiescence. This is a recurring theme in VPR's reading of his colleagues and I'll return to it later. It indicates, I think, that moves towards commodification cannot be passively resisted. Nor can traditional collegial forms of governance be relied upon to reverse excesses. When powerful administrative hierarchies are committed to a corporate agenda, only active, specific opposition is recognized or effective. Buchbinder (1993: 340) says that in "market-oriented" universities, traditional decision-making has been "replaced by a managerial hegemony in which the student and faculty groupings are marginalized and market strategies predominate." He comments further on the striking fact that the professoriate appears unmoved by the enormous transformations taking place in the university, and surmises that apathy and submission must be inevitable outcomes of marginalisation (Buchbinder, 1996).

LAUNCHING THE CAMPAIGN
The university community as a whole first became aware of the campaign at NP's installation in September 1997 when, during a formal speech to an invited audience, the new president doffed her mortarboard and donned a campaign cap as the university choir broke into song. The title of both speech and song was the trademarked campaign slogan, selected according to the committee's slogan criteria: it was "easy to say, durable, engaging, honest, direct, simple, versatile, and showed no bias."[8]

Both CC and VPR are proud of the slogan and the commercial savvy they showed in registering it. The following exchange is illustrative:

> VPR: We've trademarked it. We own it. The other company that owns it is the Bic pen company which is a bit unfortunate. They own it in the US but we beat them in Canada. So we can't sell a single piece of merchandise in the US. [pause] Not that

this is designed to sell anything [pause] but we are starting to sell some products in the bookstore.

> CC: They have an exclamation mark at the end of theirs.

> VPR: Oh, is that what they have? We'd still be in trouble, I guess.

> CC: We'll get a partnership with them; we'll get an education partnership (*laughs*).

> VPR: That's right. So we'll only be able to use Bic pens. (*Both laugh.*)

There is no irony in the reference to education partnerships. The remark reflects the growing pervasiveness of exclusive arrangements with commercial sponsors. At WCU, for example, the administration actively pursues such partnerships and has concluded exclusive arrangements with, among others, a major soft-drinks company and an airline.

The official launch took place two weeks after the installation, when NP conferred honorary degrees on eight diaper-clad infant volunteers in a psychology research program. The University chancellor tapped the infants on the head with a campaign baseball cap. The Board of Governors attended the event and the Chair of the Board expressed unanimous support for the campaign. Immediately after, the campaign's three-word slogan appeared everywhere on campus: on banners, in the bookstore, and on the university's publications—all according to plan.

CAMPAIGN PLANNING
The plan—prefaced with the usual amounts of corpspeak like "margin of excellence," "excellence and innovation," "research mission," and "research vision"—outlined a campaign that would be launched as a "grassroots initiative," followed by a mainstream media campaign in early 1998.

Soft launch tactics included dressing NP, VPR, and other senior scholars and administrators in campaign T-shirts, while they bagged books at the campus bookstore and distributed campaign bookmarks. Articles were planned in WCU's house, alumni, and donor publications. Banners were to be placed around the campus and a series of brochures would be produced. As the first event, the "baby PhDs" were expected to garner favourable coverage in the print and electronic media. (Who can resist babies?) Media kits would be mailed to bureaucrats and elected officials in all four levels of government and ongoing publicity would be generated through various avenues. Paid advertising would include 3 × 30 second radio spots a week (weekly cost = $1,100) on a selected province-wide talk show, and a bus and transit-shelter campaign at $65,000.

COSTS AND BENEFITS

Both VPR and CC insist that the campaign budget is limited to $100,000. But this is only the hard costs, which anyway exclude the original $10,000 in conceptual work. The budget does not cover CC's salary and benefits, the cost of replacing his position in public affairs, nor the time that VPR and his staff dedicate to the campaign. Nor, significantly, is there any attempt to quantify the real costs of involving 22 faculty members in six months of campaign development work. ("It's part of their job," says VPR, referring to the traditional service function.) Quite simply, there is no acknowledgement that opportunity costs are involved. And without such acknowledgement, there can be no meaningful cost/benefit calculation.

The benefit side of the equation is also problematic, since no one considered in advance the appropriateness of setting up milestones against which the campaign could be assessed. Certainly, the strategic plan specifies objectives, but not ones that can be measured in any meaningful way. How can one tell whether or not the following objectives have been achieved?

1. To raise awareness of, and support for, WCU's research.
2. To reposition WCU as a vital and innovative contributor to social and economic health in the eyes of the public, corporations, and government.
3. To put a human face on WCU research, highlight its diversity, illustrate linkages among research disciplines, and their relevance to societal concerns.

4. To raise collegial spirit and pride among WCU students, faculty, alumni, and staff.

When questioned about measuring the campaign's success, CC and VPR thought it might be worthwhile to repeat the public opinion poll at some point (first objective), which would address awareness but not support. As to the second objective, VPR and CC speculated about possible linkages between the campaign and future increases in granting council budgets.

> *VPR:* How much credit should I take? If the government increases the councils' budgets next year by a total of $200 million, should I say my $100,000 campaign investment triggered $200 million? That would be stretching it a bit, but you give me a percentage and I'll take it. I'll feel I contributed.

> *CC:* In January last year the AUCC had that full page ad—"Breakthroughs don't just happen"—with all those companies signing the back. Next month, what do we [Canadian research universities] get? Eight hundred million bucks!

> *VPR:* Is it related? I gotta tell you, the politicians said it was related. It *is* related, but we can't do the sums.

The third objective seems to defy measurement, but the fourth might be amenable to internal polling. However, VPR couldn't see the point since "I don't know what questions we could ask them." As mentioned earlier, to a significant degree, VPR's measure of the internal success of the campaign is silence; silence is interpreted as approval. Witness the following:

> I know we're OK for at least the following reason. The launch had over 300 people there. I received one e-mail that was negative. One! . . . From a community of over 2,000 faculty and 25,000 students. . . . It was a retired professor. And I think that's important. . . . Number one, they're from a different time. But number two, and importantly, when I wrote him back I never heard from him again. He was content. So that's a sign we're on the right track.

Deriving such a conclusion appears to demonstrate almost willful ignorance of social science research methods, or of the epistemological requirement to establish justification for one's beliefs in order to pronounce them true. At best, VPR seems naive. At worst, disingenuous. Either way, his conclusion is unwarranted.

AUDIENCE AND MESSAGES

The concept of a target audience also seems misunderstood. The plan specifies no less than *eleven* key audiences, including: residents of the province; the WCU community; politicians and bureaucrats; corporate leaders; local schoolchildren and their parents; donors—past, current, and prospective; multicultural communities; the science and technology community; media executives and reporters; and the mysteriously named "international stakeholders." Rather than targeted, this seems all over the map. The lack of PR finesse is almost endearing. One senses a bumbling sort of enthusiasm about the enterprise. On the other hand, people who don't know what they are doing can be dangerous. Put in charge of selling the university, these people might actually do so.

Seven key messages are to be directed at the target audiences:

- through education and research, universities are principal agents of innovation and change.
- through education and research, universities provide people with adaptable skills to meet the changing requirements of the global economy and workforce.
- WCU is one of North America's major research universities, fostering the transfer and application of knowledge for the benefit of society.
- WCU researchers actively participate in the intellectual, business, professional, social, and cultural life of the community.
- WCU researchers undertake joint research programs with industry, government, and community organizations.
- WCU faculty, students, and staff are proud of their research achievements.

- WCU's research and teaching excellence is dependent on continued support from all sectors of society.

There is no attempt to tailor these messages to specific audiences, with one exception. Politicians, bureaucrats, and business leaders received the new report on WCU spin-off companies as soon as the ink was dry. This report isn't really part of the campaign, but the UILO which produced it falls under the supervision of the VPR. They stamped the slogan on the cover and deployed the report strategically. Otherwise, there seems little or no understanding that in an era of market fragmentation, sophisticated techniques of audience differentiation are required (Turow, 1997) together with appropriate tailoring of content to format (Ericson et al., 1991).

The first three messages are unequivocally oriented to the market, while two of the remaining four specifically mention either business or industry. The university clearly seeks to reposition itself as an economic rather than social actor. In this, WCU is isomorphic with the rest of the institutional field. It is precisely this type of economic weighting that provokes Buchbinder and Rajagopal (1996: 287) to exclaim, "Public sector institutions are at risk. The public university is at risk . . . our colleagues in universities have not recognized the coming peril."

CONCLUDING REMARKS

While wary about drawing too many conclusions from a small pilot study, I have attempted in this paper to give some sense of the issues surrounding the commodification of university knowledge, and to illustrate that process through reference to one university's public awareness campaign. As I suggested earlier, I see no indication that the university is safeguarding itself as a centre of critical enquiry. I am left with the troubling conclusion that the administration's pursuit of commodification seems unreflective, uninformed, and dominated by the assumption that there is no alternative. The ideologies of business have been seized on rapaciously by university administrations worldwide.

Yet the ideology is being selectively interpreted and applied. Unlike their counterparts in other "knowledge industries," university administrators have chosen to keep the fat, cut the muscle, and disempower the front line. This goes against the "best" wisdom of management gurus who argue that with new technologies and new forms of organising production, production workers need to be empowered and middle management eliminated (Boyett and Conn, 1990). If university administrators were really "on message," they would be downsizing the management layer (themselves). Instead, it is the highly skilled production workers (the professoriate) that are being cut. The rhetoric is in place, but management's actions seem largely self-serving and in the main go unchallenged. The lack of resistance from the professoriate is troubling and perplexing. It seems to me that the questions to be formulated about faculty attitudes to these changes would be as long and complex as the answers.

I can only gesture at the issues surrounding commodification here. Limitations of time and space preclude more detailed exploration, but such exploration is clearly needed. A more extensive study of commodification and research is planned. The larger study will attend to the power shift by which the economic has come to dominate the intellectual, and the hierarchies which valorise some spaces of knowledge production over others. Faculty involvement will be investigated, as will the ownership and control of intellectual property, products and services. As well, I will attempt to unpack university financial reports to determine the underlying costs of entrepreneurial and administrative activity (Nelson and McCoy, 1997). Meanwhile, the public awareness campaign was assessed in March 1998 when CC's initial secondment came to an end. As far as I am aware, VPR has "kept him on" and the campaign is set to move into a second phase. I will reinterview both, and continue to track the campaign, as part of the larger study.

REFERENCES

BERCUSON, DAVID, BOTHWELL, ROBERT, and GRANATSTEIN, J. L. (1997). *Petrified Campus:*
The Crisis in Canada's Universities. Toronto: Random House of Canada.

BOURDIEU, PIERRE and WACQUANT, L. J. D. (1992). *An Invitation to Reflexive Sociology.* Chicago: University of Chicago Press.

BOYETT, J. H., and CONN, H. P. (1990). *Workplace 2000: The Revolution Reshaping American Business.* New York: Penguin.

BUCHBINDER, HOWARD and RAJAGOPAL, PINAYUR (1996). Canadian universities: The impact of free trade and globalization. *Higher Education*, 31: 283–99.

BUCHBINDER, HOWARD (1993). The market-oriented university and the changing role of knowledge. *Higher Education*, 26: 331–47.

CAMPBELL, E. G, SEASHORE, LOUIS K., and BLUMENTHAL, D. (1998). Looking a gift horse in the mouth: Corporate gifts supporting life sciences research. *Journal of the American Medical Association*, April 1: http://www.ama-assn.org/sci-pubs/journals/most/recent/issues/jama/oc71719a.htm.

DiMAGGIO, PAUL J. and POWELL, WALTER W. (1983). The iron cage revisited: Institutional isomorphism and collective rationality in organizational fields. *American Sociological Review*, 48: 147–160.

EMBERLEY, PETER (1996). *Zero Tolerance: Hot Button Politics in Canada's Universities.* Toronto: Penguin.

ERICSON, R. V., BARANEK, P., and CHAN, J. (1991). Media and Markets. In their *Representing Order: Crime, Law, and Justice in the News Media.* Toronto: University of Toronto Press.

KRIMSKY, SHELDON (1997). Reported in *Chronicle of Higher Education*, February 21: A4.

LYOTARD, JEAN-FRANÇOIS (1979). *The Postmodern Condition: A Report on Knowledge.* Translated by Bennington and Massumi (1984). Manchester: Manchester University Press.

MARCUSE, HERBERT (1964). *One-Dimensional Man: Studies in the Ideology of Advanced Industrial Society.* Boston: Beacon Press.

MEYER, JOHN W. and ROWAN, BRIAN (1977). Institutionalized organizations: Formal structure as myth and ceremony. *American Journal of Sociology*, 83: 340–363.

NELSON, MORTON and COY, DAVID (1997). Let's get accountable. *University Affairs*, November: 22.

NEWSON, JANICE A. (1994). Subordinating democracy: The effects of fiscal retrenchment and university-business partnerships on knowledge creation and knowledge dissemination in universities. *Higher Education*, 27: 141–61.

NOBLE, DAVID (1977). *America by Design*. New York: Alfred A. Knopf.

NOBLE, DAVID (1997). *Digital Diploma Mills: The Automation of Higher Education*, http://www.journet.com/twu/deplomamills.html.

READINGS, BILL (1996). *The University in Ruins*. Harvard: Harvard University Press.

SAID, EDWARD W. (1994). *Representations of the Intellectual*. New York: Vintage.

SCHILLER, ANITA R. and SCHILLER, HERBERT I. (1982). Who can own what America knows? *The Nation*, 17: 461–463.

SCHILLER, ANITA R. and SCHILLER, HERBERT I. (1986). Commercializing information. *The Nation*, 4 (October): 306–309.

SCHILLER, HERBERT I. (1989). *Culture, Inc: The Corporate Takeover of Public Expression*. New York: Oxford University Press.

SHUMAR, WESLEY (1997). *College for Sale: A Critique of the Commodification of Higher Education*. Washington, DC: The Falmer Press.

SLATER, DON (1997). *Consumer Culture and Modernity*. Cambridge, UK: Polity.

TUMBER, HOWARD (1993). "Selling scandal": Business and the media. *Media, Culture, and Society*, 15: 345–361.

TUROW, J. (1997). *Breaking Up America: Advertisers and the New Media World*. Chicago: University of Chicago Press.

VEBLEN, THORSTEIN (1918/1965). *The Higher Learning in America: A Memorandum on the Conduct of Universities by Business Men*. New York: Kelley, Reprints of Economic Classics, by arrangement with The Viking Press.

WEBSTER, FRANK (1995). *Theories of the Information Society*. London: Routledge.

NOTES

1. Especially one that embraces such linguistic barbarisms as "visioning."
2. None of my informants could define "research-intensive," although the term crops up everywhere in administrative and campaign rhetoric. As a working definition, the Vice President, Research suggested that, in Canada, a research-intensive university would collect over $100 million a year in research funding.
3. Interestingly, Veblen (1918) contended that professional schools and vocational imperatives have no place in an institution dedicated to "the higher learning."
4. Because the Noble article was an e-mail post, I am unable to supply page references. The article's focus is the commodification of instruction by high-tech means, but Noble sets up this phenomenon as continuous with the commodification of research over the last twenty-five years.
5. However, figures for the last three years published by the institution's university–industry liaison office seem to indicate state support for research is stable. The structure of the university's published financial statements defies detailed analysis, so changes in the funding/expenditures mix over time are difficult to trace. It is impossible to gauge the actual cost of administration, for example, since the majority of administrative salaries are buried in the category for academic salaries. Recently, Nelson and Coy (1997) called for reform in the measuring and reporting of performance by Canadian universities.
6. Which two companies originate in the "social sciences" is unclear. Closer examination of the report indicates that 45% of the companies are classified as "Life Sciences," 39% as "Physical Sciences," with the balance as "Information Technology." Faculties of origin of the 71 companies are: Science, 27; Medicine, 18; Applied Science, 15; Law, 3; Pharmaceutical Sciences, 1; Commerce, 1. Three of the projects qualified for support from SSHRC.
7. The telephone poll of 503 subjects was piggybacked onto a research firm's July 1997 omnibus survey. It was not specific to WCU but sought public attitudes to university research in general. The main finding was that while residents in the province placed "a great deal of importance" on university research, relatively few (one-third) recalled specific research. Of this one-third, most recalled medical research. Most residents regarded teaching and research of

equal importance, with the remainder of opinion favouring teaching. One in two residents expressed moderate interest in learning more about research.

8. Quotes and details on campaign organisation come from an internal document made available to me by CC.

COMMENTARY ON THE READINGS

The Adlers wrote that they gained entry into the world of drug smugglers "largely by accident." The method they utilized is a fieldwork classical approach: They stumbled upon a research opportunity, then used informants to help them gain the trust of others in the subculture. In this way they were able to obtain a snowball sample. After six years of data collection through interviewing and observation, the Adlers were able to write an analysis of the data that includes how traffickers gained entry into the subculture, differing levels of drug trafficking, and how traffickers did (or did not) "retire" from drug trafficking.

In contrast, Janet Atkinson-Grosjean was interested in the marketing of the university to prospective students, business, and political leaders. She wanted to conduct a large research project on the topic, but where to begin? She used a combination of content analysis on documents produced by the university at various levels and fieldwork methods as a first phase to a larger project. In essence, she used fieldwork as an inductive phase: an initial stage in a large research project designed to gather data and build a grounded theory that is tested in a later stage of the project. This first phase of the project is presented here.

CONCLUSION

Fieldwork is a time-consuming method of research, but it can illuminate social life in ways that other methods simply cannot do. Most fieldwork studies are, by nature, case studies. This fact limits the generalizability of the study, but in exchange for a high level of detail. Fieldwork, through its rich descriptions and interview quotes, sheds light on the actual voices that compose a social group. Because of this, it is an indispensable tool in social research.

CHAPTER 10

EVALUATION RESEARCH

Evaluation research has also been called program evaluation, and between the two terms an accurate picture of the method and its purpose emerges. Governments, businesses, and nonprofit organizations develop programs and policies designed to have a particular effect. But how do those organizations know if programs are doing what they are supposed to do? Evaluation research is designed to answer this question.

INTERVENTION AND OUTCOME

The point of programs and policies is to guide action to desired end results. For instance, food stamps, a program administered by the U.S. Department of Agriculture, is designed to alleviate hunger. The desired result of the program is the outcome, and it is outcomes that the researcher needs to measure in evaluation research.

Evaluations are normally carried out to determine whether or not the desired outcomes have been achieved. Often, evaluation determines whether or not the program will continue to receive funding or whether changes need to be made. These are legitimate reasons for conducting evaluations.

Carol Weiss (1972) has also commented on three illegitimate reasons for conducting an evaluation. In some cases, decision makers may utilize evaluation research as a way to postpone making a decision. Since the evaluation takes time, it also buys time for the decision maker. An evaluation can also be used as a means of ducking responsibility for an unpopular decision; the decision maker essentially deflects responsibility onto the one performing the evaluation research. At other times, if the expected results are good, the decision maker may seek an evaluation for public relations purposes. The researcher needs to be aware that these motives may be present but also needs to remain unswayed by the agendas of those requesting the evaluation.

MEASURING OUTCOMES

Evaluation research is often able to evaluate interventions based on the official documents related to them. Programs often have a mission statement, a document that explains the purpose of the intervention. Mission statements tend to vary, and this variation introduces inconsistencies in developing measures for differing programs. As an example, let's examine two hypothetical programs.

Program A has the following line in its mission statement:

> The purpose of the Mathematics Tutoring service is to enhance students' knowledge of math and raise their aptitude.

This program is very specific in its goals, and so there is a clear measure to evaluate the program: participants' aptitude in mathematics. Evaluation can be accomplished by comparing students' grades before and after completing the program. Or a math aptitude test can be given to participants upon entry and completion of the program and the results compared.

Program B has the following goal, according to its mission statement:

> The purpose of the Social Science Research Center is to encourage interest in social science research.

A noble goal, indeed, but how does one measure "interest"? Because the goals of this program are fairly vague, the means of evaluating the program's effectiveness is much more difficult compared with program A. One could conduct a survey, but the definition of "interest" needs to be established first. One could also compare the amount of social science research conducted before and after the program began, but the findings may not reflect the impact of the program itself. In either case, the indicators of "success" need considerable conceptualization before the design and implementation of the study can take place.

Even when the program goals are clear, the definition of "success" or "effective" is often vague and politically vulnerable. If the goal of the food stamp program is to alleviate hunger, the program is a success. If the goal is to eliminate hunger, the program is a failure. If some people experience an elimination of hunger and others do not, is the program a success, failure, or something else? How many of those in need are allowed to fall through the cracks before a policy or program is labeled a failure? And once it is so labeled, what should be done? Reform, elimination, or replacement with a new program? Although all social science research carries with it the potential for controversy, evaluation research assumes a particularly great risk.

RESEARCH DESIGN

Evaluation research typically utilizes a variety of research designs, but some are particularly well suited for the purpose.

Experimental Design.   Experimental designs are useful in evaluation research. Experiments, of course, rely on the existence of experimental and control groups. For instance, if one wishes to study the effectiveness of a program to improve math aptitude, potential participants can be randomly divided into two groups. The experimental group would go through the program. The control group, under ideal circumstances, would not receive the treatment—in this case, the program. However, if the program requires a new style of tutoring, it would be unethical to deny subjects the services if they come to the program seeking such services. In this case, the experimental subjects would receive the new style of tutoring (the treatment) and the control group subject would receive the old style of tutoring. The differences between the pretest and posttest scores for both groups are then analyzed.

Time Series.   Realistically, the ability to randomly assign program participants to experiment and control groups is often limited. In order to evaluate a program, researchers can utilize a time-series study. For instance, a researcher who wants to evaluate the effect of raising the speed limit in Michigan from 55 mph to 65 mph on traffic deaths could use the running records that exist on traffic deaths. The researcher would analyze the number of traffic deaths on Michigan roads for a number of years prior to the treatment—in this case, the change in policy raising the speed limit—to the number of deaths on Michigan roads after the treatment. Without a control group, however, the researcher cannot be sure that any changes are specifically the result of the policy change rather than some other variable.

Qualitative Evaluation.   In qualitative evaluation, the researcher typically interviews program participants and staff. The interviews are typically unstructured but are also highly focused on evaluating the effectiveness of the program. The information is then analyzed as it would be in any other qualitative study.

THE READINGS

The first reading, "Target Efficiency of State Home Ownership Programs," by Mark Lewis Matulef (1986), evaluates the effectiveness of programs designed to allow Americans to buy their own homes. The second reading is an evaluation of performance appraisal, a management technique that seeks to improve the productivity of individuals working in a hospital environment. In "Experiencing Performance Appraisal in a Trust Hospital," G. Coates (2000) has written an article that in effect evaluates a form of evaluation.

TARGET EFFICIENCY OF STATE HOME OWNERSHIP PROGRAMS

Mark Lewis Matulef

National Association of Housing and Redevelopment Officials

The United States government has promoted home ownership for over 50 years. The U.S. tax code provides a tax exemption on income earned on state and local mortgage revenue bonds issued to finance home ownership subsidy programs. The president's tax proposals to Congress would eliminate federally tax-exempt mortgage revenue bonds (MRBs). A total of 45 state housing finance agencies (HFAs) issue MRBs and impose income limits on program participants even without a federal requirement to do so. In 1983, a U.S. General Accounting Office report concluded that most MRB-financed single-family housing programs aided higher-income households in the majority. This author's study found, however, that the majority of assistance went to low- and moderate-income households. One-third of the HFAs did provide a majority of assistance to higher-income households. The study conducted for this article determined that the income limit imposed on program participants was an effective control on the degree to which low- and moderate-income households were program beneficiaries. The existence of legislative and executive oversight powers did not, however, have a significant impact on single-family program performance. National income limits or income-limit guidelines could result in greater target efficiency in home ownership programs.

Home ownership is the aspiration of nearly every American household. The federal government has been in the business of promoting home ownership for over 50 years. The federal tax code demonstrates the government's commitment to home ownership. Home purchase interest payments, closing costs, and property taxes are deductible from personal income.

Yet the cost of home ownership is too high for most households that do not already own their homes. Since 1980 the percentage of households owning their own homes has declined (Kateley et al., 1986: 5).

For the most part active government efforts to promote home ownership are carried out by state and local government agencies. Through the federal tax code, Congress allows state and local governments to issue tax-exempt bonds to finance home purchase programs for low- and moderate-income households. To date, 49 states have created housing finance agencies (HFAs) to implement single-family programs based on the federal tax exemption. By allowing HFAs to issue tax-exempt bonds, Congress and state governments support housing sales and construction, and increase the affordability of single-family housing for persons whose incomes cannot support market interest-rate mortgages.

Tax-exempt bond finance is not unanimously popular, however. The president's 1985 tax proposals to Congress would terminate the authority of state and local government to issue tax-exempt mortgage subsidy or mortgage revenue bonds (MRBs).

The purpose of this article is to determine what factors affect the *target efficiency* of state single-family housing programs. Target efficiency is the degree to which a program benefits the intended or targeted population. In the case of bond-financed single-family housing programs, Congress and state legislatures have stated that such programs should benefit low- and moderate-income households. Most state HFAs impose income limits even without a federal standard or directive.

THE CASE AGAINST MRBs

The president's plan to overhaul the federal tax code argues that the tax code should be used for

From *Evaluation Review*, 10, 6, (December 1986) 7:15–56. Copyright © 1987 Sage Publications, Inc.

revenue-raising and not for social policy. Despite the fact that the federal government has provided single and multifamily housing subsidies for 50 years, the president's proposal to Congress labels MRBs as "non-governmental bonds" (White House, 1985: 129).

> Tax-exempt nongovernmental bonds have caused erosion in the Federal income tax base.... The revenues lost as a result of tax-exempt nongovernmental bonds represent an indirect Federal subsidy program, based in the tax code, and thus significantly free of the scrutiny that attaches to direct Federal expenditures.

The cost in forgone revenues to the U.S. Treasury in 1986 was estimated by Congress's Joint Committee on Taxation at $2.1 billion—for all outstanding MRBs. This represents nearly $100 billion in MRBs issued since 1975. The tax expenditures represented by MRBs constitutes less than half of 1% of total federal tax expenditures (National League of Cities, 1985).

Perhaps tax expenditures are not generally subjected to the scrutiny of direct spending. Yet in 1980 and 1982, Congress engaged in extensive reauthorization hearings on tax-exempt MRBs. Every few years, the legislation that authorizes tax-exempt MRBs comes up for Sunset and congressional review. Each time MRB authorization is reviewed, Congress places new restrictions on their use. For example, the Mortgage Subsidy Bond Act of 1980 (Ullman Act) required a set-aside of bond proceeds to low-income "target" areas.

STATE SINGLE-FAMILY PROGRAMS: RECORD TO DATE

In all, 49 states authorize a state housing finance agency (HFA) to issue bonds to finance home ownership programs. Morris (1976: 7) describes HFAs as "state authorities which stand independent of state executive departments." By issuing tax-exempt mortgage revenue bonds (MRBs), state and local HFAs can raise funds at below-market interest rates. In turn, these agencies can provide below-market interest rate

mortgages to single-family housing program participants.

Congress directs state HFAs to assist first-time home buyers and to limit the purchase prices. Congress does not, however, impose income limits on state single-family housing program participants. State legislation creating most HFAs *targets* single-family housing assistance to low- and moderate-income households but, like federal legislation, does not specify income limits. In 45 states, nevertheless, HFA boards of directors do set household income limits.

In 1983, Senator Robert Dole asked the U.S. General Accounting Office (GAO) to investigate single-family subsidy programs financed by tax-exempt MRBs. GAO concluded the majority of assistance went to higher-income households. GAO (1983: 3) stated that the typical assisted household earned an annual income of $20,000 to $40,000. GAO reported statistics in an appendix that showed, however, that 62% of subsidized loans went to low- and moderate-income households in 1982.

Calculations of the percentage of households with low or moderate incomes ... reveal appreciable differences in state HFA target efficiency—the degree to which state HFAs assist low- and moderate-income households. Most states were found to assist low- and moderate-income households in the majority.

To date, a convincing body of evidence has yet to be produced explaining this variation in single-family program target efficiency. No study has been undertaken to determine what would make state home ownership programs work better. The purpose of this study is threefold. First, an attempt will be made to determine whether state single-family housing programs are individually or collectively target efficient or inefficient. Second, a model will be constructed to determine which aspects of an HFA's organization (staffing, structure, and so on) and environment (markets, state political culture, and controls imposed by state elected officials) affect single-family program target efficiency. Finally, this article will suggest institutions and practices—in particular, income targeting and agency oversight institutions—that could improve single-family target efficiency.

THE HFA ENVIRONMENT AND
TARGET EFFICIENCY

The purpose of this section is to identify a range of factors that would, in theory, affect the ability of a state housing finance agency to assist low- and moderate-income households. There has been little analytical writing to date on state HFAs. It is possible, nevertheless, to consider what various authors have written about similar types of agencies and about particular elements of the HFA environment in the context of single-family housing programs.

The model developed in this study does not include federal government influences explicitly. Federal government tax policy makes state single-family programs possible. Federal spending (for example, budget deficits) and monetary policy (for example, the discount rate extended to banks borrowing from the Federal Reserve) affect interest rates. These policies affect housing programs in all states. They are assumed not to affect variation in target efficiency among states.

Markets and
State Demographics

Housing prices, interest rates, and bond ratings. In the last few years, while household income has doubled, home sales prices have tripled (HUD, 1980). The median sales price of a single-family home has increased from $26,000 in 1969 to $70,000 in 1982 (*Land Use Digest*, 1980). Rising home ownership prices relative to incomes have been blamed for a 2% drop in the national home ownership rate between September 1980 and July 1983 (*Land Use Digest*, 1983). The median price of a home continues to increase and the home ownership rate continues to decline. In particular, the cost of financing is the fastest-growing component of housing costs overall. HFAs in states with relatively higher housing prices can expect to have greater difficulties in making single-family housing affordable to low- and moderate-income households than states with lower housing prices.

With few exceptions, HFAs receive no appropriations from state legislatures. They depend on issuing mortgage revenue bonds in the municipal bond market and the federal tax exemption on interest earned on such bonds.

HFAs that provide relatively lower interest rates to program participants are more likely to help low- and moderate-income households buy homes than HFAs, which offer higher rates. Lipsey and Steiner (1975: 595) write that "a rise in the rate of interest from eight to 10 percent will lead to an increase of over 15 percent in the monthly payment necessary to buy a given home."

The interest rate an HFA offers its single-family program participants depends on many factors. It depends on the federal tax exemption on MRBs. HFAs offer MRBs to bond buyers at lower yields than taxable bond issues. The bond buyer's return on investment is tax exempt, making the lower initial return competitive with the after-tax return on taxable bond investments. HFAs can raise funds at below-market rates and pass on the lower rates to single-family program participants in the form of below-market interest rate mortgages. The interest rate depends also on broader market conditions affecting bond markets and interest rates in general.

The interest rate that HFAs can offer depends on the ratings that independent bond raters assign to HFA mortgage revenue bonds. The interest rates an HFA must pay to bond investors and, in turn, pass on to participating home buyers is determined by its respective state's credit rating and by how risky its mortgage loans are perceived to be.

Investors look to bond ratings as indicators of risk. Investors will demand higher yields from bond issues perceived to be riskier investments. The grade difference between bond ratings accounts (for example, between a Standard and Poor's double-A and single-A rating) for a 0.1 or 0.2 percentage point interest rate difference in bond yield (Betnun, 1976: 133, 144). The two most prominent raters of municipal bonds are Moody's Investor Services and Standard and Poor's Corporation. A Moody's publication describes the company's bond rating policy:

The purpose of Moody's bond ratings is to convey to the investors our opinions of the economic/financial risk in owning a given security and holding it to maturity. This involves an assessment of the probability that interest and principal will be paid in accordance with the terms of the bond contract, as well as an assessment of the bondholder's likely economic return in the event of default [Moody's, 1982: 1].

HFA bond issues tend to carry ratings a full rating below that of state bond issues backed by the state's full faith and credit (Betnun, 1976: 107–129). (MRBs are not backed by full faith and credit but by HFA reserves and mortgage payment revenues.)

Dean (1962: 81–86) associates lending risk with the incomes of households that qualify for mortgages. He points to delinquencies and foreclosures as evidence of imprudent lending to households without sufficient incomes to support mortgage payments. New York's Urban Development Corporation experienced a period of multifamily project foreclosures and obtained B-level ratings.

Alternatively, bond ratings may indicate an agency's tendency toward target efficiency or inefficiency. HFAs and other bond-issuing authorities are sensitive to bond ratings (Rabinowitz, 1979: 75). Low bond ratings one year could induce HFA administrators in the next year to increase assistance to higher-income households in hope of gaining higher bond ratings and, thus, lower fund-raising costs. A previous year's bond ratings could affect current year HFA performance.

State demographics. The ability to serve low- and moderate-income, first-time home buyers depends on the extent to which there is a population of low- and moderate-income, first-time, would-be home buyers to serve. It is likely that a target efficient HFA is one in a state with a relatively young and affluent population.

Struyk (1962: 22) has outlined a series of variables that can be used to predict whether a household is likely to own its own home: household income and size, member age, race, head of household education and occupation, housing prices, degree of racial segregation, and the availability of federal home ownership tax incentives. Struyk has found that household income is the best predictor of home ownership. The interaction of income and housing costs determines affordability. In 1983 the median income household had only 80% to 90% of the income required to purchase the median-priced home. If a state HFA's income limit is based on statewide median income and the state's median income is relatively high, the HFA should have a comparatively easier time of providing assistance to low- and moderate-income households than an HFA in a relatively lower-income state.

Reid (1962: 72) explored the relationship between owner-occupancy and various household characteristics in a 1962 regression study. Reid concurred with Struyk that income was the best indicator of home ownership. She reported also that household age seemed only to be a significant factor among households whose heads were below the age of 35. Reid's findings indicate that a state with a relatively large proportion of younger households is likely to have relatively fewer home owners than a state with a smaller proportion of such households and, thus, is more likely to have a large proportion of households eligible for HFA single-family subsidies.

Household race is also often noted as an indicator of home ownership. Struyk (1962: 122–125) found that black households must pay higher prices than white households as a premium to enter predominantly white home ownership markets. In 1983, 43% of black households owned their own homes, whereas 64% of white and other racial groups owned their own homes (U.S. Department of Commerce, 1982: 24). The difference in income does not completely explain the difference in home ownership. Among households earning less than $10,000, total and black household home ownership rates were 56% and 42%, respectively.

HFA Organization and Administration

The typical HFA is an independent public finance corporation that issues tax-exempt bonds to finance its housing subsidy programs. State HFAs keep a portion of bond proceeds in a reserve account but use most of the proceeds to fund their programs. Every state HFA operates a *mortgage purchase program.* In a mortgage purchase program, the HFA contracts with private-sector lenders to initiate below-market interest rate mortgages for eligible applicants. Each lender is given a certain volume of loans to originate and administers the necessary loan applications and credit checks. After bonds have been sold, would-be home buyers apply for the subsidized mortgages with the participating lenders. When the lenders have approved the loans for the eligible applicants, the original loans are closed and the files are sent to the HFA for approval. If it approves them, the HFA purchases the loans and assumes financial responsibility.

Agency relationship to state government. HFAs are created by acts of state legislatures, principally to take advantage of the federal tax laws that authorize state and local agencies to issue tax-exempt bonds. The oldest of these single-family programs are only 10 years old.

Betnun (1976: 184, 202) describes the HFA environment as complex and everchanging. It is an environment of changing market interest rates and housing needs. Betnun cites James L. Price's conclusion that public agencies that are autonomous of executive (gubernatorial or state department) control are "organizations which have a high degree of effectiveness and are more likely to have a higher degree of effectiveness than organizations which have a low degree of autonomy." HFA effectiveness is the ability to increase the supply of capital for housing investments, to stay out of bankruptcy, to adjust to changing market conditions, and to target housing assistance to low- and moderate-income households.

Independent HFAs can enter the bond market when they wish to take advantage of favorable borrowing rates. To take advantage of changes in bond market rates, HFAs must act quickly before the cost of borrowing increases. HFA boards of directors can set income limits that vary by locality—to address the cost of housing in various communities, and by household size, to address the space needs and higher housing costs associated with larger families.

Of the 49 HFAs, 23 can be labeled *independent* agencies. Independent agencies are directed by boards that neither report to nor are part of executive agencies. The 26 other HFAs possess a variety of legal statuses. Some of these HFAs have only an information-reporting relationship with an executive agency and some lie squarely along the executive chain of command. A total of 15 HFAs are executive or *line* agencies.

HFA board and targeting policy. In most state HFAs, the agency board of directors sets operating policy and income limits. Income limits in some states are adjusted for family size and regional differences in housing costs.

In some states, particular HFA board seats are reserved for state officials. Seats can be assigned to representatives of particular industries, such as housing construction, lending, or planning. Seats can be assigned to representatives of low-income housing residents, labor unions, or particular geographic areas. The Housing Agency has the most exacting representative scheme:

(1) a person experienced in housing development administration,
(2) a person experienced in real estate operations,
(3) a person experienced in commercial banking,
(4) a person experienced in home building,
(5) a person experienced in apartment building construction or ownership,
(6) a person experienced in mortgage banking,
(7) a person experienced in savings and loan operating,
(8) a person experienced in housing problems of low-income persons and families and moderate-income families, and
(9) a representative of municipal or county government.

The willingness of a board member to assist higher- or lower-income households may depend on his or her professional or political affiliations. For example, Morris (1976: 2) suggests that lending industry representatives on HFA boards prefer assistance to lower-income households to prevent competition between the HFA and private lending institutions for higher-income home buyers.

Staffing. Lewis (1965: 248) notes that the details of operating a public program are most often delegated to a *professional staff*. Public agency professionals have been viewed alternatively as policy neutral agents of public service or as biased on particular policy issues (Appleby, 1945: 165). Betnun (1976: 83, 163) suggests that HFA directors consider their missions as twofold: serve low- and moderate-income households and maintain financial stability. These objectives may conflict. Maintaining financial security and stability implies an aversion to risk. Providing loans to lower-income households is a riskier undertaking than providing loans to higher-income households. To avoid risk, financially minded HFA directors and staff could seek to limit the number of mortgage loans to low- and moderate-income households that the agency purchases.

The orientation of HFA directors and staff to assist lower- or higher-income households could be a product of professional training and experience. A staff composed chiefly of accountants might prefer providing home ownership assistance to higher-income households, whereas a staff of former public housing managers might prefer to assist lower-income households.

Organizational structure. Betnun (1976: 202) asserts that smaller, less departmentalized HFAs are more flexible and more able to respond rapidly to changing market conditions than larger, more departmentalized HFAs. Small HFAs may be better equipped to enter bond markets rapidly, to attain lower borrowing costs, and to pass on lower interest rates than larger, more departmentalized HFAs. Larger, more departmentalized HFAs are saddled with requirements to share information and make decisions between departments and to resolve any internal conflicts.

Mintzberg (1979: 135–160, 304–313, 348–379) suggests certain tasks are best performed by smaller, less departmentalized (simple) organizations and certain other tasks are better suited to larger, more departmentalized organizations (professional bureaucracies). Tasks that are more complex require greater specialization and division of labor and are better suited to the larger, more departmentalized organization. HFA single-family housing programs may involve specialized, technical skills—bond issuing, financial market analysis, loan application review, and income targeting to meet the needs of a diverse state population.

Political Environment
Betnun (1976: 187) writes that HFAs are subject to controls imposed by governors, auditors, legislators, and special interest groups. According to Betnun these controls "often but not always limited HFA effectiveness." Betnun (1976: 187–189) suggests that state elected officials have an interest in state housing finance programs and have used their influence to obtain housing subsidies for both higher- and lower-income households. Betnun attributes this influence to formal oversight and appointment powers and to informal powers derived from HFA deference to the governor's preferences. Various authors assert that a state's *political culture* affects the degree to which elected officials involve themselves in the implementation of state programs and, subsequently, policy outcomes.

Political party affiliation. Dye (1966: 107) concludes that policy outcomes are in part a function of which party holds the majority in each house of the legislature and which party holds the governorship. Reporting the results of correlation analyses, Dye determined that higher state expenditures for public education were associated with Democratic party leadership rather than with Republican leadership. Welsh and Peters (1982) ascribe to Democrats a greater willingness to fund public programs, and to Republicans a greater unwillingness to fund public programs or upset the status quo. Thus, Democratic officials would be expected to support home ownership assistance for low- and moderate-income households, and Republican officials would be expected to favor little or no public intervention in single-family housing. If a program were already in place, Republicans would support housing policies that did little to upset the status quo—that is, assist higher-income households.

Party competition. Elected officials are expected to avail themselves more frequently of oversight channels when there is a split in the leadership—for example, when there is a governor of one party and speaker of the lower house of another (Hevesi, 1975). Sharkansky (1970: 170–180) regression analysis relating political culture, socioeconomic, and federal government aid indicators to state expenditures also revealed that political competition "played [a] minor [role] with respect to 1962 state expenditures." Yet in a study conducted with Hofferbert, Sharkansky found that the degree of political competition in a state affected the degree to which elected state officials provided financial support for program areas like welfare and education. Sharkansky concluded that competition for political support (electoral competition) manifested itself in public agency actions to the extent that elected officials had control over agency decision making.

Election politics. Weingast (1984: 148) suggests that the involvement of elected officials in program implementation is a function of political competition and demands for goods and services by voters and organized interest groups. Of Congress and independent federal regulatory agencies, Weingast writes that "in return for electoral support front interest groups and voters, congressmen provide a flow of policy benefits." Downs (1978: 28, 34) writes that political "parties formulate[d] politics in order to win elections." In a politically competitive state, Downs writes, "the government subjects each decision to a hypothetical poll and always chooses the alternative which the majority of voters prefers. It must be so because if it adopts any other course, the opposition party can defeat it." One would expect that officials would be

willing to distribute home purchase subsidies if such benefits would attract votes. One may also expect that elected officials would be more willing to support single family programs and seek to influence state HFAs in favor of assisting low- and moderate-income households in states with larger populations of low- and moderate-income households.

Controls imposed by elected officials. Each state has its own set of formal powers given to elected officials to *control* executive and independent state agencies. Rosenthal (1983), Jackson and Howard (1976), Worthley (1976), Craft (1979), and Brown (1979) assert that the ability of elected officials to influence state agency-administered programs is, in part, a function of oversight powers afforded by state law. Control institutions can be grouped into three classes. The first is *formal oversight institutions*. The second class is *degree of professionalization*—staffing resources available to legislators and the degree to which legislators depend on working outside of elected office for their livelihood. The third class of control institutions is *informal control*—the ability to influence agency policy and actions without invoking official sanctions. Oversight institutions include the following:

Formal oversight institutions:
- gubernatorial power to appoint agency directors and board members
- gubernatorial power to remove agency directors and board members
- governor or legislator as a member of an agency board of directors
- executive review of agency budget
- executive approval of agency bond issues
- Sunset or other time limit on agency authorization
- standing agency oversight committee
- legislative review of agency budget
- appropriation of general funds to agency (executive budget submission and legislative budget approval)
- legislative veto of rules and regulations
- legislative review of rules and regulations
- legislative approval of agency bond issues

- agency as an executive (line) or independent agency
- legislative appointments of board members

Degree of professionalization:
- full-or part-time legislature
- post auditor
- professional staffing for individual legislators

Public agency officials may not have to experience sanctions imposed by elected officials. They may act accordingly with the preferences of elected officials to avoid sanctions—delays in appointments, cuts in funding, and so forth. HFAs may temper their policies and performance to satisfy elected officials' preferences for assistance to higher- or lower-income home buyers.

The legislative or independent *post auditor* is an agency for reviewing public agency performance to determine whether such performance is, first, effective toward achieving its intended purpose, and, second, in keeping with budget guidelines and legislated policy objectives. The post auditor provides an analytical resource for elected officials (Rosenthal, 1983: 96; Craft, 1979: 67–69; Brown, 1979: 146). *Sunset* laws provide for legislative review of agencies and programs. If the legislature so desires, it can use the legislative review process to recommend changes in authorization, such as changing agency powers, or allow the time limit on such legislation to run out. Sunset review takes into consideration whether there is continuing need for agencies or programs, whether agencies or programs should be merged, or whether agencies require new powers to carry out their missions (Rosenthal, 1983: 94). The Congress has set a Sunset date of December 31, 1987, for the tax exemption on mortgage revenue bonds.

The few state governments that provide general funds to HFAs can restrict or curtail such public funds if they are displeased with agency targeting policies or performance. Azama (1979: 27–34) writes that agencies that depend on bond issues for programming funds may be sensitive to the preferences of elected officials who undertake *oversight hearings* or other forms of agency review. Delays in entering bond markets could result in an agency missing out on lower borrowing costs.

Do controls work? Avery (1980: 40–44) suggests that oversight controls may not afford elected leaders any control over federal independent agencies. Reviews of the Commodity Futures Trading Commission and the Consumer Product Safety Commission were undertaken with oversight committee members disposed to cut the agencies' budgets. At the conclusion of hearings, however, the committees voted to increase the agencies' budgets.

Alternatively, Weingast argues that legislatures have used control institutions effectively to discipline program officials to accept and fulfill the overseers' policy preferences. Weingast (1984: 148) suggests that the degree to which elected officials can impose their policy preferences depends on the extent of their formal control powers. Weingast (1984: 168–179, 182) links a change from regulatory "activism" to "deregulatory" activities at the U.S. Securities and Exchange Commission to a change in Senate Securities Subcommittee chairmanship and a willingness in Congress to "market test" the deregulation of the banking and securities industries. Weingast concludes that so-called independent agencies like SEC are financially beholden to their corresponding subcommittees and, thus, implement policies in keeping with subcommittee members' preferences.

Autonomy and Control
Betnun labels the debate over the impact of executive and legislative involvement in public program implementation as "autonomy and control." *Autonomy* is a public agency's freedom to make financial, programming, and policy decisions without consulting chief executives, legislators, courts, or directors of other agencies. *Control* is the authority of elected officials to review public agency finances, operating policies, and program performance, or to make certain decisions for public agencies. These two views of public program implementation and oversight

provide alternative frameworks for predicting the impact of control institutions on programs administered by state HFAs. Advocates of autonomy would predict that imposing controls on state HFAs would result in assistance to statutorily unintended (higher-income) populations in single-family programs. Advocates of control would predict that imposing controls would result in assistance to statutorily intended (low- and moderate-income) populations.

The autonomy argument. The first autonomy argument is that oversight entails a trade-off between speed and compliance. HFA officials must act rapidly to enter the bond market and contract with participating private lenders to obtain the most attractive cost of borrowing program funds. If they divert time and energy from programming to reporting, HFAs may accept less favorable borrowing terms and make borrowing terms unaffordable to low-income and, possibly, moderate-income households.

The second autonomy argument is that oversight is not necessarily policy neutral. Appleby (1945: 156) asserts that public administrators have been trained to dedicate themselves to serve the *public interest* and counsels that the public need not question the motives of unelected public officials. Bachrach (cited in Lewis, 1976: 254) describes democratic institutions— legislation writing, oversight hearings, performance review, and so on—as means for elected officials to pursue policies favorable to the narrow economic interests of society's elites. Once a law has been adopted, interaction between elected and agency officials could provide opportunities for elected proponents of narrower-than-legislated objectives to pressure public agency officials to serve populations not targeted by legislation or regulation.

Sachs (1972: 35–36) suggests that part-time elective service is more conducive to the influence of narrow economic interests than full-time service:

> Legislative service is part-time service, and the legislator must earn a substantial portion of his livelihood on the outside. He must have a job, run a business, or have investments, or

perform services for clients. The legislator himself, as an employee or client, will therefore have particular interest in what the state government is doing.

Sachs does not expect elected official oversight to be policy neutral.

Finally, Joiner (1964: 44) suggests that public officials in *line agencies* are more susceptible to chief executives' (governors') pressures for service to narrow economic interests. Joiner expects that independent or autonomous agencies are in a better position to resist the pressure from elected officials to assist unintended populations.

The control argument. The control argument is based on faith in democratic institutions. Worthley (1976: 198) advocates oversight of public agencies by elected officials. He invokes the constitutional principle of *checks and balances* against bureaucratic unaccountability and the Aristotelian view of politics as a reconciliation of diverse interests. In this sense, politics—the involvement of elected officials in program implementation—prevents the deflection of legislated objectives to serve narrow interests.

Second, control advocates see the involvement of elected officials (as overseers, evaluators of program performance, and members of boards of directors) as preventing the unchecked influence of economic interest groups on the formulation of agency operating policy (rules, regulations, and targeting policies). HFA policy is established by a *representative board*. Such boards provide opportunities for interest groups to seek benefits for their members regardless of general legislative directions (Ash Commission, 1977: 4). Thus, oversight could block efforts by narrow interests to seek home ownership subsidies for high-income households.

Third, oversight is seen as a check against the implementation of public programs according to the professional biases of public administrators. Lewis (1976: 254) writes that public administrators are specialists, trained to solve specific problems. They are also viewed with suspicion as technocrats that possess a monopoly on information and technical expertise. These technocrats impose their biases on democratic institutions (Appleby, 1945: 154). It is possible that HFA officials trained as financial analysts, for example, consider fiscal stability as their paramount objective and seek to approve subsidies for households that represent lower risks—that is, higher-income households.

Limits to the autonomy and control arguments. The autonomy and control arguments take extreme views on the impact of executive and legislative controls on the degree to which public programs achieve their legislated purpose. There is also a question of whether gubernatorial or legislative controls have a significant effect on public policy outcomes at all.

Board-run, independently financed public agencies, like state HFAs, may not be influenced by elected officials who are granted oversight powers. Boards and commissions could be galvanized against oversight by fixed terms of office and policymaking independent of the legislative process. Oversight could have no effect on HFAs or have a negative effect if reporting and justification activities deflect agency energies from making timely bond issues and administering programs.

Yet another point of view of the effectiveness of controls comes from McCubbins and Schwartz (1983: 4–5, 15–16). They write that Congress has the authority to engage in active oversight of independent regulatory agencies but chooses to limit involvement in agency activities. Oversight is costly in time and energy. Elected officials rely, by and large, on citizen (voter) and interest group complaints or "fire alarms" that indicate constituent dissatisfaction with agency performance. Congress has responded to such fire alarms—for example, by terminating the Area Redevelopment Administration just two years after creating it. McCubbins and Schwartz argue that if the legislature appears unresponsive to independent agency actions or appears unwilling to engage in active oversight, this does not mean the legislature does not care about the agencies it creates or the programs it authorizes. A legislature may leave an agency to itself if it is satisfied with the agency's performance.

There are several examples of legislative approval of HFA performance. The Texas House of Representatives Financial Institutions Committee (1982) reported that there was no need to change the Texas Housing Agency's statutory powers. The Committee was charged with studying ongoing loan programs and home ownership benefits. No witnesses gave testimony during scheduled hearings. Congress extended the states' authority to issue tax-exempt bonds through 1986 without imposing income limits, even after GAO issued its 1983 report criticizing the HFAs' single-family programs. Even during the Congress's efforts to overhaul the federal tax code through 1985 and 1986, the tax exemption on MRBs was maintained in the House and Senate plans.

There are alternative propositions on the impact of controls available to elected state officials. First, controls imposed by or available to elected state officials on a state HFA induce the agency to assist higher-income households (the control argument). Second, controls imposed by or available to elected state officials on a state HFA induce the agency to assist low- and moderate-income households (the autonomy argument). Third, controls imposed by or available to elected state officials have no particular impact on the degree to which the HFA assists low- and moderate-income households within its single-family housing program (the null hypothesis).

METHODOLOGY
General Model

The basic statistical model for estimating the effects of HFA's environment and organization on single-family housing program targets . . . estimates a statistical relationship between the observed variation in HFA organizational and environmental aspects and the observed variation in target efficiency. These relationships, regression coefficients, are represented by the vectors b_j, c_k, and d_l.

The statistical model covers one year's HFA activity—programs for which bonds were issued between January 1 and December 31, 1983. In 1984 there were enough targeted, bond-financed mortgage purchase programs—45—to permit some generalization about the effect of HFA organization and environment on target efficiency.

Data Collection
Data were collected for this study in two ways. Secondary, published sources were consulted for data on state political culture, markets, and demographics. A copy of a survey instrument was sent to each state HFA executive director. The directors were instructed to complete the form prior to a telephone interview. All primary source data were collected over the telephone.

Variable Measures
Dependent variable. Three alternative measures of target efficiency were calculated. The first, Targeting, equals an HFA's income limit for a statewide median-sized household minus the upper limit of moderate income (120% of statewide median income). This measure of the upper limit of moderate income is based on a standard definition within the assisted housing industry. The Section 8 existing rent subsidy program and other federal assisted housing programs target assistance to low- and moderate-income households. An observation of Targeting can be positive, if the limit exceeds the upper definition of moderate income, or negative, if the limit is less than the upper definition of median income.

The dependent variable measure, Target Efficiency, equals the upper limit of moderate income (120% of statewide median income) minus the median income of households assisted in an HFA's single-family program in 1983. An observation of Target Efficiency can be positive, if the majority of single-family participants earned low or moderate incomes, or negative, if the majority of an HFA's single-family participants earned higher incomes. (The measure was not based on the actual number or percentage of loans made to low- and moderate-income households. In 1983, most HFAs were small, new, non-automated organizations without the ability easily to produce a broad range of statistics about their performance.)

The third dependent variable measure, Simple Target Efficiency, is the median income of households assisted in an HFA's single-family

program. This dependent variable is not standardized by accounting for variations in median income among states. Statewide median income is included as an independent variable. Using Target Efficiency in the regression equation would overemphasize the importance of median income in the regression findings. Simple Target Efficiency is a reliable substitute for Target Efficiency. A .64 correlation was found between the two measures of the dependent variable.

Independent variables. Many of the variables are measured as dummy variables. For example, a Democratic majority in the houses of the legislature is measured as 1, a Republican majority as 0. The degree of executive or legislative control over HFAs is summarized in two composite variables. If a certain control is available to a state's executive or legislature, a score of 1 is assigned. If a certain control is not available, a score of 0 is assigned. These scores are added together to obtain executive and legislative control indices—with maximum cumulative scores of 7 and 11, respectively.

The mortgage interest rate offered to single-family program participants and an independent variable based on HFA bond ratings are included. An integer score of 0 to 3 is assigned to the 1982 Standard and Poor's HFA bond rating—0 for bond ratings in the B-range, 1 for bond ratings in the single-A range, 2 for the double-A range, and 3 for the triple-A range. Single-family housing prices are included, measured as the median asked-for price of available owner-occupied homes. Also, state percentage of households aged 20 to 34, state percentage of black households, and statewide median income are included in the model.

The working background of HFA directors and the predominant working background of staff are divided into two categories: finance (lending, accounting, budgeting) and nonfinance (housing, community development, real estate, architecture). Working backgrounds for directors and staffs are converted to dummy variables—with non-finance backgrounds assigned 1 and finance backgrounds 0. Agency superstructure is measured as staff size multiplied by the number of departments or formal divisions.

HFA board members are grouped into five categories:

(1) state officials: elected and appointed executives, legislators;
(2) local officials: elected officials, appointed or hired executives;
(3) housing industry representatives: construction, real estate, management, services, materials, developers;
(4) lending industry representatives: commercial and mortgage banking, savings and loan associations, services (accounting); and
(5) constituent groups: individuals eligible for housing assistance, and associations representing populations eligible for assistance.

A series of independent variables equal to the percentage of HFA board seats held by representatives of each group is included in the equation. The HFA income limit is also included as a variable. The income limit is measured as the gross annual household income of a median-sized household in the state (for a family of two income earners and two dependent children).

An overall political competition index is constructed to reflect the percentage of majority party seats in the houses of a state's legislature and control of the governorship over a 10-year period. The index range, from 50, indicating the highest degree of party competition possible, to 100, indicating the lowest degree possible. As an indicator of the political salience of single-family housing programs, the percentage of a state's population eligible for home ownership assistance is included in the model. The variable is calculated as the percentage of a state's population with incomes below the HFA income limit for a median-sized household.

Analysis and Interpretation

To determine if state HFAs (overall) serve low- and moderate-income or higher-income households in the majority, the dependent variable Target Efficiency is summed over the available observations. If the sum is positive, the findings show that HFAs (overall) assisted low- and moderate-income in the majority in 1983.

The impact of income limits and other aspects of the HFA environment on single-family

target efficiency is determined by analyzing the t-scores obtained through the regression analysis. Depending on how a particular independent variable's corresponding hypothesis is constructed (as a one- or two-tailed test), one looks to the t-scores that exceed a threshold level. For a one-tailed hypothesis test and 12 degrees of freedom, an independent variable's t-score must exceed 1.782 to reject the null hypothesis that variation in the independent variable does not cause variation in the dependent variable. For a two-tailed test, the t-score must exceed 2.201. These scores indicate that there is a 5% of lower risk of erroneously rejecting the null hypothesis.

FINDINGS

The descriptive and causal statistics that follow are based on a 36-state sample of state HFAs (80% of the 45 states that impose income limits on participants in single-family mortgage purchase programs). The following states make up the sample:

| Arkansas | Louisiana | North Carolina |
| Colorado | Maine | North Dakota |

HFA officers in Alabama, Alaska, New Jersey, New York, Ohio, South Carolina, and Virginia also participated in the survey but were not included in the sample. Alaska did not have an income limit per se in 1983, but a sliding interest rate scale based on household income. New Jersey, New York, and Ohio did not impose income limits in 1983. Alabama, South Carolina, and Virginia could not provide enough data to be included in the analysis. Kansas did not have a housing finance agency.

Descriptive Findings

Single family housing program performance. The first dependent variable, Targeting, concerns how closely an HFA's single-family program income limit reflects the upper end of statewide median income. The 1983 income limits for the respective states' median-sized households are presented. Income limits ranged from $24,250 in Colorado to $50,200 in Illinois. The dependent variable Targeting ranged from –2,485 in Colorado to 22,717 in Illinois. On average HFA income targets exceeded the upper end of moderate income by \$10,955.75. Observations of Targeting varied appreciably among the 36 states.

The second dependent variable, Target Efficiency, describes whether a state HFA serves low- and moderate-income or higher-income households in the majority. Of the 36 states, 24 had positive or *target efficient* observations, and 12 had negative or *target inefficient* observations. Observations of Target Efficiency ranged from −8,661 in Arkansas to 8,418 in Maryland. The sum of the observations was 51,578 and the mean was 1,432.72, indicating that overall state HFAs assisted low- and moderate-income households in the majority in 1983. A weighted mean (by bond volume) was calculated at 1,893.94, reinforcing the finding of overall target efficiency.

The third dependent variable, Simple Target Efficiency, is simply the median income of households assisted in a state HFA's single-family housing program. Observations of Simple Target Efficiency ranged from 18,227 in Tennessee to 31,376 in Texas. The mean of observations was 23,829.06, meaning that the typical state provided half of its single-family assistance in 1983 to households with incomes above \$23,839.06 and half to households with incomes below \$23,829.06.

Independent Variables

Market and state demographics. Within the sample the average interest rate offered to single-family housing program participants was 10.4% in 1983. A total of 28 states reported interest rates in the 10% to 11% range. Because of this lack of variation, the impact of interest rates may be underestimated. The states were almost equally divided, however, between those with HFA bond ratings in the double-A range (19 states) and single-A range (17 states) in 1982.

Within the 36-state sample, the average asked-for housing price was \$52,292 in 1980. Housing prices ranged from \$31,000 to \$125,000. In the sample, the overall average percentage of younger households (age 25–34) was 26.5 in 1980 and ranged from 22.8% to 41%. The percentage of black households did vary appreciably—from 0.3% to 29.7%, with an average of 7.68%. The upper end of statewide moderate

income (120% of statewide median income) ranged from about \$19,000 in Arkansas to \$32,000 in Hawaii in 1983.

HFA organization. The following list summarizes the means and ranges of particular groups' representation on HFA boards of directors in 1983:

Group	Mean (%)	Range (%)
State officials	23.4	0–57.1
Local officials	6.8	0–28.6
Lending representatives	17.0	0–44.4
Housing representatives	30.0	0–55.5
Client representatives	2.6	0–14.3

On only four HFA boards did a group constitute a majority: housing representatives in Massachusetts and North Carolina, and state officials in Connecticut and Maryland. With respect to staff working backgrounds, finance backgrounds were predominant—28 of the 36 states. Non-finance backgrounds were most common among HFA directors.

HFA superstructure scores (staff size times number of divisions) ranged from 1 (Mississippi and Washington) to 2,408 (Hawaii). The mean score was 392.6. Staff size ranged from 1 (Mississippi and Washington) to 301 (Hawaii), with an average of 59.8. Observations of departmentalization ranged from 1 (Iowa, Utah, Mississippi, Washington) to 11 (Pennsylvania), with an average of 4.97 divisions. Only 10 states had superstructure scores over the average (Hawaii, Illinois, Maryland, Massachusetts, Michigan, Minnesota, Montana, Pennsylvania, Tennessee, West Virginia). Only 2 of these 10 had negative (target inefficient) Target Efficiency observations. These 10 may be classified as professional bureaucracies. The other 26 HFAs may be classified as small or simple organizations. This finding hints at a positive relationship between bureaucracy and target efficiency.

Political environment. In the sample, 22 states had Democratic governors and 14 had Republican governors in 1983. On average in the sample Democrats held 63.4% of seats in state legislatures. The percentage of Democrats in state legislatures ranged from 20 in Utah to 96 in Louisiana.

A total of 13 states in the sample had a governor whose political party was different from the party leadership of the lower house of the state legislature. The average overall party competition index score was 66.6 closer to the maximum possible competition score of 50 than the minimum score of 100. Competition scores ranged from 53 in Pennsylvania to 85 in Arkansas. Eligibility for HFA single-family housing programs ranged from 50.3% in Colorado to 89.9% in Arkansas.

Observations of the executive and legislative control indices were generally on the low side. The executive control index averaged 2.8 out of a possible 7. The legislative control index averaged 4.2 out of a possible 11. About half of the states had executive control indices of 2.

The actual control institutions available to state executives and legislators varied appreciably among the states. A correlation matrix revealed that a state would not necessarily have a particular control institution if it had another. The only exception was that a state whose governor appointed the HFA executive director was about 80% likely to allow the governor to remove the executive director.

In the sample 17 state HFAs can be labeled *independent* and 19 HFAs can be labeled *nonindependent*. Yet only 7 states granted the executive branch the power to accept or reject HFA bond issues. Only 3 states granted that power to the legislature or one of its committees. Individual legislators occupied seats on HFA boards in only 2 states in the sample—Colorado and Tennessee. Legislators appointed board members in only 5 states. Governors sat on HFA boards in 4 states—Georgia, North Dakota, Tennessee, and West Virginia. All states empowered the governor to appoint board members. In 25 states the governor is empowered to remove board members before the end of their terms; 10 states empowered governors to appoint the HFA executive director, and 12 states empowered the governor to remove the executive director.

Sunset legislation was enacted by 28 states in the sample. Legislators in 16 states performed some kind of regular oversight, most commonly to review agency finances. A total of 15 states employed a legislative auditor, 23 states authorized a legislative veto, and 26 states allowed legislators to review or modify agency rules and regulations. In all, 8 legislatures operated without limits on the length of legislative session; 28 states imposed time limits (part-time legislatures). Legislators in 18 sample states were allowed to have personal staffs.

Causal Findings

The regression model presented earlier included 23 independent variables and was estimated with 36 observations using a least squares regression procedure (enough degrees of freedom for causal inference). The 23 independent variables explain 56% of the variation in the dependent variable Simple Target Efficiency. The regression equation constant was estimated as 8,423 and was not statistically significant. These findings suggest, however, that measurement or other refinements made in the model could increase the degree to which variation in target efficiency is explained.

Three independent variables were found to have a statistically significant impact on Simple Target Efficiency. The HFA income limit, staff working background, and the percentage of lending industry representatives on the board of directors passed their respective tests of significance.

Each independent variable found to have a significant impact on Simple Target Efficiency was an aspect of HFA organization and internal policy. The variable Staff Background indicated whether the most common working background of an HFA's staff was in financial or non-financial services. The regression findings show that in 1983 the median income of households receiving single-family assistance from an HFA whose staff come mostly from a finance background was $4,682.96 higher than for households assisted by an HFA whose staff come mostly from a non-finance background. This finding supports the notion that HFA employees with finance backgrounds are more risk averse than employees with non-finance backgrounds (such as housing management), and, therefore, seek to approve subsidies for higher-income households.

The percentage of board seats occupied by lending industry representatives was also found to affect simple target efficiency significantly. A coefficient of −170.1 was estimated, indicating that for every percentage increase in lending industry representation on an HFA board, the median income of households receiving home purchase assistance would decline by $170.10 in 1983. For example, if an HFA with a 10-member board increased its lending industry representation from two to four seats—an increase from 20% to 40%—the model predicts that the median income of assisted households would decrease by $3400. This finding supports the proposition that lending industry representatives on HFA boards seek to prevent competition between the private and public sectors for higher-income home buyers, and, therefore, seek to assist lower-income households.

The income limit imposed by state HFAs on single-family program participants had an estimated regression coefficient of .38, suggesting that for every $1000 decrease in the income limit, there would be a corresponding $380 decrease in median income of assisted households. This finding suggests that HFAs with lower income limits do assist lower-income households to a greater extent than HFAs with higher limits.

Additional Test for Executive and Legislative Control

Neither the executive nor the legislative degree-of-control indices were found to have a significant impact on target efficiency. To determine the effect of each control institution available to elected officials, a series of *difference of means* tests was conducted. The statistic Target Efficiency was used as the dependent variable. These tests compared observations of the dependent variable between states that had instituted the particular control institutions and states that had not. All t-scores representing the differences of means fell below the score of 2.037 required to reject the null hypothesis. These tests failed to support the *autonomy argument* that such controls would contribute to single-family target inefficiency, or the *control argument* that such controls would contribute to target efficiency.

CONCLUSION

Critics of bond-financed home ownership programs contend that such programs are not effective in providing home purchase subsidies to low- and moderate-income households. They contend also that such programs are not sufficiently subjected to sufficient control. This study of state HFAs and their single-family housing programs provides evidence to the contrary.

(1) State single-family programs do assist, overall, households with low and moderate incomes.
(2) State HFAs are subject to a wide variety of control institutions, but these institutions do not appear to have a generalized effect on target efficiency.
(3) There are indications that a few internal organization strategies affect target efficiency—the presence of lending industry representatives on the HFA board of directors and HFA staffing, size, and departmentalization.
(4) Income limits do have a positive impact on target efficiency.

This study shed light also on the very different political and organizational environments in which state single-family programs exist.

HFAs are similar in some respects. Each HFA operates a mortgage purchase program and issues tax-exempt MRBs to raise program funds. Most HFAs have a board of directors that sets income limits for single-family program participants. That is about where the similarity ends. Each HFA is subject to a unique set of political controls available to elected state officials. HFAs work in different demographic settings. HFAs come in different sizes and structures, employ staffs from varying professional backgrounds, have boards with different configurations of members, and set different income limits. In sum, the HFA environment is a rich quasi-experimental research setting.

Target Efficiency Findings and Implications

In its 1983 report GAO stated that the majority of

MRB-financed home purchase assistance went to higher-income households. GAO stated that the typical assisted household earned an annual income of $20,000 to $40,000. The GAO report's appendix included, however, statistics showing that 62% of assisted households in 1982 earned low or moderate incomes. The research findings described in the previous section were consistent with GAO's appendix-reported figures.

Two-thirds of the HFAs included in this study were found to assist low- and moderate-income households in the majority. The study found that the typical household receiving an HFA subsidized mortgage in 1983 earned $23,000—appreciably lower than the $40,000 reported by GAO. The median income of assisted households exceeded $30,000 in only three states (Alaska, New York, and Texas). The findings suggest that state single-family housing programs financed by tax-exempt MRBs can be target efficient. That one-third of the states in the survey sample was found to have target inefficient programs indicates that there is room for improvement.

Factors Affecting Single-Family Target Efficiency

Three variables in the 23-variable regression model were found to affect HFA single-family housing program target efficiency. The model predicted that the median income of single-family program participants would decrease by $380 for every $1000 reduction in the annual household income limit. The implication is that HFA staff and directors are responsive to board-established targeting policies.

There is a national policy implication for the finding that the income limit imposed by the HFA board affects single-family target efficiency. This finding supports a national guideline for setting HFA single-family income limits. Stricter income limits, imposed by the federal government, could result in a higher proportion of low- and moderate-income households receiving home purchase assistance. Income limits have been suggested in the U.S. Congress, but always rejected.

The regression findings showed that target efficiency was not significantly affected by market, demographic, or political factors. The implication is that HFAs operate independently of a wide range of aspects of their environment. Internal aspects of HFAs had a greater impact on single-family program outcomes.

The regression findings suggest that an HFA that wanted to improve its target efficiency could hire more persons with non-finance backgrounds—for example, persons with housing management backgrounds—or at least try to strike a balance between staff members with finance and non-finance backgrounds. A governor who wanted to improve HFA target efficiency could increase lending and finance industry representation on the HFA board of governors.

Independence from Control Institutions

There are several ways to interpret the finding that control institutions did not affect single-family target efficiency. First, the finding suggests executive and legislative controls do not influence independent public finance agencies. Second, the finding suggests that in the case of single-family programs one would not see the impact of *potential* controls on HFA performance because elected state officials are generally satisfied with single-family program outcomes. Unless a so-called fire alarm were sounded, elected officials would not engage in active oversight. The third interpretation is that these controls have no impact on policy outcomes.

Final Note

State single-family housing programs financed by tax-exempt bonds were found to be, in general, target efficient—to serve their intended purpose. The research findings point out, however, that state single-family housing programs could use some fine-tuning. By making changes in state HFA staffing and board of directors composition and by imposing guidelines for stricter single-family program income limits, single-family target efficiency could be improved. Yet national income limit guidelines should not be so restrictive as to threaten the financial stability of state HFAs or prevent HFAs from considering regional differences in affordability within a state. State HFAs are, in general, fulfilling their public purpose to make home ownership more affordable to low- and moderate-income households. These state authorities may require additional guidance to do an even better job.

REFERENCES

APPLEBY, P. (1945) Big Democracy. New York: Knopf.

AVERY, D. (1980) "The record of Sunset Review of two agencies," in T. Clark et al. (eds.) Reforming Regulation. Washington, DC: American Enterprise Institute.

AZAMA, C. (1979) Sunset: The Concept and Its Experience. Legislative Reference Bureau, State of Hawaii. Request Number 0579-A.

BETNUN, N. (1976) Housing Finance Agencies: A Comparison between State and HUD. New York: Praeger.

BLALOCK, H. (1979) Social Statistics. New York: McGraw-Hill.

BROWN, R. E. [ed.] (1979) "Forward," in The Effectiveness of Legislative Program Review. New Brunswick, NJ: Transaction Books.

———. (1979) "Implementation lessons," in The Effectiveness of Legislative Program Review. New Brunswick, NJ: Transaction Books.

BROWNSTEIN, R. (1985) "Wagering on tax reform." National Journal (February 2). Council of State Governments (1983) The Book of the States. Lexington, KY: Author.

COUNCIL OF STATE HOUSING AGENCIES (1983) 1982 Survey of Housing Finance Agencies. Washington, DC: Author.

CRAFT, R. (1979) "Products of audit-evaluation work," in R. E. Brown (ed.) The Effectiveness of Legislative Program Review. New Brunswick, NJ: Transaction Books.

DEAN, J. (1962) Homeownership: Is it Sound? New York: Harper & Row.

DORNBUSCH, R. and S. FISCHER (1978) Macroeconomics. New York: McGraw-Hill.

DOWNS, A. (1957) An Economic Theory of Democracy. New York: Harper & Row.

DYE, T. R. (1966) Politics, Economics and the Public: Policy Outcomes in the American System. Chicago: Rand McNally.

HERZBERG, D. G. and A. ROSENTHAL [eds.] (1972) Strengthening the States. New York: Doubleday.

HEVESI, A. G. (1975) Legislative Politics in New York State, A Comparative Analysis. New York: Praeger.

INTERIM REPORT OF THE FINANCIAL INSTITUTIONS COMMITTEE (1982) Texas House of Representatives, 67th Legislature, Austin.

JACKSON, E. L. and A. J. HOWARD (1976) Legislative Oversight. Atlanta: University of Georgia Press.

JOINER, C. A. (1964) Organizational Analysis: Political, Sociological, and Administrative Processes of Local Government. Institute for Community Development and Services, Michigan State University, East Lansing.

KATELEY, R. et al. (1986) "Investment opportunities in apartments." Real Estate Research Corporation (Spring).

KRISLOV, S. and L. D. MUSOLF [eds.] (1965) "Introduction," in The Politics of Regulation: A Primer. Boston: Houghton Mifflin.

LEWIS, A. (1965) "To regulate the regulators," in S. Krislov and L. D. Musolf (eds.) The Politics of Regulation: A Primer. Boston: Houghton Mifflin.

LEWIS, E. (1976) Public Entrepreneurship: Toward a Theory of Bureaucratic Political Power. Bloomington: Indiana Univ. Press.

LIPSEY, R. G. and P. O. STEINER (1975) Economics. New York: Harper & Row.

McCUBBINS, M. and T. SCHWARTZ (1983) "Congressional oversight overload: police patrols versus fire alarms." Working Papers on Institutional Design and Public Policy WP-03, University of Texas, Austin.

MINTZBERG, H. (1979) The Structuring of Organizations. Englewood Cliffs, NJ: Prentice-Hall.

MOODY'S INVESTOR SERVICE (1982) Moody's Bond Record.

MORRIS, P. (1976) State Housing Finance Agencies. Lexington, MA: Lexington Books.

NATIONAL LEAGUE OF CITIES (1985) Tax Breaks: An Introduction to Tax Expenditures. Washington, DC: Author.

PETERSON, G. with B. COOPER (1979) Tax-Exempt Financing of Investment. Washington, DC: The Urban Institute.

PRESIDENT OF THE UNITED STATES (1985) The President's Tax Proposals to the Congress for Fairness, Growth, and Simplicity. Washington, DC: Government Printing Office.

PRESIDENT'S ADVISORY COUNCIL ON EXECUTIVE ORGANIZATION [The Ash Commission] (1971) A New Regulatory Framework, Report on Selected Independent Regulatory Agencies. Washington DC: Government Printing Office.

PRICE, D. (1978) "The diffusion of sovereignty," in J. M. Shafritz and A. C. Hyde (eds.) Classics of Public Administration. Oak Park, IL: Moore.

RABINOWITZ, A. (1979) Municipal Bond Finance and Administration. New York: John Wiley-Interscience.

REID, M. (1962) Housing and Income. Chicago: Univ. of Chicago Press.

ROSENTHAL, A. (1983) "Legislative oversight and the balance of power in state government." State Government 56: 40–49.

SACHS, H. R. (1972) "On ethics and ethical standards," in D. G. Herberg and A. Rosenthal (eds.) Strengthening the States. New York: Doubleday.

SHARKANSKY, I. (1970) Regionalism in American Politics. Indianapolis, IN: Bobbs-Merrill.

STANDARD & POOR (1977) Municipal and Industrial Bond Ratings: An Overview. New York: Author.

STRUYK, R. (1962) Urban Homeownership: The Economic Determinants. Chicago: University of Chicago Press.

U.S. ADVISORY COMMISSION ON INTERGOVERNMENTAL RELATIONS (1984) The States and Distressed Communities, Final Report Draft. Washington, DC: Author.

U.S. CONGRESS, CONGRESSIONAL BUDGET OFFICE (1982) Mortgage Bond Subsidy Tax Act of 1980. Experience under the Permanent Rules. Washington, DC: Government Printing Office.

U.S. CONGRESS, GENERAL ACCOUNTING OFFICE (1983) The Costs and Benefits of Single Family Mortgage Revenue Bonds, Preliminary Report. Washington, DC: Government Printing Office.

U.S. DEPARTMENT OF COMMERCE, BUREAU OF THE CENSUS (1982) 1982 Annual Survey of Housing. Washington, DC: Government Printing Office.

———. (1982) State and Metropolitan Area Data Book 1982. Washington, DC: Government Printing Office.

———. (1982) U.S. Census of Housing, Vol. I: General Housing Characteristics, HC80-1-A2. Washington, DC: Government Printing Office.

———. (1983) 1980 Census of Population, Vol. I: Characteristics of the Population, PC80-0-1-A1. Washington, DC: Government Printing Office.

———. (1983) Statistical Abstract of the United States 1984. Washington, DC: Government Printing Office.

U.S. DEPARTMENT OF HOUSING AND URBAN DEVELOPMENT (1980) United States Urban Policy 1980. Washington, DC: Government Printing Office.

WEICHER, J. (1980) Housing: Federal Policies and Programs. Washington, DC: American Enterprise Institute.

WEINGAST, B. (1984) "The congressional-bureaucratic system: a principal agent perspective (with applications to the SEC)." Public Choice 44: 147–195.

WELSH, S. and J. G. PETERS (1982) "State political culture and the attitudes of state senators toward social, economical, welfare, and corruption issues," in J. Kincaid (ed.) Political Culture, Public Policy, and the American States. Philadelphia: Center for the Study of Federalism.

WORTHLEY, J. (1976) Public Administration and Legislatures: Examination and Exploration. Chicago: Nelson-Hall.

■ ■ ■ ■ ■

EXPERIENCING PERFORMANCE APPRAISAL IN A TRUST HOSPITAL

G. Coates

Contemporary performance appraisal (PA) has become an important tool in the overseeing of employees in work. Little of the vast literature however, has focused on its effects on the individual, beyond simple descriptions that inform its management implementation. This article firstly examines the changing nature of employee management under PA, before it investigates the contemporary usage of PA and the effects on women. This is illus-

From *Electronic Journal of Sociology, 5, 1* (2000). www.icaap.org/iuicode?100.5.1.1. Copyright © 1999 Electronic Journal of Sociology.

trated with research, gathered from a case study in the Midlands. The article also examines the changing focus of PA as a means through which the marginal, and not so marginal performer can be controlled. Analysis focuses on the use of *subjective* images of "women," through PA, for creating functionally flexible workers in a "quality" environment. This analysis also examines management's attempts to "involve" individuals in the formulation of their own work process. It does this by focusing on the powerful subjective manipulation of knowledge over individuals. The use of a hospital case study highlights some of these issues in relation to the changes taking place in the public service sector. This sector faces fundamental transformations in its concept of "service."

INTRODUCTION AND BACKGROUND

Performance appraisal belongs to the postmodern organisational notion of a "human centred," subjective management system, manifest in Human Resource Management (HRM), Strategic Manpower Planning and Total Quality Management (cf. Harrison and Laplante 1993). For many individuals, PA conjures images of piecework and performance-related-pay (PRP), and has been seen as a less than objective principle (McArdle *et al.* 1992). This fear has become a rational one in recent times for education (Harley and Lee 1995; Miller 1991), articulating notions of surveillance and control (Reed and Whitaker 1992).

Broadly speaking, there are two camps, those who support performance appraisal (Cotton 1993; Molander and Winterton 1994; Murphy and Cleveland 1995) and those who see it as a form of control (Causer and Jones 1996; Coates 1994).

Performance appraisal has its roots in a "classical theory of organisations" with strong notions of power and control through management (Reed 1992). This management control was an attempt to overcome the problems stemming from the lack of control over manual employees. Moreover, the increasing use of performance appraisal and PRP at all levels, illustrates that the *problem* of intransigent employees is seen by organisations to have transferred itself to the non-manual sector (Ball 1990;

Causer and Jones 1996). At this white-collar level, the planning and organising of work has been removed to the higher reaches of management, as has job autonomy, similar to shop floor employees (Cutler 1992).[1]

Like many other people management concepts such as organisational commitment, performance appraisal is subordinated under a notion of the "individual as resource," to be drawn on and used to the full, much like machinery (Ramsey 1991; Coates 1992). In this, performance appraisal stresses both employer and employee should focus on the complementary purpose of the organisation's furtherance. On the one hand individuals are a potential business resource through the enhancement of their personal skills. While on the other, they are seen as any other investment in *equipment* (cf. Cutler 1992).

Performance appraisal's definition however, prescribes a "required" outcome of productive increases in performance. Individuals, as *people*, are only peripherally related to it (Bartol and Martin 1991). Performance appraisal is thus a formal organisational mechanism for controlling the performance of work tasks on a rational, subjective and continuous basis, and is according to Bevan and Thompson (1991):

1. The yearly or half-yearly setting of individual performance targets relating to the operating units' target within the overall organisation;
2. A formal review of progress towards these targets, and/or the identification of training needs;
3. The creation of a shared vision of the organisations objectives, occasionally through a mission statement communicated to all employees;

In essence, performance appraisal is an attempt to involve individuals in the regular *clarification* of their work tasks, goals and achievements, at the same time making them more accountable for them (James 1988).

Such management practices accentuate one aspect in particular for performance appraisal. With the move away from a direct and technical supervision of work towards a discretionary or self-management aspect, performance appraisal has become the means to monitor the form in which this discretion is understood and practised. This discretionary feature has come about partly through technological changes in the work process, and partly a desire to achieve flexibility through the elimination of job descriptions and union staffing requirements. It has also been the attempt to adopt "Japanese" employment practices (Abe and Gourvish 1997; Cutcher-Gershenfeld *et al* 1998). Here adoption of "shared meanings" and "strong culture"—the internalisation of corporate morals, values and attitudes—becomes primary. Performance appraisal serves as a mechanism to *measure* such internalisation. Explicit rules play a lesser role in the regulation of performance.

Recent debate goes deeper than humble *performance*, moving towards the use of performance appraisal as a way for employees to identify with their organisation (e.g. Coates 1994). Hence the debate which argues performance appraisal is a means to involve individuals in their own subordination (e.g. Sturdy *et al* 1992). Townley (1994), using Foucault, has called this the acquisition of "implicit expectation" in the performance of work; i.e. employees become drawn into "the subjective realm" of their managers' aspirations for output and performance. This for Foucault (1974) was the development of a technology of power and domination. Knowledge, he argued, always supports several truth claims that are an intrinsic part of the struggle for power within human groups. Here truth is imposed on the world by the powerful. Knowledge is therefore always the intimate of power. As performance appraisal is a form of knowledge over individuals through appraisal files, it is also power over them. Central to Foucault's argument, is the belief that knowledge reflects power and authority positions. It therefore embodies both meaning and social relationships. They:

> . . . are not about objects; they do not identify objects, they constitute them and in the practice of doing so conceal their own invention. (Foucault 1974:49)

For managers performance appraisal is seen to provide the information to direct and control employees in white-collar work where there are fewer physical performance outcomes. Moreover, over thirty years ago McGregor (1960:75) argued that:

> Appraisal programs [we]re designed . . . to provide more systematic control of the behaviour of subordinates.

This article, through case study analysis, examines the changing focus of performance appraisal as a means through which the marginal, and not so marginal performer can be controlled. Analysis focuses on the level of the experience of *subjective* images of "women," through performance appraisal, for creating functionally flexible workers in a "quality" environment (Hill 1991). This analysis also examines management's attempts to "involve" individuals, at a deep level, in the formulation of their own work process. It does this by focusing on the powerful subjective manipulation of knowledge over individuals. Space does not allow the analysis to engage with the vast literature on performance appraisal, the article focuses on the experiences of individuals who receive its demands.

METHODS

The data reported here were collected from the white-collar staff of a case study organisation, carried out between January 1994–April 1995. The data reports interviews with the white-collar members of a large Midlands trust hospital—CareCo.[2] The case study provides data on a *newly* formed trust management structure for an ex-NHS hospital. This hospital had introduced performance appraisal with an overture to *market principles for costing treatments* and GP fundholders. CareCo was chosen as it was both a first wave trust and was at the forefront of the adoption, by ex-NHS hospitals, of performance appraisal for part of its pay policy.

As a hospital, CareCo employs over 2,300 staff on a single site on the outskirts of a city, and is one of two major hospitals in the area. CareCo supplies specialised care for a number of areas. It is also a leader in the field of breast cancer and gynaecology research/treatment. These services are not duplicated at the other trust hospital.

In all, some 200 white-collar employees were studied. Significantly this group contained both business managers and ward managers. In terms of gender, the vast majority of interviewees were women, which was true for CareCo in general (80%). However, this did not reflect their power position within the hospital, where less than 1% of the studied population were in upper management (cf. Pulkingham 1992). While there were 1840 women employed at CareCo, 40% of these were part-time in some form, as opposed to 3% of men. All whitecollar departments studied had male directors; midwifery and maternity had the largest proportion of female ward managers.

The interviews were designed to seek information concerning the nature of performance appraisal at CareCo and women's role within it. It was also designed to ascertain the individuals' personal experience of performance appraisal and the experience of the internalisation of CareCo's PA policy. Interviews were semi-structured and lasted approximately an hour. These interviews were all tape recorded and later transcribed. To supplement these, a number of "informal" management group meetings were also studied, as were CareCo's newsletter meetings. These were undertaken as "observer-as-participant" (Gold 1958).

PERFORMANCE APPRAISAL
AND WOMEN

Within CareCo, management were attempting to adopt *market practises*—PRP-for white-collar staff not directly involved in patient care, and especially those involved in senior management activities. These were part of the "salary progression review scheme" that pays annual increments according to a satisfactory level of performance, determined by departmental managers and based on their individual budget surpluses.

This system had been in place for senior management since 1993 and was extended to all white-collar levels in 1994. In conjunction with this, management had particularly invested in new ways of employing individuals, including short-term contracts. Management also expressed an increasing demand for candidates who exhibited 'charismatic' rather than 'bureau-

cratic' personalities. Performance appraisal was undertaken annually by immediate managers and closely followed a printed form that contained a number of categories. These were then commented upon by the manager in discussion with the employee. The form of performance appraisal used had been through a number of internal audits and passed satisfactorily in both 1994 and 1995. The official line was that:

> The core of the [performance appraisal] process is the one-to-one dialogue, which takes place between the manager and the individual reporting directly to him or her. The effectiveness of the work process is therefore crucially dependent on the quality of the appraisal interview. (HR Director)

Performance appraisal at CareCo went beyond simple function and was designed to internalise the organisations' aims; the position of women in this is important for understanding how women are doubly burdened with presenting "correct" subjective identities (henceforth identity) that are compatible with CareCo's aims. Women were doubly subjected, being employed and judged as employees for their looks as much as their skills (cf. Hochschild 1983):

> On a number of occasions [names of two managers] have gone out of their way to employ tall blond bimbos. They aren't suitable for the job, but they don't care, it would damage their egos if they employed someone with intelligence. (HR Dept)

Cockburn (1985) has pointed out that employers harness and make use of women's feelings and emotions e.g. in retail sales. Women not only *sell* their feminine identity, they also sell their *female* emotions (Truss 1993), and this is especially true for "caring professions" and their ancillaries. The perception of those working in a hospital has a very strong resonance in the minds of the general population as a feminine, caring one (Strauss *et al* 1982). Thus women, more so than men, were subject to more than just performance appraisal images. They were also subject to societal based sexual identity management in their work lives at the hospital, where they were seen to be *natural carers* (cf. Chandler *et al* 1995).

This is almost the "inside-out" smile of Hochschild's (1983) air stewardesses. Here women at CareCo had to project the applicable *feminine* identity traits to pass their performance appraisal. Hence an emphasis on not appearing career minded (Morgan 1990:51). This was explained at CareCo as:

> Helping *all* staff balance work and home commitments thereby ensuring a healthy and better motivated workforce, able to deliver our business objectives continues to be a priority for us in 94/5.

However, those that presented an identity of professional *manager* first and femininity second, there was short shrift in store. At least two female section heads, one in the HR department and the other in the TQM department, had been placed on the "at risk" register for their outspokenness. This meant their positions were no longer permanent/viable and that they would be offered *suitable* alternative positions—if possible. One person had found themself in this situation due to a "petty feud" between herself and the male head of HR:

> My job now is *not funded* or so the director says. I'm in a worse position now than ever as I could be out of a job come April if they say there is no money and all because of that bastard saying I wasn't doing my job properly. Just because I spoke up when I thought a policy was wrong.

This is the development of a technology of power and domination (Foucault 1974) or knowledge over women. Foucault argued knowledge was always an intrinsic part of the struggle for power within human groups (1974). Performance appraisal is a form of knowledge over individuals through appraisal files, it is also power (control) over them as it regulates pay. Central to Foucault's argument, is the belief that knowledge reflects power and authority positions. It therefore embodies both meaning and social relationships. They:

> . . . are not about objects; they do not identify objects, they constitute them and in the practice of doing so conceal their own invention. (Foucault 1974:49)

Thus the knowledge on individual's appraisal files at CareCo controlled their actions and their identification with work norms. Performance appraisal at CareCo reflected a new initiative for its control of women, and a new imperative for staff to be aware of their individual identity. Thus CareCo used performance appraisal as an exercise in selfpresentation of femininity more than a tool for delivering physical productivity improvement.

Hence a major criticism of performance appraisal at CareCo, and one that could be levelled generally, is that it actually dis-empowered women, despite its opposing rhetoric (Reed 1989). It did this firstly through filtering and monitoring values, attitudes and behaviour, reducing responsibility and increasing the homogeneous nature of the work force. For example, within CareCo's HRM department (99% women), it was not acceptable for women to wear trousers despite it being allowed. This was due to the HR director's preference to see women "as women" in skirts. Defiance was followed by mild disdain concerning the culprits' legs, but issues of dress were included on the appraisal form too. Also, an image consultant was employed twice a year to ensure women were aware of what was required of them. Along with the traditional customer care doctrine, the female consultant imparted advice on styles of clothes, make-up and deportment and how to ". . . be a *woman* basically. I thought I *was* one?" (Respondent). These applied to all the women studied.

Secondly, performance appraisal required one individual making judgements of another, reinforcing authority relations and defining (inter)dependency, not individuality as performance appraisal prescribes. With the growth of white-collar jobs in CareCo, objective performance criteria were more difficult to establish given the nature of the work. As such, dependability, flexibility, initiative and personal contact became more critical aspects of performance. If performance appraisal were truly working for CareCo's employees' advantage, it would centre on empowerment, not judgement by senior managers, autonomy not productivity, thus giving women resources to conduct and "manage" work. Studies in different countries have arrived at similar conclusions: "women's work is generally less autonomous, allows fewer possibilities for regulating one's pace at work, is more restricted in space and time, and is more monotonous" (Kauppinen-Toropainen *et al* 1988:17). Performance appraisal has merely added to the burden at CareCo.

Many of the policies introduced at CareCo—*Opportunity 2000*, fostering of organisational commitment, technological changes, and training—had the potential to lead to the redesign of work and increase the role of women. However, while *Opportunity 2000* was crucial to the health service at the time, CareCo issued a carefully worded policy/mission statement with four goals that ratified their commitment to it.

Goal one of the policy document sought to highlight the need to increase the participation of women in the trust at a senior level:

> The trust currently has one woman in a general management position as defined in [document number]. This represents a negligible percentage of our total female workforce. However, this needs to be viewed against a background of only two vacancies at this level in the past 12 months. One of these vacancies resulted in the appointment of a woman.

CareCo's *Opportunity 2000* actions—creating a job share register, setting up of a working mothers' group (Careers and Progression), back to work packages offering guidance and an authorised recruiter to be aware of women's needs—while defined to ease problems, actually sustained them. Many of these had not been completed or activated and where they were, such as authorised recruiters being aware of women's needs, those authorised were men.

Additionally, CareCo used performance appraisal to appeal to employees on the grounds of "moral involvement" (Fox 1985), and the improvement of personal skills/rewards:

> The trust believes that the continuance of its policies particularly in respect of career op-

portunities, such as development programmes, training sessions, etc., will result in the near future in a ground swell of female staff from many backgrounds, who will be well equipped to compete for and achieve appointments to senior positions. (Trust Policy Document)

The emphasis was placed upon personal achievement, which contributed to CareCo's overall performance, not the individual's own, which was viewed as peripheral:

> As last year, providing continuing support to these [female] staff by encouraging flexible working arrangements is a priority. It makes economic and social sense in today's market place. (Trust Policy Document)

The unofficial line at CareCo was that performance appraisal was inseparable from trust status and therefore part of the trust's identity. CareCo believed it could not have quality and efficiency without the employment policies of similarly efficient private companies such as ICI. Performance appraisal's meanings and definitions at CareCo were therefore pre-decided by the board, not the staff as is recommended by many textbooks (cf. Tolliday and Zeitlin 1991). This was echoed in the comments of one manager:

> I know quality counts and all that, but what about my staff being worked off their feet all day, how can they be expected to smile all the time and be *happy* when they need to make a pharmacological decision in a tight spot—it's a stressful job? If I had my way, performance wouldn't be measured, if it takes 10 hours to sort someone's life out, then that's how long it takes. (Female)

The unwritten policy of CareCo's board was that performance appraisal was a management led activity, for the benefit firstly of the organisation:

> If we are to have a quality organisation providing quality care, we need a performance appraisal system which can ensure individuals meet the needs of the organisation—which are, after all, their own needs too. (Head of Finance).

Crucial for our analysis here is the understanding that the creation of identities of acceptable behaviour for performance appraisal in CareCo. belonged not to women, but to men.

> Sure I feel I've become less of a woman since I've worked here, and that's been 18 years now. At the end of the day you've got a job to do. . . . If I'm not here nothing gets done.

> While we do everything for our female staff, at least 160 of them will take their year's leave of absence to have children this year alone! With that sort of turnover it's impossible to keep fully staffed. [Why is that?] Well, we can only get 60% replacement for nursing staff and 40% replacement for non-medical staff. (Male HR Director)

Additionally CareCo's policy documents' third point stated that:

> Over the next year we will look carefully at ensuring our trawls to fill the vacancies, pays particular reference to promoting aspects of our employment practices, which would be of *particular* interest to female candidates. Jobs will be designed to allow female candidates to fulfil their potential as much as is possible.

This simply reproduced the domestic division of labour (Hearn and Parkin 1987). For example, the HR director had bought a coffee percolator for himself and guests, placing this in his room. Whenever he required a cup, he would call through to his personal assistant to come in and make him one:

> I don't feel my job is to make cups of coffee. I am a trained assistant, not a skivvy!

While this can be seen simply as a sexist act, the role of "helping guests, being courteous and other tasks" were written into this individual's performance appraisal. Here such examples illustrate who had control over self-identity and the image employees were to perform to (cf. Truss 1993). Performance appraisal was a manifestation of this power over resistance, as all appraisals in the HR Department had to go

through the HR Director. He expressed this intent in different terms as:

> Performance appraisal requires individuals to conform to certain criteria. These can be both formal and informal.

While resistance is possible, it is tempered by the need to present the correct identity to retain employment, but also by CareCo linking white-collar employees' work ultimately to patient care outcomes.

The policy document stated that CareCo's performance appraisal contract was held to ennoble the individual, to respect her "dignity", rights, and welfare, and through this focus, replace collective control with enlightened "employee relations." The general manager espoused this *dignity* as:

> The problem [of] trying to get across to the person that you're not trying to give them a bad appraisal. You're looking for the *right* responses all the time.

These "right responses" were never articulated to this interviewer, but were known throughout CareCo's board.

The difficulty with performance appraisal at CareCo was its judgmental processes, which evoked defence mechanisms aimed at protecting self-identity (Shamir 1990). Some individuals felt that while they had *performed* and were "CareCo people," CareCo did not recognise their identity with its values:

> I had my review the other day. They said that I wasn't performing to my best ability and if I didn't buck my ideas up I would be given a formal warning. I've done all I can to meet the objectives I'm set, they just keep moving them. I'm pissed off with being victimised by them because I can actually do my job and they don't want to pay me PRP.

While the preceding argument concerning identity and performance appraisal might appear based on a contemporary economic imperative for CareCo, it is also crucially based in an understanding of the subjective relationship individuals have with hospitals and the *work* that goes on within.

MAKING PERFORMANCE APPRAISAL SUBJECTIVE AT CARECO

The means through which women were made subjects was decision-making discretion. This arose through the chairman's desire to achieve flexibility in staffing. For the chairman, any explicit rules played a negligible role in the regulation of performance—though they still existed. More primary was the adoption of the mission statement and its shared meanings and values—the internalisation of CareCo values, attitudes and norms. Individuals were able to enhance their promotion prospects by *fitting in* (Keating and Witkin 1992), by becoming CareCo centred individuals, aligning reflexively towards their tasks and the co-operative environment in which those tasks were undertaken:

> There is only one way an individual is going to get anywhere here, and that's by becoming a CareCo person. . . . You have to be agreeing with the CareCo doctrine at all times. (Staff Development)

To "fit in" at CareCo, women were pressured to express their feminine traits, not overtly, but covertly as part of the doctrine of "Quality Care" specified in the CareCo mission statement (cf. Sims *et al.* 1993). This posed a contradiction for the women due to their domestic roles/commitments. They were expected, for example, to staff the human resources office 24 hours a day until someone pointed out that they had other domestic responsibilities. Afterwards they were still expected to set aside one late—7pm—evening a fortnight as *work time*, there was no overtime or *in lieu* time.

Correspondingly, there was less room for an overtly instrumental—monetary—relationship between employee and CareCo. As Keating and Witkin (1992) illustrated, implementation and effectiveness of performance appraisal policies require that employees accept the new order and fit "its" requirements. Control becomes em-

bedded within employees' commitment to the organisation and its goals. Hence managerial control at CareCo was legitimated by *market* logic and its ability to compete effectively in the local care market. Within CareCo such commitment practices constituted identifying with the Trust's notion of quality:

> We at CareCo are dedicated to the provision of a quality service, at a quality price. You can't have one without the other, not in my book. I want this hospital to be known for its quality. Staff must identify with this ethos. (General Manager)

Appraisal was thus extremely problematic in CareCo as its emphasis sought to create a flexible employee with attachment to the hospital, not jobs or departments, and not necessarily each other. It was crucially promoted through the use of performance appraisal, but also a trust magazine edited by a man (all reporters were women), who "rewrote" all copy to express what he thought was the trust view on each issue. Additionally, rituals such as meetings and worktime social gatherings were also used to evoke, or were meant to, feelings of trust community and pride (cf. Rohlen 1980).

Performance appraisal was thus viewed by the board as the need to achieve control while disguising it, to tap employee compliance and effort through delegation, ensuring its responsible use. However, within this there was little space at CareCo for women or their expression of identities not immediately recognisable as feminine.

To present the correct identity, for example, of a "CareCo manager," a woman must present the subjectified image of *womanhood* by which she was first judged. Then, and only then, does the ability to perform the task come into the reckoning. In spite of attempts to promote the identity of *good* employee, it is the feminine qualities CareCo judged women on. It was the way to identity/recognition and so to the required PA outcome:

> I wouldn't mind wearing trousers to the office once and a while, it's a lot easier and warmer—

our office is so cold. But it's not allowed, well, officially it is, but [the HR Director] doesn't like women in trousers, he's a bit of a sexist really, but he does have a point. (HR Dept)

In certain cases, emphasis on femininity has lead to sexual abuse[3] at CareCo and to individuals feeling their *self-identity* had been seriously invaded (cf. Kramer 1989). Any legal regulation and redress still proves inept and outmoded (York 1989).

This integration of CareCo's identity into their own caused women to see themselves in light of their appraisal. Hence performance appraisal at CareCo to return to Foucault's terms, was a "moral technology"—a technology of power. It is the modern equivalent of Bentham's panopticon, "a generalizable model of functioning; a way of defining power relations in terms of the everyday life of men [*sic*]" (Foucault 1979:205). The management of identity at CareCo became an exercise in control over women. Unlike the panopticon, it was not about being able to observe at all times the individual's body, but internalising control until individuals were watching over their own bodies/identities (Sewell and Wilkinson 1993). Therein lies the emphasis on performance appraisal outcomes, because once an individual structures their activity according to their review, they come to hold it to be a representation of themselves and seek, subjectively, to conform to it. Thus as Littler and Salaman (1982:259) argue:

> . . . once this conception of management has been accepted by workers, they have in effect, abdicated from any question of or resistance to, many aspects of their domination.

Within CareCo performance appraisal was a form of power (collecting performance information) laying claim to certain knowledge about individuals. This cast employees as subjects of that power and hence the recipients of the procedures enacted on the basis of it—such as disciplinary hearings. Consequently within CareCo women became over exposed to power and control, and thus subject to knowledge concerning their femininity through performance appraisal.

Excessive time off with sick children led to performance targets being missed—this being noted in appraisals.

Performance appraisal also produced the things about which it spoke—a need for appraisal. The results of appraisals *proved* to management that female employees were seen to be not meeting the individual criteria laid down, which led, for example, to the need for image consultants. Hence appraisal supported the need for its own creation. In doing this performance appraisal made women employees known—in the process disregarding their fears—through the use of personal information collected as part of the appraisal process. Thus the individual employees became their appraisal outcome.

CareCo's use of personnel files permitted women to be fixed in a web of objective codification (Rabinow 1986), allowing the line manager to become a key tool of the "moral technology" of management. Appraisal made women calculable, describable and comparable (through the disciplining practices of paid external image consultants, castigation and expectation), opening them to an evaluating eye and to its disciplinary power. Foucault (1979:175) described this as examination that "combines the techniques of an observing hierarchy and those of a normalizing judgement. . . . It establishes over individuals a visibility through which one differentiates and judges them."

Performance appraisal could be seen as insidious at CareCo as it had no feelings, respected nothing and no one. It introduced individuality in order to punish and produced written records of effort/ability in order to punish (cf. Foucault 1979:175). At CareCo the appraisal interview was used as a formal ritual of power and ceremony of visibility (appointments were made and treated as job interviews)—a technology of objectification. It linked the formation of knowledge with the display of power. Consider here the use of notions of femininity by the human resources director to constrain identity presentation and the subjugation of self. Those appraised were there to be known and recorded by the appraiser. Hence they became "known" individually through their performance appraisal outcomes. Appraisal techniques have been developed and legitimated at CareCo, insofar as they coopt women and established notions of professionalism into their subjugation. At CareCo this professionalism might well be the notion of quality care:

> Quality [is] course quality is a priority, I don't care what anyone else has said, a quality service is the goal of this hospital. Without it we fail to provide even the most basic decencies at a time of human frailty. I expect the highest quality service from *my women*, all staff in fact. Performance appraisal and performance related pay are just the mechanisms through which we reward people for a quality job well done. (General Manager)

All of this can be seen in the way performance appraisal at CareCo acted like the church confessional. Critically, the performance appraisal outcome at CareCo had elements of Foucault's confessional encounter. The authority of the confessor—heads of department at CareCo—comes from the potency of the trust's credo or mission statement to provide quality care and meet in/out-patients service standards. The premise of course is that the individual is in need of confession, that there has been transgression. Appraisal provides the information whereby employees are encouraged to display their shortcomings, to seek out or identify appropriate therapeutic (remedial) procedures and to award their own punishment (of more targets/increased output). Confession of personal failure at CareCo became part of the greater (Trust) faith; employees could not become "quality people" until they had humbled themselves before the "quality facilitator" (appraiser) and resolved to repent. The problem here was that there had to be something to confess. Individuals found themselves searching desperately for their own failures; to have none was worse than having lots. The design of the appraisal form was crucial here to a perception of the confession:

> The appraisal form has all these sections on it about what you've done wrong in the time since your last. Writing nothing is as bad as writing the truth I think, you can't win in the end, I've tried and all I get is [the appraiser]

writing in what he thought my faults were. I wanted to tell him that I was pissed off with Caroline's attitude as it was stopping me working, but that's not showing contrition about yourself is it.[4]

> I guess you could say it's like the sacrament and receiving the Eucharist, its sort of eye opening to see your faults on paper. Then you can deal with them I guess. My son writes a diary, it's sort of the same really isn't it?

Newly inspired, CareCo employees "welcomed" complaints and rejoiced at their ability to accept and learn from their failure—everything became a learning event, especially the penance usually increased workloads. Performance appraisal thus embodied revelation and redemption and brought the personal and organisational into the intimate. Here CareCo's managers could be seen as a:

> . . . partner who is not simply the interlocutor but the authority who requries the confession, prescribes and appreaciates it, and intervenes in order to judge, punish, forgive, console. (Foucault 1981:61)

The sinister development this represents is towards a situation in which even one's failure, the touchstone of one's humanity, is appropriated by the organisation in its constant drive towards cost-reduction and improved performance. Not only this, but also that for a confession to be effective it must be voluntary and freely made. Confessions are a response to what Gutman (1988:106) calls a "triumvirate of compunction, external gaze and the need for complete disclosure." While performance appraisal's examination and judgement are supposedly objective and value free, they irresistibly conjure up visions of the Grand Inquisitor (Paden 1988).

CONCLUSION
While traditional approaches towards performance appraisal have been predicated upon the "supremacy" of the subject—the individual—acted on by various practices and dominant groups, the use of a subjective analysis implies that all are implicated in the process of subordination. At CareCo we have seen that the forms

of knowledge and power were not discreet, they were part of an overt discourse—that of quality—which moulded morality, sexuality, presentation of self and purity (re: quality) of thought for CareCo. The use of performance appraisal, rather than an end in itself, can be seen at CareCo as a "will to knowledge," or power, over the individual (Foucault 1974). The analysis illustrates that the attempts by CareCo to affect individual forms of appearance and conceptions of self constituted the individuals as subjects in a pre-defined, "CareCo," likeness. Thus Foucault is essential to tease out the underlying practices, which informed the notion of performance appraisal at CareCo, and drove its engine towards the subsumption of those professions within. All without performance appraisal proving its abilities to physically improve output or individual.

CareCo used performance appraisal in order that individuals adopt the correct attitude to the increased discretion and responsible autonomy that the introduction of a market (business) mentality brought. The replacement of work rules and supervision at staff level with discretion is a key feature of the dominant HRM model, which propounds this *new* kind of employment contract (Graham 1988; Guest 1989), but leaves little actual freedom. As such, CareCo's new apparatus of control could be argued to lead to a more pernicious and coercive pattern of management for employees, through the direct attempt to manage meaning, identity and sexuality. Physical performance appears to be lost. CareCo's movement towards the management of identity is adopting a different ideology altogether, focusing on assessment of the internalisation of Trust goals and norms as an index of identification with the job and the hospital.

It would be disingenuous to argue that performance appraisal has become fully internalized by CareCo employees; however, the data does illustrate that it has made headway in this respect. Employees spoke of the need to act in a "quality" way and to put the organisations first; employees always took ownership for any failures during appraisals. This could be due to the emotive nature of hospitals where "sloppy" work causes loss of life. Despite this they did voice issues, which might be construed as resistance—

the questioning of the use of an image consultant.

However, the problem of control at CareCo appeared to be resolved by the personalising of the employment contract. By giving women appraisal records by which they can judge themselves and the organisation, CareCo has uncovered the means to elicit the commitment and internalised loyalty of its employees. The appraisal records were used as a way of impressing on individuals that their identity either reflected or refuted CareCo's. With this CareCo had a very powerful mechanism of control through which it could appeal to women's sexuality, loyalty and commitment. Hence the data pointed towards the belief that substance—measurable performance/output—was replaced with rhetoric and adoption of CareCo's identity.

This is doubly important for the identity of women at CareCo with a majority of women staff. Sexuality and its attendant presentation became an essential part of the performance appraisal process. Performance appraisal was used as a means to assess femininity and to control those who sought to overstep the bounds of acceptable action and to weed out those not internalising a CareCo identity. Here individuals adopted the identity of CareCo or their jobs were "lost" in a reshuffle.

There is an irony that as CareCo places more emphasis on competitive performance and quality (care) through an individualising practice such as performance appraisal, it seeks to turn its employees into mirror images of itself. As performance appraisal becomes more widely practised in the public sector, there is increasing need to critically unravel its implications and consequences in the pursuit of contemporary management practice.[5]

APPENDIX

What follows is an approximation of the PA form used at CareCo. Certain questions have been altered/omitted in case they identify the institution.

PART 1: INTERVIEW PREPARATION

1. Outline the main duties and responsibilities of your job during the past year and estimate the percentage of time that is taken up

by each of your principle duties. (You may wish to complete a weekly diary profile for one or more weeks.)

2. Please indicate nature and extent of administrative duties, including committee membership.
3. Please give details of how you have met your objectives of the past year.
4. Please give details of *any* difficulties you have encountered and how you overcame them.
5. Please give details of external contacts and activities.
6. Please give brief details of consultancies (i) currently held (ii) in prospect.
7. Please give details of any other professional activities undertaken, (e.g. short courses, visits overseas and services to professional bodies), and why they were of benefit to you and to CareCo.
8. Please give details of staff development activities undertaken during the year.
9. Please comment on the activities of the past year.
10. Please comment on next year's planned activities.

PART 2: COMMENTS BY APPRAISER & AMP; WORK DEVELOPMENT PLAN

1. Report on performance over the appraisal period
2. Agreed points for action to be taken by member of staff and by the Department
3. Support and training needs for carrying out the agreed action
4. Agreement on comments & action plan

PART 3: TO BE COMPLETED BY APPRAISEE WITHIN 14 DAYS OF THE APPRAISAL INTERVIEW

I have read the comments made by the appraiser and

(a) I have nothing further to add
(b) I wish to add the following

[Please delete (a) or (b) as appropriate]

These questions were also supplemented by a "score card" marked by the appraiser on a scale of 1 to 5 during the discussion phase that occurred before the appraiser's comments were written down.

REFERENCES

ABE, E., GOURVISH, T. (eds.) (1997) *Japanese Success? British Failure? Comparisons in Business Performance Since 1945.* Oxford: Oxford University Press.

BALL, S. J. (ed.) (1990) *Foucault and Education: Disciplines and Knowledge.* London: Routledge.

BARTOL, K. M., MARTIN, D. (1991) *Management.* New York: McGraw-Hill.

BEVAN, S., THOMPSON, M. (1991) "Performance Management at the Crossroads," *Personnel Management*, pp. 36–40.

CAUSER, G., JONES, C. (1996) "Management and the Control of Technical Labour," *Work, Employment and Society*, 10(1):105–123.

CHANDLER, J., BRYANT, L., BUNYARD, T. (1995) "Women in Military Occupations," *Work, Employment and Society*, 9(1):123–135.

COATES, G. (1992) "Presenting a Single Face: Understanding Workplace Commitment through Social Interaction," paper presented to the 10th Standing Conference on Organisational Symbolism, Lancaster.

COATES, G. (1994) "Performance Appraisal: Oscar Winning Performance or Dressing to Impress?" *International Journal of Human Resource Management*, 5(1):167–192.

COCKBURN, C. (1985) *Machinery of Dominance: Women, Men and Technical KnowHow.* London: Pluto.

COLLINS, H. (1992) *The Equal Opportunities Handbook.* Oxford: Blackwell.

COTTON, J. L. (1993) *Employee Involvement: Methods for Improving Performance and Work Attitudes.* London: Sage.

CUTCHER-GERSHENFELD, J., NITTA, M., BARRETT, B. (1998) *Virtual Knowledge: The CrossCultural Diffusion of Japanese and US Work Practices.* Oxford: Oxford University Press.

CUTLER, T. (1992) "Vocational Training and British Economic Performance," *Work, Employment and Society*, 6(2):161–183.

ELGER, T. (1990) "Technical Innovation and Work Reorganisation in British Manufacturing in the 1980's: Continuity, Intensification or Transformation?" *Work, Employment and Society*, 4(Special Issue):67–101.

FERRIS, G. R., *et al.* (1991) "The Management of Shared Meaning in Organisations: Opportunism in the Reflection of Attitudes, Beliefs and Values," in Giacalone, R. A., Rosenfeld, P.

(Eds.) *Applied Impression Management.* London: Sage.

FOUCAULT, M. (1974) *The Archaeology of Knowledge.* London: Tavistock.

FOUCAULT, M. (1979) *Discipline and Punish.* Harmondsworth: Penguin.

FOUCAULT, M. (1981) *The History of Sexuality: An Introduction.* Harmondsworth: Penguin.

FOX, A. (1985) *Man Mismanagement.* London: Hutchinson.

GOLD, R. L. (1958) "Roles in Sociological Field Observation," *Social Forces* 36: 217–223.

GRAHAM, I. (1988) "Japanization as Mythology," *Industrial Relations Journal,* 19(1):19–25.

GREY, C. (1993) "A Helping Hand: Self-Discipline and Management Control," paper presented to the 11th Labour Process Conference, Blackpool.

GUEST, D. (1989) "Human Resource Management: Its Implications for Industrial Relations and Trade Unions," in Storey, J. (Ed.) *New Perspectives on Human Resource Management.* London: Routledge.

GUTMAN, H. (1988) "Rousseau's Confessions: A Technology of The Self," in Martin, L., Gutman, H., Hutton, P. (Eds.) *Technologies of the Self: A Seminar with Michel Foucault.* London: Tavistock.

HARLEY, S., LEE, F. (1995) "Control Surveillance and Subjectivity: The Research Assessment Exercise, Academic Diversity and the Future of Non-Mainstream Economics in UK Universities," paper presented to the 13th Annual Labour Process Conference.

HEARN, J., PARKIN, W. (1987) *"Sex" at "Work."* Brighton: Wheatsheaf.

HILL, S. (1991) "How Do You Manage a Flexible Firm? The Total Quality Model," *Work, Employment and Society,* 5(3):397–416.

HOCHSCHILD, A. (1983) *The Managed Heart: Commercialization of Human Feeling.* Berkeley: University of California Press.

KEATING, P., WITKIN, R. W. (1992) "Culturally Mediated Employee Responses to the Implementation of Managerial Techno-Culture in the Banking Industry," paper presented to the BSA Conference, Kent.

KRAMER, L. (1989) "A Guilty Plea Confirms the Dark Rumours About Capitol Hill Aide Quentin Crommelin," *People Magazine,* 21, August, 49–50.

LITTLER, C. R., SALAMAN, G. (1982) "Bravermania and Beyond: Recent Theories of the Labour Process," *Sociology,* 16:251–268.

MCARDLE, L *et al.* (1992) "Managerial Control through Performance Related Pay," paper presented to the 10th Annual Labour Process Conference, Aston.

MCGREGOR, D. (1960) *The Human Side of Enterprise.* New York: McGraw-Hill.

MILLER, H. (1991) "Academics and Their Labour Process," In Smith, C. et al., *White-Collar Work: The Non-Manual Labour Process.* London: Macmillan.

MOLANDER, C., WINTERTON, J. (1994) *Managing Human Resources.* London: Routledge.

MORGAN, G. (1990) *Organizations in Society.* London: Macmillan.

MURPHY, K., CLEVELAND, J. (1995) *Understanding Performance Appraisal: Social, Organisational, and Goal-Based Perspectives.* London: Sage.

PADEN, W. (1988) "Theatres of Humility and Suspicion: Desert Saints and New England Puritans," in Martin, L., Gutman, H., Hutton, P. (Eds.) *Technologies of the Self: A Seminar with Michel Foucault.* London: Tavistock.

PULKINGHAM, J. (1992) "Employment Re-Structuring in the Health Service: Efficiency Initiatives, Working Patterns and Workforce Composition," *Work, Employment and Society,* 6(3):397–422.

PYM, D. (1973) "The Politics and Rituals of Appraisals," *Occupational Psychology,* 47:231–235.

RABINOW, P. (Ed.) (1986) *The Foucault Reader.* London: Peregrine.

RAMSEY, H. (1991) "Reinventing the Wheel? A Review of the Development of Performance and Employee Involvement," *Human Resource Management Journal,* 4(1):1–22.

REED, M. (1989) *The Sociology of Management.* Hemel Hempstead: Harvester Wheatsheaf.

REED, M. (1992) *The Sociology of Organisations.* Hemel Hempstead: Harvester Wheatsheaf.

REED, M., WHITAKER, A. (1992) "Organisational Surveillance and Control Under Re-Organised Capitalism: Managerial Control Strategies and Structures in the Era of Flexible Fordism," paper presented to the 10th Annual Labour Process Conference, Aston.

REES, G., FIELDER, S. (1992) "The Services Economy, Sub-Contracting and New Employment Relations: Contract Catering and Cleaning," *Work, Employment and Society,* 6(3):347–368.

Rohlen, T. P. (1980) "The Juku Phenomenon," *Journal of Japanese Studies*, 6(1):25–37.

Sewell, G., Wilkinson, B. (1992) " 'Someone to Watch Over Me': Surveillance, Discipline and The Just-in-Time Labour Process," *Sociology*, 26(2):271–290.

Shamir, B. (1990) "Calculations, Values and Identities: The Sources of Collective Motivation," *Human Relations*, 43:313–332.

Sims, D. et al. (1993) *Organising and Organisations: An Introduction.* London: Sage.

Strauss, A., Fagerhaugh, S., Suczek, B., Wiener, C. (1982) "Sentimental Work in the Technologized Hospital," *Sociology of Health and Illness*, 4(3):254–277.

Sturdy, A. et al. (1992) *Skill and Consent: Contemporary Studies in The Labour Process.* London: Routledge.

Tolliday, S., Zeitlin, J. (Eds.) (1991) *The Power to Manage.* London: Routledge.

Townley, B. (1994) *Reframing Human Resource Management: Power, Ethics, and the Subject at Work.* London: Sage.

Truss, C. J. (1993) "The Secretarial Ghetto: Myth or Reality? A Study of Secretarial Work in England, France and Germany," *Work, Employment and Society*, 7(4):561–584.

York, G. (1989) "Judge Offers an Apology for Comment on Slapping," *The Globe and Mail*, 23, September.

NOTES

1. For example, the use of temporary contracts in higher education is important in the removal, for academics, of a subtle freedom to plan their career with any certainty.

2. All names used herein are pseudonyms and some details have been purposefully omitted to protect its identity.

3. The event cannot be reported here as a legal action is still being fought.

4. The author, in promising confidentiality, cannot illustrate the form here. See the appendix for an approximation.

5. In 1995 the speaker in the House of Lord spoke out against PA on the grounds that services could not be objectively measured.

COMMENTARY ON THE READINGS

Matulef utilized a literature review to deduce a set of questions that became the focus of the research. Like much evaluation research, he used more than one source of data for this study: an analysis of published data, such as articles and statistical data, and a telephone survey. He then analyzed the data using statistics in much the same as in any other quantitative study, examining several different criteria for variation in home ownership programs.

Coates used a qualitative approach to this research. She conducted interviews of personnel at a specific hospital to learn about the experience of evaluation research for the employees of the hospital. She found that the hospital was using performance evaluation as a means of controlling the attitudes of its workers. Workers tended to accept blame for mistakes and spoke in terms that mimicked the language of performance appraisal, such as discussing the need for "quality." Coates also found that some workers were skeptical about the effectiveness of performance appraisal.

CONCLUSION

Evaluation research is critical to any modern society. It is the means by which societies evaluate their policies and companies their programs. It is the way that society learns more about itself, and thus how to improve itself.

Evaluation research is conducted in a variety of ways because there are a variety of programs that require evaluation. Programs that receive grants through government agencies and private foundations are often required to perform (or have performed) regular evaluations in order to ensure the grantsmakers that the investment is a wise one. Public and private organizations, such as schools, businesses, and government agencies, perform evaluations in order to measure their success and find ways to improve in the future. All things considered, evaluation research is an essential function of social researchers.

GLOSSARY

applied research: Research conducted for some practical purpose.

artifact: Items produced by a social group that can be used as measures of the culture and the technology of the group.

attribute: The specific values or categories of a variable.

causation: The concept that the action of one phenomenon affects the behavior of another.

code of ethics: A document adopted by a professional association that provides guidelines on understanding ethical issues in research.

coding: The collection of data and its classification as belonging to one or another variable attribute.

common sense: A form of knowledge that relies upon what appears to be obvious.

confederate: In an experiment, co-conspirators who work with the experimenter without the subject's knowledge.

conflict theory: The paradigm that assumes society to be composed of groups that have opposing interests.

content analysis: The analysis of data recorded by a target population on cultural artifacts.

control group: In experimental design, a group of subjects who are not exposed to the independent variable.

debriefing: Informing the subjects of a study of the study's true purpose.

deduction: A form of reason that stresses logic and mathematical representation in the development of theory. In deduction, theory is developed by starting with general statements about the phenomenon and logically developing hypotheses from those general statements.

dependent variable: A variable whose action is dependent upon the action of another variable. It is the dependent variable that is of interest in a study.

disclosure: The practice of informing subjects of the existence and aims of a study. Overt research refers to full disclosure and covert research refers to a study where some or all aspects are concealed.

ethnography: A school of fieldwork research that aims to understand the behaviors and attitudes of people from the perspective of those studied.

ethnomethodology: A school of fieldwork research that focuses on how meaning is created by participants in social interaction.

evaluation research: A collection of research methods that have been adapted to measure the effectiveness of particular policies or programs.

experiment: Research in which the researcher attempts to control all extraneous variables so that only the effects of the relevant variables are important.

experimental group: In experimental design, a group of subjects who are exposed to the independent variable.

fieldwork: A variety of methods that collect data through active engagement of the researcher with the subject.

functionalism: The paradigm that assumes that social organizations operate in a similar manner to biological organisms.

historical comparative research: An umbrella term to describe several related research traditions that compare social processes among different units of analysis.

hypothesis: A type of theory that elaborates a simple relationship between specific aspects of a phenomenon.

ideal type: The essential element of a given phenomenon that serves as a basis of comparison for real phenomena that are actually observed.

independent variable: A variable whose action is independent of the other variables in a relationship and exerts an influence upon them.

induction: A form of reasoning that stresses observation and description in the development of theory. In induction, a theory is developed through systematic observation from which general statements are built.

interactionism: The paradigm that assumes that people collectively create and reinforce their sense of reality through social interaction and the creation of symbols.

internal review board: A committee established by an institution to review research proposals prior to the beginning of a study involving human and other living subjects.

interval variable: A variable in which there is a set of mathematical distances between the attributes.

intervening variable: A variable that acts as a causal link between the independent and dependent variables.

middle-range theory: A type of theory that serves as a link between paradigms and hypotheses.

mysticism: A form of knowledge that relies on extraworldly or supernatural sources for information.

nominal variable: A variable whose attributes act as labels for a concept.

non-probability sample: The selection of cases for their potential of illuminating or complementing specific social problems.

nonresponse: The failure to collect data from a subject.

ordinal variable: A variable whose attributes act as labels for a concept, but they introduce a ranking or ordering to the variable.

paradigm: A general framework for understanding a large array of phenomena.

population: The total of all cases (people, organizations, etc.) that the researcher may wish to study.

probability sample: The selection of a sample in a way that will be representative of the entire population under study. Also called random sampling.

pure research: The pursuit of knowledge for the sake of gaining knowledge.

qualitative data: Data that are represented by language, pictures, or other non-mathematical devices.

quantitative data: Data that can be represented numerically.

ratio variable: An interval variable that has a starting point or zero.

rationalism: A form of knowledge that utilizes logic and complex systems of knowledge in order to understand aspects of the world.

reliability: The concept that the measurement of a research tool is consistent.

replication: The practice of repeating a study to ensure that the phenomenon can be observed.

sample: A portion of a population that is chosen to represent the population as a whole.

sampling error: The difference between the population and the sample.

science: A form of knowledge that gains knowledge through systematic observation.

secondary data analysis: The use of data for purposes other than for which it was collected.

secondary data: Documents, survey results, and other forms of data collected previously with goals that may differ from those of the current research analyst.

subject: A person who is the focus of the study.

survey: A research technique that utilizes a questionnaire to collect data on a sizable number of subjects.

text: Conceptual information conveyed by a cultural artifact.

theory: A set of abstract concepts that serve to organize knowledge.

unobtrusive measures: Data gathered through mechanisms that do not interfere in the ordinary patterns of the life of the subjects.

validity: The concept that the measurement of a research tool is accurate.

variable: A concept that has two or more values.

REFERENCES

Adler, P. A. & Adler, P. (1983). Shifts and oscillations in deviant careers: The case of upper level drug dealers and smugglers. *Social Problems, 31*, 195–207.

Ames, L. J. & Ellsworth, J. (1997). *Women reformed, women empowered: Poor mothers and the endangered promise of Head Start*. Philadelphia: Temple U. Press.

Anderson, N. (1923). *The hobo*. Chicago: U. Chicago Press.

Asch, S. (1958). *Effects of group pressure upon the modification and distortion of judgments*. In E. E. Macoby et al. (Eds.), *Readings in social psychology*. 3rd Ed. New York: Holt, Rinehart and Winston.

Atkinson-Grosjean, J. (1998). Illusions of excellence and the selling of the university: A microstudy. *Electronic Journal of Sociology, 3* (3).

Bean, P. A. (1993). The Great War and ethnic nationalism in Utica, New York, 1914–1920. *New York History, 74* (4), 382–413.

Becker, H. S. (1991 [1963]). *Outsiders: Studies in the sociology of deviance*. New York: Free Press.

Blee, K. M. (1991). *Women of the Klan: Racism and gender in the 1920s*. Berkeley, CA: U. California Press.

Cao, L. & Hou, C. (2001). A comparison of confidence in the police in China and the United States. *Journal of Criminal Justice, 29*, 87–99.

Coates, G. (2000). Experiencing performance appraisal in a trust hospital. *Electronic Journal of Sociology, 5*, (1).

Cohn, E. G. (1990). Weather and crime. *British Journal of Sociology, 30* (1), 50–64.

Donaldson, G. (1993). *The Ville: Cops and kids in urban America*. New York: Anchor.

Durkheim, E. (1997 [1897]). *Suicide*. New York: Free Press.

Fitchen, J. M. (1991). *Endangered spaces, enduring places: Change, identity, and survival in rural America*. Boulder, CO.: Westview.

Garfinkel, H. (1996 [1967]). *Studies in ethnomethodology*. Cambridge, MA: Polity Press.

Geertz, C. (1973). *The interpretation of cultures*. New York: Basic Books.

Jones, S., Martin, R., & Pilbeam, D. (Eds.). (1992). *The Cambridge Encyclopedia of human evolution*. New York: Cambridge U. Press.

Jones, J. H. (1993). *Bad blood: The Tuskegee syphilis experiment*. 2nd Ed. New York: Free Press.

Levin, J. & Thomas, A. R. (1997). Experimentally manipulating race: Perceptions of police brutality in an arrest. *Justice Quarterly, 14* (3), 577–86.

Lewis, C. & Neville, J. (1995). Images of Rosie: A content analysis of women workers in American magazine advertising, 1940–46. *Journalism and Mass Communication Quarterly, 72*, 216–27.

Likert, R. (1932). A technique for measurement of attitudes. *Archives of Psychology, 140*.

Logan, J. R. & Rabrenovic, G. (1990). Neighborhood associations: Their issues, their allies, and their opponents. *Urban Affairs Quarterly, 26* (1), 68–94.

Maryanski, A. & Turner, J. H. (1992). *The social cage: Human nature and the evolution of society*. Stanford, CA: Stanford U. Press.

Matulef, M. (1986). Target efficiency of state home ownership programs. *Evaluation Review, 10* (6), 715–56.

Merton, R. K. (1968). *Social theory and social structure*. Rev. Ed. New York: Free Press.

Milgram, S. (1969). *Obedience to authority*. New York: Harper.

Miner, H. (1956). Body ritual among the Nacirema. *American Anthropologist, 58* (3), 503–507.

Moltch, H., Freudenburg, W., & Paulsen, K. E. (2000). History repeats itself, but how? City character, urban tradition, and the accomplishment of place. *American Sociological Review, 65*, 791–823.

Neuman, W. L. (2000). *Social research methods: Qualitative and quantitative approaches.* Boston: Allyn & Bacon.

Padilla, F. M. (1992). *The gang as an American enterprise.* New Brunswick, NJ: Rutgers U. Press.

Payne, S. (1951). *The art of asking questions.* Princeton, NJ: Princeton U. Press.

Pinkerton, J. R., Hassinger, E.W., and O'Brien, D. J. (1995). Inshopping by residents of small communities. *Rural Sociology, 60* (3), 467–80.

Rubin, H. J., & Rubin, R. S. (1995). *Qualitative interviewing: The art of hearing data.* Thousand Oaks, CA: Sage.

Slater, M., Rouner, D., & Karan, D. (1994). Placing alcohol warnings before, during, and after TV beer ads: Effects on knowledge and responses to the ads and warnings. *Journalism and Mass Communication Quarterly, 76* (3), 468–84.

Tamborini, R., Mastro, E., & Assad, R. (2000). The color of crime and the court: A content analysis of minority representation on television. *Journalism and Mass Communication Quarterly, 77* (3), 639–53.

Vidich, A. J., & Bensman, J. (1968). *Small town in mass society: Class, power, and religion in a rural community.* Rev. Ed. Princeton, NJ: Princeton U. Press.

Wallerstein, I. (1979). *The capitalist world economy.* New York: Cambridge U. Press.

Weber, M. (1992 [1930]). *The Protestant ethic and the spirit of capitalism.* New York: Routledge.

Weiss, C. H. (1972). *Evaluation research: Methods of assessing program effectiveness.* Englewood Cliffs, NJ: Prentice-Hall.

Wenger, N., Korenman, S., & Berk, R. (1999). Reporting unethical research behavior. *Evaluation Review, 23*, 5, 553–70.

Zierler, S., Krieger, S., & Tang, Y. (2000). Economic Deprivation and AIDS Incidence in Massachusetts. *American Journal of Public Health, 90* (7), 1064–73.